DIARY OF INDEPENDENCE HALL

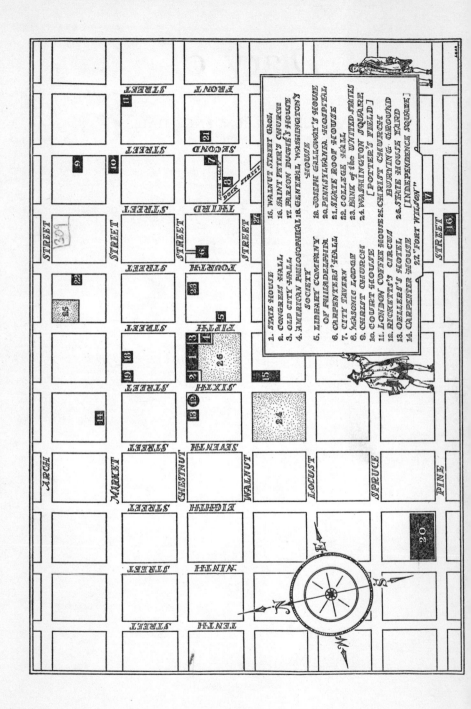

1. STATE HOUSE
2. CONGRESS HALL
3. OLD CITY HALL
4. AMERICAN PHILOSOPHICAL
   SOCIETY
5. LIBRARY COMPANY
   OF PHILADELPHIA
6. CARPENTERS' HALL
7. CITY TAVERN
8. MASONIC LODGE
9. CHRIST CHURCH
10. COURT HOUSE
11. LONDON COFFEE HOUSE
12. RICKETTS'S CIRCUS
13. OELLERS'S HOTEL
14. CARPENTER HOUSE

15. WALNUT STREET GAOL
16. SAINT PETER'S CHURCH
17. PARSON DUCHÉ'S HOUSE
18. GENERAL WASHINGTON'S
    HOUSE
19. JOSEPH GALLOWAY'S HOUSE
20. PENNSYLVANIA HOSPITAL
21. SLATE ROOF HOUSE
22. COLLEGE HALL
23. BANK of the UNITED STATES
24. WASHINGTON SQUARE
    [POTTER'S FIELD]
25. CHRIST CHURCH
    BURYING GROUND
26. STATE HOUSE YARD
    [INDEPENDENCE SQUARE]
27. "FORT WILSON"

Diary of
INDEPENDENCE
HALL

Harold Donaldson Eberlein
and
Cortlandt Van Dyke Hubbard

Prologue by
Richardson Wright

53 Illustrations from
Photographs and Engravings

J. B. LIPPINCOTT COMPANY
Philadelphia   London   New York

COPYRIGHT, 1948, BY
HAROLD DONALDSON EBERLEIN
AND
CORTLANDT VAN DYKE HUBBARD

PRINTED IN THE
UNITED STATES OF AMERICA

FIRST EDITION

To them that come from far or near to visit Independence Hall, with reverence or affection—and notably to them that come from far, again and yet again, whenever their occasions give them opportunity; to the merely curious that come to look but go away with admiration in their hearts; and, not least, to the many young that come, who—God grant—may grow up to honour and love the venerable building, this book is dedicated.

ACKNOWLEDGMENT

To the following friends, who gave countenance and steadfast support to the effort to ensure publication of this book at a price within the reach of all—the Honourables Richard S. Rodney, Edwin O. Lewis and Francis Shunk Brown, jr.; Charles J. Biddle, Esquire, Miss Gertrude Brincklé, Kirke Bryan and Thomas Francis Cadwalader, Esquires, Miss Aileen M. du Pont, Thomas Hart, Greville Haslam, S. F. Houston, Charles Francis Jenkins, Arthur M. Kennedy, Frederic R. Kirkland, Esquires, Miss Mildred W. Lee, William E. Lingelbach, Sydney E. Martin, Lawrence J. Morris, Francis R. Packard, M.D., Henry Pleasants, M.D., Esquires, Mrs. Henry Ridgely, Rodman Ward, Richard Norris Williams, II, Esquires, and Miss Frances Anne Wister; to Miss Sophia Cadwalader and Mrs. Arnold G. Talbot, for permission to use unpublished family documents; to Dr. John C. Miller, for permission to quote from his *Origins of the American Revolution;* to the Rosenbach Galleries, for permission to reproduce Mayor Wharton's letter of 1816; to the Historical Society of Pennsylvania and the Library Company of Philadelphia to quote from manuscripts and reproduce illustrations in their collections; to the officers and members of The Society of Colonial Wars in the Commonwealth of Pennsylvania, The Society of Colonial Wars in the State of Delaware, the Colonial Dames of America, Chapter II, the Delaware Society of the Colonial Dames of America, the Society of the War of 1812 in the Commonwealth of Pennsylvania and the Pennsylvania Society of Sons of the Revolution, who countenanced the effort; to the officers and members of the Historical Society of Pennsylvania, the Maryland Historical Society, the Delaware Historical Society and the Historical Societies of Chester and Montgomery Counties, who likewise supported the effort; to the Library Staffs of the Historical Society of Pennsylvania, the Library Company of Philadelphia, the Manuscript Division of the Library of Congress, the American Philosophical Society for Promoting Useful Knowledge and the Free Library of Philadelphia, for their many courtesies and helpful acts; to Richardson Wright, who has graciously contributed the Prologue; to the

Curator and Guards at Independence Hall, for their unfailing helpfulness while securing many of the illustrations; and to many friends for their interest in reading all or parts of the manuscript and in offering valued suggestions, especially Judge Lewis, Dr. Packard, Dr. Richard H. Shryock and Dr. John H. Powell, the authors here wish to record their sincere appreciation and thanks.

Harold Donaldson Eberlein
Cortlandt Van Dyke Hubbard

Philadelphia,
October, 1948

That ancient Philadelphia dowager, Independence Hall, can look back on her past with understanding, merriment and equanimity. Some things she is proud to remember, others she'd better forget.

She has known both the heights of exaltation and grubby treatment as well. She sheltered men who strove to stabilise a colony. She adapted herself to being a gaol for war prisoners and a hospital for the fever-ridden. She watched the gestation of revolt and served as midwife to the birth of a nation. She accepted the affront of being turned into a museum for curios, was tinkered at by this person and that, and long knew shabby neglect.

Now, having become a national shrine, preserved for all time, she is looked upon with affectionate regard by the local citizenry and approached with reverence by all to whom liberty is a precious heritage.

None can enter her doors but is humbled by the realisation of what happened there. We tread her halls softly. The welter of perplexities through which the young nation struggled recedes into the shadowy past of battles long ago. Yet the men who laboured there remain very much alive. They left something of themselves in her walls—something of Washington and Jefferson, Adams and McKean, Read and Rodney, Hancock, Biddle, Cadwalader, Gerry, Wolcott, Franklin, Matlack, Light Horse Harry Lee and both the youthful and the aged la Fayette.

It is a pretty poor Philadelphian who has no personal link with Independence Hall, either an ancestor or a first visit. Memory etches the graphic picture of a grandfather who devoted his life to public service, and whose other distinction lay in his being the last Philadelphian to wear a choker-collar, stock and swallow-tail coat. He cherished a private link with the Speaker's Chair, now preserved in the Hall. Once he sat in it while Speaker of the House in Harrisburg during Civil War days. Once a year, as age crept on him, he made a private pilgrimage to sit in it again.

On one of these occasions, since I bore his name, I was taken along—a very little boy grasping the hand of his very old grandfather. The guards saluted him, the custodian untied the ribbon, and then the very old gentleman sat in the chair and addressed the very little boy—told him never to forget this day.

Because he never has forgotten it, he is happy to set down these few remarks to introduce this diary of Independence Hall.

Richardson Wright

DIARY OF INDEPENDENCE HALL

NOTE

The State House doesn't become "Independence Hall" until long after the "Signers" have set their names to the Declaration of Independence.

From its very birth, the State House and its many occupants stand in the forefront of history's stage. History—Provincial, State, National—is made within the State House in continuous sequence. Even the Provincial Assembly—stodgy and humdrum as divers Members often are—nevertheless contrives to cause situations fraught with dramatic import. History's web from the outset is kaleidoscopic in colouring. In all the varied texture of events, seamy side and smooth, the colour of warm humanity appears in warp and weft. Drama so inseparably affixed to the State House is sometimes comedy, sometimes tragedy.

The first impetus towards building the State House comes from a row—Paper Money disturbances of 1728. Mobs have ever been much the same the world over—the rabble adepts at smashing windows, flinging cabbages, dead cats, stones or any other handy missiles; to say nothing of graver violence and criminal acts, under strong excitement or the urge of deep-seated rage. Which forceful displays are apt to be disconcerting to those in political disagreement with the rioters. The Paper Money outbreak so perturbs the Provincial Assembly's country Members that they beg the Governour to set some place of meeting other than Philadelphia. Which Governour Patrick Gordon does not. Instead, he tactfully sidesteps the issue, storm blows over, and Philadelphia City and County offer to build a State House for the Assembly's permanent meeting-place.

While the State House is a-building, it's "pull Dick, pull devil" between Andrew Hamilton and Doctor John Kearsley (properly pronounced *Carsley*), two of the building committee whom the Assembly appoint. Estimable gentlemen both, but with pronounced divergent notions of their own, they squabble violently about site and design alike. Andrew Hamilton comes off top dog, at which Doctor Kearsley's permanently disgruntled; the Assembly vote preference for Hamilton's design. Costs less; that appeals to the financially cautious Quakers. One usually pictures Doctor Kearsley as devoted churchman, designer and generous benefactor of Christ Church; eminent physician and a foundation-stone of

Philadelphia's later medical celebrity; finally, founder and en-
dower of Christ Church Hospital, that peaceful old-age haven of
refuge for "decayed gentlewomen." Hamilton's name recalls the
eminent jurist whose legal and administrative abilities are indispensable to the Province; defender of John Peter Zenger in New
York and vindicator of the freedom of the press in 1735, when
his masterly pleading (reckoned the "greatest oratorical triumph
won in the colonies prior to the speech of James Otis against
writs of assistance") wins him the "keys" of New York City in a
gold box (now preserved at the Historical Society of Pennsylvania),
and makes a profound impression on legal circles in England.
Politically at daggers' points for a long time past, we catch these
two worthies in an unaccustomed light, stubborn Scot pitted
against equally stubborn Yorkshireman.

Before the building's anywhere near finished—the workmen are
just about raising the "bush"—Hamilton makes all the artisans a
lavish "raising" feast in one of the still incomplete rooms. Behold! A grand leather-apron frolic; plenty of beer and beef and
lots of other victuals and drinkables suitable to the occasion.

Scarcely are the Assembly settled in the new State House than
they employ brisk young Benjamin Franklin as Clerk. Benjamin,
'tis said, is "far from being a nice young man"; in modern par-
lance, he's a "roughneck," but wide-awake, aggressive and *very*
efficient. Obviously chock full of promise and latent capacity,
afterwards to bear fruit in the mature philosopher and diplomat.

Soon (October, 1737) Sheik Sidi appears with his entourage and
the blessing of his Majesty, George II. Some call this colourfully-
clad Oriental the "Emir of Syria," some "the Eastern Prince."
Since he comes with the King's recommendation (and soliciting
contributions for Heaven only knows what), he gets marked attention and goes off with a substantial sum in his jeans, or in
whatever kind of garment he carries his pounds, shillings and
pence. The Assembly are not sitting at the time, but they foot
the bill for his entertainment—£37. 2. 3.

On a November day in 1747, Indian chiefs resplendent in paint
and feathers do a War Dance in the Council Chamber!—an "exhibition piece" performed in all friendliness. In November, five
years later, James Hamilton's giving a splendid ball at the State
House to celebrate the King's Birthday; supper's spread in the
Banquetting Hall and the many-coloured silks and brocades of

the guests' clothing, the glow of hundreds of candles and shimmering reflections from all the silver plate combine to make a picture one doesn't easily forget.

When the Earl of Loudoun, Commander-in-Chief of the British Forces in the American Colonies, comes to Philadelphia in 1757, the bells ring out a welcome, all the ships in the Delaware break out their colours and fire salutes, and the Mayor and Corporation of the City wine and dine him in the Banquetting Hall.

There's comedy in the Assembly Chamber in 1758. Provost Smith defies the Assembly. They're prosecuting him for libel, have haled him before them in that very chamber where the Declaration of Independence will be made eighteen years later. All the male portion of Philadelphia's patrician society, all the Crown and Proprietary Officers, the Trustees and Faculty of the College—all of them the Provost's friends—have crowded into the Assembly Chamber. The ladies, too, would gladly have come had it been *comme il faut* for them to appear in such a place. The belligerent Provost flatly refuses to plead before the Provincial Legislature, brands his arrest and prosecution unwarrantable and illegal, and appeals to the Crown. Whereupon all his loyal following burst into a very tempest of applause. The scandalised Assembly, bent on "saving face," order the Serjeant-at-Arms to clear the room and arrest the cheering, shouting gentry for contempt; an official gesture of bravado that has about as much effect in the end as a puff of smoke.

Eagerly curious young men, doctors' prentices belike, are entering the State House on a November evening (1762) to hear Doctor Shippen lecture on anatomy. He's just back from England and going to show the anatomical paintings Doctor John Fothergill's given the Pennsylvania Hospital. This lecture's the birth of America's first medical school.

On a Saturday afternoon in early October (1765) two black drummer-boys are beating a summons to an hastily-called meeting in the State House Yard. Feeling's tense about the Stamp Act; the city's a veritable hornets' nest of resentment towards the British Ministry. People are determined the odious stamped papers shall neither be landed nor sold. Angry thousands in the State House Yard send word to John Hughes, the appointed stamp master for Pennsylvania, demanding his instant resignation. As Pennsylvania's Colonial Agent in London, Franklin's nominated

Hughes for the job; this has done the Doctor's reputation no good. The mob have already threatened his house and obliged Deborah to resort to barricades and guns.

On a cloudless June day (1769) crowds stand watching in the State House Yard with bated breath. In the little observatory the Philosophical Society have built just south of the State House's east wing, Doctor John Ewing and his helpers are carefully recording the Transit of Venus for the Royal Astronomer at Greenwich and all the learned societies in England and on the Continent.

On a mid-October Saturday (the 16th) in 1773, excited citizens throng the State House Yard; in mass-meeting they pass the famous "Tea Resolutions" which Boston adopts *verbatim* November 5th. Philadelphia's the first city of the Colonies to organise resistance and pass resolutions against the Tea Tax; Boston, under Sam Adams's prodding, the first to exert direct action and have a "Tea Party."

Monday morning, December 27th (1773), angry crowds are streaming to a town-meeting in the State House Yard. Eight thousand are already there when the Committee call the meeting to order; they're still hastening thither from all directions. Right after the Christmas Eve news of the Boston Tea Party, the tea-ship *Polly*'s come up the river on Christmas Day; the city's in a seething ferment. A committee took Captain Ayres off the *Polly* and yesterday let him see for himself the people's dangerous temper. This morning it's speedily settled in town-meeting to send Captain Ayres, with "a flea in his ear," and the *Polly* (the tea unlanded) straightway back to England. So ends Philadelphia's "tea party"; very summary and effectual, but just as orderly as anything of the kind could be. Much more orderly, indeed, than a demonstration the following May when the mob create an uproar, Alexander Wedderburne (Attorney-General in England) and Governour Thomas Hutchinson of Massachusetts, the targets of their animosity.

Word has just come that Wedderburne lost his temper and roundly berated Doctor Franklin before the Privy Council in London—inexcusable, in view of Franklin's age, if for nothing else. As to Governour Hutchinson, the mob remember how their compeers in Boston looted his house during the Stamp Act frenzy; they likewise know the Governour's attitude on the tea question, also the gist of the "purloined letters," an unauthorised publication Franklin has taken good care to have well broadcast in America.

With this double-barrelled excuse for a rowdy show—Philadelphia can improvise mobs quite as spontaneously as Boston—the crowd make effigies of Wedderburne and Hutchinson, pin opprobrious labels on their breasts, with jeers and insults draw them through the streets on a cart, and wind up at the London Coffee House. There they hang both effigies on the same gallows, pile faggots beneath, sprinkle gunpowder thereon and start a blaze with a spark from an electric battery said to have been borrowed from Franklin's house nearby. Then, to let off their "patriotic" steam, they whoop and yell till naught remains but ashes. "Complete decorum" characterises this exhibition—say the newspapers!

News of the Boston Port Bill—Parliament's answer to the Boston Tea Party—sends all the Boston radicals into a frantic pepper-jig, Sam Adams erupting fire and brimstone like a volcano. Paul Revere comes a-riding post haste to Philadelphia with a message seeking Philadelphia's countenance and support. The Boston hot-heads are bent on entangling Philadelphia in the snarl—to force a stand for active resistance, if not for out and out independence.

Follows an adroitly stage-managed meeting at the City Tavern, the "most considerable citizens" attending—hand-picked to represent all shades of political opinion. Impassioned speeches by Joseph Reed, Thomas Mifflin and Charles Thomson; Thomson, a frail man, faints and is carried out. Utter confusion and hubbub. When a semblance of order's restored, John Dickinson advocates more moderate views. Then he slips away as angry babel bursts forth again. Before this hectic meeting breaks up, Thomson (he's revived and come back) persuades them to appoint a committee to adopt resolutions of sympathy with the Boston people. The committee meet next day (May 21st, 1774) and Provost Smith draughts a letter; a diplomatic document, this, advising firmness, moderation and the calling of a Continental Congress from all British American Colonies. With this letter Paul Revere goes galloping back to Boston.

June 18th (1774) a great mass-meeting in the State House Yard —result of busy agitation and planning. They ask Governour Penn to summon the Provincial Assembly immediately, in emergency session, to appoint delegates to a Continental Congress, to meet in early autumn. The Governour declines. Under leadership of

John Dickinson, Thomas Willing and Provost Smith (who've presided at the State House Yard meeting), invitations then go out for a Convention of committees from every county in the Province, to meet in July at Carpenters' Hall. Governour Penn suddenly changes his mind; summons Assembly for special session on July 18th—to discuss urgent "Indian affairs."

Provincial Convention meets at Carpenters' Hall July *15th*, (1774); John Dickinson prepares resolutions declaring "there is an absolute necessity to consult together and form a general plan of conduct to be observed by all the Colonies, for the purpose of procuring relief for our suffering brethren, obtaining redress for our grievances," and similar pressing matters. Thomas Willing's Chairman, Charles Thomson's Clerk.

July 21st the Provincial Convention come in a body to the State House. With great dignity they lay before Speaker Galloway, seated in his chair of office, their "Resolves on the Grievances of the Colonies and their Instructions to their Representatives in Assembly," along with the request that Deputies to the Continental Congress be appointed. (Connecticut and Maryland have already chosen Deputies; the Pennsylvania Assembly does so July 23rd.)

Sharp contrasts, on the 21st, when all the Convention members enter the Assembly Chamber together! The Convention delegates are mostly urbane gentlemen, arrayed in suitable summer garb. To John Young (eye witness), Assemblymen are just the opposite; he pictures them a group of sweating, stinking rustics—it's in the heat of summer—and writes his aunt (the well-known Mrs. Ferguson of Graeme Park):

"I assure you our Honourable House [the Provincial Assembly] made but a scurvy appearance the day the memorial was presented . . . it was enough to make one sweat to see a parcel of Countrymen sitting with their hats on, great Coarse Cloth Coats, Leather Breeches, and woollen Stockings, in the month of July; . . . not a Speech made the whole time, whether their silence proceeded from their Modesty, or from their inability to speak I know not."

A precious lot of "hick" mumchantzes, you say? Yes, doubtless, some are; but certainly not *all*. Conspicuous objectionables impress Young so unfavourably that he's blind to the exceptions, many exceptions. In the clodhopper class you certainly can't include Chief Justice Allen, Michael Hillegas, George Gray, Speaker

Joseph Galloway, Samuel Miles and many others; as for Thomas Mifflin, he's always been reckoned a dandy.

Early in September (1774), less than two squares away down Chestnut Street, about forty-odd very respectable-looking gentlemen (evidently strangers) are coming up from the City Tavern and turning in to Carpenters' Hall. They're Deputies to the First Continental Congress, going to inspect the place suggested and urged for their sessions. Even "rabble-rouser" Sam Adams is all spruced up into sartorial smartness; his admirers at home have seen to that before he leaves Boston—not forgetting new wig, new hat and "six pairs of the best silk hose."

As Speaker of the Pennsylvania Assembly, Joseph Galloway's offered them the State House; many would like to accept, but the rampageous, fire-snorting radicals know Galloway disapproves their attitude and fear pressure of his influence should they sit in the same building where he's presiding over the Pennsylvania Assembly. They'll have no favours nor courtesies at his hands. They get their way; the State House offer's declined.

When the Second Continental Congress convene in May, 1775, they meet in the Assembly Chamber at the State House. In the new Assembly—new since October 1774 elections—there's some change in membership. Galloway's no longer Speaker; Edward Biddle now holds that post. His politics different from Galloway's, the radicals are not so uneasy about sitting in the State House. The Assembly turn over their Chamber to Congress, leave all their furnishings, including the great silver inkstand on the Speaker's Table, and move across the hall into the Supreme Court Room.

Henceforth the Assembly Chamber's the established meeting-place of the Continental Congress throughout the Revolutionary War, save when circumstances dictate sitting elsewhere for the time being. For instance, during the British tenure of the city; in the hurried flight just before that, one of the Delegates leaves in such haste that he goes riding away without his saddle. Then the British troops come marching down Second Street to the brave strains of "God save the King," Hessians, cows and a flock of goats bringing up the rear.

Here, before that disconcerting episode, in the Assembly Chamber Colonel George Washington's nominated and appointed General and Commander-in-Chief of the Continental forces.

Here, also, take place all the long, anxious debates preceding the adoption of the Declaration of Independence.

At noon, Monday, July 8th, 1776, from the balcony of that same little observatory in the State House Yard, where Doctor Ewing's party watched the eclipse in 1769, clear-voiced John Nixon's reading to the gathering below him the newly-adopted Declaration of Independence. Young Deborah Norris, with a child's curiosity to see and hear, peeks from a vantage-point near her father's house (the same side of Chestnut Street below Fifth) to find out what's going on in the State House Yard. She puts it all down in her *Diary;* tells what sort of people are listening to Colonel Nixon. Not very many—very few of the "better sort."

And how about that eager, breathless throng in front of the State House; the little blue-eyed, fair-haired lad rushing from the door and shouting up to the white-headed bell-ringer waiting in the steeple, "Ring, Ring!"? Why no emphasis on that incident? *Because it never happened.* That pretty dramatic yarn's entirely the figment of the romantic novelist George Lippard's imagination, invented and published full seventy years later.

This official noonday proclamation of the Declaration seems tame and perfunctory—an anti-climax—by comparison with some of the incidents immediately preceding it (for instance, Caesar Rodney's arrival at the State House door, mud-caked and weary, just in the nick of time to cast his deciding vote for Delaware), or compared with the bonfires, bell-ringing and demonstrative jubilation that same evening.

The State House's story during the British occupation's not cheerful. Part of the time it's both hospital and gaol for American prisoners of war. At the Evacuation, it's in a filthy, dilapidated state; has to be thoroughly house-cleaned and repaired. Congress try to meet there early in July (1778); the stench drives them away. They have to sit at the College Hall for nearly a month while things are being set to rights.

Mid-July (1778) arrives the Sieur Gérard, French Minister Plenipotentiary—first accredited diplomatic representative to the infant nation. Much excitement, much impatience for Congress to receive him in due audience, much discussion about protocol. At last, August 6th—the State House deloused, set in order, and the stench quelled—Congress, in all their best clothes, await the Minister's coming. A few minutes past noon, up drives a coach-

and-six (furnished by Congress), Richard Henry Lee sitting on the back seat beside the Minister, Sam Adams opposite on the front seat. After the ceremony, *exeunt omnes* for a "grand dinner," with "an Agreeable band of Musick," and cannon booming to mark the many toasts.

On an October day (1779), from the State House steps, General Joseph Reed, "with several of his partizans & some Presbyterean preachers . . . in very mild and humble terms," is haranguing the mob and "those called the Militia," trying to quiet their rage and blood-lust and coax them to go home without further disorder. This, after their yesterday's assault on "Fort Wilson," when the mob were out to kill the "aristocrats," particularly Robert Morris and James Wilson. Only timely intervention by the City Troop, a few "regulars" and some "gentlemen" then routed the armed rabble and prevented the disgrace—almost within the shadow of the State House—of shedding the blood of three signers of the Declaration of Independence "whose patriotism is not sufficiently ardent to satisfy these American Jacobins." One of the "pleasant" episodes, this, during Philadelphia's "Reign of Terror," when rampant anarchy masquerades as democracy!

Not so serious, but bad enough's the scene on Saturday, June 21st, 1783. The country's bankrupt. Mutinous soldiers of the Pennsylvania Line gather at the State House demanding back pay; send in an impertinent message to the Supreme Executive Council of the State, giving them just twenty minutes to make terms. Although a quorum's not yet present, many Members of Congress are in the Assembly Chamber. The demonstration isn't aimed at them, but they're in consternation. Allowed to escape with only rude epithets hurled at them, they hold an emergency session in Carpenters' Hall. They're really alarmed; worse still, their dignity's suffered a galling affront. They send the Council a sharp message claiming the State's protection; insist the Militia be called to disperse the mutineers. Mutiny peters out, aggrieved soldiery are induced to go back to Barracks without violence, Militia not called out, nothing's done, and Congress rise in a huff and go off to Princeton. Never return until Philadelphia's become the National Capital, under the Federal Constitution.

From the Walnut Street Gaol, over against the State House Yard, we see "wheelbarrow-men," chained to their barrows, clanking into the scene; Washington's serene figure entering the pink and gold bedizenment of Ricketts's Circus to watch equestrian feats; to celebrate the ill-starred Dauphin's birth, the French Minister's grand fête in his nearby garden (ice-cream, cakes, confections, Madeira, claret and champagne to regale the guests); Chief Justice McKean presiding on the bench in all the majesty of powdered wig and scarlet silk robes, his associate justices likewise in scarlet; rude coffins piled on the State House pavement during the yellow-fever plague; in Congress Hall (1798) Representative Lyon spitting tobacco-juice in Representative Griswold's face—incidents, all, that come into the richly varied story of the State House.

When National and State Governments alike have left the city, the State House becomes a museum. In moves that versatile and eternally industrious gentleman, Charles Willson Peale; during the Revolution he's "fit and painted, painted and fit." The halls where Colonial Governours and Councils, the Provincial Assembly, the Supreme Court of the Province, the Continental Congress and the Constitutional Convention have sat now become a repository for mastodons' and pterodactyls' bones, stuffed birds and reptiles, the abundant fruits of Mr. Peale's brush, and the thousand-and-one ingeniosities he contrives to beguile the public.

When the Peale Museum moves out, the State House reclaims esteem as an historic structure. In 1824, when la Fayette revisits America, everybody feels there can be no more fitting place wherein to receive and honour the old General than the building where many of American history's most momentous incidents have taken place. Mr. Strickland erects a triumphal arch before the Chestnut Street front; Mr. Sully paints the City Arms on top; and Mr. Rush's sculptures adorn the sides. The Assembly Chamber, where the Declaration of Independence was adopted and signed, gets special care. At last, Tuesday afternoon, September 28th, la Fayette arrives in a barouche with six cream-coloured horses and outriders. His escort lead him up the steps and into the Chestnut Street door, while a band blares forth "See! The Conquering Hero Comes!"

"Philadelphia, yᵉ 31st Day of May, Anno Dom. 1717
The Honble William Keith, Esq., being this Day arrived from
Great Britain with a Commission from the Proprietor, & the
Royal Approbation, to be Lievtenant Governour of this province
& the three Lower Counties upon Delaware, The Honble Collᵒ.
Gookin, with the Council, attended by the Aldermen, Common-
alty & Officers of the Corporation, Received him at his Landing,
and the sd. Commission & Approbation being Produced to the sd.
Collᵒ. Gookin & Council, It was Ordered that it should be forthwith Proclaimed: accordingly, The same was Published & Proclaimed in Due Form, at the Court House in Philadelphia, The
Mayor & Corporation & Gentlemen & Inhabitants of the sd. City
attending. . . ."

No Lieutenant-Governour ever came with fairer prospects than
Keith. But soon he's tempted of the devil. He yields; ill-begotten
ambition undoes him.

He has previous acquaintance with Pennsylvania and fair
knowledge of the Province he's now to govern—he's been Surveyor-
General of Customs for the Southern Division of America, in
1714 succeeding Colonel Robert Quarry, deceased. Those who've
met Keith on his former visit like him; some of the principal men
in the Province have written the Proprietor favouring his appointment.

Keith has powerful Government friends at home; he's proved
acceptable to the Proprietary Family. Urbane and affable, he
seems to have all requisite qualifications to please King, Proprietor, Provincial Council, Assembly and people. Best of all, he's
succeeding Gookin, who's made himself thoroughly disliked and
distrusted; contrast helps Keith.

But Keith's rôle is fraught with perplexing difficulties. Christ
warned His disciples "no man can serve two Masters." *Three*
confront Keith—the Proprietor, who's appointed him; the King,
who's confirmed his appointment; and the Provincial Assembly,
who represent the people or, at least, are supposed to, and contribute his stipend. The three interests often conflict. The Assembly are strongly anti-Proprietary. A Governour must be a

consummate diplomat and skillful navigator if he's to keep in the good graces of all three masters.

Keith starts well. He effects much-needed reorganisation of criminal court procedure and speeds administration of justice; respects Quaker scruples anent oaths and secures optional affirmation; deals wisely with the Indians; and fosters commerce—his policies measurably aid the Province's prosperity. When it's plain that trade will languish and stagnate unless money circulation can be increased, he helps establish a sound paper currency, adequately secured against real estate and silver plate. By dispensing "sugar plums" he becomes tremendously popular. His administration, "after witnessing the depression of the colony, inaugurates a prosperity which in time makes Philadephia the largest city in America." If the record could stop there, one would readily admit that Keith's "the greatest of the Lieutenant-Governours under the Penns."

Unfortunately, he has inherent defects of character that popularity stimulates and brings to the surface. Avid of popular acclaim, he courts it "by every means—fair and foul." His notions of personal responsibility in financial matters are, putting it mildly, elastic. He makes profuse, extravagant promises he can't keep, or doesn't intend to. Witness his contemptible treatment of Benjamin Franklin; first flatters that young gentleman and puffs him up with exalted ideas of his own importance, gives him an intolerably swelled head for the time being, then sends him off on a wild goose chase to England—minus promised funds, minus letters of introduction that were to be an "Open *sesame*" to a rosy future! (Perhaps this *contretemps*'s a blessing in disguise to Benjamin; brings him down to earth with a bump and helps teach him realistic common-sense in appraising true values in human nature.) Furthermore, Keith contracts embarrassing debts. Finally, he's not politically sagacious enough to see he's "betting on the wrong horse" by throwing his lot wholly with the Assembly, ignoring the Penn Family's wishes, and quarrelling with the Council, which body, indeed, he tries to abolish.

He knows the Crown's been treating to buy the Proprietary rights, though negotiations are now in abeyance. He knows the low state of the Penns' fortunes and that they're not able to oppose effectually if the Crown inclines to acquire the Province. He sends the Lords of Trade and Plantations misrepresentations; he schemes to detach the Three Lower Counties on Delaware from the Penns and put them directly under the Crown. Ambition and vanity lead him to hope and believe that by skillful wire-pulling he can persuade the Crown to take over Pennsylvania, then by adroit management have himself appointed Royal Governour. (It's always irked him to govern for a mere woman—Hannah Penn.) All this is black duplicity; shameless disloyalty to the Penns, to whom he owes at least a pretense of gratitude. His quarrel with Logan and the Council now becomes a boomerang.

To make a long story short, in 1726 Keith finds himself superseded in the governourship by Major Patrick Gordon. However, he procures himself to be elected a Member of Assembly. He hasn't played all his cards yet; aided by the faction he's nurtured, he hopes to make Governour Gordon so much trouble that he can overset the government and compel the Crown to intervene. Then the coveted governourship will be again within his grasp.

One of the depositions made (subsequently recorded in Assembly minutes) reveals Keith's tactics in canvassing for votes and his unblushing avowal of subversive intent:

"*Samson Davis*, of the Manor of *Moreland*, in the County of *Philadelphia*, Yeoman, on his solemn Affirmation saith, That about the Month of *September*, 1726, on the first Day of the Week, Sir *William Keith* came from the Quakers' Meeting at *Horsham* to this Affirmant's House to Dinner; after which, the Discourse turning upon the ensuing Elections... Sir *William* said, if the People would chuse him a Representative, and if he could get some good Hands to assist him, he would take Care that the People should not be imposed upon; and that if the Governour, following the Advice of his Council, should refuse to pass any Law that the House might offer to him, they would give him no Support, which would oblige him to return Home about his Business; and by this Means they would so perplex the Proprietary, and make him uneasy, that he would be obliged to throw up the Government into the Hands of the Crown; and when that was done, he said, it would then be a proper Time for him to look out, and put in his Pretensions for obtaining the Government . . ."

This dirty political trickery disgusts Samson Davis; instead of voting for Keith and abetting his design to "bring Confusion in the Province" so as to overturn the government, Davis votes against him and tries "to influence others to do the like."

For a long time (when he's still Governour), while wooing the Assembly, Keith's likewise courted the Palatines (many of them, along with some Swiss and Huguenots, substantial folk of good stock), whom he's encouraged to migrate from the Livingston Manor in New York and squat on Proprietary lands in Pennsylvania without a shadow of warrant. At the same time, he's soft-soaped and couzened all the baser element, the rabble. For there *is* a numerous rabble, in the city and throughout the Province; there's plenty of contemporary evidence—complaints about transported gaol-birds, often confirmed criminals, that England dumps on the Colonies; "wild Irish" who crowd in, squat without leave in the "back parts" of the Province, and make trouble by being "rough" to the Indians; runaway indentured servants (redemptioners), extensively advertised for and minutely described in the newspapers. There's "hopping Peg," who limps, speaks with a broad West Country accent and has a nasal twang (Strange, this! The nasal twang comes from East Anglia, especially Suffolk); there's Jonas Smith, with an old hat, a new striped Ozenbrig shirt and a "down look, surly when spoke to." There are hundreds more of the same ilk—verily an unsavoury crew, fruitful of incendiary material. By his blandishments, our "grandiloquent baronet" has attached these folk of "vile and mean Condition" to his standard, as well as sundry of the "better sort," ready to do his bidding when it suits his purpose to stage a demonstration.

Keith's first conspicuous essay in that direction's just after he's elected to the Assembly in October, 1726. Let James Logan tell the story; though strongly opposed, Logan's always honest and dependable in stating facts. He writes John Penn:

"Sir W.K. for 13 months before his Removal gave freely out, that when he should no longer be Govr, he would be Speaker of our Assembly at least, and at our last Elections he putt up both for New Castle & this County, y^t he might be in both Houses. In ye first he missed it, but in this factious town where ye lower Ranks of People, Sr Will^{ms} Partisans, are ye most numerous he was elected. On ye 14th Instant however, when ye Representatives meet to choose their Speaker, tho' he came into town wth a Cavalcade of 80 horse under ye noise of many Guns firing . . . yet he was not so much as named for Speaker, but D Lloyd. . .carried it, they say by every Vote but three. . . And tho' he [Keith] will leave no means unessayed by cajoling, wheedling and every little art, to impose on and seduce some of ye honest well meaning Countrey Members, yet it is not apprehended y^t for the current year he will be capable of much harm."

Keith's strongest, most dangerous weapon to embarrass Governour and Council, and vex the Proprietary party, is the Paper Money issue. The Lords of Trade and Plantations frown upon paper money; its issue in other Colonies has been notably unsatisfactory. By Pennsylvania's Charter, Acts of Assembly are reviewable by the Lords of Trade and Plantations; if they fail of the Royal Approbation in Council, *ipso facto* they become null and void. Pennsylvania's previous emissions of paper money never had either Royal Approbation or Censure; judgement withheld, the Home Government tolerated Pennsylvania paper currency since it met a real need and was adequately secured. Still better, it worked. James Logan himself admits "it is really of service to yᵉ Countrey." But since the earlier issues, the Province has increased greatly in population and commerce. Obviously, more currency's needed in circulation; from every side come "loud Cries for more Paper Money."

Governour Gordon agrees more money's needed in circulation; favours a controlled emission of paper, following the precedent set. But his instructions from England preclude signing any paper money bill he knows the Crown will disallow. And the people, egged on by Keith and his faction, clamour for a *large* issue, regardless of proper security. Disastrous inflation will further Keith's plans.

As party leader, Keith never misses a chance to keep himself in the limelight; he's a good showman. The sorely vexed Logan writes John Penn:

"Sir Wᵐ Keith appears resolved as far as he can to perplex us. He went on board yᵉ Ship that brought thy last wᵗʰ Musick [Like a modern politician's stunt:] as we are told that yᵉ Capᵗ (Newton) might talk of him here and roar wᵗʰ his Party to keep up their Spirit."

Of the ten Assemblymen for Philadelphia City and County, the 1727 October elections return Keith himself and eight avowedly Keithians. "More Paper Money!"—*ostensibly* the sole Keithian election issue—has done it. The Keithians loudly proclaim the Governour and country Assemblymen oppose *any* new emission. That's a lie.

Keith attends October and January Assembly sessions; to outward appearance he behaves well. But there's constant *"More Paper Money!"* agitation and pressure; well-engineered petitions reach the Assembly from various quarters. While the hubbub's stewing and steaming at boiling point, Sir William finds it expedient to slip away to England. His going, says Logan,

". . . is told two different wayes, for some assure us, that not only Springet Penn but several great Lord Dukes &c have sent for our late glorious man to Europe to give him a new Commission, for this Governm^t, & y^t he is very speedily to return wth it to bless this Countrey again. While others presume to say of ye same pson y^t being made uneasie by some judgem^ts ag^st him, & informed of a fresh Demand on him from Europe for about 500 ^lbs Sterl. he thought. . . .

However it be, this is ye Truth in fact, that Sir Wm Keith about 12 dayes Since went very privately from hence in a Boat to Newcastle attended only by his great fr^d Wm Chancellor, & ye Rowers, & went wth one Small Trunk only on board Capt Colvil's ship, then lying before that Town bound for Europe, & y^t he staid in her 2 dayes so very privately that not one in ye place knew of it besides ye Coll his son in law & ye Parson G[eorge] R[oss] . . . ."

When the Assembly reconvene in April, Keith's gone. Never comes back. Returned to England, he has a chequered career of success and misfortune. He dies, 1749, in the Old Bailey. God rest his soul!

After Keith's hegira, his faction still function vigorously, quite capable of causing the confusion he wished to create. Their chance comes when the 1728-29 Assembly meet, October 14th. Outbreaks of hooliganism directed at Assemblymen offend their dignity as legislators. They remember Sir William's myrmidons "burnt the pillory and some market stalls" when he made his first sensational entrance into the city as a new Assemblyman. Whether "honest well meaning Countrey Members" dread personal violence added to verbal insults, most Assemblymen are thoroughly out of patience with the annoyances and indignities they're being subjected to in Philadelphia, where Keithian malcontents can count on the hoodlum element (country rowdies helping) to do their political dirty work. On the 16th, because of the "several Indecencies used towards the Members of Assembly . . . by rude and disorderly Persons," the Assembly pray the Governour and Council to set for next session some meeting-place other than Philadelphia that "to them shall seem most safe for the Members of Assembly." Then they adjourn to December.

When the Assembly regather in December, the hoodlums have quieted down. In his Speech, the Governour tells the House he thinks they'd better continue in Philadelphia for the time being because of the "Severity of the Season . . . and . . . the Settlement of the public Accounts, which . . . can no where so conveniently be done as where the Offices are Kept." Also tells them that a "Legislative Assembly is invested with a very great Authority" to punish "any Indignity," hopes they'll use it, and promises full support. Despite this pep talk, the Members still have misgivings, but settle down to business about the paper currency, with occasional digressions on "Swine running at large," pounds for stray animals, bounties on wolves' heads and the like.

February 20th, 1728, amidst absorbing money discussions, the *Votes of Assembly* record:

> "The Petition of divers Inhabitants of the City and County of *Philadelphia,* praying the House would, by a Law, impower the said City and County to build a Market and State-House in High-Street, near the Prison; was presented to the House, read, and ordered to lie on the Table."

The Assembly's October petition for some meeting-place other than Philadelphia's set responsible Philadelphians hard a-thinking:— It will be bad for the city to have the Assembly meet elsewhere (possibly for good and all); they've little material cause for attachment to the city; have no fixed place of meeting; sometimes have met at the Bank Meeting House; more recently have rented one or another private house to sit in; never know from year to year where they'll meet; have to depend on what they can get, often at the last minute; disconcerting to Members; scarce befitting the dignity of a prosperous province's legislature! If the Assembly can have a worthy structure built for them, it will tie them permanently to the city; make them feel they're appreciated, and become a matter of pride. Hence the State House Petition.

While the State House Petition's lying "on the Table," the Assembly adjourn to March 24th. Meantime turbulence crops up afresh. The £50,000 Paper Money Bill's been sent to the Governour; there's widespread feeling he'll refuse to sign it. The unthinking crowd are bound it *shall* pass, willy-nilly; are getting ready to take matters into their own hands.

The first day of the New Year, March 25th, 1729, the Governour vetoes the Paper Money Bill. Straightway the brewing hostility of the lawless element breaks forth. While the Bill's being reconsidered in the light of the Governour's suggested amendments, rumours are rife, disorderly clamours arise. On the afternoon of March 28th the Assembly resolve that

"the House enter upon the Consideration of the Peace of this Province, and the Safety of this House, prior to all other Business."

Then the Speaker issues warrants to the Serjeant-at-Arms to arrest four apparent ringleaders of the mob.

Next morning a committee (Andrew Hamilton one of them) frame an Address to the Governour; to wit, that

"great Numbers of dissolute and disorderly Persons have of late been imported, and daily do come from our neighbouring Colonies, and knowing we have no military Forces . . . have of late taken the Liberty to menace and threaten not only many private Persons, but likewise some of the Members of this House, to the great Terror of the Inhabitants of the City . . . the Disturbance of the Peace, and . . . Delay of the publick Service of the Country." The Assembly are outraged at "such riotous and tumultuous Attempts" and "the Promoters of such Tumults." Since an "Act of the General Assembly of this Province" provides *That Riots and Rioters shall be punished according to the Laws of England,"* they beg the Governour will proclaim the Riot Act.

Hamilton's hand in framing this Address proves it's a straightforward statement of an alarming condition; neither a panicky appeal, nor an exaggeration of facts.

The Governour forthwith proclaims the Riot Act of George I and bids the Sheriffs hold themselves ready "to raise the Posse Comitatus . . . to quell & reduce by Force all Tumults, Riots & Disorders." There's been a plot for armed rioters, several hundred strong, to march on the Assembly, force them—then and there—to pass a Paper Money Bill such as the mob demand, then bludgeon the Governour into signing it. Hamilton's got wind of it and it's at his instance the Assembly have asked the Governour to proclaim the Riot Act. Logan says the day the Assembly reconvene, the very day (March 31st) the Riot Act is

"proclaimed here about 200 Countrey men had agreed to come to this town wth Clubs. . . and with such of this place as would joyn them of whom they might have had large. . . numbers to apply first to the Assembly & then storm the Govern^r but with the Council, at least some of them, it was to have gone the hardest. Of these between 3 & 4 score came ye next day almost to ye town's" edge but "upon notice sent them of the measures taken here they retired."

The Riot Act makes rioting a felony punishable with death; that's damped the rioters' ardour and explains why "they retired" without breaking heads or shedding blood.

Though the riot's been nipped in the bud, people are keenly aware they've been "in real danger of Insurrection." Logan's letter to John Penn continues, there's

> "little room to doubt but there are those here who would be well content to see some here knock'd on the head, their Estates plundered & their Houses in Ashes for their private Satisfaction only, & that such a publick confusion might oblige the Crown to take the Govm^t out of your hands under its immediate care."

In case the Crown should disallow whatever Paper Money Bill may be enacted, he adds,

> "Pray be pleased to shew so much regard to those who are rendered obnoxious here [the Council] as to give them timely notice that such of them as may think their lives worth saving. . . may remove out of the reach of popular fury which on that occasion would I believe rage as high here as it has been known in any Countrey. . . S^r W^m [Keith] . . . was so mad as. . . industriously to sett up the lowest part of the People, wch make by far the greatest number in all Countreys above all others . . ."

James Logan's no hysterical "scary cat"; he's cool, clear-headed, matter-of-fact; above all, he's truthful, knows the inhabitants of the Province as few others know them, and sees with dispassionate calm how serious was the imminent Paper Money Riot—abortive only because of Hamilton's foresight and Gordon's prompt action.

When the House meet on April 28th, the ringleaders of disorder have been summarily dealt with; three of them fined, made to apologise and reprimanded; the fourth obliged also to beg the House's pardon on his knees. The Assembly's abated the proposed £50,000 issue to £30,000; the few remaining differences between their provisions and the Governour's conditions are being ironed out; by May 1st everyone's confident the Governour will sign the Bill.

On that date—May 1st, 1729—the *Votes* record:

> "Upon a Motion made, the House took into Consideration the necessity of a House for the Assembly of this Province to meet in; and the Question being put, that *Two Thousand Pounds* of the *Thirty Thousand Pounds*, now to be emitted, be appropriated for the Building of the said House? *Passed in the Affirmative, N.C.D.*"

The *unanimous* passage of this resolution plainly shows the change of feeling since the October (16th) petition. Furthermore, the

Assembly are undertaking the job as a body—not leaving it up to the City and County of Philadelphia.

Governour Gordon signs the Bill May 10th; it becomes the Paper Currency Act; the Great Seal of the Province is forthwith attached to it. One clause of the Act—the 16th; it's a long document—reads:

> "And forasmuch as a House for the Representatives of the Freemen of this Province to meet and sit in General Assembly in the City of *Philadelphia*, is very much wanted: Be it therefore enacted by the authority of the aforesaid, that the sum of two thousand pounds of bills of credit made current by this act be delivered by the Trustees of the Loan Office to Thomas Lawrence, Andrew Hamilton, and John Kearsley, who are hereby appointed for the building and carrying on the same."

Thus does the *Act for Emitting Thirty Thousand Pounds in Bills of Credit for the Support of Government and the Trade of this Province* implement the Assembly's "Resolve"; it appoints the Committee and provides initial funds to start building the State House.

The genesis of the State House, the Paper Money Disturbances and the Paper Money Act are inseparably bound together. The October (1728) turbulence upsets the Assembly and causes their petition to the Governour; without this provocation, the petition would not have been made. The Assembly's petition sets Philadelphia people a-thinking and occasions their own petition and offer to the Assembly; had there been no disturbances and no petition to the Governour for a different meeting-place, the project of building an House for the Assembly "to meet and sit" might have slumbered indefinitely—the petition awakened city sentiment and forced the question to the front. The quelling of mob tumult and final amicable agreement for a new paper money issue produce the Assembly's favourable attitude; hence the unanimous resolution of May 1st and the rider to the Paper Money Act. It's like a "House that Jack Built" sequence.

Even after Governour Gordon's signed the Paper Money Act, and the Great Seal of the Province is attached, there's still the possibility the King may disallow it. Knowing the Home Government's sentiments about paper money in general, and hoping to forestall adverse action by the Crown, the Assembly appoint a committee—Doctor John Kearsley, Andrew Hamilton and William Webb—"to prepare an address to the King, and another to the Penns, in favour of the law as passed." Their main concern is the paper money emission; building the State House, although coupled with it in the Act, is secondary. As a matter of fact, the Act never comes before the King in Council; the currency emission's adequately safeguarded and the Lords of Trade and Plantations let it receive permanent sanction of law by lapse of time.

Although the Paper Money Act, signed May 10th, 1729, is the enabling measure to start work on the State House, it's October 14th, 1730, before any land's secured for the site; they don't break ground until the summer of 1732. Long delay in starting is partly attributable to prudence in waiting to see what reaction the Act will cause in England; chiefly it's because of dissension between two members of the Building Committee—Hamilton and Kearsley.

When the people of Philadelphia petitioned the Assembly to let them "build a Market and State-house," the intended site mentioned was "High Street near the Prison." Doctor Kearsley wishes to stick to that site; Andrew Hamilton has other views, and contention starts right there. Thomas Lawrence keeps out of it. Hamilton decides to change the proposed location, "either upon his own responsibility" (trusting to his weight as Speaker of the Assembly, a post of almost autocratic power to which he's succeeded in 1729 on David Lloyd's retirement), or, "probably with the tacit consent of his fellow-commissioner, Lawrence." Hamilton envisions a building with ground enough around it to make a worthy setting. No such site's available in "High Street near the Prison." In Chestnut Street there is.

The whole square bounded by Chestnut, Walnut, Fifth and Sixth Streets was long ago set off for "bonus lots." When William

Penn first began to sell land in his Province, to each purchaser of a substantial farm site or "country lot" he gave also a city lot as a bonus. Two squares in his "greene Countrey Towne"—from Fourth Street to Sixth, between Chestnut and Walnut—he marked for the Welsh Friends who'd bought considerable acreage in the Welsh Barony. The eastward portion of the "Welsh Lots" was for colonists in Merion and Haverford Townships; the westward—the ground now taken up by the State House and Yard—was for the Radnor Welshmen. By 1730 most of the early grantees have sold their lots so that nearly the whole of the Radnor square's in the hands of only a few owners.

Hamilton delegates wealthy William Allen (later to become his son-in-law) to begin buying land in the Radnor square. The first ground acquired (deed dated October 14, 1730) has 198 feet frontage on Chestnut Street; on this earliest purchase the State House now stands. By 1732, Hamilton and Allen together, have secured the whole Chestnut Street frontage from Fifth Street to Sixth; the ground extends in depth half way to Walnut Street. Several small houses are already built on it; one of them the Assembly subsequently use to meet in for a time, just prior to moving into the State House.

Doctor Kearsley, his reputation established by the design for Christ Church, submits a design for the State House, opposes Hamilton's scheme every way. Hamilton, not to be swerved, goes ahead and breaks ground on the Chestnut Street lot.

This incessant friction necessitates a "show-down." It comes, in the Assembly, August 8th (1732). "Mr. Speaker" Hamilton tells the House the "said *John Kearsley*" has "opposed the Work, both on account of the Place where it is begun to be built, and of the Manner and Form of the Building," and has insisted the House "never agreed it should be erected in that Place"; he desires, therefore, to "know the Sentiments of the House thereupon." At that, Doctor Kearsley rises and has his full say. Then Mr. Speaker moves that the House "resolve itself into a Committee of the whole House" so he may "have an Opportunity of answering the said *John Kearsley*." Of what's said while the Assembly are in Committee of the whole House we have no record; there's doubtless plenty of "spice" in a discussion lasting several days. Hamilton's thoroughly disgusted with the whole situation. With constant wrangling, prejudiced opposition and animosity to contend with, besides serious loss of time from his law practice, he's quite ready to chuck the job. It's fortunate for posterity the Assembly back him whole-heartedly when the row's thrown into their laps.

August 11th, the Assembly minutes say, "Mr. Speaker produced a Draught of the State-house, containing the Plan and Elevation of that Building; which being viewed and examined by the several Members, was approved by the House." Hamilton's full vindication comes August 14th; Jeremiah Langhorne, Chairman of the Committee of the whole House, makes his report and the Assembly resolve "That Mr. Speaker both in regard of the Place whereon the Building of the State-house is fix'd, and of his Manner of conducting the same Building, hath behaved himself agreeable to the Mind and Intention of this House."

Jerry-building's not favoured in early eighteenth-century Philadelphia, especially for important structures. The State House rises with due expenditure of time; it's the object of daily scrutiny and criticism. Members of Assembly—others, too—get keenly building-conscious. They're also beginning to understand that public records ought to have a suitable repository. (Would that the present generation of Pennsylvanians had a deeper sense of the same obligation!) On the last day of the year (March 24th), 1732, the House resolve "That for the greater security of the publick Papers of this Province (agreeable to a Plan now produced before the House) two Offices be built adjoining to the State-house." Thus do the House arrange to start the east and west annexes—the low flanking buildings at each end of the main structure—during the summer recess of 1733.

Whence came Hamilton's design for the State House? Often asked and often answered, this question seems still to puzzle many. In 1732, some knowledge of architecture was deemed essential to a gentleman's education. Hamilton was a cultivated gentleman, familiar with all the best England had to offer in education and culture; and Hamilton was somewhat of a connoisseur and had a good library. We know, too, that one or more of the many splendidly-published books of architectural design held a place in nearly every private library worthy of the name.

Acquaintance with building styles enabled the amateur architect to indicate, however roughly, the kind of structure he wished to have built. The contracting builder (*architect-builder* might be a better term), whose job it was to translate the idea into tangible reality, could interpret his patron's rough sketch, cope with all technical and structural problems, supply all appropriate details from his pattern-books, execute them with masterly finish, and bring to final realisation a structure deserving and commanding posterity's lasting admiration. Edmund Woolley who, with Ebenezer Tomlinson, bore the most significant physical task in making the State House a reality of bricks, mortar and joinery, stood for all that was best in the practice of the building craft.

Hamilton's draught for the north elevation and floor plans of the State House (in the Collection of the Historical Society of Pennsylvania) is a rough sketch—exactly the kind of thing an amateur architect of the period would turn over to his architect-builder—drawn on parchment; not unlikely one of the skins from his law office, kept on hand for engrossing deeds. Lacking details, it nevertheless fully conveys the essential character of the building Hamilton had in mind. And Edmund Woolley was capable of putting it into acceptable execution.

There still remains the question of immediate inspiration. Joseph Jackson thought it came from James Gibbs's *Book of Architecture,* published in 1728. This seems not unlikely, although lacking proof. Hamilton, likely enough, knew Gibbs's book, and two plates in it show features closely resembling items in the State House design. Whether Hamilton used them or not, he unquestionably had breadth of vision, sound taste and a generous outlook. Nothing can lessen his right to be reckoned the father of America's most famous building.

Notwithstanding the Assembly's blanket endorsement of Hamilton's whole scheme and his direction of the work, certain self-appointed critics slander him, badger and carp at him till he loses all patience. In December, 1733, the Master Carpenters, in view of the "extraordinary Trouble and Expence they are put to," pray that "some Addition may be made to the Price now allowed them." The work is, quite true, much more exacting than house-building; this request—they don't strike and *demand*—is altogether reasonable and the Assembly accede to it. But the Master Carpenters' prayer gives the itching opposition the handle for a renewed chorus of clamours. Less than a month later (January 18th, 1733-34), Hamilton offers the Assembly a written "Remonstrance" wherein he rehearses all that's occurred to date—especially that the "whole Blame" for the delay in starting the State House "was charged upon the said *Andrew Hamilton*"; that he had "exhibited to the two Gentlemen concerned with him. . . a Plan and Elevation. . . and the same was compared with several other Plans and Elevations, one or more of which were produced by one of the Gentlemen joined in the said Undertaking; and that at last the Plan and Elevation now erected. . . was not only agreed upon as the least expensive, but also as the most neat and commodious, by the Persons entrusted to build the same, but likewise approved by the then House of Representatives." He continues that since "the Gentlemen employed with him. . ." declined to attend, he "proceeded to purchase Materials, and, with the Approbation of the several Assemblies. . . hath carried on the principal Building, with the Offices. . . ; in doing of which he hath not only undergone a great Deal of Trouble and Fatigue; but he hath sustained very great Loss in his Business," being obliged to almost constant supervision.

He concludes, "But forasmuch as many Persons, imagining it might recommend them to the People, have made it their Business unjustly to charge the said *Andrew Hamilton* with being the sole Projector of building a" State House, "and of his own Head running the Country to a much greater Charge than was necessary; The said *Andrew Hamilton* humbly requests of this House (to many of whom the Falsehoods of those Charges are well known) that they would be pleased to discharge him from having any further Concern in carrying on, or taking Care of the said Building, he being unwilling to bear the unjust Reproaches of malicious Persons, for doing what he conceived, and is well satisfied, is not only necessary, but, when finished, will be a Credit to the whole Province."

Irritated beyond endurance, thus does the magnanimous mastiff growl and show his teeth at the tribe of yapping curs. The "bombshell" has the desired effect. As a remonstrance, it requires no corporate action by the Assembly, but it serves timely notice both on them that actually hear it read, and on the outside busybodies, to whom it's doubtless fully reported. The "request" at the end, the Assembly are too wise to accede to, or even consider.

The Remonstrance—worth reading if only as a bit of good, vigorous, straight-forward English that has almost the majestic surge of Elizabethan diction—gives certain definite data. It settles beyond question that the Assembly are sitting in one of the small houses (already standing there when the State House property's acquired) while the principal block of the State House is a-building; likewise that *several* plans have been submitted and discussed, the final decision based on considerations of cost and suitablity; also, that the building's intended to house the Supreme Court as well as the Assembly; and that the "Offices," east and west of the principal building, are already well under way. It's easy to see why Hamilton must spend so much time in consultation and superintendence; the State House is the largest and most important building that's yet been undertaken in the Province—in any of the American Colonies, save the Wren building of William and Mary College, the Capitol at Williamsburg, and Old Harvard and Massachusetts College at Cambridge (the Old State House in Boston is 10 feet longer but has no "Offices" or wings)—and problems constantly arise to perplex the contracting-builders.

According to custom, a "raising" feast is given the workmen on completing the main portion of a structure, the "finishing" still to be done. For the State House and its "Offices," there are several "raising" spreads, apparently on a lavish scale, to judge from Hannah Powell's "Petition" to the Assembly, October 14th, 1734, wherein she says "that she had exhibited an Account to the last Assembly, of Victuals, Drink, and other expensive Articles, provided for the People who were employed in raising the State-house, for a great Part of which she herself stands indebted at this Time," and prays speedy payment. The two Members, to whom the last Assembly have referred Hannah's bill, think it excessive and "have come to no Resolution thereupon," notwithstanding Hannah's "insisting strictly upon the Justness of her Charge." To quiet her present insistence, the House give an order to pay the "said *Hannah Powell . . . Sixty-one Pounds,* in Part of her said Account," the remainder to be examined at their next sitting. £61, in 1734, is a sizeable sum; either the workmen were very numerous, or they were overfed with expensive delicacies.

Hannah's not to be fobbed off with partial payments. She's right after the Assembly at their next sitting. March 28th, 1735, the *Votes* record:

"*Hannah Powell,* pursuant to the Leave given her, having exhibited to the Committee her Account, not mentioned in the Articles hitherto charged. . . the said Committee. . . reported. . . they had examined the said Accounts, and, upon the whole matter, find a Ballance in her Favour of *Fifteen Pounds, Nineteen Shillings,* and *One Penny* besides what hath been formerly allowed. . . in the Whole, amounting to *Eighty-eight Pounds, Nineteen Shillings,* and *One Penny.*"

Still "pursuant" and clamourous, if not altogether business-like in rendering her bills (she's omitted to charge for her own services in *cooking* the food), Hannah next day bepesters the Assembly with a further claim that "she hath not charged any Thing in her Accounts, formerly exhibited, for the Trouble she was at in dressing Victuals . . . at the several Raisings of the State-house." After "Debate thereupon," the Assembly silence further importunities by giving her £10. Thus endeth the unbusiness-like Hannah episode.

Towards the end of September, 1736, there's a "house-warming" feast in the Banquetting Hall. The *Pennsylvania Gazette* of September 30th says:

"Thursday last William Allen, Esq., Mayor of this City. . . made a Feast for his Citizens at the State-house, to which all the Strangers in Town of Note were invited. . . considering the Delicacy of the Viands, the Variety and Excellency of the Wines, the great Number of Guests, and yet the Easiness and Order with which the Whole was conducted, it was the most grand, the most elegant Entertainment that has been made in these Parts of America."

This "house-warming" dinner mustn't be confounded with the previous "raising" feasts for the workmen, about which Hannah's made such a pother. Mayor Allen pays for this dinner out of his own pocket; the Assembly contribute not one penny. This banquet's the first of many that will be spread in the Banquetting Hall through the years—to mark Royal Birthdays, to honour the coming of a Commander of the Royal Forces in British America, to celebrate occasions of public rejoicing, or to welcome a new Governour or some member of the Proprietary Family.

On October 14th, 1736, when the Assembly meet for the first time in the Assembly Chamber, that noble room's by no means nearly finished; the walls yet unpanelled, the windows not fully glazed. That same day, the Assembly minutes say:

"A Petition from *Benjamin Franklin* was presented to the House, and read, setting forth, That he hath been informed this House have a disposition to change their Clerk, and if so, he humbly offers his Service to them in that Station;
Resolved, That *Benjamin Franklin* be appointed Clerk to the House of Representatives for the current Year.
And he was called in and qualified accordingly."

Difficulties about getting skilled workmen keep the building in an unfinished state until, in the summer of 1741, the impatient

Assembly insist that at least "the plaistering and glazing [of the Assembly Chamber] shall be finished for the next session, even if the ceiling and upper work must be delayed till workmen can be procured from England." They insist also "that the whole building. . . shall be finished without delay. . . for the use intended." "Use intended" includes accommodation for the Supreme Court in the west end of the ground floor, across the hall from the Assembly Chamber. The Supreme Court Room isn't ready for the Judges till 1743; it's 1745 before the Assembly Chamber's full finished. The Council Chamber (southwest room upstairs) isn't ready for the Governour and Council until the summer of 1747, and Mr. Secretary Peters has to nag Mr. Speaker Kinsey to have it ready by then.

Notwithstanding. long delays, and difficulties about skilled labour and materials, some very able craftsmen contribute their part to making the building what it is. Besides Edmund Woolley and Ebenezer Tomlinson, there are John Harrison, joiner and carver; Thomas Kerr, "plaisterer"; Brian Wilkinson, wood-carver; Thomas Ellis, glazier, and later, Thomas Godfrey, inventor of the quadrant; and Gustavus Hesselius, who subsequently makes a great name for himself as a portrait painter, paints the woodwork.

The exact date at which the tower's begun is uncertain. That it formed no part of the original scheme, we know; there's no sign of it on Hamilton's parchment draught. In spite of the oft-repeated assertion that Hamilton *forgot* the stair in his strictly rectangular lay-out of the building, examination of the parchment plainly shows the place indicated (on the plan of the upper floor) for the stair; it was to ascend from the south end of the central hall. In all likelihood, it soon becomes apparent that this arrangement's too crowded and the addition of a stair tower will much enhance both the appearance and convenience of the building. Presumably Hamilton has something to do with this generous extension and improvement of his earlier design, or, at least, approves it, for the tower's lower stages (probably up to the eaves of the main body) are completed in 1741, either just before or after his death.

Confirmation of this date is the bill Edmund Woolley presents on November 4th, 1741, "For expences in raising the Tower of the Stadt House." The items prove the "expences" are incurred for a "raising feast," which implies the structure's about completed. The feasters are evidently numerous, or else have an abnormal capacity for stowing away meat and drink. They consume, amongst other things, 44 pounds of mutton, 30 pounds of venison, 61¾ pounds of bacon, 37¾ pounds of veal, 148½ pounds of beef, besides turkeys and chickens, a barrel and a half of beer, and a reasonable allowance of punch, for there's a charge for 800 limes.

That the tower's steeple superstructure is fully determined upon, and the design settled by 1750, is evident from the Assembly's order of January 27th, in that year, "That the Superintendents of the State House proceed as soon as conveniently they may to carry up a building on the south side of the said house to contain the staircase, with a suitable place thereon for hanging a Bell." The words "carry up" indicate the addition of another storey or stage of the tower's brickwork, to provide a place "for our books" and for the use of committees; the "suitable place thereon for hanging a Bell" means the steeple superstructure surmounting the heightened brick tower. In 1750, also, Scull and Heap publish a map of the city, at the top of which is an engraving of the State House with the "completed" steeple, the completion, however, not yet a fact but only a cherished hope. This engraving's published in London two years later in the *Gentleman's Magazine*, for the edification of our British kin.

In October, 1751, the Assembly direct the State House Trustees —Isaac Norris, Thomas Leech and Edward Warner—to order a bell from England. In sending the order to Robert Charles, the Provincial Agent in London, Norris writes:

"We hope and rely on thy care and assistance in this affair, and that thou wilt procure and forward it by the first good opportunity, as our workmen inform us it will be much less trouble to hang the bell before their scaffolds are struck from the building where we intend to place it, which will not be done till the end of next summer or beginning of the fall."

This shows the steeple's not finished till 1752.

Bell arrives at the end of August; steeple ready for it. To everyone's great disappointment, it cracks while being tested. Two "ingenious workmen" in Philadelphia, Pass and Stow, recast the bell; it goes up in the steeple early in 1753. Hanging the bell calls for another "raising feast"; Edmund Woolley sends in a food and drink bill, as before. This time there's only a barrel of beer, with 300 limes and 3 gallons of rum; victuals also in less quantity.

After the bell, the next important acquisition's the silver inkstand, from which the Declaration of Independence will be signed twenty-odd years later. February 12th, it's

"*Ordered,* That the Superintendents of the State House do provide a suitable inkstand of silver for the use of the Speaker's table."

Philip Syng, the Elder, makes it; the Assembly pay £25. 16. 0. for it.

Having ordered a bell for the tower, and a massive silver inkstand for the Speaker's Table, the Assembly next decide (March 11th, 1752) to have a "large clock," with a "suitable dial plate to show the Hours and Minutes," which shall "strike on the Bell in the Tower." The clock-making they entrust to Peter Stretch, of Philadelphia. Isaac Norris says they expect Stretch's clock

"will prove better than any they would send us from England, where once they had put it out of their hands, they have done with it; but here the workman would be made very uneasy if he did not exert his utmost skill, as we do not stint him in the price of his labour."

The clock movements are placed right under the roof, in the middle of the main building and close to the tower. Rods connect with the dial plates at the ends of the main building; the dials, just below the eaves, are set on piers or jambs, projecting slightly from the walls, their design inspired by the familiar tall-case clock.

By Act of February 17th, 1762, the Assembly declare

"no part of said ground lying to the southward of the State House" shall "be made use of for erecting any sort of buildings thereon, but that the same shall be and remain a public green and walk forever."

At this time the State House Yard extends only half way to Walnut Street. A committee, however, have been treating to get the rest of the property bounded by Walnut, Fifth and Sixth Streets, so that the Province may own the whole square. This committee report favourably and an Act of May 14th, 1762, orders the Trustees to purchase the residue of the square "to and for the same uses, intents, and purposes to which the said [State] House and its appurtenances are appropriated." By the spring of 1769 the purchases are all completed and the Province in full legal possession of the whole State House Yard (Independence Square, as we now know it). In 1770, the Assembly enclose the whole Yard with a brick wall seven feet high; in the middle of the Walnut Street front, there's an high arched gateway with wooden doors.

For many years after the State House is built, delegations of sundry Indian tribes visit Philadelphia from time to time. During James Logan's lifetime, they often camp on the grounds at Stenton; Logan they trust and respect above all others. On these official visits, they're naturally guests of the Provincial Government. As such—especially since Logan's death—they're frequently entertained in the State House Yard at public expense; prior to 1759, they're often lodged in one of the wings or "Offices" of the State House. Few Indians are house-broken; besides the disconcerting filth after their departure, there's the constant risk of fire while they're here. These considerations lead to putting up two long, low sheds for the Indian visitors where are now the County Building (Congress Hall) and old City Hall (U. S. Supreme Court Building) at the respective corners of Sixth and Fifth Streets. These sheds appear in some of the early illustrations.

As early as 1736, Andrew Hamilton got the Assembly to convey certain lots to designated trustees who should "hold them in trust for the use of the City and County of Philadelphia." These two lots, one at the southeast corner of Sixth and Chestnut, the other at the southwest corner of Fifth and Chestnut Streets, have each a frontage of 50 feet on Chestnut Street and are 73 feet deep. The Assembly's resolution stipulates that the buildings to be erected thereon shall be

"of the like outward form, structure and dimensions, the one for the use of the County and the other for the use of the City, and to be used for the holding of courts or common halls and not for private buildings"; likewise that they shall be of design consistent with that of the State House.

Nothing's done about these buildings till the spring of 1785, when the Assembly begin to consider starting them. March 29th, 1787, they pass an "ACT *to enlarge the lots in the State-House square, appropriated for building thereon respectively county and city court-houses.*" The enlargement's but trifling, meant to remedy an error in setting the building-line farther back from the street than originally intended. After sundry delays and adjustments, work begins and the County Building's finished early in 1789, partly paid for by the sale of the "old gaol and workhouse" at Third and Market Streets.

Meanwhile, at the end of 1784, the Philosophical Society have applied for a site in the State House Yard whereon to put up a building for themselves. In spite of considerable opposition, the Assembly grant the request on March 28th, 1785; work's begun and, about 1788, the Society take possession of their "neat, sufficient Building, on the ground aforesaid," south of City Hall and fronting on Fifth Street below Chestnut.

March 4th, 1789, the Pennsylvania Assembly and the Representatives of the City and County of Philadelphia consider, and on the 5th unanimously resolve

"That the members of the Senate and House of Representatives of the United States, from this State, be authorised to make a respectful offer to the Congress of the use of any or all the public buildings in Philadelphia, the property of the State and of the building lately erected on the State House Square belonging to the City and County of Philadelphia, in case Congress should at any time incline to make choice of that city for the temporary residence of the federal government."

This offer's accepted, Philadelphia becomes the National Capital for ten years, and the United States Senate and House of Representatives begin to occupy Congress Hall, December 6th, 1790.

The City Building, at Fifth and Chestnut Streets—partly paid for by a lottery—isn't completely finished until the fall of 1791, although it's near enough completion for the Supreme Court of the United States, Chief Justice John Jay presiding, to begin sitting there February 7th, 1791. The Supreme Court occupy the large back room upstairs.

Before the Revolution, the old steeple (the wooden structure raised on top of the brick tower) has become decayed and is taken down in 1781. The brick tower is then roofed over, as it appears in the Birch prints. Not until 1828 is the present steeple built (approximately a restoration) from designs by William Strickland.

In 1811, the two old wings or "Offices," with the arcades joining them to the main building, are removed; Robert Mills designs more compact buildings to replace them. (Mills's structures have since been removed and replaced by restorations of those originally there.) About this period, and also later, other and worse acts of vandalism are perpetrated and remain as eyesores until the final and complete restoration.

When the State Legislature leave Philadelphia, in 1799, the State House falls on evil days. In 1816, the Legislature wish to sell the State House and State House Yard—the Yard to be cut up into building lots! However, they *graciously* give the City an option to buy the entire property for $70,000. The City raises the money, becomes the owner, and saves the State House for posterity.

1738

Tuesday, August 22—Govenour Thomas sends the Assembly a special Message:

"Gentlemen.

At the Desire of the Council, I herewith send you two Accounts, amounting to *Thirty-seven Pounds, Two Shillings* and *Threepence,* for the Entertainment of the Scheick Sedi, a Christian Nobleman from Syria, who came to this City in October last, and produced Credentials and a Recommendation from his Majesty's principal Ministers of State. As the Assembly was not sitting at that Time, the President and Council could not consult them; but from the private Instances of Humanity and Generosity . . . exercised here towards that Unfortunate Nobleman, I have no room to doubt of your ordering the Bills to be paid." The Assembly thereupon,

"*Resolved,* That the Accounts. . . be allowed."

The Sheik Sidi Alhazar makes a sensation. A lusty person clad in flowing Eastern robes, impressive black whiskers, a "turbant" on his head, he comes with the King's blessing to solicit contributions—'tis said, to raise a ransom to free wife and children from the Sultan's gaol. People are generous; he gets about £250.

James Logan's the only person in Philadelphia able to converse with the Sheik. Logan says:

"He appeared to be a gentleman, whatever else he might be besides. As he spoke nothing but Arabic and a little Syriac, he put me on scouring up what I had formerly gotten and forgotten of these, and we exchanged some little in writing."

The Sheik Sidi, of Beyrout, described as an "Eastern Christian" (probably Greek or Maronite), comes hither from Boston and New York. His credentials from England call him "*Unus ex nobilibus civitatis Berytus*"; commend him to the "charity of all Christian people."

It seems his province has been devastated by locusts, famine and other misfortunes. Consequently, he can't furnish the tribute and quota of soldiers the Sultan demands. The Sultan, savagely impetuous, shouts "Off with his head!" The friendly Russian Ambassador tips Sidi off to this bad news; he flees to Russia. Sultan claps Sidi's wife and children into gaol.

In Russia, Czarina Anne, niece of Peter the Great, takes pity on

Sidi, promises her interest in his behalf when a treaty's made with the Sultan, then ships him off to the Muscovite Ambassador in London. That obliging gentleman commends him to the Royal Clemency, whereupon Sidi obtains a "brief" to solicit aid in England and the American Colonies. Hence his arrival in Philadelphia. Various churches, as well as the Quaker Meeting—and probably some private individuals—contribute to his necessities. He goes hence to Barbadoes; is last heard of there.

Votes of Assembly; *History of Philadelphia*, Thompson Westcott, ch. xcii; *Chronicles of Pennsylvania*, C. P. Keith, ii, 729; *The History of Nova-Caesaria or New Jersey*, Samuel Smith, 1765, 2nd ed. 1877, 425; Contemporary Newspapers.

1739

Tuesday, October 16—This morning at 11 o'clock the Assembly wait on Governour Thomas to present their new Speaker, John Kinsey. The Governour acquaints them he has something important to communicate—requires their attendance at 4 this afternoon.

At 4 the House go back to the Governour. His Honour, with Council present, warns of immediate likelihood of war with Spain, also with France. He tells them the King's orders for seizure of Spanish ships; paints the miseries of a city sacked, or province ravaged by invaders; bids them consider the "defenceless State of this Province," and put it in a posture of defense "before it be too late." His Honour looks hourly for his Majesty's commands "to lay before him the Strength and Circumstances of this Government"; concludes,

> "I hope your Resolutions will be such, as will tend to preserve his Majesty's Regard for you. . . that you will not be unmindful of his Majesty's, your own, and the general Honour and Interests of these Parts. . . when the neighbouring Provinces are vigorously pursuing these laudable Ends."

To the convened Assembly, this is the first official announcement of the impending War of the Austrian Succession—generally called "King George's War" in the Colonies. Defense isn't a popular subject with the Pennsylvania Assembly.

When the Members return to the Assembly Chamber much tongue-wagging breaks loose; general disquietude's evident. They finally decide to consider the Governour's Speech again to-morrow; then adjourn.

Of course, before this, the Members know what's in the wind. Their reply to the Governour's Message will be their first opportunity to register their corporate "sentiment" about war in general, Provincial defense in particular.

When Governour and Council met August 20th, his Honour laid

> "before the Board His Majesty's Warrant. . . for granting Letters of Marque & Reprisal against the Spaniards. . . with a draught of a Proclamation for making the same Publick."

The Proclamation his Honour's issued thereupon, after reciting

England's grievances, has given directions for taking out letters of marque—fitting out privateers. Thomas's supplement to the Royal Proclamation's warned the people of Pennsylvania to be

"upon their Guard to prevent any Mischief they might otherwise suffer from the Spaniards, in Revenge for the Measures His Majesty" is obliged to take, and bids them "annoy the Subjects of Spain in the best Manner they are able."

The Proclamation also enjoins—this is really serious—

"That no Ammunition or Stores of any Kind whatsoever be carried to the Spaniards" in the West Indies "under Pain of His Majesty's highest Displeasure, and of being rigorously prosecuted for the same."

It's an embargo on Pennsylvania's trade with the Spanish West Indies! Gall and wormwood!

Assemblymen are fully aware—have been from the first—of all foregoing particulars; know quite as well what's been going on in England, what's led to present developments. (Through various channels the Colonials keep thoroughly conversant with political, civil and military affairs in England and on the Continent. Witness the newspapers; newspapers are only one medium of information. Innumerable private letters and the "grapevine" speed news.)

Every Member knows England's as much to blame as Spain; knows how combative and ready to pick quarrels fellow-subjects in Great Britain are; knows Sir Robert Walpole's been trying his utmost to stave off hostilities, for which the Opposition in Parliament have roundly damned him; knows how the mercantile jingoes, with their "Jenkins's ear" propaganda, have whipped up present war fever;

"that no allowance was made for the counter claims on the side of Spain; and that in many instances their [British ship-captains'] alleged hardship, when stripped of its colouring, amounts only to this, that they were not permitted to smuggle with impunity."

This knowledge explains the Assembly's refusal to take sudden alarm; it doesn't in the least excuse their refusal to take measures of defense.

Colonial Records, iv. 350 et seq.; Votes of Assembly; History of England, from the Peace of Utrecht to the Peace of Versailles, 1713-1783, Lord Mahon, ii, 264 et seq

Wednesday, October 17—Towards the end of the afternoon—
they've discussed the Message at both morning and afternoon sessions—the Assembly send five Members to tell the Governour the
House "conceive" the nature of his Message so important that an
answer requires "time and deliberation"; that since his Honour
must soon go to New Castle for the Lower Counties' Assembly,
and this is a

> "season of the Year in which the House rarely sits for the Dispatch
> of Publick business," they think "no Inconvenience can arise by
> postponing Consideration thereof until their next Meeting; there-
> fore, if the Governour has nothing to object to it, the House
> incline to adjourn until the Thirty-first Day of December next."

Whenever an inconvenient issue arises, the Assembly are prone
to take refuge in adjournment and scuttle out of the way. Very
ostrich-like!

Seated in their noble Assembly Chamber, the thirty-odd Members give the impression of prevailing homespun, rustic drabness.
Moore of Moore Hall, Andrew Hamilton, William Allen and a
few more of the City-dwelling Members, to be sure, contribute a
leaven of urbanity, but there aren't enough curled wigs, bright-
hued waistcoats and lace ruffles to offset the weight of sartorial
dulness. Collectively, they're unprepossessing; it takes vigorous
effort of the imagination to picture them as ever having been
lovable babies or winsome children—and thus stimulate a measure
of charitable regard for them.

If not dramatically exciting in appearance or behaviour, the
Assembly nevertheless precipitate numerous situations a dramatist
would grasp at and turn to effective account. The outbreak of
war, plus grounds of contention already existing between them
and the Governour, cause a sequence of episodes with both comic
and tragic aspects.

Quit-rents are cousins-german to irredeemable ground-rents.
The latter, eighteenth-century Quakers never object to holding;
payment of the former makes them squirm and squeal. It isn't
a question of just and legal obligation; it's purely a matter of
who's the "goat." The Quaker Assembly are always trying to do
the Penns out of their quit-rents; at this particular juncture
they're bitter at Governour Thomas because he won't sanction
payment in paper currency but insists quit-rents be paid the Proprietaries in full sterling value. The Governour's attitude's per-

fectly logical; he's abiding by the Proprietaries' instructions, whose appointee he is. Worse still, he's fished up (or rather, Richard Peters has fished up for him) the hitherto unpublished and almost forgotten Address of 1729 to the Proprietaries (*v.* p. 33) wherein the Assembly then definitely engaged that quit-rents were to be paid at sterling value. This is an awkward cat to let out of the bag.

The smouldering animus springing from quit-rents bursts into flame at appeals for defense.

Colonial Records, iv, 355; Richard Peters to John Penn, *Peters Papers, Letter Books,* Historical Society of Pennsylvania.

Thursday, October 18—This morning the Members who waited on the Governour yesterday report he'll consider their message and send an answer as soon as possible. While they're waiting his Honour's answer, the House go through some current business, one item of which is a petition from the Library Company of Philadelphia (probably sent at Franklin's instance) for leave

"(for the better Security of their Books from Fire)" to "deposite them in a Room over one of the Offices of the State-house, till such Time as the Publick have Occasion to use the same."

Anon comes the Governour's Secretary with a written message. His Honour knows it's not usual for the Assembly to sit for business at this season but, in view of the threatening danger, he'd hoped the House would waive a "Rule, nowise essential." "Forewarned" should be "fore-armed." They ought to have a

"suitable Regard for his Majesty's Honour, and our own Safety." However, since "the Time of adjourning is a Privilege of your House, I must be content with having so far done my Duty, and heartily wish there may be no further Occasion to call you together again before the Time mentioned."

Then the House grant the Library Company's petition and adjourn to December 31st—nearly three months off! They've been determined all along to do just that. And so, ignoring impending dangers, regardless of growing discontent and alarm throughout City and Province, they disperse until mid-winter. Their one satisfactory act at the October session is granting the Library Company's petition.

"On April 7th, 1740, the Library was transferred 'to the upper room of the westernmost office of the State House' (now Independence Hall). Here it remained for close upon thirty-four years, serving in a measure as the Library of the Provincial Assembly and the Supreme Court of Judicature."

Austin Gray mentions Jacob Duché's *Observations on a Variety of Subjects* (Philadelphia, 1774)—a

"series of letters about Philadelphia ostensibly written by a 'Gentleman of Foreign Extraction' to noble lords and ladies in England and elsewhere"

—which gives further details about the Library Company at that time, besides considerable other matter of contemporary interest. In June, 1771, the Directors of the Library sought permission to put up a building in the State House Yard. This permission was refused, and the Library moved to Carpenters' Hall in December, 1773. There, in 1774, Members of the First Continental Congress were given the use of its valuable collection of books.

The Library Company of Philadelphia, founded in 1731, was the first public library in America. Being the oldest public library in America, it possesses an exceptional collection of treasures, both printed and manuscript; it is one of the few libraries to which the British Museum refers readers when they seek a rare book the British Museum itself has not. In 1696 came a consignment of books to Philadelphia for Christ Church, but the small library then established (and still in existence) can hardly be called a *public* library; it was intended mainly for the clergy.

Benjamin Franklin's Library: *A Short Account of the Library Company of Philadelphia*, Austin K. Gray, 1936; *Votes of Assembly*; *Colonial Records*, iv, 355-356.

Tuesday, January 1—Yesterday the House reassembled and sent the Governour word they were met. This morning, the gentlemen who attended the Governour report his Honour was "pleased to say, he had nothing further to offer the House than what already lies before them."

They still have the Governour's troublesome Speech of October 16th to answer. After re-reading it, they decide to consider it again to-morrow.

The House also receive to-day

"A Petition from a great Number of the Inhabitants of the City of *Philadelphia,* setting forth the defenceless State of the Province in Case of a general War, and praying that the House would take the same into Consideration, and enter into such Measures for the common Security, as to their Wisdom shall seem meet."

After reading it, the House order this Petition to lie on the table. Procrastination is one of their pet devices.

Benjamin Franklin, we know, believes in defense measures; it's not unlikely he's had—directly or indirectly—some connection with this Citizens' Petition presented in a time of real danger. As Clerk of the Assembly, he's their employé and has neither voice nor vote in their proceedings, but it must irk him to see this appeal sidetracked and know it will probably have no effect on the obdurate majority of the House.

Votes of Assembly.

Saturday, January 5—This morning the Committee who framed the answer to the Governour's Speech—approved by the House—go and present it to his Honour.

This morning, also, the House read again the Petition from the People of Philadelphia praying for defense measures. The answer that "to their Wisdom seems meet" is

> *"Resolved,* That the Sentiments of this House, on the Subject Matter of the said Petition, are fully expressed in the Address of the House, in Answer to the Governour's Speech, made at the opening of this Session"

Thus do the Assembly—elected representatives and guardians of the people—summarily brush aside the City's very urgent, very reasonable, appeal in the face of a danger by no means imaginary. The citizens are snubbed—not even paid the courtesy of a separate answer; merely referred to the House's reply to the Governour's Speech.

The reply to the Governour's Speech of October 16th (it's now January 5th), just handed his Honour, admits

> "due Regard for the concern Expressed therein for the Safety of this Province"; that the present state of affairs in Europe gives "some reason to fear a Rupture may ensue"; that the Assembly are under "many Obligations to the Crown and present Governments"; but "as Loyal Subjects, Lovers of our Religion and Liberties" they think "in a Manner not exactly Conformable to the Governour in the Matters recommended."

The Province, say they, was originally settled chiefly by the "People called Quakers" who are "principled against" the bearing of arms, but conditions are now much altered—

"many others are since come amongst us under no such restraints, some of whom have been disciplined in the Art of Warr, and may. . . think it their Duty to fight in defence of their Country, their Wives, their Famillys, and Estates"; Quakers "do not (as the World is now Circumstanced) condemn the use of Arms in Others,"

but it would be inconsistent with the Constitution to make a law compelling some to bear arms while exempting others; the Royal Charter gives full authority to the Proprietaries or their Lieutenant-Governours, under which provision his Honour is free to act without consulting the Assembly.

The House are

"fully perswaded that Whatever Preparations may be made here they will prove ineffectual without the aid of our Mother Country" whence, "morally speaking, Wee must hereafter, as heretofore, principally depend for Preservation from the Insults of our Enemies"; at the same time, they express "a due dependence" on the Almighty and remember "the Words of the sacred Text, That 'Except the Lord keep the City, the Watchman waketh but in vain.'"

They choose to ignore the truth that "Heaven helps them that help themselves." They're not even willing to *help* watch; leave it *all* to the Lord and "our Mother Country." There's no allusion to appropriating any *funds* for defense.

Compared with some of their communications to his Honour, this reply's remarkably mild and restrained; also leaves ingenious verbal loopholes whence one might, perhaps, extract hints looking towards accommodation. Some opine that if the Governour could have understood the hint implied in the reply, he might have avoided much subsequent trouble; that from intimations therein

"it was clear that the House would have been willing to vote a sum as 'a present to the King,' without any reference to its being used for warlike purposes."

This had been done at previous times.

Governour Thomas

"either did not understand the easy method of circumventing the difficulty which was offered him, or he was determined to make the Assembly do what he considered their duty," says Westcott.

His Honour, according to Richard Peters (Letter to John Penn, April 10, 1739), is "candid, open and very ingenuous," sticks to his point, says all he has to say and then stops. Being a direct and forthright person, it's scarcely to be expected he'll be expert in penetrating the subtleties of devious verbiage and the intricate methods of circumventing their consciences, at which the Assemblymen are adepts. They're resourceful casuists; the Governour isn't a casuist at all

The State House is a serene, cheerful, magnanimous-looking building; one sometimes marvels how so much devious, concentrated meanness, like a mephitic exhalation, could have emanated from such surroundings.

Votes of Assembly; *Colonial Records*, iv, 366; *History of Philadelphia*, Thompson Westcott, ch. xciv; *Peters Papers*, *Letter Books*, Historical Society of Pennsylvania.

Friday, January 11—The Members of Assembly are "buzzing like bees in a tar barrel"; country Members, particularly, much nettled. The Governour's Message causes all the tongue-wagging—a rejoinder to the House's Address of last Saturday. The Governour's Secretary brought it this morning. It wasn't unexpected; the Governour and Council met yesterday. The Message's tone can't be called conciliatory; his Honour's getting very riled at the Assembly's refusal to do anything about defense.

Circumstances considered, the Governour's Message is as temperate as one can expect. He's under great provocation; feels the weight of responsibility on his shoulders. City's in a ferment of apprehension; the non-Quaker element—and not a few of the Quakers, too—enraged at the Assembly's point blank refusal to heed their Petition.

True, the sloop *George*—the first privateer ever fitted out at Philadelphia—sailed in November, under letters of marque the Governour issued in August. And the *George*, with its "10 guns and 10 swivels," will soon be followed by others. This measure of warlike preparation may have allayed current uneasiness in slight degree; may have lulled some Assemblymen into a false sense of security so they think the Governour's getting needlessly perturbed. But sending out privateers is a mission of *offensive* warfare; it's not anywise providing for *home-defense*.

In his Message, the Governour regrets having to press a matter so disagreeable to the Assembly's sentiments, but he thinks himself obliged

"by the Duty I owe to His Majesty in Discharge of the Trust reposed in me by your Honourable Proprietors, and from a dis-

interested Regard for the Lives and Fortunes of the People under
my Government, to warn you of the impending Danger"; he has
no desire to criticise anyone's religious principles, but "now from
what you yourselves have declared, I must lament the unhappy
Circumstances of a Country, populous indeed, extensive in its
Trade, bless'd with many natural advantages, and capable of
defending itself, but from a religious Principle of its Representatives against bearing Arms, subject to become the Prey of the first
Invader, and more particularly of its powerful Neighbours, who
are known to be well armed, regular in Discipline, inured in
Fatigue, and from thence capable of making long Marches, in
Alliance with many Nations of Indians, and of a boundless ambition."

The allusion is, of course, to the French.

His Honour continues,

"The Freeholders of the Province have chosen you for their Representatives; and many of the principal Inhabitants have publickly
petitioned you that some Measures may be taken for the Defence
of the Country."

There's no intention to compel conscientious objectors to bear
arms, but why can there not be a properly organised and supported militia raised from those willing to serve?

"Whatever Expence it shall be attended with," it will with reason
be expected that "you shall bear your proportion of it, as was
done here in the sum granted to Queen Anne. . . and as has
always been done by Men of the same religious Persuasion in
Britain for carrying on a War against the Publick Enemy."

His Honour agrees with the Members that

"we have reason to hope for a share of" his Majesty's protection,
along with his "other Subjects in America, but should we declare
we are unwilling to be at any Expence or to expose our Persons
to any Danger, and at the same time implore the Assistance of
our Mother Country, I fear we shall rather expose ourselves to
Derision and Contempt than obtain Compassion and Protection."

Trying thus to shame the Assembly for patent dereliction of
duty, the Governour goes on:

"without preparing ourselves the necessary means for our Defence,
I confess can no more be reconciled to my understanding than
that Because the Lord stills the raging Waves of the Sea, the
Seamen may therefore leave the Sails of the Ship standing, and
go to sleep in a storm; Or that Watchmen are therefore unnecessary, because Except the Lord keep the City the Watchman
waketh but in vain."

He ends by beseeching

"you out of the sincerest Affection for your Interests, to act as will undoubtedly be expected of you by His Majesty, for the Security of this Part of His Dominions."

Most people will doubtless agree with the Governour. It's unreasonable, it's despicable, to claim protection of the Lord and King George when they won't lift a finger for their own defense. The unpleasant trick of trying to "get something for nothing" isn't wholly a monopoly of twentieth-century America.

The *Votes of Assembly* give no report of the debates in the Assembly Chamber; the sharp differences of opinion amongst Members; the vigorous opposition time and again offered by minorities when crucial matters are under discussion; nor (at this period) any tally of how individual Members vote. A little more information occasionally leaks out through minutes of the Governour's Council. We must depend mostly on other sources.

The disappointing silence and outward serenity of the *Votes* don't mean that the public passively acquiesce in the Assembly's majority declarations of "wisdom." At this particular time, one visible evidence of the liveliest and most outspoken opposition is the outfitting of privateers. If the Assembly, supposedly their representatives and guardians, turn a deaf ear to corporate appeals, the people of Philadelphia are not such a spineless lot of nincompoops as to sit supine, fold their hands, and then yelp for divine assistance in their necessity. The citizens make their own decision that the best available *defense,* in this juncture, lies in *offense.* They may well cast in the teeth of the Scripture-quoting Assembly Saint Paul's injunction—"Quit you like men, be strong."

Votes of Assembly; *Colonial Records,* iv, 368 *et seq.*; *History of Philadelphia,* Thompson Westcott, ch. xciii; *History of Philadelphia,* Scharf & Westcott, i, 208; *History of Philadelphia,* Ellis Paxson Oberholtzer, i, 170-172.

Saturday, January 19—Yesterday, with great deliberation, the Assembly read an Address to be sent to the Governour. The committee appointed to draught it have been working on it all week. After yesterday's consideration, the House approved it, ordered it engrossed. To-day, a delegation of five Members carry it to his Honour. His Honour won't like the sarcasm. It's bitter, too.

The Address is a wordy outpouring of sarcasm and gall. With mulish obstinacy, the Assembly refuse to do anything at all.

They're by no means convinced any real danger exists. As the product of "passive resistance" to sound arguments, the Address is exceptionally irritating—probably meant to be so.

In a thoroughly exasperating paragraph, the House say:

"That we have many natural Advantages is true; we are situate upon a River of difficult Navigation, far distant from the Sea, and not easily to be attacked from thence. New Jersey lies between us and the Ocean; New York and New England between us and the principal Settlements of the French; Maryland, Virginia, South Carolina and Georgia between us and the Spaniards; and besides all these Advantages, a considerable Number of Inhabitants, equal, perhaps, to those of any other Colony, who, we *suppose, have been disciplined and inured to the Art of War.*"

Could any attitude be more pusillanimous? "O, yeah! Why should *we* worry? We're sitting pretty and the enemy can't get at *us*. Let the other fellows take the knocks!" That's what it amounts to in to-day's colloquial, unvarnished English. A choice instance of eighteenth-century isolationism!

Votes of Assembly; Colonial Records, iv, 371-375.

1741

Thursday, June 4—At 3 o'clock this afternoon, in the Hall of the State House, the Honourable Andrew Hamilton heads a numerous body of distinguished gentlemen who wait outside the Assembly Chamber's closed doors. They're indignant through and through at the Assembly's "do nothing" policy in this hour of the city's grave peril; they've come to lay before the Assembly a Petition— or rather, a *Representation,* for it's not at all humble and contains some very plain speaking. The Assembly usually treat memorialists in a curt, summary manner, whether they come singly or in a group. But Andrew Hamilton and his company are too important and influential for the high-and-mighty Assembly to be rude to them; they're admitted to the Chamber. Hamilton reads his paper to the House, delivers it at the Table, then he and his party withdraw.

Thereupon, the Governour's Message about the Spanish privateers' depredations, and their immediate threat to the city, is reread, and then

"The Paper presented to the House by *Andrew Hamilton,* Esq; and others, was again read, and follows in these Words, *viz.*

To the Honourable, the Speaker, and House of Representatives, for the Province of Pennsylvania,

The humble REPRESENTATION of divers of the Merchants and Inhabitants of the City of *Philadelphia,* in Behalf of themselves and others.

The daily Accounts we have of our Capes being infested by [Spanish] *Privateers, and of some Vessels being actually taken, induced us to hope, that you, our Representatives, being at this Time met in General Assembly, would have made some Provision to guard us against these Mischiefs: But being informed, your House is this Day about putting an End to your present Meeting, or Session of Assembly, without taking any Notice of our defenceless Condition, we thought it our Duty, once more to represent to you our Dangers, and what we conceive we have a Right to expect from you, who at this Time have the Honour to represent a large and flourishing Province. As it is well known that the Prosperity of the Province is chiefly owing to our Trade, we humbly conceive, it ought to be our principal Care both to encourage and protect that Trade, by which the whole People receive such considerable Advantages.*

His Majesty is engaged in a just and necessary War; it is a

War enter'd into with the Consent of all his Majesty's loyal Subjects; and his Parliament have shewed a Readiness and Zeal in supporting his Majesty in the Prosecution of that War; And though his Majesty is ever watchful for the Safety of all his People, yet he justly expects that they themselves, in their several Stations, and according to their Abilities, whenever it shall be found necessary, will contribute what is in their Power, for their own Safety at least.

We have amongst us a loyal and willing People, and a Treasury sufficient to support such a Charge as may be necessary for our Safety upon this Occasion: And as it will be agreed, no Man, nor Number of wise or good Men, ever undertook, far less sought for a Trust, which, for any Reasons whatsoever, they could not discharge for the Good of those that entrusted them; give us Leave therefore to say, we have a Right to expect from you, who only have it in your Power at this Time, some publick Provision to be made for the Safety of our Trade, and our Inhabitants, who are at this Time equally exposed to the Insults and Depredations of the Enemy.

And tho' former Applications of this Kind have been disregarded; yet, as our Trade is now suffering, and greater Dangers daily threaten us, we hope at last you will shew a due Regard for the Safety of the Province; and this only can free us from the unhappy Necessity of applying to his Majesty for Relief."

This paper's signed by Andrew Hamilton and eighty-four more of the most considerable gentlemen of City and Province. And what do the Assembly do after this very urgent and justifiable communication? We shall see anon.

Less than two years ago—January, 1739, to be exact—in a long, tedious Message to the Governour, the Assembly gave a choice exhibition of their pusillanimous "isolationist" attitude, their unwillingness to co-operate with the other Colonies, and their confidence in geographical position to protect the Province, to say nothing of the Lord and King George. Their communications to his Honour at that time, albeit punctiliously couched in superficially polite phraseology, were really compounds of casuistical clap-trap, Scripture-quoting, sarcastic insinuation, obtrusive piety and vitriolic innuendo. Verily,

"the words of their mouths were softer than butter, having war in their hearts; their words were smoother than oil, and yet be they very swords . . . they have sharpened their tongues like a serpent; the poison of asps is under their lips."

Less than three months later—April 14th, 1740—war with Spain was proclaimed at the Court House, with "repeated acclamations of 'God save the King'; some Cannon on Society Hill. . . discharged on drinking the Loyal Healths, and some Barrels of Beer given to the Populace."

When the Governour called for enlistment of volunteers to go and fight the Spaniards, his relations with the Assembly worsened, if that were possible. They quarrelled about a new bill for taxing the city; about enlistment of indentured servants; about transport of troops; about supplies and clothing for the King's army and navy; and when the Assembly voted a sum "for the King's use"— finally shamed into an apparent measure of acquiescence to royal requirements, for fear of being deemed treasonably disloyal if they didn't—they either inserted such conditions in the bill that the Governour couldn't sign it without direct disobedience to the Royal and Proprietary Instructions that bound him, or else, if no strings were attached, they made a niggardly appropriation manifestly insufficient for the needs it was supposed to meet. The Governour's every appeal for defense only increased their mulish resolution to do nothing.

No one quarrels with the Quakers for their "passive resistance" and their being "principled against war," so far as they themselves are concerned; it's when they try to impose the same rules of conduct on the whole Province that they rouse bitter resentment. Numerically, the Quakers are about only one-third of the population, or less, but the smooth-running Quaker political machine— thanks to suffrage restrictions and unbalanced county representation—keeps them in power, and the Monthly and Yearly Meetings make and regulate the Assembly's policy.

Wise old James Logan, who could never be accused of either narrowness or lack of political acumen, sees clearly how the "hardshell" obstructionists of the Society are heading the whole Province for trouble. Opposed like other Friends to offensive war, he's always approved defense. He strongly disapproves the political meddling by the Meetings and, only a little while after Hamilton and the "eighty-four" have made their "REPRESENTATION" to the Assembly—being lame, ailing and unable himself to attend —he *sends* a communication (September 22nd) to the Yearly Meeting, held just before the October Provincial election. In a letter to John Penn, Richard Peters tells the story:

"The Yearly Meeting being held the Week before the general Election Mr. Logan by his Son Willm sent them a Lre [letter] wherein he is said to enlarge on the defenceless State of the

Province & of the ill Consequences that may ensue on Men of
their Principles procuring themselves to be return'd to Assembly,
but his good Design was eluded by the following Expedient. Some
Members moved that a Committee might be appoint^d to peruse
the Lre & to report whether it contained matters proper to be
communicated to the Meeting at large, accordingly Robt Jordan
J^{no} Bringhouse [Bringhurst] Ebenezer Large John Dillwin [Dill-
wyn], & Robt Strethill [Strettell] were appointed to inspect the
Epistle & report whether it contained Matters wch were fit for the
Meeting to take into Consideration; On Examinacon they reported that the Lre containing Matters of a Military & Geographical Nature it was by no means proper to be read to the
general Meeting, but some Persons who understood those Matters
might be desir'd to consider and answer it."

When the inspection committee render this verdict, Robert
Strettell rises to register a dissenting "minority report," whereupon John Bringhurst

"pluck'd him by the Coat and told him with a sharp Tone of
Voice 'Sit thee down, Robert, sit thee down! Thou art single in
thy Opinion.'"

(This same Robert Strettell, soon to become a Member of the
Provincial Council and, *ipso facto,* in opposition to the Assembly,
will also a little later—like some other prominent and wealthy
Quakers—become involved in the heinous sin of helping to fit out
privateers, and thus be the subject of "concern" to Meeting. John
Smith tells all about it in his *Diary.*) Yearly Meeting "inspection
committee"—all scandalised save Strettell—thus see fit to suppress
Logan's letter. Logan thereupon has it printed and, though never
generally circulated, enough copies get abroad for Richard Peters
to be certain about what he tells John Penn.

When Hamilton and the "considerable Number of the Inhabitants" visit the Assembly on June 4th, conditions are thoroughly
alarming. Without attempting to chronicle all the disturbing
incidents (contemporary newspapers, letters and other documents
give the particulars), suffice it to say that for some time past the
Bay and Capes have been infested by the enemy's privateers, raids
have been made on both sides of the lower Delaware—to the great
terror of the helpless victims—and there appears to be every likelihood the privateers will come all the way up to the city, and sack
and burn it. And all this while the perverse, supine Assembly
won't do anything about it. No wonder the non-Quakers—and a

good many of the less "stiff" Quakers, too—feel outraged and apprehensive.

Now then, on Saturday (June 6th), two days after receipt of the "REPRESENTATION," the committee appointed to consider "what may be proper for the House to do thereupon," make their report. They insinuate the Governour's inspired the "REPRE-SENTATION"; that it's merely a rehash of previous protests; imply that many of the signers, though "intending well," have been so muddle-headed as to be "drawn in to sign it" without knowing its purport; that the sponsors are liars; and, finally, see fit to deem this protest an insult and threat to the Assembly!

With this "smack in the face" to Hamilton and the citizens of Philadelphia, the Assembly adjourn to August 10th—more than two months hence—characteristically scuttle away in time of peril and notoriously neglect their obvious duty. Such behavior paves the way for the "Bloody Election" of 1742.

Votes of Assembly; John Smith's *Diary*, MS. in Library Company of Phila-delphia; Letter of Richard Peters to John Penn, October 20, 1741, *Penn MS.S.*, in Collection of Historical Society of Pennsylvania; James Logan's Letter to Meeting, September 22, 1741, printed in *Collections of Historical Society of Pennsylvania*, i, 36 *et seq.*; *Colonial Records*, iv, *passim*; *Chron-icles of Pennsylvania*, C. P. Keith, ii, 792 *et seq.*

1746

Thursday, July 24—By last Thursday's Proclamation, Governour Thomas appointed to-day to be observed throughout the Province and the Three Lower Counties on Delaware

"as a Day of Publick Thanksgiving" for the Duke of Cumberland's victory at Culloden Muir on April 16th, and directed that "the several Ministers of the Gospel do compose Prayers and Sermons suitable to the Occasion, and perform Divine Services in their respective Churches or Houses of Religious Worship." His Honour likewise recommended that the people "do abstain from all servile Labour on that Day."

The Governour got word of Prince Charlie's defeat Friday evening the 4th; early next morning the *Gazette* published a handbill with the news. On the 10th, the regular Thursday issue of the *Gazette* had six pages, instead of the usual four, most of the space given to a description of the battle; then, two days later, a four-page war supplement with the latest despatches and further details.

The news has caused much excitement and pretty general satisfaction. Of course, some folk have Jacobite leanings, and some of the Scots and Roman Catholic Irish are sympathetic to the Stuart cause, but most of the people have a strong sense of loyalty to the Crown as now held by the House of Hanover and are sincerely thankful and gratified, as their behaviour shows.

The day's being generally kept as the Governour recommends. In the forenoon "Great Numbers of People" attend "at all the Places of Worship," and the Reverend George Whitefield delivers "a discourse at the 'new building,' in Fourth Street below Mulberry [Arch] on the occasion of the late victory."

Culloden's a set-back to the French; in slight degree it lessens the threat of French attack on Philadelphia. Now, the Assembly, after all these weary years of contention with the Governour about defense, enlistment of volunteers and support of military requirements by the Home Government, will be more obdurate than ever in their pacifism.

To mark the occasion worthily and testify his own rejoicing—aside from all the artillery salvoes and bonfires—the Governour entertains "near a hundred of the principal Gentlemen and Inhabitants of the City at Dinner; where our Happiness under the present Constitution, both in Church and State, and the great Obligation we have to the Family on the Throne" are "properly and decently remembered."

(Although no direct statement to that effect seems to exist, the Governour must be giving this dinner in the Banquetting Hall at the State House. Apart from the "New Building" in Fourth Street, at this time it's the only place in the city large enough to seat "near a hundred" guests. The "New Building" isn't equipped for dinner-giving; besides [even if it were], after Whitefield's sermon there in the forenoon there wouldn't be time to get ready for a big public dinner at half-past two or three.)

Pennsylvania Gazette, July 5, 10, 12, 17, 31, 1746; *History of Philadelphia,* Thompson Westcott, ch. c.

1747

Tuesday, August 18—At last President and Council are sitting for the first time in the newly-finished Council Chamber, the big, sunny southwest room on the upper floor of the State House. Thither they summon the Assembly this morning to deliver them an important Message. To-day the Assembly are first sitting since Governour Thomas went back Home; the proper official announcement has to be made that President and Council are acting in the Governour's place until a new Lieutenant-Governour's appointed and comes out to govern the Province.

Benjamin Franklin's entries in the Assembly minutes show both Council and Assembly standing very rigidly on their dignity. The *Votes* record:

"A Message from the President and Council, by *Robert Strettell* and *Thomas Hopkinson,* Esquires, Members of Council, viz.
'Mr. Speaker,
The President and Council desire to speak with the House of Representatives in the Council Chamber.'
Then the Gentlemen of the Council withdrew."

The House straightway consider the Message; then the record continues:

"*Ordered,*
That the Gentlemen of the Council be desired to walk in."

The Speaker then acquaints them the House will attend, which they forthwith do.

Mr. Abraham Taylor, Mr. Benjamin Shoemaker and Mr. Thomas Hopkinson, of the Council, have draughted the main part of the Message. The "Speech" that's "spoke" to the Assembly's alarming enough. It recites that

"A notorious insult hath lately been committed in New Castle County by a. . . Party of French & Spaniards in conjunction with some Englishmen, Traytors to their King and Country, and who we are informed have dwelt in this City and are too well acquainted with the Condition of it."

They'd been bold enough to come up the whole length of the Bay and River to within eighteen miles of New Castle; there they'd

"plunder'd two Plantations, the Owner of one of them they bound and abused and dangerously wounded his Wife with a Musket Ball, carrying off their Negroes and Effects to a considerable value. On their Return they met with a valuable Ship in the Bay, bound to this Port from Antigua, which they likewise took and carried off." The message continues that the marauders had shown "a thorough Knowledge of our defenceless State" and had hinted "a Design of shortly paying this City a Visit. . . . The Terror and Confusion, the Ruin of vast numbers of Families, the Destruction of Trade, the Bloodshed, Cruelty, & other fatal Consequences which must unavoidably attend the Plundering or burning this City, are too obvious to need a Description."

The Council therefore ask the Assembly,

"Is it not then absolutely necessary, for the Security of this so valuable a Part of His Majesty's Dominions, & the Preservation of the Lives and propertys of the Inhabitants, that some Method be fall'n upon to prevent the Evils which threaten Us, and to which we lie exposed?"

The Message further mentions pressing Indian affairs—imminent border hostilities instigated by the French, immediate need of presents to the friendly tribes, and the like.

Before the Assemblymen leave the Council Chamber, Mr. Secretary Peters delivers a copy of the complete Speech to Mr. Speaker Kinsey.

Facing an impending threat of the city being sacked and burnt, the President and Council have done all that in them lies to meet present emergencies but, in absence of a Governour, their powers are straitly limited; they can do nothing involving expenditure of public funds. The Assembly have sole and absolute control of the money-bags.

After they've heard the Message, and Speaker and Assemblymen have gone back downstairs to their own Chamber, they're in a pretty dither. They know all about the excitement in the city and the general clamour for defense measures but, of course, that "weighty Friend," the elder Israel Pemberton, and the other "stiff" Quakers—especially the country Members from Bucks and Chester —who are "principled" against defense, will oppose any measures to save the City and drive the French and Spaniards out of the Bay.

Votes of Assembly; Colonial Records, v, 68, 95, 96 *et seq.*

Friday, November 13—Indians in the Council Chamber to-day— ten warriors from Ohio; came to town several days ago. Mr. President Palmer's called the Council especially to receive them.

Conrad Weiser, Provincial Interpreter, fetches the Indians in as soon as the Council are ready for them. When they enter the Council Chamber, the ten young warriors all sit down solemnly and silently. Then their spokesman rises up and delivers their message; he gives the Council several belts and strings of wampum in the course of his speech.

These Ohio Indians, belonging to the Six Nations, are disturbed about the war with France. It isn't going as they think it should; they've come to urge the English colonists to more active war measures.

"How comes it to pass," say they, "that the English, who brought us into the War, will not fight themselves?" Well may they complain thus and ask "How come?" with the Pennsylvania Assembly obstinately refusing to lift a finger or give one penny for defense!

The warrior spokesman goes on:

"This has not a good appearance, and therefore we give you this string of Wampum to hearten and encourage you, to desire you wou'd put more Fire under your Kettle."

After this, the warriors, all in their feathers and best trappings, silently get up and file out; they're a dignified lot of fine-looking men.

Colonial Records. v, 145 et seq.

Saturday, November 14—Four worried Members of the Council are in the Council Chamber this morning, discussing what had best be done immediately.

"The President being indisposed [Anthony Palmer's advanced in years and in frail health] & the other Members not attending, there could be no Council," but the Members present "judg'd. . . it was necessary previously to learn from Mr. Weiser the particular History of the Indians, their real disposition towards Us, and designs; and accordingly sent for him [before answering the Indians' yesterday's speech]. . . .

The Members likewise judged that it might be of Service to know Mr. Logan's Sentiments about what might be proper to be said to the Indians. . . ."

In view of the Assembly's adamant mulishness about defense measures, framing an answer to the Indians is a bad enough worry. But there are other matters a-plenty to perplex and perturb the

Councillors, though the day's minutes contain only the brief notes quoted.

There's been the embarrassment of answering letters from Governour Shirley, of Massachusetts, Admiral Knowles and Governour Clinton, of New York, about the pay and maintenance of the volunteer companies enlisted from Pennsylvania—much embarrassment, indeed, for the Assembly will do nothing helpful and, anyhow, they've adjourned till next May, leaving President and Council "holding the bag." Because of Governour Shirley's and Governour Clinton's letters, the President and Council have had to summon the Assembly back to meet the 23rd of this month.

Another worry—the *Euryale* has arrived from pest-ridden Barbadoes, ignored quarantine regulations, and landed passengers and crew; now probably spreading infection in the Province.

Likewise, the old Assembly, just before adjourning August 26th, sent a long-winded reply to the Message of President and Council —evasive, petulant, disclaiming responsibility to protect the people, and belittling the very real peril to City and Province, in short, a typical missive. They had the effrontery to say,

"The Plundering of the two Families in New Castle County is indeed an Instance of the Boldness of our Enemies, but we think it will be difficult, if not impossible, to prevent such Accidents. . . We. . . could have wished you had been pleased to have spared that Part of the Speech which mentions the defenceless State of the Province, and the Consequences which might attend the plundering of the City; the tendency to which, in our Opinion, is rather to beget or Augment Fears than to prevent those Dangers which thro' the favour of Providence we have hitherto escaped. Besides, as this Speech from the President & Council may be sent beyond Sea, if it should fall into the Hand of our Enemies it may possibly induce them to make an Attempt they otherwise would not have thought of. We may also add, that the Defence of the Province hath been a matter already much controverted, and you cannot be unsensible of the different Sentiments of our late Governour and former Assemblies, . . . nor can we understand on what Grounds You are pleased to alledge the Length & Difficulty of the Bay are now less Security than heretofore; . . . it would not be an easy Task to persuade us that the measures which have been proposed for the Defence of the Province, either by erecting Fortifications or building Ships of War, would be of any real Use to the Province. . . ."

Rare adepts at "bush-beating"; they could beat an whole *host* of devils about a *forest* of bushes.

When the *new* Assembly met October 14th (to sit only until the 17th), President and Council again recounted the repeated depredations by Spaniards and French in the Bay and River, the sufferings of the people exposed to their raids, and urged the imperative need of putting the Province "in a Posture of Defence." To which the Assembly replied:

". . . The Transactions you are pleased to mention in the former Part of your Message we observe is only an abridged Account of what was laid before us the last Assembly . . . As to any Enterprise against the City, we hope there is no Danger . . . . As the Members of the present Assembly are mostly the same with the last, & their Sentiments the same as at that time, it will be unnecessary, we think, to add to what is before contained [in the previous answer] . . . ."

Thereupon, they adjourned for seven months! It's hard to say whether they're more like cuttle-fish or ostriches. An entry, September 17th, 1747, in John Smith's *Diary*—he's one of the "stiffest" Quaker shipping-merchants—may help to make the Assembly's "do-nothing" attitude faintly comprehensible to us in the present age. John writes:

". . . heard as I returned home the Certainty of Our Ship Bolton's being taken at our Cape by a privateer Sloop who has likewise taken several Vessells—Endeavoured to be Resign'd in this great Loss and disappointment, & to say without murmuring Shall we receive Good & Shall we not also receive Evil &ca."

While seeking to emulate Job's resignation to sore boils, prudent insurance doubtless cushions John's "Loss and disappointment," but he may have trouble and delay in collecting it.

Plainly, the Councillors sitting this 14th of November in the Council Chamber have cause for anxiety, enough and to spare. The only bit of silver lining to their black cloud of worry (they can't yet discern it) is the publication this very morning of *Plain Truth* by "A Tradesman of Philadelphia." That "Tradesman" happens to be Benjamin Franklin.

With eleven years' experience as Clerk of the Assembly, Benjamin's native shrewdness has enabled him to take full measure of the "stiff" Members' ability to circumvent their consciences by adroit phraseology, susceptible of several interpretations. He knows that a great many of the Quakers (like James Logan, Robert Strettell and others), however much they deplore war, are not "principled against" *defense;* also, that the "stiffest" of them are not averse to being defended if somebody else does the defending. He knows, too, the intense feeling on the subject amongst the preponderant non-Quaker element in Philadelphia; that, in the present crisis, they'll gladly support vigorous defense measures, once initiative, some systematic organisation, and leadership are forthcoming. Furthermore, Benjamin has the happy knack of presenting practical commonsense in a logical, convincing way.

In leading up to his concrete suggestions for effective defense measures, the "Tradesman" observes:

"Pennsylvania, indeed, situate in the Centre of the Colonies, has hitherto enjoy'd profound Repose; and tho' our Nation is engag'd in a bloody War, with two great and powerful Kingdoms, yet, defended, in a great Degree, from the *French* on the one Hand by the Northern Provinces, and from the *Spaniards* on the other by the Southern, at no small Expence to each, our People have till lately, slept securely in their Habitations.

There is no British Colony excepting this, but has made some Kind of Provision for its Defence; many of them have therefore never been attempted by an Enemy; and other that were attack'd, have generally defended themselves with Success. . . But whatever Security [the Bay and River] might have been while both Country and City were poor, and the Advantage to be expected scarce worth the Hazard of an Attempt, it is now doubted whether we can any longer depend upon it. Our Wealth, of late Years much encreas'd, is one strong Temptation, our defenceless State another, to induce an Enemy to attack us; while the Acquaintance they have lately gained with our Bay and River, by Means of the Prisoners and Flags of Truce they have had among us; by Spies which they almost every where maintain, and perhaps from Traitors among ourselves; with the Facility of getting Pilots to conduct them; and the known Absence of Ships of War, during the greatest Part of the Year, from both *Virginia* and *New York,* ever since the War began, render the Appearance of Success to the Enemy far more promising, and therefore highly encrease our Danger."

Then he enlarges upon spies; points out the French are sparing no artifice nor expense to win the Six Nations (hitherto friendly to the English) to their interest; reprobates the despicable selfishness of them that think themselves remote enough not to be endangered by invasion and therefore refuse to co-operate in defense measures; urges the Province's obligation to bear its share of the general burden of defense for the whole of British North America; and warns that, as things are now going, the Province's trade will infallibly be ruined in another year.

He continues:

"The Enemy, no doubt, have been told, That the People of
Pennsylvania are *Quakers,* and against all Defence, from a Principle of Conscience; this, tho' true of a Part, and that a small
Part only of the Inhabitants, is commonly said of the Whole;
and what may make it look probable to Strangers, is, that in Fact,
nothing is done by any Part of the People towards their Defence."

He vividly pictures the sack and burning of the city, with all the
other horrors of war, then asks,

"On whom may we fix our Eyes with the least Expectation that
they will do any one Thing for our Security? — Should we address
that wealthy and powerful Body of People, who have ever since
the War governed our Elections, and filled almost every Seat in our
Assembly; should we intreat them to consider, if not as Friends,
at least as Legislators, that *Protection* is as truly due from the
Government to the People, as *Obedience* from the People to the
Government; and that if on account of their religious Scruples,
they themselves could do no Act for our Defence, yet they might
retire, relinquish their Power for a Season, quit the Helm to freer
Hands. . . . [Bravo, Benjamin! That's hitting the nail squarely
on the head.]

Should we remind them, that the Publick Money, raised *from
All,* belongs *to All;* that since they have, for their own Ease, and
to secure themselves in the quiet Enjoyment of their Religious
Principles (and may they long enjoy them) expended such large
Sums to oppose Petitions, and engage favourable Representations
of their Conduct, if they themselves could by no Means be free to
appropriate any Part of the Publick Money [A painful stab!] for
our Defence; yet it would be no more than Justice to spare us a
reasonable Sum for that Purpose, which they might easily give to
the King's Use as heretofore, leaving all the Appropriation to
others, who would faithfully apply it as we desired: . . . they have
already been by great Numbers of the People petitioned in vain.
Our late Governour did for Years sollicit, request, and even
threaten them in vain. The Council have since twice remonstrated to them in vain. Their religious Prepossessions are un-
changeable, their Obstinacy invincible. Is there then the least
Hope remaining, that from that Quarter any Thing should arise
for our Security?"

While he can't resist taking an incidental fling at several individuals in the Proprietary or Governour's Party for what he
thinks insufficient will to co-operate in defense projects, the
"Tradesman of Philadelphia" champions the "middling people,"
the great mass of citizens outside the Quaker fold, and speaks as
one of them; as an apostle of self-help, he points the way to con-

certed action independent of what the Quaker hierarchy may do or approve. Not only does he furnish an articulate voice for the "common folk" the Assembly's hitherto disregarded and snubbed, but he cuts the Gordian knot that's kept the Province tied in a state of inaction. The Governour can call out volunteers, but can't provide military equipment and support; the Assembly can, but will not, grant funds needful for defense, nor take any steps to create a Provincial militia. The "Tradesman" shows how the exasperated people of City and Province can effect what the Governour (in his absence, President and Council) cannot, and the Assembly will not, do. By voluntary co-operative self-help they can put the Province in that "Posture of Defence" so long and so justly clamoured for.

Plain Truth supplies the spark to kindle the flame of popular resistance. This epoch-making little book produces amazing results. The upshot of its publication is that just one week after it comes out, there's a meeting to form an Association. Forthwith, Articles of Association are drawn up and left for signature at the New Building. Within three days 500 volunteers sign up, and volunteering goes rapidly forward in both City and throughout the Province; it's not long before a goodly number of the men available in Pennsylvania (60,000, by Franklin's estimate), ready and willing to bear arms, have signed.

Meanwhile, the Mayor and Corporation petition the Proprietaries for "aid & an early Supply of Cannon, &c." The Associators likewise petition them for a "Supply of Cannon & Arms." The Merchants of the City petition "the Board of the Admiralty for a Man of War to be sent early enough to protect the Trade, & to prevent or defeat the mischievous designs of our Enemies" by patrolling the Delaware Bay and River.

When the neighbouring Governments, too, get an appeal for help, Pennsylvania's agents hear a few plain truths about the Assembly's despicable policy. Mr. Secretary Peters, writing the Proprietaries, says that when "Mr. Allen, Mr. Lawrence, Mr. Taylor & Mr. Franklyn" went to New York to ask for cannon,

"they met with an ill natur'd disposition in the generality of the People who said Pennsylvania deserv'd nothing at their hands, as they had ask'd them to join with them in defending their Frontiers against the Indian and French Enemy, & they always refus'd, & were at none or little Expence, tho' it cost New York Government the annual Sum of £ 45000. and at first Mr. Chief Justice Delancy from his Love of Popularity, or rather a regard to his

Interest among the People prov'd averse, but soon came to think of the application in another Light, & the Governour & Council in a very handsome manner acceded to the Petition." Governour Clinton and his Council lend 12 twelve-pounders and 2 eighteen-pounders.

Franklin and his defense party lose no time in starting a lottery to raise £3,000—the proceeds to build and equip a battery. Some of the most substanital and influential men in the city are managers—William Allen, William Masters, Joshua Maddox, Samuel McCall, Doctor John Kearsley, Edward Shippen, Thomas Leech, Charles Willing, William Clymer, Thomas Lawrence, jr., William Coleman and Thomas Hopkinson. The Mayor and Corporation subscribe heavily, and there's enthusiastic support.

December 6th, 500 or 600 Associators, "consisting principally of the Merchants & tradesmen of the City," present themselves under arms to the President and Council, who assure them their measures are acceptable to the Government and, as soon as they choose officers, commissions will be forthcoming.

December 9th, President and Council proclaim Friday, January 7th, as a day of fasting and prayer for the Province. Parson Currie, Rector of St. David's, Radnor, and St. Peter's-in-the-Great Valley, then preaches a rousing sermon urging the men to military enlistment, and bids his hearers read *Plain Truth*. Both on the Fast Day and at other times, the clergy hold forth on the duty of defense, and "Hell Fire" Tennent preaches his famous sermon from the text, "The Lord is a Man of War"—which sets John Smith to scribbling a tedious, indignant pamphlet rejoinder, Quaker *vs.* Presbyterian.

Friday, January 1st,

"ten Companies consisting of about 800 Men appear'd under Arms at the State House Drums beating & Colours flying & presented their Officers to the President & Council who having order'd me [Mr. Secretary Peters] to prepare blank Military Commissions, they were immediately filled up with the Names of those who were upon the Returns and deliver'd to them— Then the subaltern Officers proceeded to chuse their superior Officers & . . . Commissions were accordingly order'd to be prepared for them. . . ."

For the several companies of these citizen soldiers, the women of the city have made flags and banners exhibiting a variety of devices—lions, eagles, elephants, coronets and plumes of feathers, castles, David and Goliath—all with appropriate mottoes, some of them in very bad Latin. "Stiff" Quaker John Smith notes this

January 1st parade to the State House in his *Diary* and comments, "It is very remarkable that upon this occasion though people of other persuasions are so universally afraid, there was not above 10 or 12 under our proffesion that bore Arms in this City." John's very disturbed because some of the wealthy Quakers have contributed to fitting out privateers.

The ardent Associators set energetically to work on two batteries—a small one, under Society Hill (near Lombard Street wharf), the city carpenters and joiners build gratuitously, and finish it between a Monday morning and Tuesday night, gun-mounting and all; the other, the Grand or Association Battery, mounting 27 guns, the Associators build below the Gloria Dei Church, and there they mount guard until, August 24th, comes news of the Peace of Aix-la-Chapelle.

Votes of Assembly; *Colonial Records*, v, 124-174, *passim*; John Smith's *Diary*, in MS.S Collection, Library Company of Philadelphia; *Pennsylvania Gazette*, November 12, 19, 1747; *ibid*, January 5, 1747; Letters of Richard Peters in *Penn MS.S, Official Correspondence*, Historical Society of Pennsylvania; *Plain Truth*, by a Tradesman of Philadelphia, published November 14, 1747; *History of Philadelphia*, Scharf & Westcott, i, 214-216.

Monday, November 16—An Indian War Dance this afternoon at the State House—actually! Paint, waving feathers and all!

Since the Indians came to the Council Chamber four days ago, the Council have had several talks with Conrad Weiser, who knows the Indians well and is fully aware of their sentiments. Governour and Council can always depend on his information. Weiser and Mr. Secretary Peters have also been to get James Logan's advice. So now, President and Council bid the ten Ohio warriors come to the State House at 4 o'clock.

When the Indians are seated cross-legged on the floor in the Council Chamber, Mr. President Palmer makes them a speech; Weiser translates it to them. The speech is conciliatory and appreciative; President Palmer promises them substantial presents for their tribe. (The Assembly are always willing to pay for presents to the Indians.)

This the Indians take so well that

"in Testimony of their entire Satisfaction & Devotion to the English Interest they gave the Indian Marks of Approbation and Danced the War Dance."

Colonial Records, v, 149, 150.

1751

Monday, July 1—Some thirty or more of Philadelphia's most public-spirited and substantial gentlemen, the "Contributors" to a new undertaking, meet to-day in the State House to organise a needed public institution—an hospital for the Province of Pennsylvania. The State House is the official and actual birthplace of the Pennsylvania Hospital, the *first* hospital founded within the territory of the present United States.

(Other charitable institutions that have subsequently undertaken the functions of hospitals antedate the Pennsylvania Hospital, but their assumption of the hospital rôle is later than 1751. For instance, the Philadelphia "Almshouse and House of Employment" was established in 1731, but not until 1769 were physicians appointed to attend ailing inmates, and not until 1836 was the institution designated the "Philadelphia Hospital and Almshouse"; not until 1902 was the part reserved for the sick styled the "Philadelphia General Hospital." Other similar instances, in other places, may be cited also, but the Pennsylvania Hospital is first in point of time to be established as specifically an *hospital* for the care of the physically and mentally sick.)

January 23rd, 1750-51, a Petition's been presented to the Provincial Assembly setting forth the urgent necessity of establishing an hospital in Philadelphia for "the Relief of the Sick Poor." The idea of this charitable foundation has originated with that truly philanthropic physician, Doctor Thomas Bond, but it needs an aggressive "publicity man" to advertise it and win the essential popular support. Benjamin Franklin's the very man for this purpose; has the happy knack of getting the public ear. He writes about the project in the newspapers and arouses considerable interest, but soon perceives government aid will be indispensable. Hence the Petition.

The Petition's in Franklin's handwriting and is signed by thirty-three of the most representative and influential men in the city, including the Mayor and Chief Justice Allen. (Franklin himself is not one of the signers, presumably because he's Clerk of the Assembly and also a candidate for public office.) The Petitioners' prayer right away encounters opposition from some of the penurious country Members—they're not convinced an hospital's really needed; if it's established, it will benefit only city people, and the city, therefore, ought to pay for it without getting help from the whole Province; besides, it will cost too much to keep it up and pay the doctors, and they doubt whether the citizens themselves generally approve the idea.

In spite of these peanut-minded objections, January 29th the Petition gets a second reading in Assembly. Some of the country opposition abates when it becomes known that Doctor Zachary, Doctor Thomas Bond and Doctor Phineas Bond will serve the proposed hospital without compensation. As Clerk of the Assembly, Franklin knows exactly what's going on "within doors" and exactly how the individual Members view the hospital scheme. As a result of this second reading and Franklin's astute tactics, the House give the Petitioners leave to bring in a Bill "for incorporating the contributors according to prayer of their petition, and granting them a blank sum of money." Franklin says this

> "leave was obtained chiefly on the consideration that the House could throw the bill out if they did not like it."

The Bill's forthwith introduced several days later (February 1st). Again Franklin's political ingenuity scores. He says,

> "I drew it [the Bill] so as to make the important clause a conditional one, viz.: And be it enacted by the authority aforesaid, that when the said contributors shall have met and chosen their Managers and treasurer and shall have raised by their contributions a capital stock of two thousand pounds value, the yearly interest of which is to be applied to the accommodation of the sick poor in the said hospital, and free of charge for diet, attendance, advice and medicines, and shall make the same appear to the satisfaction of the speaker of the Assembly, for the time being; that then it shall and may be lawful for the said speaker, and he is hereby required to sign an order on the provincial treasurer, for the payment of two thousand pounds in two yearly payments, to the treasurer of the said hospital, to be applied to the founding, building and finishing the same."

Some of the tight-fisted opponents imagine it will be utterly impossible for the supporters of the scheme to raise £2000 through individual subscriptions; therefore assent to the Bill's passage. The Bill passes the House February 7th; Governor Hamilton signs the enactment May 11th, in the Council Chamber.

From this point let Franklin tell the story. In his *Autobiography* he writes:

> Thanks to the conditional clause "the members who had opposed
> the grant, and now conceived they might have the credit of being
> charitable without the expense, agreed to its passage; and then in
> soliciting subscriptions among the people, we urged the condi-
> tional promise of the law as an additional motive to give, since
> every man's donation would be doubled; thus the cause worked
> both ways. The subscriptions accordingly soon exceeded the req-
> uisite sum [by nearly £800], and we claimed and received the
> public gift, which enabled us to carry the design into execution.
> . . . I do not remember any of my political manoeuvres, the success
> of which at the time gave me more pleasure; or wherein, after
> thinking of it, I more easily excused myself for having made use
> of some cunning."

It's refreshing to think of anyone outwitting Chester County
Quakers. The end's abundantly justified the means.

As eventually passed, the "Act to encourage the establishing of
an Hospital for the Relief of the Sick Poor of this Province, and
for the Reception and Cure of Lunaticks," is so drawn that it's
both an enabling Act and a Charter combined in the one instrument. The Charter clauses vest the government of the Hospital in
a Corporation of "Contributors" (who are defined as those who
have severally given, or shall give, £10 or more for the use of the
Hospital), and prescribe that they shall "meet on the first Day of
the Month called *July* next" to elect Managers and appoint a
treasurer.

At the "Contributors'" meeting at the State House this "first
Day of the Month called *July*," they choose twelve Managers (of
whom Benjamin Franklin's one) and a Treasurer to serve until
the

> " 'first second day in the Month called May,' and from that day
> to the present time the Annual Meeting of the Contributors and
> election of Managers has always been held on the first Monday
> in May."

July 6th, 1751, the Managers meet and choose Joshua Crosby
their President and Benjamin Franklin their Clerk. The original
Minute Book in Franklin's handwriting is one of the Hospital's
treasured possessions. Also in July, 1751, the Managers appoint
Doctor Thomas Bond and Benjamin Franklin a committee to
prepare a seal for the Corporation. The Seal finally adopted bears

a device of the Good Samaritan conveying the sick man to an inn, with the inscription "Take care of him, and I will repay thee."

The History of the Pennsylvania Hospital, 1751-1895, Thomas G. Morton, M.D., revised ed., 1-10; *Some Account of the Pennsylvania Hospital of Philadelphia from 1751 to 1938,* Francis R. Packard, M.D., 1-7; *Votes of Assembly; Colonial Records,* v, 525, 526; *Autobiography,* Benjamin Franklin.

1752

Friday, November 10—His Majesty, King George II, is seventy years old to-day; his loyal subjects in British North America are celebrating the Birthday in becoming manner. To crown the day's festivities, his Honour, Governour James Hamilton's giving a ball to-night at the State House.

Possessed of great wealth and given to lavish hospitality, James Hamilton dispenses social functions pertaining to the Governour-ship with a dignity befitting the office. At mid-day he's host to a large gathering at his country house, Bush Hill, and he keeps up the round of entertainment without cease until the evening's brilliant function.

> Edward Shippen, writing Colonel Burd several days before, says, "all the gentlemen of the town are to drink to his Majesty's health at Bush Hill, and after dinner they are to wait upon the ladies in town & conduct them to the State-House to a Ball in the Assembly-Room, & after a dance or two, all hands are to go upstairs."

We may be sure the company have more than "a dance or two" in the Assembly Chamber before "all hands. . . go upstairs" to a sumptuous supper laid in the "Long Gallery." The Banquetting Hall's a noble room judged by any standards; compares favourably with like apartments in many an Old World palace. Lighted by the mellow glow from hundreds of candles; alive with the kaleidoscopic play of rustling brocade and silken frocks, the multi-coloured attire of the men, the bright hues of officers' uniforms, or the occasional glint of a jewel; and filled with an assemblage marked by beauty, elegance and distinction, the Banquetting Hall presents a picture that may well cause Governour Hamilton a thrill of filial pride that his father had the vision to plan so worthy and gracious a chamber.

The Governour himself's not the least striking figure in this gathering. In his *Recollections,* Joshua Francis Fisher says of James Hamilton,

> "He was, according to my recollections of West's full length picture of him, a short stout man with a handsome, full, but not ruddy face; altogether in dress and air, personifying the dignity of his station. I once was dressed in some of his embroidered habiliments. . . ."

The West portrait alluded to shows Hamilton in a brown velvet coat, with a long-skirted waistcoat of yellow brocade embroidered with little flowered sprigs. Whatever his Honour may be wearing on this particular evening, his presence embodies the courtly elegance of the occasion. At this Birthday Ball are "present upwards of one hundred Ladies, and a much greater Number of Gentlemen," and all agree it's the most splendid "Assembly that has ever been seen in this Province."

While "all the gentlemen of the town" have been at Bush Hill at noon, toasting the King and Royal Family, there's been a

"Discharge of Cannon from the Association Battery, and many of the Ships in the Harbour, which being near 100 Sail, with their Colours display'd, &c." have "made a fine Appearance."

In honouring the King's Birthday, Philadelphia's not alone in the Province. The *Pennsylvania Journal* (November 23rd) says:

"We hear from *Reading,* in the County of *Berks,* that HIS MAJESTY'S Birth Day was kept in a very joyful, decent and loyal Manner, and that at Night the Town was very handsomely illuminated and all the Powder that could be got expended on the Occasion."

It's worth noting that in 1752 the King's Birthday was kept on November 10th, instead of in October, because in that year took place the change from the Julian (Old Style) calendar to the Gregorian (New Style) calendar. New Year's Day, in 1752, was January 1st, instead of March 25th as formerly. To rectify the calendar reckoning, 11 days were dropped. This skip came in September; the 14th immediately followed the 2nd.

Pennsylvania Gazette, November 16, 1752; *Pennsylvania Journal,* November 23, 1752; *History of Philadelphia,* Ellis Paxson Oberholtzer, i, 192; *Annals of Philadelphia,* J. F. Watson, ii, 274; *Recollections,* Joshua Francis Fisher, 77 *et seq.*

1754

Monday, November 11—Yesterday King George II was seventy-two; it being Sunday, the Birthday celebration was postponed till to-day. At noon, his Honour, Governour Robert Hunter Morris, has entertained a numerous company of gentlemen at his house in the city. This evening, he's giving a Birthday Ball at the State House. About an hundred ladies attend, and a somewhat larger number of men. Dancing's going forward in the Assembly Chamber and the scraping of fiddles resounds through the building.

His Honour's provided handsomely; an elaborate supper's laid in the Banquetting Hall. At supper, the first healths are to his Majesty the King and all the Royal Family; then follow toasts to the Proprietaries and to the Prosperity of the Province.

Pennsylvania Gazette, November 14, 1754; *Recollections*, Joshua Francis Fisher, 79, 81; *Annals of Philadelphia*, J. F. Watson, ii, 274.

1755

Monday, September 22—The Gentlemen of the Army are giving a ball at the State House this evening for "the Ladies and Gentlemen of the City." The hosts are the surviving Officers of General Braddock's defeated and broken army who came here to "lick their wounds" after the disaster of July 9th at Fort Duquesne. Any day now they're expecting orders to march northwards.

There's a twofold motive in giving the ball. It's ostensibly to celebrate Sir William Johnson's victory over the French at Lake George, for which, last Wednesday and Thursday evenings, there were bonfires, illuminations and "many curious Fire-works plaid off"—demonstrations of public rejoicing in which the troops in the city took active part. But the ball's also to mark the Officers' grateful appreciation of kindnesses the citizens have shown the shattered, sick and discouraged remains of Braddock's army when they reached Philadelphia the latter part of August.

At that time, notwithstanding the general consternation—amounting almost to panic—that had seized the city; the threat of riots, the imminence of French and Indian attack; and an expected avalanche of terrified, destitute refugees from the "back parts" of the Province, the incurably obdurate Assembly balked at making any proper provision to care for the officers and dejected troops. But the citizens, in spite of their own great anxiety, showed a better spirit. In his *Journal*, Duncan Cameron writes:

> "The Philadelphians' hearts and houses were open to us in the most affectionate and tender manner; and I must not forget the tender compassion of their good housewives, for they, being informed that our living had been chiefly on flesh, the women of Market Street and Church Alley, as I was told, formed an association for regaling us with apple pies and rice puddings, which they generously effected, and their example was followed by a great many women in the city."

So, then, the military ball at the State House this evening's partly the outcome of charitably bestowed "apple pies and rice puddings." Incidentally, the eighteenth-century prototype of the Emergency Aid exemplifies the adage that "the shortest way to a man's heart is through his stomach"; an homely bit of truth of which the modern Red Cross, with canteens and doughnuts, has not been unmindful.

Invitations to the ball, as is the custom of the time, are printed or written on the backs of playing cards. Many years afterwards, amongst old family papers was found an invitation on a card-back to this very ball—addressed to Mrs. Jekyll (*née* Shippen), begging "the favour of her company to a Ball at the State-House on Monday, September 22nd, 1755." Invitations to the City Assemblies are "written on the backs of playing cards, & signed by two of the Managers." Another method of bidding guests,

"which seems to have descended to a pretty late day, was by verbal invitation, delivered personally by Dolby, the sexton of Christ Church."

There are still people (in this twentieth century) who like to send written invitations by hand of footman or chauffeur rather than by post.

Pennsylvania Gazette, September 25, 1755; *Recollections*, Joshua Francis Fisher, 79, 81; *Colonial Records*, vi, 504, *et seq.*; *Diary* of Daniel Fisher, *Pennsylvania Magazine of History and Biography*, xvii, 274; *Journal* of Duncan Cameron, 1756 ed. 14, 15; *History of Philadelphia*, Ellis Paxson Oberholtzer, i, 194, 195; *History of Philadelphia*, Scharf & Westcott, i, 247.

Saturday, November 8—Tears of sorrow and indignation trickling down the cheeks of an Indian warrior must betoken some poignantly tragic situation. A tragic situation, indeed, has reached a climax this afternoon in the Council Chamber. In this time of black foreboding since Braddock's defeat, the horrors of the French and Indian War stand forth in grim relief.

Last night, along with two other chieftains and Conrad Weiser, came to the city Scarroyady—the long-time faithful friend of the Pennsylvania colonists—and desired an audience. He was in the utmost anxiety.

This morning, while Governour Morris and the Council were considering a Message to the Assembly, the Indians came to the Council Chamber and Scarroyady

"acquainted the Governour that he had a Message to deliver from the Sasquehanna Indians to the Governour, Wisemen, and People of this Province, & desired to be heard in publick, and that the Assembly might be present."

Accordingly, when the Indians had gone,

"The Governor sent a Message by the Secretary to give the Assembly notice of this, and appointed three o'clock in the afternoon. . . to hear the Indian Message."

Then, when the Assembly gather in their Chamber in the afternoon—before they come upstairs to the Council Chamber to hear Scarroyady—the Secretary delivers them a Message from the Governour:

"Gentlemen:
You have now been sitting six days, and instead of strengthening my Hands and providing for the safety and defence of the people and Province in this Time of imminent danger, You have sent me a Message wherein you talk of regaining the Affections of the Indians now employed in laying waste the Country and butchering the Inhabitants, and of inquiring what injustice they have received, and into the Causes of their falling from their alliance with us and taking part with the French. Such Language at this time and while the Province is in its present Circumstances seems to me very extraordinary, as no Complaint has ever to my knowledge been made by them of any Injury done them. . . ."

The Governour's allusion to Indian atrocities is no idle exaggeration. A Petition the people (some of them in the Quaker fold, too) have already sent the King, sets forth how Colonists in the "back settlements," less than 100 miles from the city, live in constant jeopardy and expect

"every Day to be attacked by Blood-thirsty Savages, a mere Handful of whom might, without the least Resistance, carry Fire and Sword into the very Heart of the Country."

About the middle of October—this from a contemporary Philadelphian whose blood's boiling—a large body of Indians,

"chiefly Shawonese, Delawares, &c, . . . fell upon this Province from several Quarters almost at the same Instant, murdering, burning, and laying waste; so that in the five Counties of *Cumberland, York, Lancaster, Berks,* and *Northampton,* which compose more than half the Province, nothing but Scenes of Distraction and Desolation were to be seen."

The Reverend Thomas Barton, brother-in-law to David Rittenhouse and one of the missionaries maintained by the Society for the Propagation of the Gospel, musters what men he can in his widespread mission field and leads them to stem, so far as they're able, this flood of devilish savagery.

At Gnaddenhutten, a small Moravian settlement in Northampton County,

"the poor unhappy Sufferers were sitting round their peaceful Supper, when the inhuman Murderers. . . stole upon them, butchered them, scalped them, and consumed their Bodies, together with their Horses, their Stock, and upwards of sixty Head of fat

Cattle (intended for the Subsistence of the Brethren at *Bethlehem*) all in one general Flame; so that next Morning furnished only a melancholy Spectacle of their mingled Ashes.

At the *Great Cove* in *Cumberland,* at *Tulpehockin* in *Berks,* and in several other Places, the Barbarities were still greater if possible. Men, Women, Children, and Brute-beasts shared one common Destruction; and where they were not burnt to Ashes, their mangled Limbs were found promiscuously strewed upon the Ground, . . . Nay, Stakes were found driven into the private parts of the Women, and the Men's private Parts cut off, and put into their Mouths; so that the *Savages* seem to riot and triumph in the most deliberate Acts of infernal Cruelty. . . .

One Family, consisting of the Husband, his Wife, and a Child only a few Hours old, were all found murdered and scalped in this manner;— the Mother stretched on the Bed with her new born Child horribly mangled and put under her Head for a Pillow, while the Husband lay on the Ground hard by with his Body ript up, and his Bowels laid open.

In another Place, a Woman with her sucking Child finding that she had fallen into the Hands of the Enemy, fell flat on her Face, prompted by the strong Call of Nature to cover and shelter her innocent Child with her own Body. The accursed Savage. . . struck her in the Head with a *Tomahawk,* tore off her Scalp, and scoured back into the Woods. . . . The Child was found some Time afterwards under the Body of its Mother, and is yet alive. . . ."

If the pacifist Assembly, who talk of regaining "the Affections of the Indians," wish to know "the Causes of their falling from their alliance with us and taking part with the French," it might possibly be salutary for them if they could be made to understand that the Indians' defection from the "English interest" is mainly because of their own persistent "principled" refusal to give the Indians the protection and assistance they've repeatedly begged against hostile and vastly more powerful tribes allied to and directed by the French. The Indians not unnaturally reason that if the English won't fight along *with* them, they can't expect the Indians to fight alone *for* them against the whole power of the French. Therefore, they feel obliged to make the best terms they can with the more enterprising enemy, who have greater courage and can protect them.

However some individual Members may feel, it's apparently the policy of the Assembly, as a body, to belittle these outrages. They certainly haven't lifted a finger to prevent or stop them.

Less than a fortnight after Scarroyady's impassioned appeal at the State House, a sorely-tried "Inhabitant" in Lancaster writes that

"a Member of the Assembly sent back to inform himself and Brethren of the Truth of the Ravages and Inhumanities committed amongst us, finding that Things were full as bad as they were represented," said "with great Indifference, that *there were only some Scots-Irish killed, who could well enough be spared.* This is the common Language of many of these People. It is our Crime not to be Dupes to Quaker Politics. . . ."

Is it any wonder the Presbyterians hate the Quakers! The author of this callous comment is Nathaniel Grubb, a Member for Chester County.

Scarroyady, grieved and alarmed at what's been taking place, and knowing full well the dire perils overhanging the few Indians still faithful to the English, hastens to Philadelphia. Now, in the Council Chamber, with the Governour and Council, the whole House of Assembly, and sundry citizens besides, gathered to hear him, he says:

"Brethren—

I let you know I am returned from my Journey, which when I was last here I told you I intended to take. I went as far up the Sasquehannah River as where the Nanticokes live. I told them that I had undertaken that Journey purposely to alarm them. . . I bid them rouse and awake and hearken to the noise that was all about them, and that if they did not now awake the first noise they would hear would be the noise of the Tomahawk upon their Heads. I went in this manner to all the Indians and I know their Sentiments, I want to know Yours. . . . I must now know if you will stand by us; to be plain, if you will fight or not. You must be as sensible of Danger as the Indians, and therefore speak plain to us, We shall then know What to do. Be persuaded that we are determined to know the certainty of your Measures before we take any of our selves.

I told them [the Susquehanna Indians] that the Defeat of General Braddock had brought about a great turn of affairs. It was a great Blow. But what then, tho' we were struck half way to the Ground I told them we had strength enough left to recover. . . .

At the same time they told me that. . . whoever sent to them first they would go to first, whether it should be their Brethren the English or the Six Nations, whoever sent first should be first assisted, and that it was further agreed by all the nations of Indians on Sasquehannah that I should go to Philadelphia and apply immediately to the Government and obtain an Explicit answer from them whether they would fight or no.

I must deal plainly with You, and tell you if you will not fight with us we will go somewhere else. We never can nor ever will put up the affront. If we cannot be safe where we are we will go somewhere else for protection and take care of ourselves.

We have more to say, but will first receive your answer to this, and as the times are too dangerous to admit of our staying long here, we therefore entreat you will use all the Dispatch possible, that we may not be detained.

We are charged with having been concerned in a late Engagement that the Enemy had with your people. We absolutely deny it. We. . . cannot help taking it very much amiss to be thus Charged by your people.

For a proof of our Innocence we let you know that as soon as we had the news of your people being attacked we went immediately, we did not stay two Minutes, to the place of attack; we found no Enemy there, but we found an Indian that was killed by your people, a French Indian, we did not kill him but we scalped him, and have brought you the Scalp, which we would not have done if he had been of the number of our Friends. Brethren, I have done for the present."

Besides presenting the scalp, Scarroyady has laid symbolic wampum belts on the table at intervals.

Towards the close of his address, tears welling from the old man's eyes bespeak his deep emotion. Indians, they say, generally keep impassive faces, no matter what their feelings. At Fort Duquesne, where an ally has accidentally shot and killed Scarroyady's son, and Scarroyady himself has used up all his ammunition and there's naught for him to do but wait the end of the battle, he sat down under a tree, with true Roman stoicism, and smoked his pipe. Now, the strain's too much for him; his composure completely breaks down.

When Scarroyady's finished speaking, Governour Morris thanks him for his friendly visit and warning; assures him that the "Government. . . of this Province have never accused the Six Nations of any Breach of Faith"; explains that he himself is unable to grant funds or send men and supplies—that the power to do so lies with the Assembly, as does also the decision whether the Province will fight or not; and that he, as Governour, will use his utmost endeavours to get an early and favourable response to this urgent appeal.

Then, turning to the Speaker, Governour Morris says:

"Mr. Speaker and Gentlemen of the Assembly:
You have heard what the Indians have said; Without Your aid

I cannot make a proper answer to what they now propose and expect of us. I therefore desire you will return to your House, consider well of it, and whenever you will strengthen my Hands and enable me to give them a full and proper Answer I shall most readily do it."

(Exeunt omnes)

For the third time this anxious Saturday, this time by candle-light, the Governour and Council meet in the Council Chamber. At the Governour's direction, Mr. Secretary Peters goes downstairs to the Assembly Chamber to deliver the copy of an Indian treaty they've asked for. The Assembly have adjourned!

To-night the Governour's torn between two minds. His impulse is—indeed, he's convinced it's his bounden duty—to set out straightway, with some of the Council, for the "back settlements" to give what measure of organisation, help and protection they can effect with such local volunteer aid as they can muster. At the same time, he sees he ought to stay in the city and try by every means to induce the Assembly to take appropriate and speedy action. After consulting Mr. Weiser, and at the earnest entreaty of the Indians, he decides to remain.

On Sunday, the Governour and Council are in the Council Chamber again. The result of this meeting's another urgent Message to the Assembly:

"Gentlemen:

After the Indians had in publick demanded the Assistance of this Government and desired to know what we intended to do, & whether they were to depend upon us for Protection or take care of themselves, They came to me in Council & informed me by Mr. Weiser. . . that they and their Brethren living upon the Sasque-hannah, who were about three hundred fighting men, were now the only Indians in this part of the Continent besides the Six Nations that remained firm in the English Interest . . . ; that the French & those their Allies were coming down against the English and had given them notice to get out of the way; That the Body of the Six Nations were employed in protecting their own Country and assisting the English to the Northward, and could not, therefore, afford them any help at so great a Distance, where-fore they declared that they and their Brethren were willing to act in Conjunction with the English against the French and their Allies, but that in their present Situation and Circumstances they could not take the weight of the War upon themselves.

What they desire from us at present is, that we would put the Hatchet into their Hands; that we would send a number of our Young Men to act in Conjunction with their Warriors and furnish the necessary Arms, Ammunition, & Provisions; That we would build some strong Houses for the Protection of their old men, Women, and Children, and that they may be supplied from time to time with necessaries.

They further insist upon knowing the resolutions of this Government. . . & upon having an explicit answer without further Delay, that they may prepare to act with us or to take the necessary measures for their own Security. . . .

. . . I cannot but look upon this as one of the most important matters that ever came under your Consideration. You know your own critical Situation, and cannot be strangers to theirs . . . it cannot be expected that these Indians will expose themselves, for us to the fury of nations far more powerful than themselves unless we vigorously support and assist them . . . If, therefore, they find that we continue to refuse either to act in defence of ourselves or them, they must necessarily leave us and throw themselves for protection into the hands of the French. . . .

. . . if through refusal these Indians should be obliged not only to leave us but to act against us, all the dreadful Consequences of it must be left at your door. . . ."

The Assembly don't meet for business till Tuesday, and then do nothing!

On November 24th, 400 terrified Germans come down from the "back parts" begging the Assembly to protect them.

On December 14th, a party of Germans from the "back settlements" only 60 miles away, drive a big Conestoga waggon into the city, lay the bloody corpses of their scalped countrymen at the door of the State House and call on the Assembly to "behold the Fruits of their Obstinacy"!

Colonial Records, vi, 681-761; *Votes of Assembly; A Brief View of the Conduct of Pennsylvania, for the Year 1755*, Rev. William Smith, D.D., *passim*.

1756

Monday, August 23—In the Banquetting Hall the Assembly are giving a very handsome dinner in honour of the newly-arrived Governour, the Honourable William Denny. The Assembly are keen to impress the new Governour favourably; have spared neither pains nor expense to make this dinner a memorable occasion—an occasion when they deem it politic , to splurge. Mr. Speaker Norris, though a Quaker, has a strongly-developed taste for elegance; under his watchful control, every detail of arrangement's been punctiliously carried out. As a point of pride, this dinner must in no wise be less splendid than the dinner Mayor Plumsted and the City Corporation gave his Honour at the Masonic Lodge last Saturday; the viands must be as fine and varied, the Madeira as old and mellow.

Amongst the guests at the State House are the Civil and Military Officers of City and Province, the Provincial Council, Officers of the Royal Army, the Mayor and Corporation, the Judges, the Clergy, and whatever distinguished strangers may chance to be in the city. It's a striking gathering to behold. Although most of the country Members, of course, wear plain Quaker garb—Quakers still dominate the Assembly, in spite of recent political unrest— there are enough of the "World's People" present, and enough of the "worldly" or "wet" Quakers (who have a taste for fine dress and aren't afraid of bright colours, gold lace and embroidery), to make the scene anything but dull.

Amongst the non-Quakers, one can readily picture Mayor Plumsted with curled and powdered wig, brown velvet coat and small clothes, and goffered wristbands of finest lawn; Colonel Duché and other military officers in resplendent uniforms, swords by their sides; Chief Justice Allen, portly, bewigged, and arrayed in all the rich elegance of attire to be expected of one of the wealthiest men in the Province; and all the rest of Philadelphia's "silk-stocking" gentry, never one whit behind current London modes in their apparel. Provost Smith, though in clerical black, makes a figure one would notice anywhere. Governour Denny, a man of forty-seven, sprung of an old East Anglian family and an Oxford graduate, is doubtless diverted (perhaps a bit puzzled) by the sharp contrasts he sees—the courtly urbanity in dress and bearing of many of the assemblage, the dour aspect of some of the hard-bitten, drab, "stiff" Quaker country Members from Chester and Bucks.

The arrival of a new Governour's the signal for alert politicians to vie one with another "in reaching him first to make a good impression and establish themselves in his favour." This is especially true in Governour Denny's case because of the intense bitterness of complex Pennsylvania politics and the critical condition of military affairs at the moment. Under all the outward show of hospitality and friendliness, poor Denny's being landed in a hotbed of animosities and dissension.

The Governour reached New York in the *Stirling Castle,* August 15th. Watchful Richard Peters, Secretary to the Provincial Council (of which former Governor James Hamilton's President), writing Thomas Penn, says he sped to New York as soon as word came of the Governour's likely time of arrival,

> "and found Mr. Denny had come up in a Pilot Boat from the Sterling Castle the day before. I had lodged a Letter for him in the Hands of Mr. William Alexander, which he gave him on his Arrival, and by that he knew the necessity of hastening to Philadelphia which he was prepared to do when I came to him, and therefore we set out immediately all alone, and wou'd have remained so, at his Request, till we shou'd come to Bristol, where Mr. Morris [Robert Hunter Morris, the retiring Governour] and the Council were to meet us. But Mr. Pemberton and some other Friends hearing of Mr. Denny's Arrival, he came as far as Princes Town [Princeton] and about twenty more came to Trenton and supped with the Governour."

This hasty scramble by Israel Pemberton and his clique to meet the Governour-designate is a patent attempt to get his ear first and ingratiate themselves with him; the axe they have to grind is primarily to circumvent the Council and Proprietary Party and to enlist his sympathy for their particular Indian policy.

Mr. Secretary Peters continues in his letter:

> "the next Morning Governour Morris, Mr. Hamilton, Mr. Hockley, Mr. Lardner, Mr. Mifflin and others [Members of the Council and foremost men of the Proprietary Party] met us at Trenton."

From Bristol, on Friday the 20th, says the *Pennsylvania Gazette,*

> "his Honour and the Company proceeded on their Way to Town, and were received near the Line of this County [hard by the *Red*

Lion, on the Bristol Pike] by Colonel Duché, of the Philadelphia County Regiment, with his Officers, and a Company of Grenadiers, who escorted him from thence to the City. When they came near Frankford, they were joined by a Part of the Troop of Horse, and the Company of Independents, and a great Number of the principal Inhabitants. . . . Before the Governour enter'd the Town, as many of the City Regiment, as the Shortness of the Notice would admit of, were got together, and drawn up in Second-street, near the Church [Christ Church], where they received him with rested Firelocks, and the Officers gave him the proper Salutes."

After this entry to the accompaniment of fife and drum, the Governour-designate confers with Governour Morris and the Council (possibly in the Council Chamber at the State House, possibly at Governour Morris's house) to settle some matters in connection with the Proclamation, matters dictated by the urgent war situation. Meanwhile, the troops have been drawn up on both sides of Market Street from the Court House down to Front; the Artillery Company are farther down, between Front and Water; the Grenadiers are on Second Street between the Court House and Christ Church; and "the Horse and Independents" are marshalled immediately about the Court House.

As soon as Governour Denny's Commission's been read and he's been duly proclaimed from the Court House balcony,

"the Guns of the Association Battery, of the Artillery Company, of the Privateer *Denny,* and of some other Vessels were fired off; the City Regiment made three general Discharges; the Vessels in the Harbour shewed their Colours; the Bells were set a Ringing; Bonfires were lighted; and a general Joy appeared in the Countenances of People of all Denominations."

The next day (Saturday, August 21st) Mayor Plumsted and the City Corporation give Governour Denny a dinner at the Masonic Lodge. Being a notable function under the auspices of members of the Proprietary Party, this dinner's a challenge and sets a mark for the anti-Proprietary Assembly to measure up to on Monday.

Before Monday's dinner at the State House, Mr. Speaker Norris utters an Address of welcome on the Assembly's behalf. After congratulating the Governour on his "Accession," the Address assures his Honour the Assembly

"hope, from the excellent Character we have received of him, his Administration will be as happy for the Province, as we shall endeavour to make it easy and comfortable to himself."

Then they present him with "an Order on the Provincial Treasurer for Six hundred Pounds." For all of which (flattering
address, dinner and advance stipend) his Honour graciously
thanks "the House for this obliging mark of their Esteem."

This order for £600 is an almost too obvious attempt to curry
favour—almost savours of bribery. Less than a year hence, when
the Assembly are again behaving "true to form," poor Denny will
be trying hard to borrow enough ready money to entertain Lord
Loudoun decently. Whereupon the Mayor and Corporation come
to the rescue.

Little does the new Governour reckon of what's in store for
him ere his recall three years later. In spite of the Assembly's
brave show of cordiality, there's to be the same old perennial contest between Governour and obdurate Legislature, the same be-
devilment to which his predecessors for years have been subjected.
When the Assembly find they can't "twist him around their
finger," there's the usual mulish balking, the usual succession of
vitriolic, abusive addresses (sometimes politely, but sarcastically
phrased, sometimes bluntly rude); these addresses all begin, "May
it please the Governour," or "May it please your Honour," when
all the time the House well know their communications will be
anything but pleasing, and do not intend they shall be. Yet, even
after five months' experience of bitter bickering and hectoring,
the Governour can still write home, "Philadelphia is a fine city."

Pennsylvania Gazette, August 19, 26, 1756; Pennsylvania Journal, August
19, 26, 1756; Votes of Assembly; Colonial Records, vii, 228; History of
Philadelphia, Thompson Westcott, ch. cxli; Minutes of Common Council;
Israel Pemberton, King of the Quakers, Theodore Thayer, 120 et seq.;
William Franklin in Gentleman's Magazine, September, 1757, xxvii, 417-
420; Penn MS.S, Official Correspondence, viii, 141, 151, 241, Historical Society of Pennsylvania.

1757

Friday, March 18—The Right Honourable John Campbell, Earl of Loudoun, Captain General of his Majesty's Forces in British North America, is guest of honour this afternoon at a dinner in the Banquetting Hall. The Mayor and Corporation of the City are the hosts.

Governour Denny can't be the host; he can't afford the necessary outlay for a state dinner because, at this time, he's much embarrassed for lack of ready money. Why? His Honour and the Assembly are at loggerheads about defense and military support and the House, as usual, are withholding his stipend to mark their displeasure. The Assembly, who *ought* to be the hosts—Lord Loudoun's visiting the Province for a conference with four Provincial Governours whom he's summoned to meet him in Philadelphia, the Colonial metropolis—are not inclined to be gracious and fulfill the obligations of official courtesy. The Mayor and Corporation, for the honour of the City and its reputation for hospitality, have stepped into the breach and determined to receive and treat his Lordship handsomely, in a manner befitting the dignity of the City and Province.

Early in February, when his Lordship was first

"expected to be in Town by the 17th Instant; it was proposed that an Address from this Board [the Mayor and Corporation] be presented to him on his Arrival in this City. . . and the Recorder was desired to make a Draught of an Address for the Purpose. It was also agreed that Provision be made at the Expence of this Board for entertaining his Lordship, and such of his Officers, &c., as may be then in Town, at Dinner." [Thanks to the "grapevine," they're aware the Governour's been trying to borrow £300 or 400.] And later in the month, "it being represented to the Board that it is imagined it would be agreeable to his Lordship, that a convenient House should be taken and furnished for his Reception; the Board agreed that this should be done at their Expence: which is also recommended to the Care of the Committee, and also to make provision of Wine, Fuel, or other Necessaries, which they may think will be acceptable. And the Mayor & Recorder, with the said Committee, are desired to meet him at his Arrival, and conduct him to his Lodgings."

When Lord Loudoun at last gets here, Monday, March 14th,

94

"the Guns of the Association Battery, and of some Vessels in the
Harbour, were fired, and the Bells were rung,"
and all the programme planned by the Mayor and Corporation
duly carried out.

Lord Loudoun's twofold task in America's no sinecure—"to
make the British army in North America into an efficient fighting
unit, and to unite jealous and divided colonies in support of the
war." The purpose of his meeting the Governours of Pennsylvania, Maryland, Virginia and North Carolina in Philadelphia is
to consult with them "what is best to be done in these Parts" at
this juncture of the French and Indian War and effect, if possible,
more unity of action in a serious crisis.

The dinner itself at the State House is all one could wish;
Philadelphia's ever been noted for good food and good wine, and
an able committee have made all arrangements—Samuel Mifflin,
John Inglis, Andrew Elliott, Edward Shippen, junior, William
Bingham and Thomas Willing have assisted Mayor Attwood Shute
"in making Preparation for the said Entertainment."

It is, indeed, a brilliant State function. Besides the chief guest
of honour, described as "short, strong made," with a countenance
"full of Candour, his Eyes Sprightly & good Humoured," the other
guests ranking next in honour are Governour Sharpe from Maryland, Governour Dinwiddie from Virginia, Governour Dobbs
from North Carolina and, of course, Governour Denny and the
Council. Then there are "Officers of the Royal Americans," a
"Number of the principal Inhabitants of the Town," and the
"Gentlemen Strangers in the Place." Resplendent military uniforms mingle with civilian brocaded waistcoats, silk stockings,
lawn ruffles and silver buckles. In view of the Assembly's un-
sympathetic attitude towards anything or anybody connected with
the war, Members of the honourable House are not conspicuous
by their numbers on this occasion.

Their staffs attend the several Governours, and one of these
"Gentlemen Strangers" is Colonel George Washington. Gov-
ernour Dinwiddie's been rather unwilling to have him come. In
February he's written Washington,

"I cannot conceive what Service You can be of in going there, as
the Plan concerted will in course be communicated to You & the
other Officers; however as You seem so earnest to go I now give
You Leave."

Washington's met with a flattering reception from Lord Loudoun, "who solicited and duly valued his counsels."

Pennsylvania Gazette, March 17, 24, 31, 1757; *Letters to Washington*, S. M. Hamilton, ii, 44; *Pennsylvania Journal*, March 17, 31, 1757; *Life and Writings of George Washington*, W. C. Ford, i, 431; *Lord Loudoun in North America*, S. M. Pargellis, 218; *Minutes of the Common Council of Philadelphia, 1704-1776*, 602 *et seq.; Penn MS.S, Official Correspondence*, Historical Society of Pennsylvania; *Dictionary of National Biography*.

Sir William Keith, Bart., Lieutenant-Governour of Pennsylvania, 1717-1726.

The Honourable Andrew Hamilton, who Designed the State House and Presided over its Building. From Portrait copied by Wertmüller (1751-1811) from an Original now lost.

Self-Portrait of Charles Willson Peale in his Museum in the State House.

Carpenters' Hall, built 1770. "First Carpenters' Company of the City and County of Philadelphia" founded 1724. From Water-Colour Sketch in Kennedy Collection.

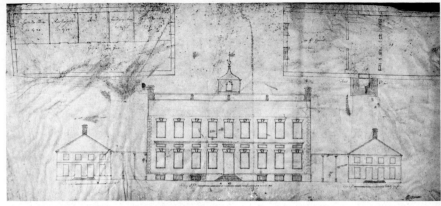

Andrew Hamilton's Design, North Elevation of State House, with Arcades and East and West "Offices." Drawn on Parchment.

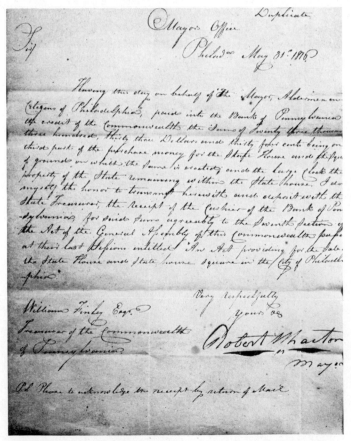

Mayor Robert Wharton's Letter to State Treasurer of Pennsylvania, enclosing Cheque in Part Payment for State House and State House Yard.

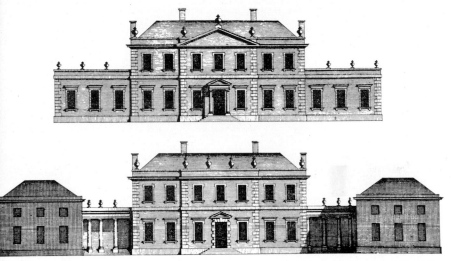

"A Draught done for a Gentleman in Essex," Plate 63 in James Gibbs's *Book of Architecture*.

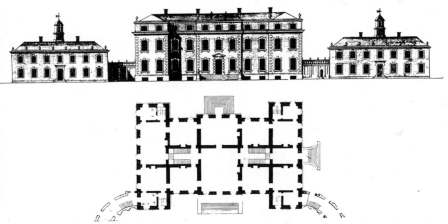

"The Plan and Upright of the Right Honourable the Earl of Litchfield's House at *Ditchley* in *Oxfordshire*," Plate 39 in James Gibbs's *Book of Architecture*.

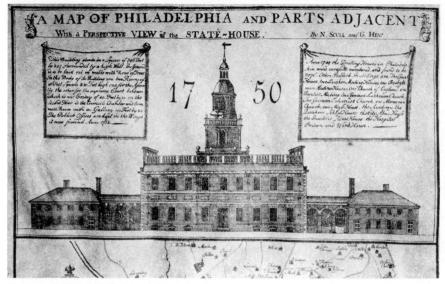

Engraving of State House from Top of Scull and Heap Map of 1750, showing *old* Steeple, not finished till two years later.

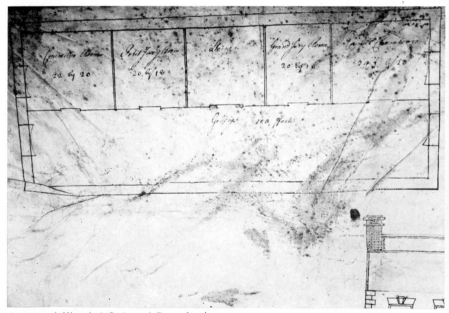

Upper Floor Plan of State House, from Judge Hamilton's Parchment Draught; plainly shows Place for Stair before Tower was built.

"A N.W. View of the State House in Philadelphia, *taken* 1778." Engraved by Trenchard for *Columbian Magazine* (1790) from Peale's Painting.

The State House in 1776, from John McRae's Engraving.

North Front of State House and Indian Sheds, c. 1776. Engraved by J. Rogers after Peale's Painting.

"View of Several Public Buildings in Philadelphia," from *Columbian Magazine*, 1790. Left to right (1) Episcopal Academy; (2) Congress Hall; (3) Main Body of State House, showing Steeple not then there; (4) Hall of American Philosophical Society; (5) Library Company of Philadelphia.

Old Court House, Second and Market Streets, Christ Church in Middle Distance. From Engraving by W. Birch, 1799.

South Front of State House and State House Yard, 1800. From Engraving by W. Birch.

North Front of State House and Supreme Court Building (Old City Hall), 1798. Engraving by W. Birch.

State House Yard, 1798. Engraved by W. Birch.

Congress Hall and Ricketts's Circus, Sixth and Chestnut Streets. From early Water-Colour Sketch.

City Tavern, Second between Chestnut and Walnut Streets. From Water-Colour Sketch in Kennedy Collection.

Joseph Carpenter's House, where the Chevalier de la Luzerne gave his Great Feast, July 15, 1782.

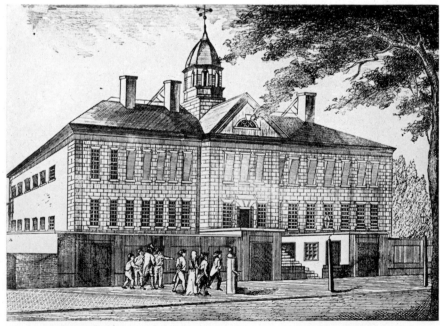

Old Walnut Street Gaol, from Engraving by W. Birch.

Chestnut Street Front of State House Group c. 1820. From Childs's Print of Strickland's Engraving.

Robert Mills's Coloured Rendering for County Offices of 1811.

A Row in U. S. House of Representatives, from William Cobbett's *House of Wisdom in a Bustle*, 1798.

Election Day at the State House. From Water-Colour by John Louis Krimmel, c. 1815.

Printed Linen Handkerchief, Souvenir of la Fayette's Visit to Philadelphia in 1824.

Triumphal Arch, built in Front of State House for la Fayette's Visit in 1824. From Water-Colour Sketch in Kennedy Collection.

Old Painting of Parson Duché's House, Third and Pine Streets. After Confiscation assigned Chief Justice McKean as his Official Residence.

Stair Landing in Tower.

U. S. House of Representatives, Ground Floor, Congress Hall.

Provincial Council Chamber, Southwest Room, Upper Floor.

Pennsylvania Supreme Court Room, West Room, Ground Floor.

1758

Wednesday, January 25—A grand rumpus in the Assembly Chamber! The Assembly are trying—or attempting to try—Provost Smith for what they're pleased to call a libel on their "Honourable Body." The trial's the talk of the town and the Assembly Chamber's packed with most of the gentry of Philadelphia, all Doctor Smith's friends.

This so-called "trial" is the merest travesty of justice, nothing but a high-handed "Star Chamber" proceeding. Infatuated with their own self-importance, and without a shadow of legal justification, the Assembly have constituted themselves *plaintiff, court* and *judge* all in one!

Doctor Smith's

"Charged with being a promoter and abettor of the Writing and Publishing a Libel, entitled the Address of William Moore one of the Justices of the Peace for the County of Chester."

When the Provost was brought for a hearing, accompanied by his counsel, on January 17th, these "Resolves" were read to him:

"Resolved.

1st That Mr. Smith or his Council [counsel] shall not be allowed to Speak or Argue against the Authority or Power of this House to take Cognisance of the Charge against him.

2nd That Mr. Smith or his Council shall not be allowed to argue that the Address aforesaid is not a Libel."

(Note, at this point, that legally a non-existent body or person can't be libelled. If there *were* any libel, it was on the Assembly that ceased to exist in September, 1757. The prosecuting Assembly are a *new* body, elected and beginning existence in October, 1757. Although the membership is substantially the same as that of their *non-existent* predecessor—now legally dead as a mullet—rancour's impelled them to this legally and technically indefensible course.) The Provost's counsel—John Ross and William Peters, two very able lawyers—thus precluded from speaking on the two vital issues, and the whole affair virtually settled beforehand by the Assembly, the Provost's determined not to plead but to appeal directly to the Crown.

To-day, when the Provost's brought again to the Bar of the

House, the Speaker (now Thomas Leech) delivers his sentence thus:

"Mr. Smith, this House having enquired into the charge against you, have found you guilty of promoting and publishing the Libel entitled the Address of William Moore, Esqr. and do order that you be committed to the Gaol of this County, untill you make satisfaction to this House."

Thereupon the Provost reads and tenders the House his appeal to his Majesty in Council:

"To the Honourable the Representatives of the Free-Men of the Province of Pennsylvania —
I apprehend that I have an indubitable Right as an English Subject of appealing from the Sentence given against me by this House to his Majesty our Gracious Sovereign, in Council, and agreeable to such right I do now make such appeal and desire that it may be granted me. I offer myself ready to give such Security and comply with such reasonable and legal Requisites as the House may prescribe for the prosecuting such appeal, and I request that I may have Copies of all such Papers and Minutes of the proceedings of the House in this Case as may be necessary to enable me to prosecute the said Appeal with Effect.
And I further pray that Admission of this my Appeal may be entered on the Minutes of this House."

The House utterly reject the Provost's appeal and return it to him. On his desiring

"that the Tender and Refusal [of the appeal] might be enter'd on their Minutes, they Ask'd with anger, if they were to be directed by him how to keep their Minutes."

The Speaker then reads an irrelevant "Form of an Acknowledgment" and insinuates "as if the same wou'd be sufficient from Mr. Smith." The Provost arising, answers the Speaker that he's not conscious of having done any offense. Then, "drawing himself to his full height, and striking his breast with his hand," he says with "great vehemence and dignity":

"Mr. Speaker, I cannot make acknowledgments nor express contrition. No punishment which this Assembly can inflict upon me would be half so terrible to me, as suffering my tongue to give my heart the lie."

Delighted with this "dramatic defiance of the Assembly," the throng of the Provost's Proprietary Party friends burst forth into a veritable storm of applause. For some minutes uproar and confusion reign. The House, amazed and enraged at this insult to their dignity, order the doors closed; bid the Serjeant-at-Arms arrest the applauding gentry, some of them Officers of the Crown. The Provost's hustled off to gaol

> "without suffering him to open his Mouth, when he attempted to Vindicate himself from some unjust Charges alledged against him on Account of the Tumult among the People."

For several days there are arrests and "informations" (in other words, tattling) which lead to arrests, the culprits bearing the most honoured names in the city. Fines are imposed, and there are some perfunctory apologies for creating a disturbance— enough, at least, to soothe a little the jolted self-esteem of some of the Assemblymen, smarting under the consciousness of first having made fools of themselves to satisfy their vindictive rancour, and then having their folly clinched by that "odious Proprietary minion," Provost Smith.

From gaol, on January 30th the Provost sends a communication to the Speaker in order

> "to acquaint the House of Assembly with his intentions, that they might be ready to answer his Complaints immediately before the King in Council, and have no Pretence for delaying the Affair by Suggestion of Surprise, and accordingly wrote the following Letter:
> 'As I do not think that the Refusal of your House to receive or admit the Appeal I tendered to them, on Wednesday the Twenty Fifth Instant, can either deprive His Majesty of his Royal Prerogative to hear Appeals from any Judgment in this Province; nor any of his Subjects of their Right to make such Appeals, I think it proper to acquaint You and this House of Assembly, that I am still determined to lay my Appeal, Case and Complaint before His Majesty in Council; and to prosecute the same in such Manner as I shall be advised; in Order to obtain that Redress which I have reason to hope from the Royal Clemency and Justice. I do therefore require of You and the House that You will be pleased to order your Clerk to sign the Deposition and Papers which he has already delivered to me or my Counsel, by your Order, and likewise that You will grant me Copies under his Hand of all the other Papers, Minutes, Orders and Resolves of your House concerning me, or my Case, which may be necessary to enable me to prosecute the same with Effect; for which Copies I am ready to pay.' "

Many of these papers the Assembly, in their spite, never supply so that depositions have to serve in lieu of them when the appeal comes before the Crown.

In the meanwhile, the Assembly do all they can to make it uncomfortable for the Provost. The Vestry of Christ Church and many of his other friends wish to bail him out of gaol, and the Trustees of the College represent to the Assembly the inconvenience and disorganisation the enforced absence of the Provost occasions. All to none effect. The Assembly have passed a resolution ordering the Sheriff not to

"obey any Writ of Habeas Corpus, or other Writ whatsoever, that may come to his Hands for Bailing and discharging the said William Smith, or otherwise discharge him from his Custody on any Pretence whatsoever; And that this House will support him in his Obedience to this Order."

And because of a confusing technicality irregularly inserted in the mittimus to the Sheriff, Chief Justice Allen's unable legally to override the Assembly's action and release the Provost by a writ of *Habeas Corpus,* although there's nothing he'd more gladly do. So the Provost stays in gaol till April, but on February 4th the College Trustees pass a resolution that the Assembly of the Province

"having taken our Provost into custody, and a great inconvenience arising thence, it is ordered that his classes shall attend him at the usual hours, in the place of his present confinement."

For more than two months, the gaol's the Provost's office and classroom.

To shorten a very long and involved story, Provost Smith sends his appeal to England and he himself sails in December (1758). In England, he's looked upon as a "distinguished and accomplished young man [he's only twenty-eight] . . . martyred and persecuted by an Assembly of Quaker fanatics, who would not fight the French." Both Oxford and Aberdeen confer on him the degree of Doctor of Divinity, and he's made much of wherever he goes. The Committee of Trade and Plantations of the Privy Council (who control all colonial affairs) hear the case, at which counsel represent both the Provost and the Assembly, and the Attorney-General appears for the Crown. The outcome is that the Provost's fully upheld, while the Assembly are severely censured under his Majesty's high displeasure, and roundly reprimanded for unwarrantable behaviour in assuming powers that do not belong to them; likewise, for invading both the Crown's prerogative and the indefeasible liberties of the subject. And they're sharply cautioned that hereafter,

"in all cases in Pennsylvania, His Majesty's writs [of *Habeas*

Corpus] should issue freely, according to law, and that no person whatsoever [*sic*] should presume to disobey them."

When Doctor Smith comes back to Philadelphia, his standing's vastly enhanced by this deserved victory over arrest and persecution on a flimsy pretext, trumped up to gratify a long-standing political grudge.

To get at the Assembly's motives in attacking the Provost, one has to go back more than two years. Early in November, 1755, when Indian outrages had thrown the Province into the utmost anxiety, bordering on popular panic, and the Assembly stubbornly refused to take any measures of defense, Judge Moore, of Moore Hall, sent the Assembly a sharply-worded protest (signed by many of the substantial free-holders of Chester County) bidding them cease from "unnecessary Debates" and demanding "that Protection from them which they undoubtedly owed to the People who had chosen them their Representatives." Not long after, Colonel Moore (Judge Moore was commissioned Colonel in 1748, when the Associators were organised) let it be known that unless the Assembly bestirred themselves for defense, he'd march down from Chester County with 2000 volunteers and compel them to action. The protest and this threat the Assembly, of course, took as a grievous insult, and not only the Assembly but the whole Quaker oligarchy and their political machine. They bided their time for revenge; it came when a vacancy for Chester County occurred in the Assembly in November, 1756, and they procured the election of Isaac Wayne (father of General Anthony Wayne), Judge Moore's personal enemy.

To injure and punish the "obnoxious" Moore,

"the Party got one *Isaac Wayne,* (who they knew had a Quarrel with Mr. Moore) elected. . . in the Room of some Member resign'd, very few Townships in the County having had regular Notice to attend. This Man, to ingratiate himself with the old Interest and secure his Election, had declared in the Hearing of many, that tho' he would rather give *Fifty Pounds* than serve in the Assembly on any other Occasion, yet as he had quarrelled with 'Squire *Moore,* he would spend or give *Fifty Pounds* sooner than not be elected; for, if he should be chosen an Assemblyman, he would endeavour to ruin the said *Moore,*' or words to that effect; which many are ready to make Proof of."

Sworn depositions indicate the indefatigable industry of the "enemy" in procuring, from irresponsible persons, twenty-seven single petitions to the Assembly with trifling or wholly imaginary complaints against Judge Moore. Many of those approached said they "had always taken Mr. *Moore* to be an able and discerning Magistrate in his Office, and . . . they would have no concern in the Matter" of complaints. As so frequently happens with persons of strong convictions, imperious manner and blunt speech, Judge Moore often greatly offended them that disagreed with him, and one of the people whose bitter animosity he had thus aroused was Isaac Wayne, a gentleman also of blunt speech and vigorous behaviour. Admirable as Captain Wayne may ordinarily have been, on this occasion his deep-seated resentment impelled him to become the catspaw of the revengeful Assembly and imbrue his hands in dirty politics. Few great or good men, indeed, can present a lifelong blameless record.

Following this smear campaign, and the string of complaints presented to them, the Assembly summoned Judge Moore to appear before them and answer to the charges against him. Judge Moore appeared on the day set, but declined to plead before the House and declared they had no jurisdiction in the matter. Later, when he'd received copies of the complaints, he sent the Assembly an Address (September 22nd, 1757) in which he took up the accusations seriatim and showed they'd all been procured from "Persons of mean and infamous Characters"—wife-beaters, notorious drunkards, adulterers, cheats and evaders of debts, bigamists and horse-thieves, a scurvy lot of rapscallions of indubitably barnyard morals and scarcely to be credited with better than barnyard standards of probity.

On the 28th, the Assembly retorted by sending Governour Denny an Address in which they charged Judge Moore with "divers misdemeanours, fraudulent and extortionate Practices," and general misbehaviour in office,

> "Wherefore we do intreat your Honour to remove the said William Moore from the Offices of Judge of the Court of Common Pleas and Justice of the Peace, and from all other Publick Offices, Posts, and Employments, whatsoever, under his Majesty within this Government."

Having shot this shaft at Judge Moore, the Assembly followed it with a long venomous, contumacious and insulting Message to Governour Denny that led the exasperated Governour to say, in part of his reply Message, that he was not surprised at their abuse

and malevolence towards him when he considered that "Several
Worthy Gentlemen," his predecessors in office,

"have not been better treated, which must convince every unbiassed Judgement that you are not so much Displeased with the
Person Governing, as impatient of being Governed at all."

This was an uncomfortable statement of truth, after which his
Honour sent the Assembly a separate Message concerning Judge
Moore—

in "Common Justice. . . no man should be condemned unheard in
any matter that affects his Life, Fortune, or Character." He cannot remove "Mr. Moore from his Publick Employment till I have
made him Acquainted with the Complaints and Evidence exhibited against him, and given him an Opportunity of Making his
Defence; I therefore desire you will furnish me with Copies of the
Petitions and Proofs on which your Application to me against him
is grounded, and you may assure yourselves that on a full Hearing
of the Matters, strict Justice shall be done both to him and the
Publick."

Then, as the old Assembly were dissolving before the annual election, they saw to it that their attack on Judge Moore was published in the newspapers.

Judge Moore very naturally felt that since his character had
been severely aspersed in public print, he had a perfect right to
defend himself in public print, and soon afterwards published in
the same newspapers his Address to the Governour in which he
defended his character and conduct, and animadverted pretty caus-
tically upon his accusers. This was the Address alluded to in the
accusation against Provost Smith, and this is where the Provost
comes into the picture. The Moore controversy makes a long,
complex and highly illuminating story; however, the rest of it has
little connection with the State House, so will not be told here.
Suffice it to say that after the Address has been published in the
Gazette, Provost Smith has it reprinted in the German newspaper
he helps to edit, published as part of the policy to educate the
German element in the Province into becoming intelligent and
responsible citizens. This German reprint offers the long-awaited
opportunity the Assembly eagerly pounce upon to vent their
malice on the Provost.

They hate the Provost on several counts, are bent on revenge,
and hope to punish and silence a dangerous political adversary.
In the first place, the Provost's a valiant supporter of the Proprie-

tary or Governour's Party, and at this very moment Benjamin
Franklin's in England whither they've sent him to try to upset the
Proprietary Government and have the Province taken over by the
Crown. In the second place, they're still smarting under the scath-
ing (and deserved) strictures in *A Brief View of the Conduct of
Pennsylvania, for the Year 1755,* published in London in 1756.
Although published anonymously, everybody knows the Provost
wrote it, but there's been no sufficient evidence to prosecute him
for it.

The *Brief View* is merciless towards the Quaker political machine whose iniquity it exposes and the methods by which it keeps
itself in power. Besides James Logan's opposition to the machine
(and incidental proof of its existence), there's an illuminating bit
of unintentional confirmation from one of the foremost Quaker
politicians himself. Under date of October 3rd, 1749, in his *Diary*
John Smith writes:

". . . Wm. Plumstead having a desire to be Chose a Burgess, he
with some of his fr^{ds} took a great deal of pains for it; which Occasioned some of us to take some that he might not, and the old
ones were chosen by a great majority."

The Assembly don't relish having the *Brief View* label them a
"factious Cabal"; nor allusions to their corrupting the German
vote; nor being told their incurable pacifism's been contributory
to Braddock's defeat; nor being charged with the injustice of "not
allowing the Back Counties their due Proportion of Representatives" in Assembly; nor expressions about an "Antidote to
Quaker-Poison"; nor mention of the need "for a Change of our
Quaker Rulers, whose Principles have almost undone their Country, and its Constitution, too"; nor the forthright assertion that
as long as they "keep the Power in their own [political machine]
Hands, it will be as impossible to reconcile Light and Darkness, as
to make them prefer the general Interest of the Province to that
of their own Party." The truth hurts.

The Provost's uttered a bit of prophecy for himself when he's
said,

"If we. . . blame the Administration, and *probe* into the Bosom
of prosperous Villainy, it is like waking a Nest of Hornets, who
will be sure to sting and pursue, if they can, to Destruction."

A touch of romance comes in as happy ending to the story.
While Judge Moore and the Provost are in gaol together, Rebecca

Moore frequently visits her father. The Judge is soon fully exonerated by the Governour and Council (to the great mortification
of the Assembly), restored to his home and family, and continues
for many years as Presiding Judge of Chester County. When the
Provost comes back from England, he marries Rebecca Moore,
the marriage celebrated at Moore Hall.

Colonial Records, vii, 742-783; vii, *passim*; *Votes of Assembly*; *Penn MS.S*,
Historical Society of Pennsylvania, v (most of the volume); *Diary* of John
Smith, MS. in Collection of Library Company of Philadelphia; *Pennsylvania, Colony and Commonwealth*, Sydney George Fisher, 198, *et seq.* &
498 *et seq.; Balch Papers, Shippen*, Historical Society of Pennsylvania, i,
39, 51, 53, 62; *Portrait of a Colonial City*, H. D. Eberlein and Cortlandt
V. D. Hubbard, 142-151 & 401-403.

1762

Tuesday, November 16—An entertaining show at the State House this evening! At 6 o'clock Doctor William Shippen, junior, who's just back from his medical studies in England and abroad, gives his "introductory" to the course of anatomical lectures he's been advertising in the newspapers; he's showing the anatomical paintings the celebrated Doctor John Fothergill, of London, has just given the Pennsylvania Hospital.

Thus, within the State House, is born America's first medical school.

Hitherto, the only medical training available in the American Colonies has been through apprenticeship to a practising physician. Practising physicians vary widely in their own store of knowledge; also in their capacity to impart information. Busy practitioners have but little time for instruction of apprentices; there's a woeful lack of all manner of professional equipment.

The paintings Doctor Fothergill's given the Hospital have cost him "about 200 guineas. . . the work of Van Rymsdyk, a Dutch painter living in London, reputed the best anatomical artist of his day." (They're now in the Library of the Hospital).

Doctor Fothergill's said in a letter to James Pemberton (one of the Hospital Managers):

"I have recommended it to Doctor Shippen to give a Course of Anatomical Lectures to such as may attend." He adds that Doctor Shippen "will soon be followed by an able Assistant Dr. Morgan, both of whom I apprehend will not only be useful to the Province in their Employments but if suitably countenanced by the Legislature will be able to erect a School for Physic amongst you that may draw Students from various parts of America & the West Indies."

Doctor Fothergill has truly prophetic vision.

Doctor Shippen's asked permission to show the Fothergill paintings at his lecture; the Hospital Managers (November 8th) have consented. The newspaper advertisements of November 11th

"inform the Publick that a Course of Anatomical Lectures will be opened this Winter in Philadelphia for the Advantage of the young Gentlemen now engaged in the Study of Physick, in this and the neighbouring Provinces, whose Circumstances and Connections will not admit of their going abroad for Improvement, to

the Anatomical Schools in Europe; and also for the Entertainment of any Gentlemen, who may have the Curiosity to understand the Anatomy of the Human Frame . . . The Necessity and
publick Utility of such a Course in this growing Country . . .
will be more particularly explained in an introductory Lecture
to be delivered the 16th Instant at 6 o'Clock in the Evening, at
the State House. . . ."

How many gentlemen "Curiosity to understand the Anatomy
of the Human Frame" prompts to attend this lecture, we know
not; medical apprenticed students eagerly grasp the opportunity
to hear the State House "introductory" and enroll themselves for
the rest of the lectures. These Doctor Shippen gives in a small
building at the rear of his father's house at Fourth and Market
Streets.

Dissection of cadavers is a prime desideratum for the course,
but the community at large have a strong prejudice against dissect-
ing human bodies. With considerable difficulty, Doctor Shippen
gets permission to use the bodies of criminals—suicides and those
hanged for felonies. Less than a month after the course starts,
there's a "windfall" in the shape of a negro body. In its local news
notes of December 2nd, 1762, the *Pennsylvania Gazette* says:

"We hear that a Negroe Man was found last Tuesday in his
Master's Cock-Loft, with a Piece of Glass Bottle under him, with
which he had cut his Throat in such a terrible Manner, that notwithstanding all the Assistance that could be had, he died in a few
Hours: and after the Coroner's Inquest had pronounced him
guilty of Self-Murder, his Body was immediately ordered, by Authority, to Dr. Shippen's Anatomical Theatre."

Such fantastic rumours get afloat about the means of obtaining
bodies, and so inflamed is public sentiment against dissection,
that mobs several times beset Doctor Shippen's anatomical theatre.
During one of these attacks, it's said the Doctor barely escapes
with his life.

Doctor John Morgan's been studying in England and on the
Continent at the same time as Doctor Shippen, but has continued
longer overseas. While in England, these two young Philadelphians have seen much of each other and Doctor Rush says that

"it was during his [Morgan's] absence from home that he concerted with Doctor Shippen the plan of establishing a Medical
School in this city."

When Doctor Morgan comes back to the city in 1765, with

Philadelphia's first "umbrelloe" and the Proprietary endorsement of the idea for a medical school—backed by letters of like tenour from former Governour James Hamilton and the Reverend Richard Peters—he lays before the Trustees and Faculty of the College the plan he and Doctor Shippen have together devised in England. After reading Thomas Penn's letter, the Trustees and Faculty (May 3rd) elect Doctor Morgan "Professor of the Theory and Practice of Physic," thus creating the "first medical professorship in America." In September, the Trustees unanimously elect Doctor Shippen "Professor of Anatomy and Surgery."

Thus comes into full corporate being the first American medical school (now the Medical Department of the University of Pennsylvania), for which Doctor Shippen's paved the way more than two years before by his "introductory" lecture at the State House, and his subsequent dissections at his little anatomical theatre.

History of the Medical Department of the University of Pennsylvania, Joseph Carson, M.D.; Some Account of the Pennsylvania Hospital of Philadelphia from 1751 to 1938, Francis R. Packard, M.D.; Pennsylvania Journal & Weekly Advertiser, November 11, 1762; Pennsylvania Gazette, November 11, 1762.

1765

Saturday, October 5—Muffled bells tolling all afternoon and evening—the State House bell and Christ Church bells, with others joining in! Since a little before 4 o'clock, two negro lads (one belongs to Alderman Samuel Mifflin) have been marching the streets, beating their crêpe-festooned muffled drums; they're calling the citizens to a meeting in the State House Yard. Alderman Benjamin Shoemaker meets them and asks "by whose authority they're doing it, and what they mean by summoning people to a riot?" They "sass" him back and go on with their rub-a-dub-dub. Alderman Shoemaker hastens to find the Mayor, to put a stop to this unseemly performance. No Mayor, no Magistrates anywhere to be found; nothing for Alderman Shoemaker to do but go home in sputtering wrath.

In the forenoon, the "leading English merchants" have sent "two deputies" to Doctor Mühlenberg, Pastor of the German Lutheran Church,

> "to say that, in the afternoon at high water, a ship from London, under the protection of a ship of war, would reach the city and land the stamped papers. . . all the bells on the high church and on the State House would be tolled, all the ships at the wharves and in the stream would hang out signs of distress, and the drums muffled in crape would be beaten along the streets, and a general town meeting at the State House would take place. . . and they wished to know whether I would allow our bells on the school house to be muffled and tolled."

Doctor Mühlenberg tells them he can't say "yes" without consulting his Vestry. The Germans decide they'd better keep out of it.

By 4 o'clock, several thousands have crowded into the State House Yard, mad as hornets about the Stamp Tax. This afternoon, the *Royal Charlotte* with the Stamps on board, has come up the river, in company with a man-of-war, and anchored in front of the city—greeted by all the rest of the shipping with their colours displayed upside down and menacing crowds on the wharves. The citizens are bound the Stamped Papers shan't be landed; their tempers hotter than ever against John Hughes, the Member of Assembly appointed Stamp Master for the Province on Doctor Franklin's nomination.

Hughes calls the meeting a

"mob. . . chiefly Presbyterians and proprietary emissaries," with Chief Justice Allen's "son at their head, animating and encouraging the lower class."

Doctor Mühlenberg, a less-biassed witness, says they're "the principal merchants and lawyers of the English nation." The bells keep on tolling solemnly at regular intervals.

The meeting quickly decide a deputation—James Tilghman, Robert Morris, Charles Thomson, Archibald McCall, John Cox, William Richards and William Bradford—shall go and demand Hughes's immediate resignation as Stamp Master. While they're gone, the citizens wait with simmering wrath in the State House Yard.

John Hughes is sick a-bed—seriously so, 'tis said. Nevertheless, he sees the gentlemen. They argue for half an hour. Finally, Robert Morris suggests that just now Hughes must at least agree he'll not attempt to put the Act into execution "until his Majesty's further pleasure be known." Hughes, in a subsequent letter to the Commissioners of the Stamp Office in London, says he complied

"because I had many informations by my friends that the mob intended to proceed to the last extremity if I did not resign."

The committee go back to the citizens in the Yard and report that Mr. Hughes refuses to resign now—his commission hasn't come yet; says he can't resign from a post he doesn't yet hold—but engages "no Act of his shall tend to carry that Law into Execution here, until it is generally complied with in the other Colonies." At this reply, the people are (to quote the contemporary newspapers)

"instantly transported with Resentment, and it is impossible to say what Lengths their Rage might have carried them, had not the Gentlemen who waited on Mr. Hughes represented him in the Light he appeared to them, at the Point of Death; his Situation raised their Compassion, and they happily communicated their Feelings to all the People assembled; and instead of the Multitude repairing instantly to his House for a positive Answer, they agreed to make their Requisition in Writing, and gave Mr. Hughes until Monday Morning to make a Reply."

Then they draw up a paper to the effect that

"a great Number of the Citizens of Philadelphia, assembled at the State House, do demand of Mr. John Hughes, Distributor of Stamps for Pennsylvania, that he will give them Assurance, under

his Hand, that he will not execute that Office; and expect that he
will give them a candid, fair and direct Answer by Monday next,
at Ten o'Clock, when he will be waited on for that Purpose."

Young Thomas Bradford, William's son, carries this written
demand to Hughes; the people leave the Yard and go home.
Meanwhile, the Stamped Papers have been put on the *Sardine*
for safety; the mail's been taken to the post-office. There, young
Bradford's seen a large official-looking envelope from the Stamp
Office in London, addressed to Hughes, so he knows Hughes's
commission's come.

Hughes tries to avoid signing the demanded resignation—reit-
erates his commission hasn't come, and he knows of his appointment only "by common report." Says Thomas Bradford in his
Journal:

"He equivocated and said he did not *know* he was appointed. I
told him I had seen the package containing his commission, and
that he had received it that day. This he could not deny, and
made many trials to put me off. I compelled him to call his son
and draw up his resignation. . . ."

The "resignation" can be called such only by courtesy; it's
merely a cagey repetition of his afternoon's verbal engagement
reported to the town meeting. Even pending its promised delivery in writing on Monday, Hughes calls in Charles Thomson
Sunday morning to see if there isn't some way he can wriggle out
of it. Thomson tells him plainly there isn't. So the so-called "resignation's" read to the people Monday forenoon.

It's approved at first with some applause,

"but [say the newspapers in their next issue] we find many People much dissatisfied with it since, as they think, he ought to have
resigned his Office without Reservation; . . . we have Reason to
think this Declaration would not have quieted the Inhabitants,
had Mr. Hughes been in better Health."

Philadelphia newspapers of the day are given to understatement.
Doctor Mühlenberg thinks

"a single spark would have set the whole inflammable mass in a
blaze, and then the house of the collector of stamps would have
been destroyed, so that not one stone would have remained on
the other."

The newspapers add,

"Captain Hawker having taken the Stamp Papers on board his
Majesty's Ship, prevents them from being exposed to the Resent-

ment of an injured and enraged People. . . . cool thinking People among us congratulate themselves" that the citizens are "Men who had Moderation not to proceed to any unnecessary Acts of Violence."

So ends this immediate phase of the episode. The newspapers' allusion to absence of unnecessary turbulence in the city, however, is hardly warranted. Prior to the *Royal Charlotte*'s arrival with the Stamped Papers, there's been considerable uneasiness; beginning in April at the first tidings of the Stamp Act's passage, it's swelled with continuing *crescendo* to the dramatic outburst of October 5th.

One Colonial Governour's complained that the British Government, deaf to all remonstrance, have virtually told Americans, "Obey the Act and be damned!" To which Americans have naturally replied, "We'll be damned if we do!" The Act strikes

"directly at the interests of some of the most influential groups in the colonies. . . tavern owners (often the leading politicians of their neighbourhood), printers, lawyers, and merchants were alike injured."

Doctor Franklin's counsel of resignation to the inevitable, when he finds, "We might as well have hindered the sun's setting" as to try to stop the Stamp Act's passage, is rejected with wrathful indignation. "But," continues the Doctor, "since 'tis down [liberty's sun], . . . let us make as good a night as we can of it. We may still light candles"—such bland advice from London's extremely unpalatable in Philadelphia. Tame submission's not Philadelphia's idea of making the best of it.

Franklin's severely censured and roundly damned as a complacent betrayer of the people's trust. Nominating his friend and political supporter, John Hughes, as Stamp Master's further enraged the citizens. Besides the sore issue of the Stamp Act's passage (March 22nd, 1765), to which they believe Franklin's assented, the bitterness of the anti-Proprietary struggle's been injected into the strife; in the Assembly (against strong opposition from John Dickinson, Robert Morris, Thomas Willing and most of the saner element), Hughes has been the chief means of having Franklin sent to England to effect the end of Proprietary Government and put Pennsylvania directly under the Crown. With anti-Franklin-anti-Hughes feeling at white heat, "Franklin might well be thankful the Atlantic was between him and the City of Brotherly Love."

Ominous mutterings against Hughes, increasing ever since news of his appointment came in May, cause him in September to complain to Franklin of the "storm of Presbyterian rage" assailing him; he adds, "when a mob is on foot, my interest may fall a sacrifice to an infatuated multitude."

On Sunday, September 15th, comes news of a change of Ministry in England. On Monday, the bells ring all day; in the evening there's health-drinking to the King, bonfires blaze and John Hughes is burned in effigy. The mob—Hughes accuses the printers of having raised

> "a Rabble of Boys, Sailors and Negroes" — "surrounded his house and threatened violence, which caused him to load his gun, with a determination to defend himself if attacked."

Hughes's own account, written from hour to hour inside the house, records at 8 o'clock that sober persons are in readiness nearby to suppress the mob, he himself's well armed, but "every noise or bustle" puts them on the alert; at 9 it's reported the "rabble begins to decrease"; at midnight, "several hundreds of our friends" have been ready to suppress the mob, but the "rabble is dispersing." All the public jubilation, the bell-ringing and the effigy-burning, however, are premature; not yet has the Stamp Act been repealed.

An "outside" account Joseph Galloway writes Franklin on the 20th:

> "We should not have been free from riots here [on the 16th], if another method had not been taken to prevent them, viz., By assembling quietly at the instance of Mr. Hughes's friends (and not by an order from the government of the city) near 800 of the sober inhabitants posted in different parts, ready to prevent any mischief that should be attempted by the mob, which effectually intimidated them, and kept all tolerably quiet, only they burnt a figure they called a Stamp Man, and about midnight dispersed."

In a long complaint to the Commissioners of the Stamp Office in London, Hughes blames the newspapers for the disquiet; stuffed with inflammatory matter, they put mischievous notions in people's heads. Certainly the Philadelphia papers don't conceal what's going on in other Colonies—tarrings and featherings, and the like. Also, Hughes says:

"Common justice calls upon me to say, the body of the people called Quakers, seemed disposed to pay obedience to the Stamp Act, and so do that part of the Church of England and Baptists that are not some way under proprietary influence. But Presbyterians and proprietary minions spare no pains to engage the Dutch and lower class of people, and render the royal government" odious in their eyes.

Hughes is bitter against Presbyterians, especially the Allen family —both Presbyterians and "proprietary minions" are they—with the Chief Justice at their head (the same William Allen who, 33 years ago, helped Andrew Hamilton secure the land and build the State House). The Chief Justice and Hughes have long been implacable political enemies.

"Proprietary minions" have disturbed Galloway, too; deploring his inability to keep party lines intact, he writes Franklin in November, "Too many of our friends were inclined to unite with those wretches [the Proprietarians] against the Stamp Act." There's bitter enmity, likewise, between Galloway and John Dickinson. Philadelphia politics have always been complex and rancorous.

While Hughes has been the centre of the September disturbances, Mrs. Franklin, too, has been apprehensive of mischief; her personal safety a source of anxiety to her friends. Writing Franklin on the 22nd, she says:

"I was for nine days kept in a continual hurry by people to remove; and Sally was persuaded to go to Burlington for safety; but on Monday last we had very great rejoicings on account of the change of the ministry, and a preparation for bonfires at night, and several houses threatened to be pulled down.

Cousin Davenport came and told me . . . towards night I said he should fetch a gun or two, as we had none. I sent to ask my brother to come and bring his gun also, so we [turned] one room into a magazine; I ordered some sort of defence upstairs, such as I could manage myself. . . but if any one came to disturb me, I should shew a proper resentment . . . I was told there were eight hundred men ready to assist any one that should be molested. . . .

Billy [Franklin's bastard son William, Governour of New Jersey] came down to ask us up to Burlington. I consented to Sally's going, but I will not stir. . . ."

After all this preliminary unrest, with sporadic turbulence, small wonder the citizens are ripe for a determined stand on

October 5th; more than ready to answer with alacrity the black drummer-boys' summons to the State House Yard.

Votes of Assembly; Journal of Rev. Henry Melchior Mühlenberg, *Historical Society of Pennsylvania Memoirs,* vi, 78; *History of Philadelphia,* Thompson Westcott, chs. clv, clvi; Jacob Hiltzheimer's *Diary; Writings,* Benjamin Franklin, x, 226-227; *Life of Benjamin Franklin,* John Bigelow, i, 460, 467; *Pennsylvania Journal & Weekly Advertiser,* October 10, December 19, 1765; *ibid,* Supplement, September 4, 1766; *Pennsylvania Gazette,* October 10, December 19, 1765; *Origins of the American Revolution,* John C. Miller, 115, 119, 136.

1766

Wednesday, May 21—The Stamp Act's repealed! A sumptuous dinner this afternoon in the Banquetting Hall to celebrate! Three hundred places laid; of the choicest food and drink there's great plenty. The "Worshipful Mayor" of the City, John Lawrence, does the "Honours of the Table," assisted by some of the Aldermen.

The distinguished guests include "his Honour the GOVERNOUR [John Penn], and the Officers of Government; the Military Gentlemen; Captain Hawker, of His Majesty's Ship *Sardine,* the other Gentlemen of the Navy, and the Strangers in this City."

The Province's cannon are in the State House Yard to fire salutes; they keep up a great booming most of the afternoon. In the evening, the bells are all ringing merrily, the people flock about blazing bonfires, and there's "Strong Beer for the Populace."

On Monday (May 19th), the brig *Minerva,* Captain Wise, drops anchor before the city ere it's known whence she comes or what news she's brought. As early as March 24th, Thomas Willing's brought back a report from Maryland that the Stamp Act would be repealed; this occasions bell-ringing, bonfires and health-drinking. Again, on April 6th, an express from Maryland's brought further tidings—the repeal bill's passed one House in Parliament. "For which news the bells rang all day"; more bonfires and healths to the King and Royal Family. Still, there's been no official confirmation of the repeal.

Meanwhile, since October 5th (1765), things have by no means been standing still. On the 25th, the merchants draw up the Non-Importation Agreement; about 400 sign it. The retailers follow suit. October 31st, the morrow of the day when the Stamp Act goes into effect, all the newspapers appear in heavy mourning for the death of Liberty and conspicuously display skulls and crossbones. November 1st, muffled bells toll all day. No Stamped Paper's used in the city; whenever a stray piece from a distance turns up by chance, it's publicly burnt at the Coffee House. Somebody in Philadelphia has a fine dramatic flair; the people show singular spontaneity in playing up to spectacular demonstration.

On December 5th, the Heart and Hand Fire Company, of which Mr. Hughes is a member, request him to resign. He refuses. They expel him and resolve that he shall "be held in the greatest contempt by each member." Notwithstanding the common odium heaped upon him, Mr. Hughes survives with health unimpaired, hating Presbyterians and "proprietary minions" (not forgetting Chief Justice Allen) as cordially as ever. In witness of his continued robust health, there's a punch-drinking in June, 1767, "at John Hughes's, who lately married Stephen Paschall's daughter," and we subsequently hear of his attending barn-raisings, cock-fights and bull-baitings.

As the *Minerva* drops anchor this auspicious May morning in 1766, "one of the Inhabitants"—Would that we knew his name!—goes aboard and "receives the Glorious Tidings." He brings

> "the Law on Shore [the Act of Repeal, printed by Baskett, the King's printer], proclaims the News [the Act of Repeal's obtained the Royal Assent March 18th, 1766], and reads it aloud at the London Coffee House, and, a Multitude being by this Time collected, three loud Huzza's testified their Approbation."

The gentlemen at the Coffee House thereupon send a deputation to fetch Captain Wise. They make the ship's company a present; "with Colours flying" they bring Captain Wise to the Coffee House, where a "Large Bowl of Punch" is made ready against his coming; and all drink "Prosperity to America." Then, to top off the occasion, they present Captain Wise with "a gold-laced Hat" in token of their esteem.

> "The Inhabitants then appointed the next Evening [the 20th] to illuminate the City, which was done to the universal Satisfaction of all Spectators; the Houses made a most beautiful Appearance, to which the Regularity of our Streets [Refreshing to hear an occasional good word for our monotonous, depressing chequer-board system!] contributed not a little; the Scene was, however, variegated, by the different Manner of placing the Lights, Devices, &c; for which the Publick is indebted to the Ladies, who exercised their Fancies on the Occasion.
>
> It was very remarkable, that the City was not disturbed by any Riot or Mob, as is common on such Occasions, but the whole was begun, continued and ended [the writer evidently knew his Prayer-Book] to the universal Satisfaction of the Inhabitants. A large Quantity of Wood was given for a Bonfire, and many Barrels of Beer to the Populace."

At the State House dinner got up by the "principal Inhabitants" on the 21st, there are 21 toasts; first the King, second the Queen, third the Prince of Wales and all the Royal Family; the rest of the toasts are all prompted by the general rejoicing. On "drinking the King," the cannon in the Yard belch forth the Royal Salute. After every succeeding toast there are seven guns. The occasion's marked by "the greatest Elegance and Decorum."

Before leaving the State House, the dinner company unanimously adopt a resolution—a kind of farewell to the Non-Importation Agreement:

"That to demonstrate our Affection to Great Britain, and our Gratitude for the Repeal of the Stamp Act, each of us will, on the Fourth of June next, being the Birth Day of our most gracious Sovereign George III, dress ourselves in a new Suit, of the Manufactures of England, and give what HOME-SPUN we have to the Poor."

Pennsylvania Gazette, November 7, 14, 21, December 19, 1765, May 22, 1766; *Pennsylvania Journal & Weekly Advertiser,* November 7, 14, 21, December 19, 1765, May 22, 1766; *History of Philadelphia,* Thompson Westcott, ch. clvii; Jacob Hiltzheimer's *Diary.*

1768

Tuesday, February 2—At 6 o'clock this evening, in the Council Chamber, there's a meeting of the American Philosophical Society. It's the first time they've met at the State House. There are James Hamilton, former Governour of the Province, Doctor Thomas Cadwalader, both Doctor Thomas Bond and Doctor Phineas Bond, Provost Smith, along with Doctor Alison, Mr. Kinnersley and Doctor Ewing from the College, James Allen, George Bryan, Thomas Willing, Doctor William Shippen, junior, Israel Pemberton and sundry more—twenty-two in all, most of them amongst the most distinguished personages in the American Colonies. In the flickering light from the fire and the glow of the candles, a handsome picture do these worthy gentlemen make.

The American Philosophical Society, founded in 1743, has been rather inactive in recent years until, in January, they have a "stir-up" meeting at Mr. Byrnes's tavern and decide to ask Governour John Penn to become Patron. Just a week ago they had another meeting at the *Indian Queen* and

> "Agreed that an application be made to the governour by Mr. Secy. Shippen, and to the Trustees of the State House by Mr. Galloway, for the use of the Council Chamber, to hold our subsequent meetings in. . . ."

The Governour's accepted the invitation to become Patron. The request for the use of the Council Chamber's been granted.

At this first State House meeting, Candlemas Day, 1768, an important matter's come up for consideration—a suggested union with the American Society for Promoting Useful Knowledge. A paper from "sundry Gentlemen of this City" is read, to wit:

> "A Society having subsisted for some time in this City under the name of the American Society held at Philadelphia for promoting and propagating useful Knowledge [they didn't mind long, double-barrelled names] whose Views have been nearly the same with those which are published of the American Philosophical Society, and it being judged that the Ends proposed by both could be carried on with more advantage of the Publick if an Union could take Place between them, it is proposed that such Union take place. . . ."

It seems likely that the American Society (with the rest of the long name), founded in 1766, was formed "to take the place of an organisation that had ceased to function," namely the American Philosophical Society.

The names attached to the paper presented for consideration sufficiently attest the American Society's "respectability"—Charles Thomson, Doctor John Morgan, Samuel Powel, John Dickinson, Owen Biddle, Nicholas Waln, David Rittenhouse (corresponding member), Thomas Mifflin and fifteen more of like worth.

The Philosophical Society forthwith act favourably upon the proposal; agree to take the American Society in by an "omnibus" election. This doesn't satisfy the American Society; they wish an outright "union," presumably with some idea of preserving their identity. So nothing comes of the scheme for some time.

Meanwhile,

"Andrew McNair agrees to wait on the Society [at the State House], make the Fires, light ye Candles and extinguish them, & keep the Room clean, for four shillings a Night for the current year."

Also, David Rittenhouse (he's been previously elected to, and accepted, membership in the Philosophical Society) communicates

"(through Dr. Smith) a Description of his new invented Orrery." Subsequently, the committee on the orrery report "they think Mr. Rittenhouse deserves great applause for having projected so useful and curious a machine. . . they are of opinion that it will do honour to himself & to this Province, the Place of his Nativity; and beg leave. . . to recommend it to the Society to order his Description to be published. . . ."

Doctor Hugh Williamson reports a new kind of plough and shows a model of it. Doctor Bond's paper on the Hessian Fly is ordered printed "that it may be communicated to the Publick without Loss of Time" and thereby help farmers to combat the wheat pest. Thus does the American Philosophical Society set a precedent to be followed many years later by the Department of Agriculture with its farm bulletins.

While the union of the two organisations is still in abeyance, and the Philosophical Society are still meeting in the Council Chamber, Provost Smith and Doctor Ewing bring forward and elaborate their schemes for observing the Transit of Venus in 1769.

While this project's taking shape and enlisting the interest of the members, they don't disdain the claims of domestic wine. At the June meeting,

"Two samples of American Wine were exhibited by Dr. Alison,

who was requested to obtain the receipt for making it 'that it may be recommended to the Public.' " In July, the Society are interested in the "best Means of destroying Garlic out of the Fields, where it grows," and likewise they "would be obliged to any Gentleman that would communicate to them any Method of making Wine of the American grape, without Sugar or Water or the best way of making it with that addition." By way of reward for their concern about wine-making, at the September meeting in the Council Chamber, Doctor Syng exhibits "a specimen of Wine made of the American black grape, without water or sugar, in 1765, 'which appears to be perfectly sound and delicious to the Taste.' "

Most of the members are good judges of wine; they doubtless have an all-round tasting then and there.

At the end of the year, the scheme of union between the two societies comes up again. This time both parties are fully satisfied; the two unite under the style of *The American Philosophical Society, Held at Philadelphia, for Promoting Useful Knowledge.* Doctor Franklin (although absent in London) is elected President in the stead of former Governour Hamilton, who's been President during 1768; Doctor Thomas Cadwalader, Doctor Thomas Bond and Joseph Galloway are elected Vice-Presidents; Philip Syng's Treasurer, and the four Secretaries are Provost Shith, Charles Thomson, Thomas Mifflin and Doctor Ewing. The Curators are Doctor Kuhn, Doctor John Morgan and Lewis Nicola.

Following the union (January 2nd, 1769), the Society meet at the College. Provost Smith's been one of the leading spirits and most active promoters of the Philosophical Society, and has been largely instrumental in effecting the union. Ultimately, the Society change their meeting place to Christ Church schoolhouse, which comes to be called "Philosophical Hall." There they continue until the erection of their own building in the State House Yard.

Early Proceedings of the American Philosophical Society, Held at Philadelphia, for Promoting Useful Knowledge, Philadelphia, 1884, pp. 1-24.

1769

Saturday, June 3—From the Observatory in the State House Yard members of the American Philosophical Society are meticulously recording observations of the Transit of Venus across the Sun's disc, a phenomenon that won't occur again for more than an hundred years. Scientists the world over eagerly await results of these observations, made in a latitude particularly favourable for recording the eclipse. Directly the findings have been digested and duly tabulated, they'll be sent to the Reverend Nevil Maskelyne, Astronomer Royal at Greenwich; thence communicated to all the learned societies in England and abroad.

Curious, expectant, silent crowds fill the Yard as the hour of the Transit draws near. They've been asked to keep very quiet so as not to disturb the observers at their delicately precise task. Some are going to do their own observing through pieces of "smoaked" glass.

There's been long, careful preparation for this event. It's been decided to take readings from three places—the State House Yard, David Rittenhouse's farm at Norriton (now Norristown), and the lighthouse at Cape Henlopen. Doctor John Ewing, Vice-Provost of the College and Pastor of the First Presbyterian Church, heads the State House party; Joseph Shippen, Doctor Hugh Williamson, Thomas Pryor, Charles Thomson and James Pearson assist him. At Norriton are Provost Smith, David Rittenhouse, John Sellers and John Lukens. Owen Biddle's watching at Cape Henlopen.

When the Philosophical Society first determine to make these observations, no adequate telescope's available in the British Colonies in North America. They therefore petition the Assembly that

"some provision should be made by the government for 'the purchase of a reflecting telescope of about three feet focus, and to defray expenses.'"

The Assembly accordingly procure a suitable telescope in London, through Doctor Franklin, now Provincial Agent in England. Thomas Penn sends another excellent telescope, to be used at Norriton; after that, to be given to the College. By dint of diligent exertion, all the requisite equipment's ready in time.

The Philosophical Society supplement their first petition to the Assembly by another asking leave to build an observatory in the State House Yard, "with such public assistance as you may think convenient for erecting the same." The "public assistance" the Assembly "think convenient" is a grant of £100, along with permission to put up an observatory in the Yard. Of the Observatory, Colonel Etting says:

"While no trace of this building is now [1876] visible, the foundations were discovered when recently perfecting the sewerage of the Square. It appears to have been of circular shape, and was erected about forty feet due west from the rear door of the present Philosophical Hall, and about the same distance south from the wall of the present (eastern) wing" of the State House.

Watson's statement that the structure was "about twenty feet high" may be true enough; his assertion that it was "twelve to fifteen feet" *square* is obviously incorrect as well as illogical. The enclosing *balcony,* however, may have been square in plan. Unfortunately, neither pictures nor plans of it are known to exist.

Before the day of eclipse, the weather's been a source of anxiety; the outlook discouraging—sky generally overcast, frequent heavy rains.

"But, by one of those sudden transitions, which we often experience here," writes Doctor Smith, in his report to the Society, "on Thursday evening the weather became perfectly clear, and continued the day following, as well as the day of the Transit, in such a state of serenity, splendour of sunshine, and purity of atmosphere, that not the least appearance of a cloud was to be seen."

Dr. Ewing and his assistants have been going daily to the State House Yard Observatory

"to adjust our instruments, and to remove every local obstruction that might hinder our Observations.

Some of us gave particular attention to the regulation of the time-piece . . ." When the "long expected Day of the Transit came. . . The committee assembled in the morning at the Observatory, examined the adjustment of their Telescope anew, and appointed two assistants to observe the clock, one to count the seconds with an audible voice, and the other to write down the minutes as they were completed, to prevent a mistake in that article.

Every Observer being fixed at his Telescope, at least half an hour before the beginning of the Transit,"

the tense expectancy of the little group in the Observatory spreads to the waiting crowd in the Yard; the minutes seem like hours. You can hear a pin drop.

Doctor Smith says of the throng of spectators at Norriton that during the 12 minutes of the eclipse

"there could not have been a more solemn pause of silence and expectation, if each individual had been waiting for the sentence that was to take his life."

The results of this day's successful observations win the unqualified praise of the scientists in England and abroad.

Votes of Assembly; Life and Correspondence of the Reverend William Smith, D.D., Horace Wemyss Smith, i, 436, 439, 447 (incorporating part of Provost Smith's report to the Philosophical Society); *An Historical Account of the Old State House of Pennsylvania*, Frank M. Etting, 64; *Annals of Philadelphia*, J. F. Watson, i, 402; *Transactions of the American Philosophical Society held at Philadelphia for Promoting Useful Knowledge*, i (from January 1st, 1769, to January 1st, 1771) p. 44 *et seq.* (containing "Account" of the Reverend John Ewing, D.D. to the Society).

1773

Monday, August 30—This morning a notable gathering of gentlemen in the Council Chamber. They're met for the proclamation ceremonies of the new Governour, the Honourable John Penn, who's just come back from England.

On such occasions the dignitaries and officials of the Province and City gather at the State House, thence escort the new Governour, with pomp and circumstance, to the Old Court House at Second and Market Streets. There, from the balcony, his Honour's Commission's read, the Chief Justice administers the oath of office to him, and he's duly proclaimed to the "good people of Pennsylvania."

This August morning, besides the Governour-designate, are assembled in the Council Chamber the Honourable James Hamilton, twice before a Governour and now President of the Council, the honourables Joseph Turner, Lynford Lardner, Benjamin Chew, Doctor Thomas Cadwalader, James Tilghman, Andrew Allen (the Governour's brother-in-law), and Edward Shippen, junior, all of the Council. Leaving the State House, the Governour and his Council, the Chief Justice and Associate Justices of the Supreme Court of the Province in their wigs and scarlet robes, the Recorder of the City, the Mayor and City Corporation, and a number of the Clergy, preceded by the High Sheriff and his Officers with their wands of office, go in stately procession to the Court House.

The Governour's Commission being "published with the usual Solemnities. . . in the presence of a very great Concourse of People," the eight bells of nearby Christ Church break forth in a loud peal, other bells throughout the city answer, the people cheer, and the artillery boom a salute, taken up by the ships in the Delaware. Then the procession goes back to the State House. Knowing the habits of the time and Philadelphia's love of punch, it needs no stretch of imagination to picture a cheering bowl of cold punch awaiting the returned notables in the Council Chamber.

But one important personage is conspicuously absent from the morning's function. It's customary for the outgoing Governour to attend the ceremonies and make the public civilities of transfer and congratulation to his successor. Richard Penn doesn't once appear; his name isn't even mentioned in connection with the swearing-in and proclamation.

News of the coming change in governourship's had ample time to reach Philadelphia; Richard's had ample time to ponder and nurse his grievance. James Allen writes in his *Diary*, August 23rd,

"The 20th of this Month, Mr. John Penn, and my Sister [Mrs. John Penn], & Brother John arrived at New York in the *Grovenor Mast* Ship, & are daily expected here."

On Sunday, the 29th, "a great number of Gentlemen & Ladies" meet them at Bristol and escort them into the city. As Sarah Eve notes in her *Diary*, the new Governour makes "a public entry into Town with a large train." Meanwhile, Richard's disappointment and deep resentment at being supplanted in the governourship have already become common topics of conversation. James Allen says John

"comes to assume the Government & to supersede his Brother; to his [Richard's] great dissatisfaction. This step, tho' highly approved by Mr. John Penn's friends, it is thought will lay the foundation of lasting animosity between the brothers. Mr. John Penn's reasons for this measure are that his Brother has set up a claim to the Proprietary Estate in reserved Lots & Manors, & immediately on his coming to the Government entered a Caveat in the Proprietary Offices, declaratory of his right, which he still reserves, notwithstanding his signing Patents as Governour."

During his brief term as Governour, Richard Penn's become highly popular; people are genuinely sorry to see him relegated to private life. At the same time, John's never especially endeared himself to the Province; he's suffered some measure of unpopularity, partly because of the 1771 excise tax of 4d. a gallon on all wines and spirits. Popularity and sensitive pocketbooks are closely related. Sarah Eve fairly reflects the general sentiment when she says,

"For my part I had rather be his brother [Richard] than he [John], the one possesses the hearts of the people, the other the Government."

Colonial Records, x, 91, 92; *Pennsylvania Journal & Weekly Advertiser*, September 1, 1773; Sarah Eve's *Diary*, in *Pennsylvania Magazine of History and Biography*, v, 197; James Allen's *Diary*, in *Pennsylvania Magazine of History and Biography*, ix, 181.

Monday, September 13—This afternoon the City Merchants are giving the Honourable Richard Penn a splendid testimonial dinner in the Banquetting Hall. The Commanding Officer at the Barracks has lent the regimental band to furnish the music; the artillery gunners, also sent down from the Barracks and posted in the State House Yard, greet each of the many after-dinner toasts with a roaring salvo from their field-pieces. Robert Morris is presiding, Governour John Penn seated on one side of him, Richard Penn on the other. Although Richard's the guest of honour, John, as the person of highest rank present, sits at the host's right.

A little more than two years ago, when John Penn went back to England at his father's death, Richard succeeded him in the governourship. Richard's all along expected to continue Governour indefinitely, even after John's return to Pennsylvania, whenever that might be. Now, when John re-appears on the scene with a new commission to resume the governourship and supersede Richard, Richard doesn't hesitate to let people know he's sorely upset and wounded. Tension in the Proprietary Family's been expected, as James Allen's said quite plainly. The brothers aren't on speaking terms. Uncomfortable for the host!

By this time, everybody knows about the ill feeling between the Penn brothers. James Allen says they've met at the Club the preceding Tuesday evening (the 7th),

"but they took no notice of each other, Mr. Penn [Richard] never having visited his Brother, and being determined to continue at variance."

Edward Shippen, writing Colonel Burd, says of the dinner:

"Mr. Bob Morris, the head man at the Merchants' feast, placed Governour Penn on his right hand, and his brother, the late Governour, on the left; but not a word passed between the two brothers."

The Philadelphia merchants, who've conceived a cordial regard for Richard Penn during his governourship (besides their personal liking for him before he took office), are dining him in token of their universal sincere esteem. It's really a "consolation party" at his return to private life.

Earlier in the day, "the Merchants of this City" have waited on the "Hon. Richard Penn, Esq., our late Governour," at his house on Market Street below Sixth—the house General Howe will later occupy; after him, Benedict Arnold; and after him, Holker, the French Consul. (Eventually, Robert Morris will buy the house and live there; Washington will stay there with the Morrises during the Constitutional Convention, in 1787; and, in 1790, when Philadelphia becomes the National Capital, President Washington will live in it and remain there until 1797.)

Arrived at his house, the merchants address Richard:

"Sir,

Influenced solely by a sense of the justice due to your public character, and highly pleased with the moderation, wisdom and humanity of your late administration," we thank you for the "protection and attention you have invariably shown" towards the Trade of the Port "which has equalled the most sanguine expectations . . . We must consider your unexpected removal. . . as unfortunate to the people" over whom you have so happily presided.

Then, out of obligatory deference to the newly-returned Governour John, they assure Richard their regret would be greater still, if a member of the same estimable family were not succeeding him. After this polite reference, they continue:

"Your declared intention of residing amongst us is particularly pleasing, as we are confident your social virtues and private character will secure the continuance of an affectionate regard from your Fellow-Citizens, as your public merits have gained their utmost esteem and confidence."

To this handsome address Richard makes gracious reply. He can't refrain from alluding to his being "unexpectedly DE-PRIVED of the power of being serviceable in a public character," but hopes in his private capacity "as a Fellow-Citizen" amongst them he'll prove not unworthy the public mark of esteem they've paid him.

After which,

"the Merchants, in a body, attend Mr. Penn to the State-house, where. . . are present the Governour and Council, the Corporation of the City, the Clergy, the Gentlemen of the Army and Navy, with most of the strangers and principal inhabitants of the city. . . ."

Just what "appropriate airs" the Eighteenth Regimental Band performs during dinner, we're not told—amongst other tunes, the musicians probably treat the diners to "Hearts of Oak" and the "Grenadiers' March" (that stirring composition already 200 years old), both of which are great favourites with the people, who often go to the Barracks to hear the band play at parade.

When Robert Morris rises, lifts his glass and says, "Gentlemen, I give you the King," the whole State House resounds as the military brasses peal forth the majestic strains of "God Save the King," every man in the silk-stockinged and lace-beruffled gathering on his feet, glasses of old Madeira raised aloft, the cannon in the Yard thundering the Royal Salute of 21 guns. The toasts immediately following are "The Queen," "The Prince of Wales and all the Royal Family," "The Honourable Thomas Penn and the Proprietary Family" and "The Land we live in."

From the rest of the toasts—there are 20 in all—one may fairly judge the political sentiment of the time. "Prosperity to and Unanimity between Great Britain and the Colonies," "The City of Philadelphia and its Commerce," "The British Navy and Army" and "The Immortal Memory of William Penn" share the Madeira and artillery honours with "The Glorious Memory of General Wolfe," "Lord Chatham," "Lord Dartmouth," "General Gage," "Daniel Delany [sic], Esq.," "Mr. Burke" and "The Friends of American Freedom."

Pennsylvania Journal & Weekly Advertiser, September 15, 1773; *Pennsylvania Gazette,* September 15, 1773; *History of Philadelphia,* Thompson Westcott, ch. clxvii; James Allen's *Diary,* in *Pennsylvania Magazine of History and Biography,* ix, 181; *Letters and Papers Relating to the Provincial History of Pennsylvania,* Thomas Balch, 232; *The Family of William Penn,* Howard M. Jenkins, 189-194.

Saturday, September 18—For the second time in one week there's an "elegant dinner" in the Banquetting Hall. This afternoon Mayor Gibson and the City Corporation are giving a dinner of welcome to "his Honour," the newly-returned Governour, John Penn—an official ceremony prescribed by custom, as well as an expression of good will; it's also in some measure a balance to the testimonial feast the City Merchants gave Richard Monday afternoon. After dinner come the usual loyal and patriotic toasts, accompanied by patriotic din from the artillery in the State House Yard. The most "respectable" citizens in great number attend to-day's function as they did last Monday's.

Present are "the late Governour, Richard Penn, Esq; the Members of the Council, the Clergy"—"gentlemen of the cloth" apparently as ready then as now to attend public dinners—"the Gentlemen of the army and navy, with most of the strangers and principal inhabitants of the city." ("Strangers and principal inhabitants" gets to be a stock newspaper phrase.) It's awkward when the Governour and his brother aren't on speaking terms.

Next Wednesday's *Journal* acquaints its readers that "the whole" is "conducted with much decent festivity." The "decent festivity," however, doesn't dispel the Penn family tension. Nearly three weeks after this second dinner, Judge Yeates writes Colonel Burd:

> "The accounts from Philadelphia tell us there is no connection between the present and the late Governours, though they have dined together twice in public. Mr. Richard Penn takes no notice of his brother, nor even speaks to him."

Although the breach continues for some time, it

> "appears to have been healed within a twelvemonth; a letter from Lady Juliana Penn to John Penn, at the end of 1774, expresses her satisfaction in learning from his letters that a reconciliation has been effected."

In a subsequent letter, John mentions "the reconciliation between me and my brother."

> *Pennsylvania Journal & Weekly Advertiser*, September 22, 1773; *Pennsylvania Gazette*, September 22, 1773; *History of Philadelphia*, Thompson Westcott, ch. clxvii; *Letters and Papers Relating to the Provincial History of Pennsylvania*, Thomas Balch, 232; *The Family of William Penn*, Howard M. Jenkins, 189-190.

Saturday, October 16—Organised American opposition to the Tea Tax begins at the State House in Philadelphia. There's a Town Meeting this mid-October Saturday; the most responsible citizens attend in goodly number; Doctor Thomas Cadwalader presides. The eight resolutions, then and there adopted, formulate the first definite and logical justification for opposing the new tax. These resolutions of October 16th prompt and stiffen the spirit of resistance throughout the Colonies.

Especially do they hearten the people of Boston; at a "very full" Town Meeting in Faneuil Hall, November 5th, it's

> "*Resolved,* That the sense of this town cannot be better expressed, than in the words of certain judicious resolves, lately entered into by our worthy brethren the citizens of Philadelphia."

Forthwith the Bostonians adopt the Philadelphia resolutions. The Philadelphia Town Meeting at the State House on October 16th, in other words, is the direct antecedent and primary cause of the Boston "Tea Party" (staged with its own local details) exactly two months later.

And what preceded the Town Meeting at the State House? In October, 1791, the *Pennsylvania Mercury* published an *"Anecdote of the late William Bradford"*:

"After the Tax on Tea imported into America was reduced to 3d. per pound by the British Parliament, there appeared to be a general disposition in the Colonies to pay it. In this critical situation of the Liberties of America, Mr. Bradford stopped two or three citizens of Philadelphia, who were walking by the door of his house in Front-street [the London Coffee House], and stated to them the danger to which our country was exposed, by receiving, and paying the tax on, the tea. Many difficulties stared the gentlemen, to whom he spoke, in the face, in setting on foot an opposition to the landing of the dutied tea which was expected from London; and it was particularly mentioned that the citizens of Philadelphia were tired out with town and committee meetings, and that it would be impossible to collect a sufficient number of them together, to make an opposition to the tea, respectable and formidable. 'Leave that business to me (said Mr. Bradford),—I'll collect a town meeting for you—Prepare some resolves;—and,—they shall be executed.' The next evening he collected a few of such citizens as he knew were heartily opposed to the usurpations of the British Parliament, who drew up some spirited resolutions to reject the dutied tea, and to send back the tea ship."

The October 16th Town Meeting at the State House, thanks to Mr. Bradford's "pudding-stick" efforts, is well attended. The "spirited resolutions," previously draughted, are put and promptly carried. They are:

"1. That the disposal of their own property is the inherent right of freemen; that there can be no property in that which another can, of right, take from us without our consent; that the claim of Parliament to tax America is, in other words, a claim of right to levy contributions on us at pleasure.

2. That the duty imposed by Parliament upon Tea landed in America is a tax on the Americans, or levying contributions on them without their consent.

3. That the express purpose for which the tax is levied on the Americans, namely for the support of government, administration of justice, and defence of his Majesty's dominions in America, has a direct tendency to render Assemblies useless, and to introduce arbitrary government and slavery.

4. That a virtuous and steady opposition to this ministerial plan of governing America is absolutely necessary to preserve even

the shadow of liberty, and is a duty which every freeman in America owes to his country, to himself, and to his posterity.

5. That the resolution lately entered into by the East India Company to send out their Tea to America, subject to the payment of duties on its being landed here, is an open attempt to inforce this ministerial plan, and a violent attack upon the liberties of America.

6. That it is the duty of every American to oppose this attempt.

7. That whoever shall, directly or indirectly, countenance this attempt, or in any wise aid or abet in unloading, receiving or vending the Tea sent, or to be sent out by the East India Company, while it remains subject to the payment of duty here, is an enemy to his country.

8. That a committee be immediately chosen to wait on those gentlemen, who, it is reported, are appointed by the East India Company to receive and sell the said Tea, and request them, from a regard to their own character, and the peace and good order of the city and province, immediately to resign their appointment."

As the 8th resolution directs, the Committee wait upon the appointed consignees of the expected cargo and represent the sense of the Town Meeting. Some of the consignees—Thomas Wharton, senior, and others—renounce their expected commissions "in a manner that gives general satisfaction, others, in such equivocal terms as require explanation."

The newspapers take care the agitation started by the Town Meeting's kept alive. They frequently report reactions in other Colonies to the measures launched in Philadelphia. Meanwhile, twelve new members join the Committee the Town Meeting's appointed. It's the unanimous opinion that

"the entry of the tea ship at the Custom-House, or the landing of any part of her cargo, would be attended with great danger and difficulty, and would directly tend to destroy that peace and good order which ought to be preserved."

Nothing's left undone to stimulate vigilance, "keep up a proper correspondence and connection with the other colonies," and take suitable precautions against the coming of the tea-ship.

All sorts of rumours are rife about the date of the tea-ship's sailing from England and the likely time of her arrival at Philadelphia. Some of these reports are premature, some mere canards. It's a time of much anxiety and suspense. At last, December 1st, the newspapers definitely give the date of the tea-ship's departure from Gravesend. The *Pennsylvania Gazette* says:

"The Ship Polly, Captain Ayres, from London, for this Port, having the DETESTED TEA on board, sailed from Gravesend the 27th of September, and may be hourly expected.—*Americans! be wise—be virtuous.*"

Messers James & Drinker, one of the importing firms nominated as tea consignees, have been hesitant when other reported consignees promptly complied with the Committee's request. On December 2nd, they get this pointed reminder in the shape of a public "card":

"The Public present their Compliments to Messieurs JAMES and DRINKER. *We* are informed that you have this day received your commission to enslave your native Country; and as your frivolous Plea of having received no Advice, relative to the scandalous Part you were to act, in the Tea-Scheme, can no longer serve your purpose, nor divert our Attention, We expect and desire You will immediately inform the Public, by a Line or two to be left at the Coffee-House, Whether you will, or will not, renounce all Pretensions to execute that Commission? . . . That we may Govern ourselves accordingly."

It's said a crowd of citizens wait upon Abel James, the head of the firm, and demand he then and there resign his commission. He does so; on the surety of his word and property, he guarantees the tea shan't be landed and the ship shall go back to England. "Then pointing to his young daughter, Rebecca, who stands near him perched on the head of one of her father's hogsheads, he pledges her (a *vivum vadium*) to the fulfillment of his promise."

Several days before this, a "Committee of Tarring and Feathering" have sent the Delaware pilots a handbill:

"We took the Pleasure, some Days since, of kindly admonishing you *to do your Duty,* if perchance you should meet with the (Tea) Ship Polly, Captain Ayres; a Three Decker which is hourly expected.

We have now to add. . . that *much is expected from those Lads who meet with* the *Tea Ship*—There is some Talk of a handsome Reward for the Pilot who gives the first good Account of her— How that may be, we cannot *for certain* determine; But all agree, that Tar and Feathers will be his Portion, who pilots her into this Harbour."

That part of the handbill addressed to Captain Ayres bids him keep away from Philadelphia so that

"taking Time by the Forelock, you may stop short in your dangerous Errand—secure your Ship against the Rafts of combustible Matter which may be set on Fire, and turned loose against her;

and more than all this, that you may preserve your own Person, from the Pitch and Feathers that are prepared for you. . . .

You are sent on a diabolical Service, and if you are so foolish and obstinate as to compleat your Voyage, by bringing your Ship to Anchor in this Port; you may run such a Gauntlet, as will induce you, in your last moments, most heartily to curse those who have made you the Dupe of their Avarice and Ambition.

What think you Captain, of a Halter around your Neck—ten Gallons of liquid Tar decanted on your Pate—with the Feathers of a dozen wild Geese laid over that to enliven your Appearance?

Only think seriously of this—and fly to the Place from whence you came—fly without Hesitation—without the Formality of a Protest—and above all, Captain Ayres, let us advise you to fly without the wild Geese Feathers."

A further handbill to the Delaware pilots, December 7th, corrects the previous description of the *Polly*—not "a Three Decker, but an *old black Ship, without a Head, or any Ornaments*"—and describes Captain Ayres as a *"short fat Fellow,* and a little *obstinate* withal."* Lest there be any mistake in identifying him, the handbill repeats he's a *"thick chunky Fellow."*

Smuggling explains the early lethargy about fighting the tax on tea still in force before the new Tea Act of 1773. People haven't bothered about the tax; just avoided it. Instead of buying taxed British tea, they've been getting vast quantities of smuggled Dutch tea—and the smugglers have been reaping rich profits. Not only in the American Colonies, but also in eighteenth-century England, smuggling's looked upon as a really not immoral, but individual, way of evading exorbitant Government exactions. If you can "get away with it," there's no stigma of moral obliquity attached; you don't even have to salve your conscience, as do some Philadelphia merchants, with the piously smug reflection that "every man has a natural right to exchange his property with whom he pleases and where he can make the most advantage of it."

The Tea Act of 1773 cuts the ground from under the tea-smugglers' feet; it gives the East India Company a government-supported monopoly and enables them to sell tea, including tax, at 10/- a pound. Smuggled Dutch tea, at 20/- a pound, or even considerably less, can't compete with that. It's now really serious. Hence the "loudest yelps" for liberty, coming from the smugglers.

"It is significant that the first outcry against the [1773] Tea Act came from Philadelphia and New York, the smugglers' strongholds, while Boston remained relatively quiet—an unaccustomed rôle for the 'metropolis of sedition.'" The Commissioners of Customs, with their headquarters in Boston, and a British fleet stationed in the harbour, leave little chance there for illicit trade; the port of Philadelphia is virtually wide open for contraband. Smugglers and law-abiding merchants alike join in opposition to the Tea Act. The menace of monopoly unites them. "Viewed in this light, the Tea Act was more inimical to the interests of American merchants than were the Townshend duties."

> History of Philadelphia, Thompson Westcott, ch. clxviii; Pennsylvania Journal & Weekly Advertiser, October 20, December 1, 8, 1773; Pennsylvania Gazette, October 20, December 1, 8, 1773; Pennsylvania Packet, October 18, 1773; Pennsylvania Mercury, October 1, 1791: "How the Landing of Tea was Opposed in Philadelphia" etc., Frederick D. Stone, in Pennsylvania Magazine of History and Biography, xv, 385-393; Origins of the American Revolution, John C. Miller, 338-341.

Monday, December 27—At 10 o'clock this morning there's a crowded Town Meeting in the State House Yard. At first they try to hold the meeting inside the State House, but so many people come there isn't room enough; they have to move outside. They say 8000 persons are present.

"The tea ship having arrived, every inhabitant who wishes to preserve the liberty of America is desired to meet at the State House this morning, precisely at ten o'clock, to consider what is best to be done in this alarming crisis."

Such is the notice the newspapers carry. Printed notice is entirely unnecessary; everybody knows the meeting's to be held and what it's for. The whole town's been waiting for it; a welcome outlet for pent-up feelings. The state of universal suspense, anxiety and repressed excitement, ever since last Friday afternoon, has been almost unbearable.

Last Friday (Christmas Eve) at 2 o'clock,

"arrived in this city a Gentleman, who came express from New York, with. . . advices from BOSTON, which were sent there by express also." The news "being read to a crouded audience at the Coffee-house, a loud shout of applause was given, and the bells immediately set to ringing. Several gusts of Indignation broke forth against Governour Hutchinson and the tribe of pensioners, who had compelled the people to such a disagreeable step, and at the same time was expressed a general approbation of the spirit and resolution of the Bostonians."

The newspapers immediately print "postscripts" with accounts of the Boston Tea Party on December 16th, though omitting the picturesque detail of "Indians" and tomahawks. By early evening, the whole city's agog. Late on Christmas Day (Saturday), an express from Chester brings word the tea-ship's there—has followed another ship up the river. Apparently pilots have heeded the warning given them.

Gilbert Barclay, one of the tea consignees, has come passenger on the *Polly,* and disembarked at Chester. Directly he reaches the city, members of the Committee visit him and explain the tea situation. He thereupon renounces his commission; that's a point scored for the Committee.

Early Sunday morning, some of the Committee hasten down to Chester to stop the *Polly* there if they can. They're too late. The *Polly*'s already headed up the river.

Meanwhile, others of the Committee have gone to Gloucester Point to intercept the *Polly* there in case the Chester deputation's missed Captain Ayres. When the *Polly* reaches Gloucester Point, the captain wisely heeds the Committee's hail, drops anchor and comes ashore as he's bid. If he'd had any doubts before about the gravity of the situation, the doubts are soon dispelled. He accompanies the Committee to the city; from what he sees and hears on all sides, he's readily convinced his only possible course is to abandon any attempt to land his cargo and sail straight back to England.

On Monday morning, the Committee take Captain Ayres to the State House Yard meeting. "This meeting is allowed by all to be the most respectable, both in numbers and rank of those who attended it, that has been known in this city." The meeting called to order, they promptly pass these resolutions:

"1. That the Tea, on board the ship Polly, Captain Ayres, shall not be landed.
2. That Capt. Ayres shall neither enter nor report his vessel at the Custom-House.
3. That Capt. Ayres shall carry back the Tea immediately.
4. That Capt. Ayres shall immediately send a pilot on board his vessel, with orders to take charge of her, and proceed to Reedy-Island next high water.
5. That the Captain shall be allowed to stay in town till to-morrow, to provide necessaries for his voyage.
6. That he shall then be obliged to leave the town and proceed

to his vessel, and make the best of his way out of our river and
bay.

7. That a Committee of four gentlemen be appointed to see these
resolves carried into execution."

Captain Ayres solemnly engages at the meeting that he'll "literally
comply with the sense of the city, as expressed" in the resolutions.

Disposing quickly of the immediate business for which the
meeting's been called, the citizens are quite in the humour to en-
dorse and applaud the Boston "Tea Party." While the crowd's
excitement's at white heat, the speaker proposes a resolve

"That this assembly highly approve the conduct and spirit" of
the Bostonians and "return their hearty thanks to the people of
Boston for their resolution in destroying the Tea rather than suffering it to be landed."

A shout of popular acclaim goes up and carries this last motion
before the more moderate majority of the guiding Committee
have a chance to counsel restraint (as they'd intended doing) in
any message to the people of Boston about the hasty, lawless act—
inevitably fraught with serious consequences—to which Sam
Adams has egged them on; restraint at least in the *wording* of the
resolution. But the fervid tension of the moment leaves no place
for any counsel of restraint or calm judgement.

During the rest of Monday and on Tuesday forenoon, Captain
Ayres gets together the necessary supplies for his return voyage.
Thomas Wharton, senior, writing his brother Samuel in London,
says:

"We and J. Brown advanced him [Captain Ayres] what money he
wanted to victual his ship, &c:—and as poor Gilbert [Barclay] returns with the Ship, I leave him to give the further account of
matters."

On Tuesday afternoon, at a quarter to 3, a pilot boat loaded
with provisions, Captain Ayres and Mr. Barclay aboard, leaves
Arch Street wharf to go down to Reedy Island where the *Polly*'s
moored. As soon as the supplies are transferred, the *Polly* weighs
anchor and starts her return voyage, bearing "the East India Company's Adventure to its Old Rotting Place, in Leadenhall Street."
By discreet acceptance of conditions he's powerless to change,
Captain Ayres has disarmed popular resentment; the crowd
gathered on the wharf "wish him a good voyage."

At Monday's meeting in the State House Yard,
"the public think the conduct of those gentlemen, whose goods

are returned aboard the Tea-ship, ought not to pass unnoticed, as they have upon this occasion generously sacrificed their private interest to the public good."

Thanks (words and sentiments are cheap), but nothing said about compensation for serious losses and inconvenience! The public are quite willing to accept the "sacrifice." Over and above the tea in the *Polly*'s cargo, are very considerable consignments of goods, besides Thomas Wharton's new "charriott," which,

"though it might be fit to visit Pine Street meeting in, must once more be landed in Brittain, and thereby share the same fate with every other article on board the ship. . . ."

Thomas Wharton, in the same letter to his brother Samuel, says: "I hear the Doct. [Franklin] has wrote J. G. [Joseph Galloway] (which I shall as soon as I can see him know the truth of) that if the Americans refuse to receive the tea, but send it back, it will more over-sett the ministry than any thing that could happen. . . ."

Governour John Penn gets "hauled over the coals" for Philadelphia's treatment of the *Polly*. Lord Dartmouth writes him:

"The insult that has been offered to this Kingdom by the inhabitants of Philadelphia in the case of the Polly, Captain Ayres, is of a very serious nature. . . . It is a matter of equal surprise and concern to the King that such a transaction should have happened in any of his Colonies without the least appearance of an endeavour on the part of the Government either to check or oppose the violences that have been committed."

History of Philadelphia, Thompson Westcott, ch. clxix; "*Letters of Thomas Wharton*," in *Pennsylvania Magazine of History and Biography*, xxxiii, 321; *Pennsylvania Journal & Weekly Advertiser*, December 29, 1773; "*How the Landing of Tea was Opposed in Philadelphia*," Frederick D. Stone, in *Pennsylvania Magazine of History and Biography*, xv, 385-393; *Pennsylvania Gazette*, December 29, 1773.

1774

Friday, September 16—A great public dinner this afternoon in the Banquetting Hall; about 500 places are laid. The Gentlemen of the City are entertaining the Members of the General Continental Congress, now meeting in Carpenters' Hall. Toasts (32 of them) come after dinner, the cannon in the State House Yard firing salutes the while. The party tarry till late; all the guests seem pleased.

This is one of the notable acts of welcome the city pays the Delegates to the First Continental Congress. The *Pennsylvania Journal* of September 21st reports:

"On Friday last the Honourable Delegates, now met in General Congress, were elegantly entertained by the gentlemen of this city. Having met at the City Tavern about 3 o'clock, they were conducted from thence to the State House by the Managers of the entertainment, where they were received by a very large company composed of the Clergy, such genteel strangers as happened to be in town, and a number of respectable citizens, making in the whole near 500.—After dinner the following toasts were drunk, accompanied by musick and a discharge of cannon. . . . The acclamations with which several of them were received, not only testified the sense of the Honour conferred by such worthy guests, but the fullest confidence in their wisdom and integrity, and a firm resolution to adopt and support such measures as they shall direct for the public good at this alarming crisis."

The first four toasts are "the King," "the Queen," "the Duke of Gloucester" and "the Prince of Wales and all the Royal Family." Then follow "Perpetual Union to the Colonies"; "May the Colonies faithfully execute what the Congress shall wisely resolve"; the "Much injured town of Boston"; "May Great Britain be just and America free"; "May the cloud which hangs over Great Britain and the Colonies burst *only* on the heads of the present Ministry"; and "A happy reconciliation between Great Britain and her Colonies, on a constitutional ground." The City of London, Lord Chatham, Lord Camden, Doctor Franklin, Mr. Burke, Mr. Hancock and the Marquess of Rockingham likewise come in for toasts and applause. The thunder of the cannon in the Yard seems incessant.

Silas Deane, writing Mrs. Deane, says:

"Friday we had a grand entertainment at the State House. Sammy Webb must describe it. About five hundred gentlemen sat down at once, and I will only say there was plenty of every thing eatable and drinkable, and no scarcity of good humour and diversion. We had, besides the delegates, gentlemen from every province on the Continent present."

John Adams notes in his *Diary*:

"Dined with Mr. Wallace with a great deal of company at an elegant feast again."

John's keenly food-conscious; usually enumerates the good things to eat, as after one Philadelphia dinner—

"Turtle and every other thing, flummery, jellies, sweetmeats of twenty sorts, trifles, whipped sillabubs, floating islands, fools &c. and then a dessert of fruits, raisins, almonds, pears, peaches. Wines most excellent and admirable. I drank Madeira at a great rate, and found no inconvenience in it."

At this State House dinner, however, he's evidently preoccupied with conversation; writing Mrs. Adams shortly afterwards, obviously alluding to this occasion, he says:

"The esteem, the affection, the admiration for the people of Boston and the Massachusetts which were expressed yesterday, and the fixed determination that they should be supported, were enough to melt a heart of stone. I saw the tears gush into the eyes of the old grave pacific Quakers of Pennsylvania."

He's carried away by his own feelings; he's wrong about the "tears." The "old grave pacific Quakers" are not, and never were, weepy folk.

Pennsylvania Journal & Weekly Advertiser, September 21, 1774; *Pennsylvania Gazette,* September 21, 1774; *Letters of Members of the Continental Congress,* E. C. Burnett, i, 32, 35; *Diary* of John Adams, *Writings,* ii, 379.

1775

Tuesday, April 25—At 4 o'clock this afternoon a huge public meeting in the State House Yard—thousands present—"to consider the measures to be pursued." Plenty of handbills and notices have been distributed to bring people to the meeting, but they've not been necessary; everybody's tremendously excited and notice has gone around by word of mouth before the handbills are off the press.

Yesterday afternoon, about 5, came galloping a messenger from Trenton. He went straight to the City Tavern and gave news of a fight at Lexington, in Massachusetts, last Wednesday morning (April 19th). Like wildfire the story spread through the city. Many think it means real war between England and the Colonies.

When tidings of the Battle of Lexington reach the city, there are already in being three military organisations—the City Troop, organised in November, 1774, commanded by Captain Markoe, later by Captain Samuel Morris; the infantry "Greens" or "silk-stocking company," commanded by John Cadwalader; and the "Quaker Blues," a light infantry company made up of young Quakers who have swerved from the pacific tenets of the Society of Friends, commanded by Sheriff Joseph Cowperthwait. There's considerable rivalry between the "Greens" and the "Quaker Blues"; both have acquired proficiency in the practice of drilling. It's said the "Greens,"

"seventy in number, drill twice a day, and usually in Cadwalader's yard, he having the kindness to set out his Madeira for the men to refresh themselves after drill."

Now, under impetus of the news from Lexington, the thousands gathered in the State House Yard eagerly follow the lead of the Committee of Correspondence; forthwith they adopt a resolution to

"associate together, to defend with arms their property, liberty, and lives against all attempts to deprive them." It's agreed to form right away "two troops of light horse, two companies of riflemen, and two companies of artillery, with brass and iron field-pieces."

The Philadelphia Association of Volunteers ("Associators") is organised into three battalions under the respective commands of

John Dickinson, Daniel Roberdeau and John Cadwalader as colonels. Drilling goes on constantly in every available place; the recruits are at it night and day—many of the new-formed companies drill twice a day.

April 29th, Christopher Marshall goes "to State House Yard to help consult and regulate the forming of the militia." May 1st, he notes in his *Diary*:

"This day a number of the associators to the militia met in each of the wards of the city, to form themselves into suitable companies, and to choose their respective officers." May 2nd, he views "some companies learning the use of fire-arms." On the 3rd, Quaker though he be, he notes with evident satisfaction, "a company of young men, Quakers, who this day asked leave. . . to learn the military exercise in the Factory yard, which was granted, and they began this evening." Next day, quite proudly—"The Quaker company. . . about thirty, exercised in the Factory yard, and such is the spirit and alacrity of them, that few, if any, of the companies will sooner learn the military art and discipline, and make a handsomer appearance, nor be more ready to assert, at the risk of their lives, the freedom of America on Constitutional principles."

The State House Yard, too, becomes a drill ground; the afternoon of the 6th, Christopher Marshall goes there, "from thence to the commons, seeing the various companies exercise."

Early in June, in a letter to Mrs. Deane, Silas Deane tells about the "Associators' " battalions:

"The uniform is worth describing to you. It is a dark-brown (like our homespun) coat, faced with red, white, yellow, or buff, according to their different battalions, white vest and breeches, white stockings, half boots, and black knee-garters. The coat is made short, falling but little below the waistband of the breeches, which shows the size of a man to great advantage. Their hats are small. . . with a red, white, or black ribbon, according to their battalions, closing in a rose, out of which rises a tuft of fur of deer (made to resemble the buck's tail as much as possible) six or eight inches high. Their cartouch-boxes are large, with the word LIBERTY and the number of their battalion written on the outside in large white letters. . . their cartouch-boxes are hung with a broad white horse-leather strap or belt, and their bayonets, etc., on the other side, with the same, which two, crossing on the shoulders diamond-fashion, gives an agreeable appearance. . . . The light infantry are in green, faced with buff; vests, etc., as the others, except the cap, which is a hunter's cap or a jockey's. . . . They have, besides, a body of irregulars, or riflemen, whose dress it is hard to describe. They take a piece of Ticklenbergh, or tow-

cloth, that is stout, and put it in a tan-vat until it has the shade
of a fallen or dry leaf. Then they make a kind of frock of it,
reaching down below the knee, open before, with a large cape.
They wrap it around them tight on a march, and tie it with their
belt, in which hangs their tomahawk. Their hats are the same as
the others. They exercise in the neighbouring groves, firing at
marks and throwing their tomahawks, forming on a sudden into
line, and then, at the word, breaking their order and taking their
parts to hit their mark. West of this city is a large open square of
nearly two miles each way, with large groves each side, in which,
each afternoon, they collect, with a vast number of spectators."

We're much indebted to Mrs. Deane for being the cause of such
full description.

Notwithstanding all this enthusiasm for drilling and smart appearance, "all is not gold that glitters." Many volunteers, unfortunately, have little sense of the need of discipline. They've no
inclination to curtail their personal independence; respect for
officers and obedience to orders go much against the grain. Hence,
some of the companies, formed in the fervour of the moment and
while the enemy's still far distant, are little better than a mere
"rabble in arms."

James Allen, although later he's strongly opposed to independence, is quite ready to take up arms against the distasteful measures of the British Ministry and, in October, joins a company of
the Associators. He says in his *Diary*:

"Last Thursday & the preceding Tuesday I appeared in Battalion
in my uniform, as a private man in Captn Shees company. I have
no opinion that this association, will be very useful in defending
the City: as they have refused to be bound by any Articles & have
no subordination. My Inducement principally to join them is;
that a man is suspected who does not; & I chuse to have a Musket
on my shoulders, to be on a par with them; & I believe discreet
people mixing with them, may keep them in Order."

Christopher Marshall's *Diary; History of Philadelphia*, Scharf & Westcott,
i, 295, 296; *History of Philadelphia*, Ellis Paxson Oberholtzer, i, 240, 241;
Diary of James Allen, in *Pennsylvania Magazine of History and Biography*,
ix, 186.

Wednesday, May 10—In the Assembly Chamber this afternoon are
met for organisation the Delegates to the Second Continental
Congress. The Pennsylvania Assembly have invited the Second
Congress to use the State House for their sessions, instead of Carpenters' Hall, as did the First Congress; the new Congress have

accepted the invitation. The Assembly have turned over their own Chamber to Congress and have moved across the hall to the Supreme Court Room.

Nearly all the Delegates have come to town and, at this initial meeting, they elect Peyton Randolph, of Virginia, President; Charles Thomson, of Pennsylvania, Secretary. They decide to ask Parson Duché to read prayers at the opening of to-morrow's session.

Some of these gentlemen have never laid eyes on each other before; some are acquainted since last September and the First Congress. Each is making mental appraisals of his fellow-Members. Thanks to John Adams and several others, we catch occasional revealing glimpses of what's going through their minds.

There's Colonel Washington, in his early forties, "a fine figure and of a most easy and agreeable address," neat and dapper, as always, in military uniform. There's Peyton Randolph, "a large, well looking man," as John Adams sees him; of conspicuous urbanity and unfailing tact, "none was ever more beloved and respected by his friends," says Thomas Jefferson, then adds:

"Somewhat cold and icy towards strangers, but of the sweetest affability when ripened into acquaintance. Of attic pleasantry in conversation, always good humoured and conciliatory. With a sound and logical head, . . . well read in the law [admitted at the Middle Temple, 1739; called to the Bar in London, 1744] . . . his opinions . . . highly regarded, presenting always a learned and sound view of the subject but generally, too, a listlessness to go into its thorough development; for being heavy and inert in body, he was rather too indolent for business. . . ."

Benjamin Harrison, Peyton Randolph's brother-in-law, a conservative "well acquainted with the forms of public business," elicits Adams's enthusiasm at first; later, he complains that Harrison's "an indolent, luxurious, heavy gentleman, of no use in Congress." Harrison's conservatism riles Adams; Doctor Rush says he has "strong State prejudices and was very hostile to the leading characters from the New England States," which explains Adams's subsequent pique.

William Paca's a "good tempered worthy man, with a sound understanding" which he's "too indolent to exercise." Samuel Chase possesses "more learning than knowledge, and more of both than judgement." Edward Rutledge is "a sensible young lawyer, of great volubility in speaking." Roger Sherman's a "plain man of slender education" and "deeply religious." Robert Treat Paine, educated a clergyman and become a lawyer, of amiable temper and useful on committees, labours under some "obliquity of understanding" that impels him to oppose "nearly every measure proposed by other people." He will come to be nicknamed "the Objection-Maker." George Ross has "great wit, good humour and considerable eloquence."

Richard Henry Lee's "a tall, spare man," and Richard Bland "a learned, bookish man," as John Adams describes them; and there's John Adams himself, neat, alert-looking and somewhat plump. Sandy-haired young Thomas Jefferson, tall, loose-jointed and freckle-faced, won't be here for a month yet, but there's John Hancock, portly and impressive, peevish at times when the gout's bothering him. And there's the placid rotundity of Doctor Franklin who's come in with Thomas Willing and John Morton—the last a "plain farmer and capable Judge," who'll become a bitter opponent of the Pennsylvania "State Constitution of 1776." So much for contemporary impressions of some of the Delegates. They're all men of strongly marked character in their several ways.

The advent of all these gentlemen from the other Colonies causes not a little stir in the city. Christopher Marshall (May 9th) says:

"This morning, arrived four of the delegates from South Carolina, in the brig Charleston Packet, Captain Barton, in four days passage, viz., Henry Middleton, Christopher Gadsden, John Rutledge, and Edward Rutledge, Esq's . . . This day arrived these sundry delegates, viz., Peyton Randolph, George Washington, Patrick Henry, Richard Henry Lee, Edmund Pendleton, Benjamin Harrison, and Richard Bland, Esq's., from Virginia; Richard Caswell, and Joseph Hewes, Esq's., from North Carolina; Samuel Chase, Thomas Johnson, and John Hall, Esq's., from Maryland; Caesar Rodney and George Read, Esq's., from the counties of New Castle, Kent, and Sussex, on the Delaware." [Marshall's wrong about Patrick Henry, who doesn't take his seat till the 18th.]

To meet and greet "these sundry delegates" coming up yesterday from the South, the "officers of all the companies in the city, and . . . many other gentlemen, on horseback, to the amount of five hundred" (besides others in coaches and chairs) went out some miles from the city. At Gray's Ferry (the "Lower Ferry" over Schuylkill), the infantry and riflemen, with a band of music, turned out as a further escort.

To-day, round about noon, have come the New England Delegates and the rest from the northward. They've had an ovation
all the way hither. Silas Deane gives a full account in writing
Mrs. Deane. After leaving Fairfield, they

> "dined at Stamford with a company met at a wedding, which
> honest Mr. Cushing took for a company convened to wait upon
> us; and in he stumped, and led us to the head of the table, where,
> toward the close of our dinner, we found out our mistake, and
> were merry eno' on the occasion." The next morning "from
> Greenwich or Horse Neck" they have an armed escort of twelve,
> "extremely well mounted and armed, and their two officers in
> scarlet and gold. Eight preceded us; Jnº Webb as Aid-de-camp,
> followed singly; then the carriages; then the other four of the
> Guards, and our servants in the rear of the whole; so that we
> cut a considerable figure."

Arrived at New York, they get an uproarious welcome. At Princeton, they're "received by a Company under arms, the president
and students, &c."

They stay the night at Bristol; setting out in the morning for
Philadelphia, they

> "were met at about six miles this side of the City by about two
> hundred of the principal gentlemen, on horseback, with their
> swords drawn; here we alighted and baited. Thence began a
> most lengthy procession; half of the gentlemen on horseback, in
> the van; next to them, ten men on horseback, with bayonets
> fixed; then Hancock and Adams," John and Samuel "in a phae-
> ton and pair," Hancock, according to Curwen, "looking as if his
> journey and high living, or solicitude to support the dignity of
> the first man in Massachusetts, had impaired his health." Silas
> Deane says Paine came next, "next Mr. De Hart, next Col. Floyd
> and Mr. Boerum in a phaeton with two most elegant white
> English horses; then your humble servant and Col. Dyer; then
> Father Cushing and Jnº Adams" in a single-horse chaise, "Mr.
> Sherman next; then Mr. P. Livingston, who took Jnº Webb in
> his carriage, as one of his servants had tired his horse and took
> Johns. Mr. Alsop tired all four of his fine bay horses and was,
> with Mr. Duane, put into other carriages. Our rear closed with
> carriages [about 100] from the City. At about two miles distance
> we were met by a Company on foot, and then by a Company of
> Riflemen in their uniform, which is very curious. Thus rolling
> and gathering like a snow-ball, we approached the City, which
> was full of people and the crowd as great as at New York."

All the Philadelphia bells start a-ringing, a "band of music"
accompanies the procession, and the thronging "people of all

ages, sexes and ranks" break forth a-cheering and rend the air "with shouts and huzzas."

"My little bay horses were put in such a fright," concludes Deane, "that I was in fear of killing several of the spectators; however, no harm was done, and after much fatigue we were landed at the City Tavern."

Christopher Marshall's *Diary; Letters of Members of the Continental Congress*, E. C. Burnett, i, 90; *History of Philadelphia*, Ellis Paxson Oberholtzer, i, 241; *History of Philadelphia*, Scharf & Westcott, i, 296; *Dictionary of American Biography; Journal of Samuel Curwen*, ed. George Atkinson Ward; *Deane Papers*, Collections of New York Historical Society, i, 43, 46; *Memorial of Dr. Benjamin Rush*, privately published; *The Pennsylvania Evening Post*, May 13, 1775.

Thursday, June 15—By 9 this morning Congress are in the Assembly Chamber. For some days past there's been much discussion about whom to appoint in command of the armies being raised, and how much to pay him. The other day, John Adams suggested Colonel Washington; that apparently put President Hancock's nose out of joint. Finally, to-day, Congress elect Colonel Washington and the Members agree to make the vote unanimous.

The *Journals of Congress* this day record:

"*Resolved,* That a General be appointed to command all the continental forces, raised, or to be raised, for the defence of American liberty.

That five hundred dollars, per month, be allowed for his pay and expences.

The Congress then proceeded to the choice of a general, by ballot, when George Washington, Esq. was unanimously elected."

Ford adds, in a note: "Washington was nominated by Thomas Johnson of Maryland, and the election was unanimous."

When John Adams first suggests Washington as a proper person for Commander-in-Chief, there's some pointed opposition; President Hancock's visibly annoyed. Opposition is not because of any objection to Washington personally; it's occasioned by sectional jealousies, sectional prejudices, and fear that a Southern general with Northern army elements—and, *vice versa,* a Northern general with Southern contingents—may cause mischievous friction. Furthermore, the Middle Colonies and Southern Members are apprehensive lest New England, should American arms be victorious, may then try to dominate the other Colonies. Local animosities and mistrusts are not much in evidence in the early days of the

Continental Congress; but they soon crop up and become increasingly destructive of the unity essential to effective Congressional functioning at a crucial period. Eventually, they weaken Congress to an alarming extent.

Irked and anxious at the impasse, the "brace of Adamses" have a walk and an heart-to-heart talk in the State House Yard. Although it's not yet time, perhaps, to nominate a General, John determines to force the issue. He addresses Congress on the serious condition of affairs in general; when, in the course of his speech, he mentions the chief command, he declares he has in mind

"a gentleman from Virginia who is among us and very well known to all of us. . . better than any other person in the union." Adams continues: "Mr. Washington, who happened to sit near the door, as soon as he heard me allude to him, from his usual modesty, darted into the library-room. Mr. Hancock, who was our President, which gave me an opportunity to observe his countenance, while I was speaking on the state of the Colonies, the army at Cambridge, and the enemy, heard me with visible pleasure; but when I came to describe Washington for the commander, I never remarked a more sudden and striking change of countenance. Mortification and resentment were expressed as forcibly as his face could exhibit them. Mr. Samuel Adams seconded the motion, and that did not soften the President's physiognomy at all. The subject came under debate, and several gentlemen declared themselves against the appointment. . . because the army were all from New England, had a general of their own, appeared to be satisfied with him, and had proved themselves able"

to bottle up the British in Boston. That, at this time, they seemingly consider the chief desideratum. The subject of appointment's postponed to a future day.

Meantime, 'pains are taken out of doors to obtain a unanimity, and the voices are generally so clearly in favour of Washington, that the dissentient members are persuaded to withdraw their opposition and Mr. Washington is nominated' (by Thomas Johnson, jr.) and unanimously elected on June 15th.

Writing his brother, after his appointment, Washington says he "neither sought after the honour nor desired it, but that 'the partiality of Congress, joined to a political motive,' really left him without choice."

Additional light on the "sectional jealousies to be appeased," and the "political motive" mentioned in Washington's letter, comes from John Adams. In his *Autobiography* (written years after-

wards), noting the various hindrances to "getting on with the job"
immediately pressing at this time, he says there was

"a Southern party against a Northern, and a jealousy against a
New England army under the command of a New England
General. Whether this jealousy was sincere, or whether it was
mere pride and haughty ambition of furnishing a southern
General to command the northern army, (I cannot say); but the
intention was very visible to me that Colonel Washington was
their object, and so many of our staunchest men were in the plan,
that we could carry nothing without conceding it. Another embarrassment, which was never publicly known. . . the Massachusetts and other New England delegates were divided. . . . Mr.
Hancock himself had an ambition to be appointed commander-
in-chief. Whether he thought an election a compliment due to
him, and intended to have the honour of declining it, I know not.
To the compliment he had some pretensions . . . But the delicacy
of his health, and his entire want of experience in actual service. . .
were decisive objections to him in my mind. In canvassing this
subject, out of doors, I found too that even among the delegates
of Virginia there were difficulties. The apostolical reasonings
among themselves, which should be the greatest, were not less
energetic among the saints of the ancient dominion than they
were among us of New England . . . I found more than one very
cool about the appointment of Washington, and particularly Mr.
Pendleton who was very clear and full against it."

Sectional jealousy and mistrust of New England find another
witness in Eliphalet Dyer. Writing Governour Trumbull (June
17th), he says he thinks Washington's appointment

"will be Very agreeable to our officers and soldiery," and also that
"it removes all jealousies, more firmly Cements the Southern to
the Northern and takes away the fear of the former lest an Enterprising eastern New England Genll. proving Successfull, might
with his Victorious Army give law to the Southern or Western
Gentry. this made it absolutely Necessary in point of prudence,
but he is Clever, and if anything too modest. he seems discreet
and Virtuous . . . ."

Members of Congress like Washington personally. Silas Deane
(writing Mrs. Deane the day after Washington's appointment)
says:

"I have been with him for a great part of the last forty-eight
hours, in Congress and Committee, and the more I am acquainted
with him, the more I esteem him . . ."

By no means are sectional antipathy and fear of New England's motives confined to Members of Congress. Colonel Frazer

(afterwards General Frazer) of Chester County, in Pennsylvania, writes Mrs. Frazer (August 6th, 1776) from Ticonderoga:

"No man was ever more disappointed in his expectations respecting New Englanders in general than I have been. They are a set of low, dirty, griping, cowardly, lying rascals. There are some few exceptions and very few . . . You may inform all your acquaintance not to be afraid they will ever Conquer the other Provinces (which you know was much talked of), 10,000 Pennsylvanians would I think be sufficient for ten times that number out of their own Country."

Colonel Frazer's highly uncomplimentary opinion of the New England soldiery he's met, one can readily understand after reading *Oliver Wiswell;* a very large proportion of the substantial and responsible element in New England have been either driven out or ruthlessly suppressed by the boisterous, well-organised and more vocal "lower orders" who've seized most of the power and form no inconsiderable contingent of the local soldiery. It's some of that ilk that Colonel Frazer's met with. A respectable New Englander could truthfully say much worse things about some of the Pennsylvania soldiery—the armed mob intent on tarring and feathering Doctor Kearsley; the riotous militia that will attack "Fort Wilson" and would willingly kill three Signers of the Declaration of Independence; the mutinous soldiers of the Pennsylvania Line who will besiege Congress in the State House, men whom a Pennsylvania Member of Congress calls the "scum of the earth," whose conduct General Washington scathingly condemns in unqualified terms. New England certainly has no monopoly of undesirables.

Answering Colonel Frazer's letter, Mrs. Frazer writes:

"The people seem middling well reconciled to independency, but very much fear the heavy taxes that are to come upon us, but above all they fear the New Englanders should the Americans gain the day."

At the bottom of the antipathy is the still widely prevalent dread in the Middle Colonies and the South lest, in case of victory for the American arms, the New Englanders will "substitute their own tyranny for that of the mother country over the other Provinces."

Ignorance, ignorance of one's neighbours—perhaps "insufficient acquaintance" would be a better term—has nearly always been the mother of local antipathies, misunderstandings, distrust and

unfriendliness; it has ever been so, and still is. (There are plenty
of villages in England now, where people who have moved thither
from the next village are considered "outsiders" and regarded with
suspicion or even unfriendliness for two or three generations;
families that moved to Florence from Rome and Siena in the
sixteenth century, many Florentines still look upon as "Romani"
and "Senesi"; instances can be multiplied indefinitely.) It's one
mark of Washington's greatness (not always sufficiently recognised)
that, in spite of the sectional jealousies, distrust and antipathies he
has to contend with—and they cause him endless anxiety—he can
achieve enough harmony to win ultimate victory to American
arms.

Letters of Members of the Continental Congress, F. C. Burnett, i, xix-xxi,
126, 128; *Autobiography* of John Adams, *Works,* ii, 415 *et seq.; Pennsylvania Magazine of History and Biography,* xxxi, 129 *et seq.; Journals of
Congress.*

Friday, June 16 At 8 this morning Congress are in the Assembly
Chamber. Mr. Hancock, the President, sitting in the Speaker's
chair, tells Colonel Washington he's been unanimously elected
General and Commander-in-Chief of the armies. Then Colonel
Washington stands up in his place and makes a speech:
"Mr President,
    Tho' I am truly sensible of the high Honour done me, in this
Appointment, yet I feel great distress, from a consciousness that
my abilities and military experience may not be equal to the extensive and important Trust: However, as the Congress desire it,
I will enter upon the momentous duty, and exert every power I
possess in their service, and for support of the glorious cause. I
beg they will accept my most cordial thanks for this distinguished
testimony of their approbation.
    But, lest some unlucky event should happen, unfavourable to
my reputation, I beg it may be remembered, by every Gentleman
in the room, that I, this day, declare with the utmost sincerity, I
do not think myself equal to the Command I am honoured with.
    As to pay, Sir, I beg leave to assure the Congress, that, as no
pecuniary consideration could have tempted me to have accepted
this arduous employment, at the expence of my domestic ease
and happiness, I do not wish to make any proffit from it. I will
keep an exact Account of my expences. These, I doubt not, they
will discharge, and that is all I desire."
Spoken like the conscientious gentleman he is!
    The record continues in the *Journals of Congress*:

"Upon Motion *Resolved,* That a committee of three be appointed to draught a commission and instructions for the general.

The committee, to consist of the following Mr. [Richard Henry] Lee, Mr. [Edward] Rutledge, and J[ohn] Adams."

Journals of Congress.

Friday, October 6—To-night about 11 o'clock some of the Committee of Inspection bring Doctor John Kearsley, junior, to the State House, along with James Brooks and Leonard Snowden, the Quaker. Here they leave them for the night, with a strong guard to prevent their getting away. It's a new thing for the State House to become a lock-up.

Doctor Kearsley's a nephew of old Doctor John Kearsley, who died several years ago and left his estate to found and endow Christ Church Hospital. The younger Kearsley's an outspoken Loyalist; last month he was the centre of all that hullabaloo that began when the Associators were carting Isaac Hunt (father of Leigh Hunt, the essayist) around town, with fife and drum playing the "Rogues' March." The Doctor then narrowly escaped a coat of tar and feathers from the mob.

Doctor Kearsley's arrest and confinement in the State House is the outcome of that September 6th disturbance. That rumpus started when a number of Associators were "dealing" with lawyer Hunt because he'd undertaken the defense of a so-called "engrosser" and refused to drop the case at the Committee of Inspection's arbitrary bidding. Hunt was altogether within his technical and legal rights; for such rights, the excited tempers of the time have scant regard.

Indignant because they opined Hunt was flouting the Committee of Inspection's authority, these ardent Whigs adopted drastic measures. In the words of Christopher Marshall, one of the most zealous members of the Committee of Inspection:

"Between eleven and twelve this forenoon, about thirty of our associators waited upon and conducted Isaac Hunt from his dwelling to the Coffee House, where having placed him in a cart, he very politely acknowledged he had said and acted wrong, for which he asked pardon of the public and committed himself under the protection of the associators, to defend him from the gross insults of the populace. This, his behaviour, they approved him, and conducted him in that situation, with drum beating, through the principal streets, he acknowledging his misconduct

in divers places. But as they were coming down town, stopping
at the corner where Dr. Kearsley lives [Front Street just below
Market, nearby the Coffee House], to make his declaration, it's
said the Dr. threw open his window, snapped a pistol twice
amongst the crowd, upon which they seized him, took his pistol,
with another in his pocket from him, both of which were loaded
with swan shot. In the scuffle, he got wounded in the hand. Then
they took Hunt out of the cart, conducted him safe home, put
Kearsley in, brought him to the Coffee House, where persuasions
were used to cause him to make concessions, but to no effect. They
then, with drum beating, paraded the streets round the town, then
took him back to his house and left him there, but as the mob
were prevented by the associators, who guarded him, from tarring
and feathering, yet after the associators were gone, they then
broke the windows and abused the house, &c."

This choice exhibition of Jacobinism, of course, created a tremendous stir and called forth severe denunciation of the per-
petrators. So much so, that one of the said Associators sent the
Pennsylvania Journal (September 20th) a long unsigned letter
trying to justify the lawless performance. The anonymous con-
tributor enlightens us with further details—the "laudable" plan
to humiliate (also tar and feather) Hunt "met with such opposition from some who ought to have stood foremost in support of
the Committee" that they agreed "only to cart him around the
Town"; also, while the cart, with Hunt in it, stood in front of
Kearsley's door, "a lad. . . one of the crowd, took hold of one of
the window shutters and partly opened it, upon which the Dr.
threw up the sash." Being an irascible gentleman, and seeing his
house attacked by hoodlums, the Doctor very understandably took
to pistols.

The nameless apologist of organised disorder then goes on:

"He [Kearsley] was then carted to the Coffee House, with a determined resolution to tar and feather him, if it could be done
with safety to his life; but the people flocked together in such
numbers, and were so exasperated at the insolence [!] of his behaviour, that the men under arms were afraid to proceed to the
operation, lest the violence of the people should put it out of their
power to protect his person. . . ."

The armed guard, we're assured, then returned the Doctor to his
house; it was after they left that the excited rabble made an on-
slaught with stones and brickbats. All the damage was done by a
"number of hearty jolly tars, market people, and others out of

the crowd," disappointed of a tar and feathering show. We're also assured the "gentlemen" who staged this spectacle, and by their own conduct had incited the rabble, were not in the least "mobbish." Indeed, the whole affair "was conducted with sobriety, decency and decorum"! The verbose "gentleman" winds up his newspaper screed with truculent snarlings.

Smarting under these indignities at the hands of those he deems lawless rebels, Doctor Kearsley not unnaturally writes letters to his relatives in England and to those in some authority there. His letters, along with others, are intercepted and taken off the ship at Chester. From the Whig point of view, Kearsley's letters are unquestionably treasonable; from his own, they are accounts of unwarrantable outrage and bids for help against rebellious subjects of the Crown.

This very day (October 6th) Congress have recommended to the several Provincial Committees of Safety the arrest of persons "whose going at large may. . . endanger the Safety of the Colony." It's at this juncture the intercepted letters are brought from Chester. Here Christopher Marshall's *Diary,* for October 6th, takes up the story:

"About six [P.M.], was called to Committee Room, where were twenty-nine members, some of whom by information had been down to Chester after some letters which they were informed were going to England. . . it was directed that three of the authors be immediately taken into custody, which was immediately put into practice by securing Dr. Kearsley, James Brooks, and Leonard Snowden. . . and they were confined under a guard in the State House until next morning. A seal was put on the Doctor's desk, and a guard placed at his house. All this was done by eleven o'clock."

October 7th, three members of the Committee of Safety bring word from Congress to the Committee of Inspection that "all suspected persons" are to be "delivered over for trial. . . to the Committee of Safety, they only being invested with that power and not" the Committee of Inspection. The Committee of Inspection are loath to surrender their quarry, but finally comply. The Committee of Safety try Doctor Kearsley and the others and send them to gaol. Robert Morris, then the Committee's President, signs the warrant.

Later, escorted out of the city by Captain Markoe with a detachment of the Light Horse (City Troop), Doctor Kearsley's imprisoned first at York; afterwards at Carlisle. He dies at Carlisle.

Diary of Christopher Marshall; *Pennsylvania Journal & Weekly Advertiser,* September 20, 1775; *Colonial Records,* x, 358-385, *passim,* 397, 403, 408, 455, 467, 773; *Journals of Congress.*

Friday, December 22—The United States Navy's birthplace is the Assembly Chamber in the State House. The exact *date* may be matter of dispute—whether we reckon it to-day, or one of the recent days when reluctant Congress have been obliged to commit themselves to definite action in this matter of paramount import. The Navy may be credited, indeed, with *four* birthdays to choose from; personal inclination must decide which seems most appropriate.

To-day the "Committee appointed to fit out armed vessels" lay before Congress the list of "officers by them appointed." "Ezek Hopkins, Esqr." is to be "commander in chief of the fleet"; it seems still undecided whether he's to be called "Captain" or "Commodore." The four other captains appointed are "Dudley Saltonstall, Esqr., of the *Alfred*, Abraham Whipple, Esqr., of the *Columbus*, Nicholas Biddle, Esqr., of the *Andrea Doria*, and John Burrows Hopkins, Esqr., of the *Cabot*." John Paul Jones heads the list of five 1st Lieutenants; five 2nd Lieutenants and three 3rd Lieutenants are also listed.

Joseph Hewes and John Adams have disputed sharply over these appointments; strong sectional jealousy's cropped up, just as it did in June before Virginia's Colonel Washington's appointment as "General and Commander-in-Chief" of the Continental armies. In recognition of his ability and of very substantial help he's given during naval preparations, Hewes has wished John Paul Jones appointed a captain. Adams, tireless (and somewhat prejudiced) watchdog of New England's interests, was determined all the captaincies should go to New Englanders. Mr. Hewes says:

"The attitude of Mr. Adams was in keeping with the always imperious and often arrogant tone of the Massachusetts people at that time. They contended that they had shed the first blood, both their own and that of the enemy. They urged that they had already yielded everything to Virginia and Pennsylvania in the organisation and command of the Army; that they, representing the principal maritime Colony, were entitled to the leading voice in the creation of the Naval force."

Mr. Adams further objected that Paul Jones had "never commanded any but English ships with English crews, had no acquaintance with Colonial seamen," and had not lived in the Colonies more than about two years. When Hewes proposed "to make six captains instead of five," Adams "demurred on the ostensible ground that there would be no ship for him to command." Adams evidently "wished to keep Jones in the grade of lieutenant so that Captain Saltonstall, who was to command the *Alfred* if Mr. Adams could bring it about, might have the benefit of Jones's services as first lieutenant of that ship."

When Hewes, knowing Jones's "sensitive spirit" and fearing an "indignant protest," tells him the Committee's decision, Jones says:

"I am sorry Mr. Adams holds a poor opinion of me; but I am here to serve the cause of human rights; not to promote the fortunes of Paul Jones. If, by devotion to the one I can secure the other, well and good. But if either must wait, let it be my fortunes. Do not debate the point further with Mr. Adams. Let the Resolution go as it is. Leave me at the head of the lieutenants' list. I will cheerfully enter upon the duties of first lieutenant of the *Alfred* under Captain Saltonstall. Time will make all things even."

It's only through Robert Morris's pertinacity that Pennsylvania gets one captain—"the brave and accomplished, but unfortunate, Nicholas Biddle."

This same Friday (December 22nd) commissions are issued to the officers named, and the "Committee for fitting out armed vessels" are instructed to issue "warrants to all officers employed in the fleet under the rank of 3ᵈ lieutenants"; likewise

"(as a secret committee) to give such instructions to the commander of the fleet, touching the operations of the ships under his command, as shall appear to the said committee most conducive to the defence of the United Colonies, and to the distress of the enemy's naval forces and vessels. . . ."

The Committee's also charged to apportion between officers and men whatever prize money may accrue from captures. Altogether, the day's doings in Congress seem sufficient to warrant celebrating this as a birthday.

But "much water's gone over the dam" since the first Member proposed establishing a Continental Navy, whereat an alarmed and vociferous minority, with yowling and protest, have opposed this wild project that will "mortgage the whole continent." It was "sheer madness to send ships out upon the sea to meet the over-whelming naval force of England"; it was visionary and fore-doomed to disastrous failure. Edward Rutledge rouses the irasci-bility of John Adams (a strong naval advocate from the first). He says of the South Carolina Member:

He "never displayed so much eloquence as against it [the pro-posed navy]. He never appeared to me to discover so much in-formation and sagacity, which convinced me that he had been instructed out-of-doors by some of the most knowing merchants . . . . It [an American Navy] was an infant, taking a mad bull by his horns; and what was more profound and remote, it was said it would ruin the character, and corrupt the morals of all our seamen. It would make them selfish, piratical, mercenary, bent wholly upon plunder, etc. . . ."

On this score, Adams might have spared his indignation and Rut-ledge his solicitude; privateering and smuggling had long since affected American nautical morals as much as they were ever likely to.

Unfortunately, the question of establishing a Continental Navy's inextricably bound up with the matter of maritime trade, intercolonial jealousies, and the non-importation policy, so that the course of the story's peculiarly devious. The stoppage or regu-lation of sea-borne traffic's already occasioned much bitter wran-gling and peppery oratory, as well as honest perplexity, when the naval defense issue's injected into the deliberations of the harassed Congress.

The first "feeler" towards naval defense the *Journals* mention is on July 18th. Congress recommend

"That each colony, at their own expence, make such provision of armed vessels . . . as their respective assemblies. . . shall judge expedient. . . for the protection of the harbours and navigation on their sea coasts, . . . against all . . . depredations from cutters and ships of war."

October 3rd, it measurably strengthens the hands of Navy advo-cates when one of the Rhode Island Delegates lays before Congress part of the Instructions given them by their House of Magistrates, as of August 26th, to the effect that

"this Assembly is persuaded, that the building and equipping an American fleet, as soon as possible, would greatly. . . conduce to the preservation of the lives, liberty and property of the good people of these Colonies and therefore instruct their delegates to use their whole influence at the ensuing congress for building at the Continental expense a fleet of sufficient force for the protection of these colonies, and for employing them in such manner as will most effectually annoy our enemies and contribute to the common defence of these colonies. . . ."

Two days later (October 5th), Congress having learned of Captain John Manley's application to General Washington, and having heard about two unconvoyed supply ships bound for Quebec—too tempting a prey for the Colonies, so sadly in need of ammunition and all other military stores—they appoint a committee to prepare plans of interception and seizure. They write General Washington by express, directing him to

"apply to the Council of Massachusetts bay, for the two armed vessels in their service, and despatch the same. . . in order, if possible, to intercept s[d] two Brigs and their cargoes, and secure the same for the use of the continent . . ." The resolution continues, "That a letter be wrote to the s[d] hon[ble] council, to put s[d] vessels under the General's command and direction. . . at the expence of the Continent.

Also that the General be directed to employ s[d] vessels and others, if he judge necessary, to effect the purposes afores[d]; informing the General that the Rhode Island and Connecticut vessels of force will be sent directly after them to their assistance."

Congress despatch letters of similar purport also to the Governours of Rhode Island and Connecticut; then add a confirmatory paragraph

"That the s[d] ships and vessels of war" are "to be on the continental risque and pay, during their being so employed."

Thus do Congress unquestionably sponsor naval-resistance activities but, up to this point, there's only a loosely-devised arrangement of divided responsibility between Congress and the several participating Colonies—a sort of elastic Colonial-Continental partnership, with emphasis on the Colonial element of the combination.

At last, Friday, October 13th, after considering the report of the Committee "to prepare a plan, for intercepting vessels coming out with stores and ammunition," Congress resolve

"That a swift sailing vessel, to carry ten carriage guns, and a proportionable number of swivels, with eighty men, be fitted with all possible despatch, for a cruize of three months. . . for intercepting such transports as may be laden with warlike stores and other supplies for our enemies, and for such other purposes as the Congress shall direct.

That a committee of three. . . prepare an estimate of the

expence, and lay the same before the Congress," and contract "with proper persons to fit out the vessel." Also, "That another vessel be fitted out for the same purposes, and that the said committee report their opinion of a proper vessel, and also an estimate of the expence."

This is indubitably a clear-cut act whereby Congress, quite independently of the several Colonies, move towards creating a Continental Navy, responsible to Congress alone. One so inclined, may consider October 13th, 1775, the *first* of the American Navy's four optional birthdays, despite the fact that the Declaration of Independence is still nearly ten months in the future, and that all persons concerned are still subjects of the British Crown, not rebelling against the Crown but in arms against the Ministry, and many of them hoping for reconciliation with the Mother Country.

Before the next "birthday" (and perhaps the means of delaying it a little), comes the Macpherson interlude. Captain John Macpherson, that picturesque, adventurous, eccentric and, above all, versatile, one-armed sea-faring Scot, who built Mount Pleasant on the Schuylkill—John Adams calls it "the most elegant seat in Pennsylvania"—pops up with a secret panacea for the ills the British Navy's causing. He's "invented a method, by which," with leave of Congress, "he would take or destroy every ministerial vessel in North America." He refuses to divulge his plan to any but the committee appointed to confer with him. They think well of it and Congress—some of them still trying to dodge the inevitable—vote $300 travelling expenses for Captain Macpherson to go to Cambridge and lay his scheme before Washington. The General's apparently not convinced of its merit. So ends the interlude.

Monday, October 30th, Congress do enough navy-making to warrant calling it the *second* birthday. Having considered the report of the committee "to prepare an estimate, &c and to fit out the vessels," Congress forthwith resolve

"That the second vessel ordered to be fitted out on the 13th Inst, do carry 14 guns, with a proportionate number of swivels and men. That a Committee. . . carry into execution with all possible expedition the resolution of Congress of the 13th Inst, the one of ten and the other of 14 guns, and, That two other armed vessels be fitted out with all expedition; the one to carry not exceeding 20 Guns, with a proportionate number of swivels and men, to be employed in such manner, for the protection and

defence of the united Colonies, as the Congress shall hereafter
direct."

Congress seem to be getting almost reckless!

'Ere the third "birthday," (really the birthday of the Marine
Corps), Congress consider naval finances and naval pay; decide to
raise two battalions of Marines, whose officers, in addition to other
qualifications, are to be "good seamen or so acquainted with maritime affairs as to be able to serve to advantage by sea when re-
quired"; rule on the disposal of captured British cargoes; get all
befuddled with the intricacies of the boundary row between Pennsylvania and Connecticut; and, November 28th, adopt a set of
"Rules for the Regulation of the Navy of the United Colonies"
(usually ascribed to John Adams's industrious compilation).
Amongst other provisions, these rules quaintly prescribe that

"The Commanders. . . are to take care that divine service be performed twice a day on board, and a sermon preached on Sundays,
unless bad weather or other extraordinary accidents prevent"; if
any shall be "heard to swear, curse, or blaspheme. . . the Commander is strictly enjoined to punish them for every offence, by
causing them to wear a wooden collar, or some other shameful
badge of distinction. . . . If he be a commissioned officer, he shall
forfeit a shilling for each offence, and a warrant or inferior officer
six pence. He who is guilty of drunkenness, if a seaman, shall be
put in irons until he is sober, but if an officer, he shall forfeit
two days' pay"; "all ships furnished with fishing tackle, being
in such places where fish is to be had, the Captain is to employ
some of the company in fishing. . ."; "if there shall be a want of
pork, the Captain is to order three pounds of beef to be issued to
the men in lieu of two pounds of pork"; besides a suet ration,
there shall be "once a year, a proportion of canvass for pudding-
bags, after the rate of one ell for every sixteen men. . ."; and
there shall be a rum ration of "half a pint of rum per man every
day, and discretionary allowance on extra duty, and in time of
engagement."

No wonder John Adams says, writing Mrs. Mercy Warren, November 25th,

"I am really engaged in constant business from seven to ten in
the morning in committee, from ten to four in Congress, and from
six to ten again in committee. Our assembly is scarcely numerous
enough for the business; everybody is engaged, all day in Congress, and all the morning and evening in committees."

Monday, December 11th, which we may reckon the *third*
"birthday," Congress create an enlarged Naval Board or perma-

nent Marine Committee with competent authority to order naval affairs, and definite responsibility for their execution and management. This Committee, established December 11th, consists of one member from each Colony. There's a slight rearrangement of personnel on the 14th, but the significant membership remains substantially unchanged; continuity of functioning's not impaired. One duty of this Committee is to "devise ways and means for furnishing these colonies with a naval armament," and they have considerable discretionary power in divers directions.

At this new Naval Board's recommendation, Congress order the United Colonies' main armament to consist of 5 ships of 32 guns; 5 of 28 guns; and 3 of 24 guns, thirteen in all. With this business, and not a little besides, the Committee find their hands full until the *final* birthday, December 22nd.

While all these things have been going on in connection with the Birth of the Continental Navy, as recorded in the proceedings of Congress (hence directly associated with the State House), much has been happening "out-of-doors" of no less importance to the final result. Unfortunately, for lack of space it's impossible to give the chronicle here, in spite of its interest. However, if the reader's disposed to seek further details—how merchant ships were bought, refitted and armed; how seamen were recruited; how and when discussion of naval preparations really began; how Paul Jones was drawn into the discussion, and the diversity of valuable assistance he gave, both technical and general—the second section of the following references will blaze a trail leading to a wealth of fascinating Navy lore.

Journals of Congress; Letters of Members of the Continental Congress, E. C. Burnett, i, 174-280 *passim* and 261, 274, 282, 284, 285; *Writings of Washington,* W. C. Ford, iii, 174, 202, 226, 238, 256, 270, 274, 341, 397; *Notes on Debates,* John Adams, *Works,* ii, *passim; Diary,* John Adams, *Works,* ii, 424, 428; *Papers of the Continental Congress,* MS.S Division of the Library of Congress; *Paul Jones, Founder of the American Navy,* Augustus C. Buell, i, 44; *Portrait of a Colonial City,* H. D. Eberlein & Cortlandt V. D. Hubbard, 341 *et seq.*

Papers of the Continental Congress, MS.S Division of the Library of Congress; *A Calendar of John Paul Jones MS.S in the Library of Congress,* C. H. Lincoln; *John Paul Jones in the American Revolution,* A. T. Mahan, in *Scribner's Magazine,* July & August, 1898.

1776

Wednesday, May 1—An election's going on at the State House all day long and all evening; the votes aren't all counted till about midnight. The Assembly's ordered this election so as to choose *four* burgesses to represent the City, instead of two, as there have always been till now. Electioneering, talk, and letters to the newspapers have been bitter; there's been a veritable war of handbills and pamphlets, in which Provost Smith, Tom Paine and John Dickinson have taken active part.

The Congress didn't sit to-day; yesterday they adjourned till to-morrow morning because the voters hand their ballots in at the Chestnut Street windows of the Assembly Chamber, and the whole ground floor's used for election purposes.

Christopher Marshall's *Diary* entry for this anxious day says: "Thence to the State House; stayed till one; went in company with Thomas Paine and dined at son Christopher's. Went back to the State House; engaged till past five; then went with James Cannon to his house; drank coffee there; then we returned to the State House; stayed till eight; then I came home, eat supper and went back. Stayed till past ten, the Sheriff having proclaimed to close the poll in half an hour. This has been one of the sharpest contests, yet peaceable, that has been for a number of years, except some small disturbance among the Dutch, occasioned by some unwarrantable expressions of Joseph Swift, viz., that except they were naturalised, they had no more right to vote than a Negro or Indian [quite true!]; and also, past six, the Sheriff, without any notice to the public, closed the poll and adjourned till nine to-morrow and shut the doors. This alarmed the people, who immediately resented it, flew to the Sheriff and to the doors and obliged him again to open the doors and continue the poll till the time above prefixed. I think it may be said with propriety that the Quakers, Papists, Church, Allen family, with all the Proprietary party, were never seemingly so happily united as at this election, notwithstanding Friends' former protestation and declaration of never joining with that party since the club or knockdown Election [the "Bloody Election"]. (O! tell it not in Gath, nor publish it in the streets of Askalon, how the testimony is trampled upon!) About midnight, casting up the poll, it turned out thus, viz. . . ."

The four successful conservative candidates for the City are Samuel Howell, Andrew Allen, Alexander Wilcox and George

Clymer. The three first named belong distinctly to the old order
—ready to bear arms against the present British policy, but opposing independence. George Clymer is a "moderate" Whig—advocate of independence, but not at all in accord with the views
of the extreme radicals. The election result faithfully represents
the feeling of the great majority of substantial citizens.

> Christopher Marshall's *Diary; History of Philadelphia*, Scharf & Westcott,
> i, 311; *Journals of Congress; Votes of Assembly.*

Monday, May 20—From 9 this morning till well towards noon a
great crowd—about 4000, they say—stand in the State House Yard
in the rain. This meeting's been planned and called by the City
Committee of Inspection. John Bayard, Chairman of the Committee, states the purpose of the meeting. They make Daniel
Roberdeau chairman of the meeting; Colonel Thomas McKean's
the chief speaker.

After Colonel McKean's speech, they adopt resolutions, and a
protest to the Provincial Assembly. Most of the Whigs are bent
on doing away with the old Assembly and setting up a new
Provincial Government. A good many of the people attending
the meeting show an unpleasant temper.

While the citizens are having their meeting outside in the rain,
the Congress begin their session in the Assembly Chamber at 10
o'clock. The Assembly are due to meet this afternoon, but not
enough come to make a quorum.

May 10th, Congress have adopted a resolution

"That it be recommended to the respective Assemblies and Conventions of the united colonies, where no government sufficient to
the exigencies of their affairs has hitherto been established, to
adopt such government as shall, in the opinion of the majority
of the people, best conduce to the happiness and safety of their
constituents in particular, and of America in general."

On the 15th, they add a preamble giving the intent of the resolution—"totally to suppress the exercise of every kind of authority
under the British Crown." Resolution and preamble have been
a pet project of John Adams. To end the "exercise. . . of authority
under the British Crown," there's no immediate need to change
the Pennsylvania Government which is *Proprietary,* not Royal,
and fully "sufficient to the exigencies of . . . affairs"; furthermore,
Congress recommend initiation and adoption of governmental

changes to the legally existing *legislatures,* not to Committees of Inspection or other self-constituted bodies, and stipulate as a requisite condition of such changes "the opinion of the majority of the people."

Without ado, nevertheless, the crowd readily twist the Congressional recommendation to their own interpretation. Preamble and resolution give the Whigs (both moderate and radical) the chance they've been itching for. Hence the rain-soaked meeting in the Yard "to take the sense of the people respecting the resolve of Congress."

The victory of the Moderate Whigs and Loyalists, at the May 1st election for the Provincial Assembly, has incensed the radicals and brought incessant hornet-like attacks from the "furious" Whigs. In tavern and coffee-house throughout the city, hot discussions have raged from morning till night; also, there's been a lively war of vituperative language and vilification in "letters to the editors" of the newspapers. Everyone's conversant with all the questions at issue. Not a few of the extreme "left" have fully espoused the levelling doctrines Tom Paine and James Cannon have been preaching.

Colonel McKean (a Whig, though by no means a "furious" radical) tells this morning's meeting the Assembly are unworthy of confidence; they've not rescinded the "instructions" of last November 9th to the Pennsylvania Delegates in Congress, although the people have petitioned them to do so; they have no authority to form a new government because the "present House was not elected for the purpose of forming a new government, and to attempt to do so would be to assume arbitrary power"; the existing government is incompetent; and the people ought to choose a Provincial Convention to frame a new one.

Agreeable to the tenour of this address, the crowd gathered in the Yard adopt a protest to the Provincial Assembly, pass resolutions, and determine upon a Provincial Conference to arrange for the election of a Provincial Convention. Since "some difficulties may arise respecting the mode of electing Members for the said Convention," the Philadelphia Committee of Inspection are to work with the Committees of Inspection throughout the Province. By means of this co-operation, representatives will meet in a Provincial *Conference* in Philadelphia on June 18th; the Conference will set up the election machinery for the Convention in

July. The plan's been fully worked out; there'll be plenty of grease for the wheels and cogs.

That the wet State House Yard meeting's peaceful in neither temper nor behaviour, Doctor Clitherall's one witness. He notes in his *Diary:*

". . . the people behaved in such a tyrannical manner that the least opposition was dangerous. They came seemingly with a determined resolution to comply strictly with the recommendations of the paper [put forth by the Committee of Inspection], and Colonel Cadwalader. . . was grossly insulted for proposing a different form. . . . The questions were put, at the first of which, a man, because he would not vote as they did was insulted and abused, I therefore thought it prudent to vote with the multitude. . . ."

The "insulted and abused" man who disturbs the unanimity of the resolutions by his "one dissenting voice," Christopher Marshall tells us, is "Isaac Gray."

Christopher Marshall also gives us an insight into the "machinery" for putting into execution the political programme sprung at the State House Yard. This same "rainy Monday" he goes afterwards "to Committee [of Inspection] Room at Philosophical Hall [Christ Church schoolhouse], where were confirmed the resolves at the State House, and directions, with proper persons appointed to go with the said resolves to the different counties." The Committeee of Inspection "machine" seems to keep grinding till late at night. When the astute manipulators finish their protracted session, they've worked out all the details of an efficient propaganda scheme. Amongst the "proper persons appointed to go with the said resolves into the different counties" are such "furious" zealots as Timothy Matlack, James Cannon and Doctor Young.

May 23rd, Edward Shippen writes Jasper Yeates, in Lancaster, he's

"advised by some friends to notify him 'that a certain bawling New England man called Doctor Young, of noisy fame together with Joseph Barge' was gone up to Lancaster to endeavour 'to persuade the people there to join in the late attempt to dissolve our Assembly and put everything into the hands of a Convention, . . .' In what way your people may stand I know not, but surely they would not be willing to give up all our Charter privileges at one stroke; many of the people here who even wish for our Independence are averse to the measures now proposed as tending to deprive us of some valuable Rights, without an

Assurance of a Substitute; and the Assembly can as well carry the Resolve of Congress into Execution as a Convention."

Edward Shippen's not alone amongst Philadelphians in feeling it necessary to warn people in the interior of the propaganda barrage about to fall on them. The methods of the propagandists are not above criticism; in York County, for instance, the "proper persons" stop not at opening mail addressed to people they suspect of differing with them politically.

Meanwhile, the State House Yard proceedings have raised a storm of censure and opposition in Philadelphia; the Counties, too, are showing resentment. The Philadelphia Moderate Whigs hasten to inform the Assembly of their dissidence from Monday's action. Their address says:

> "We, the Subscribers, Inhabitants of the City and Liberties of *Philadelphia,* sensible of the many Advantages derived to us from our excellent Constitution and anxiously solicitous that they may be continued to us and our posterity, deem it our indispensable duty to declare, that we are not represented in the said Protest [to the Assembly by those attending the Yard meeting], neither have we empowered any Person or Persons whatever, on our Behalf, to sign the same."

The day following the Yard meeting, a considerable number of responsible Philadelphians draw up a resolution and send it around for signatures. This paper, says Christopher Marshall, is

> "carried by numbers, two by two, into all parts of the town, to be signed by all (tag, longtail and bob), and also sent into the country, and much promoted by the Quakers."

Though Marshall's scornful about it, this paper gets 6000 signatures of people minded

> "to claim and support our Birthright, in the Charter and wise Laws of Pennsylvania"; who reprobate the State House Yard meeting's "Protest" because it holds up "the Resolve of Congress. . . as an absolute Injunction. . . Whereas the said Resolve is only a conditional Recommendation" [which is quite true]; furthermore, they deplore a "Measure which tends to Disunion, and must damp the zeal of Multitudes of the good People of *Pennsylvania,* in the common Cause, who. . . never conceived, when they engaged. . . for the support of the Charter-Rights of another Colony, that they would be called upon to make a Sacrifice of their own Charter."

Notwithstanding Marshall's sneers at this paper signed by "tag, longtail and bob," 6000 signatures would *appear* to represent a majority over the 4000 claimed attendance at the Yard meeting!

This bit of opposition, "to counteract our proceedings last Second Day [Monday] at the State House," causes the Philadelphia Committee of Inspection so much concern, indeed—Marshall admits it—that they hold a meeting at Philosophical Hall to prepare a rejoinder to send to Congress.

The ultra-Whigs of the Philadelphia Committee of Inspection are upset also because the Philadelphia *County* Committee of Inspection denounce the State House Yard action; view with extreme concern the fact

> "that the ground on which the opposition to the British Ministry was first made has been so totally changed"; declare a "System has been adopted by some Persons, in the City and Liberties of *Philadelphia*, which tends immediately to the Subversion of our Constitution"; and voice strenuous objection to "changing or altering, in any the least Part, of our invaluable Constitution, under which we have experienced every Happiness."

A vigorous protest from Chester County repudiates the doings of May 20th; the signers consider

> "such a change in Government to be of hurtful and dangerous Consequences, and which we cannot consent to, but do earnestly desire, that the Charter and good Constitution of this Province may be preserved inviolate."

From other counties, too, comes similar opposition.

Caesar Rodney, whom no one could ever accuse of being either a Loyalist or an half-hearted Whig, writes from Philadelphia (May 22nd):

> "The people of this City I think have acted rather Unwisely—They have called a town-Meeting—by which they have determined to apply to the Committees of Inspection of the Several Counties" to summon a Convention. "This mode for Establishing a Government appears to be, and really is verry fair—Yet I think they are unwise" in view of the acute military situation which demands every united exertion at every point, "and we well know how necessary Regular Government is to this End—and by their mode it will be impossible for them to have any Government for three months to Come,—and during that time much Confusion—If the present Assembly should take order in the Matter, the work would be done in one Quarter of the time. . . ."

He clearly sees the perils of Pennsylvania's political chaos. He also knows the kind of hot-heads pushing for this measure. Colonel Persifor Frazer, of Pennsylvania, another honest Whig blessed with common-sense, writes from the Army on Long Island (June

7th), that he's opposed to the Convention scheme; it's "very impolitic and unnecessary at this time."

"Impolitic and unnecessary," truly! Much more than that! The whole affair's radically and destructively revolutionary, revolutionary in a way honest advocates of independence from British rule do not intend—in a way they would heartily condemn did they fully realise the sinister implications of the movement now launched. The few who do see through its inherent folly and iniquity at the outset, and oppose it, get roundly damned by the unreasoning enthusiasts who have the "bit in their teeth."

The State House Yard meeting of May 20th is the "opening gun" of a *revolution within the Revolution*. This Pennsylvania internal revolution's to bring a veritable reign of terror to City and State, with violence, bloodshed, misery, injustice and bitter dissension for years to come. It will both seriously weaken the State and hinder the American cause.

The resolution of Congress—which the pro-Conventionists choose to regard as mandatory—expressly mentions the concurrent "opinion of the majority of the people" as a pre-requisite sanction for any new form of government to be adopted. With respect to that point, what happens?

When the Conference meets at Carpenters' Hall on June 18th, the hand-picked "representatives" (ostensibly returned by the local Committees of Inspection) are *not* representative of the whole of Pennsylvania at all. They represent only a noisy minority within the *Whig party itself;* the Moderate Whigs are "in the dog-house." They have no show. As for the entire Pennsylvania population, fully one-half to two-thirds are either Loyalists or "neutrals"; their opinions and votes, of course, are not asked. Not only have the Quakers been shouldered aside from having any voice, but all whom the "yeasty" local committeemen suspect of being unfavourably inclined towards the measure in hand have been ignored or silenced by intimidation. The "representatives," who are going to create the *election machinery* for the Convention to frame a new Constitution, must be of the ultra-Whig stripe. The more substantial, responsible element, who refuse to be rushed off their feet by the perfervid rantings of noisy radicals— "excited by what they're pleased to regard as patriotism"—are shoved to the rear. The most numerous constituents of these carefully-picked "representatives" are the "leather-apron" men; the few "silk stockings" who've given any countenance at all to the movement, and tried to exert what restraint and reason they could, are hopelessly outnumbered. Men like Charles Thomson, Secretary to Congress, John Dickinson, James Wilson, or even John Adams—whose lead the "furious" Whigs *profess* to follow—are in high disfavour.

The Pennsylvania Constitution of 1776, J. Paul Selsam, *passim;* Christopher Marshall's *Diary; Journals of Congress; Votes of Assembly; Journals of the Pennsylvania Assembly; The Referendum in America*, Ellis Paxson Oberholtzer, *passim;* John Adams, *Notes of Debates, Works*, ii, 489-491, *Autobiography, Works* ii, 510; *Pennsylvania Magazine of History and Biography*, xxii, 469-470, and xxxi, 140; *Life and Letters of John Dickinson*, C. J. Stillé, *passim; George Bryan and the Constitution of Pennsylvania*, Burton Alva Konkle, *passim; The True History of the American Revolution*, Sydney George Fisher, 229-237; *History of Philadelphia*, Scharf & Westcott, i, 311 *et seq.; History of Philadelphia*, Ellis Paxson Oberholtzer, i, 240; Contemporary Newspapers, Pamphlets and Broadsides.

Friday, June 7—Richard Henry Lee, of Virginia, rises in his place and offers Congress a resolution that will bear fruit less than a month hence in the Declaration of Independence.

The *Journals of Congress* laconically record:

"Certain resolutions respecting independency being moved and seconded,

Resolved, That these United Colonies are, and of right ought to be, free and independent States, that they are absolved from all allegiance to the British Crown, and that all political connection between them and the State of Great Britain is, and ought to be, totally dissolved.

That it is expedient forthwith to take the most effectual measures for forming foreign alliances.

That a plan of confederation be prepared and transmitted to the respective Colonies for their consideration and approbation."

Though this resolution has the effect of a blast—set off with due warning, whereafter the workmen can swarm to resume their task—the *Journals* give no indication of the tense atmosphere in the Chamber immediately beforehand; no hint of the anxieties, dissents, excitements that have preceded this bomb-like culmination loosing a torrent of heated debate; they don't even mention that Richard Henry Lee makes the motion and that John Adams eagerly seconds it.

The other Members have been generally aware that Lee will offer his resolution this morning (hence the expectant suspense)

—have been waiting for it, though with mixed feelings. It comes pursuant to the "Instructions" the Virginia Convention have unanimously adopted on May 15th.

For months past there's been a ferment of agitation throughout the Colonies on the question of independency. Congress have been waiting for a clear-cut pronouncement by the *vox populi*, however impatient some of the Members have been to force a decision. There's been much bitterness amongst them about it. In March, Joseph Hewes has written:

> "We do not treat each other with that decency and respect that was observed heretofore. Jealousies, ill natured observations and recriminations take the place of reason and argument. Our tempers are soured. Some among us urge strongly for Independence and eternal separation, others wish to wait a little longer and to have the opinion of their Constituents on that subject."

North Carolina's been the "first of the colonies to speak out in unmistakable tones." On April 12th her Provincial Congress "impowered" her Delegates "to concur with the Delegates of the other Colonies in declaring Independency." By the beginning of May, the concurrence of South Carolina and Georgia's assured.

James Duane, of New York, and James Wilson, of Pennsylvania, strongly oppose adoption of Lee's resolution; Robert R. Livingston, John Dickinson and Edward Rutledge back them up. Robert Morris, too, feels as they do—the time's not yet ripe for such a declaration. Before Congress adjourn this memorable Friday, they resolve the consideration of Lee's resolution "be referred till tomorrow morning; and that the members be enjoined to attend punctually at 10 o'clock."

Saturday morning, the House resolve themselves into a committee of the whole, Benjamin Harrison in the chair, debate all day, reach no decision, and "beg leave to sit again" on Monday. Saturday night, Edward Rutledge writes John Jay:

> "The Congress sat till 7 o'clock this evening in consequence of a motion of R. H. Lee's rendering ourselves free and independent State[s]. The sensible part of the House opposed the Motion—they had no objection to forming a Scheme of a Treaty which they would send to France by proper Persons and uniting this Continent by a Confederacy; they saw no Wisdom in a *Declaration* of Independence. . . rendering ourselves ridiculous in the Eyes of foreign powers by attempting to bring them into an Union with us before we had united with each other. For daily experience evinces that the Inhabitants of every Colony consider

themselves at liberty to do as they please upon almost every occasion. And a Man must have the Impudence of a New Englander to propose in our present disjointed state any Treaty (honourable to us) to a Nation now at peace. No reason could be assigned for pressing into this Measure, but the reason of every Madman, a shew of spirit. The event. . . was that the Question was postponed; it is to be renewed on Monday when I mean to move that it should be postponed for 3 Weeks or Months. In the mean Time the plan of Confederation and the Scheme of Treaty may go on. . . I wish you had been here. the whole Argument was sustained on one side by R. Livingston, Wilson, Dickerson [*sic*] and myself, and by the Power of all N. England, Virginia and Georgia at the other."

Monday morning, the Congress take "into consideration the report from the Committee of the whole" and resolve

"That the consideration of the first resolution be postponed to this day, three weeks [July 1st], and in the meanwhile, that no time be lost, in case the Congress agree thereto, that a committee be appointed to prepare a declaration to the effect of the said first resolution. . . ."

Next day, the committee's appointed to draught the Declaration —Thomas Jefferson, John Adams, Benjamin Franklin, Roger Sherman and Robert R. Livingston.

Journals of Congress; The Continental Congress, Edmund Cody Burnett, 146-174; *Letters of Members of the Continental Congress,* E. C. Burnett, i, 476-477 *et passim.* The resolution on Independence, in the handwriting of Richard Henry Lee, is in the *Papers of the Continental Congress,* No. 19, iii, folio 169, MS.S Division of the Library of Congress.

Tuesday, July 2—This afternoon the Congress declare "these United Colonies" are "Free and Independent States."

After noting various items of current business, the *Journals of Congress,* for July 2nd, record:

"The Congress resumed the consideration of the resolution agreed to and reported from the committee of the whole; and the same being read, was agreed to as follows:

Resolved, That these United Colonies are, and, of right, ought to be, Free and Independent States; that they are absolved from all allegiance to the British crown, and that all political connexion between them, and the state of Great Britain, is, and ought to be, totally dissolved."

After that, the Members as a committee of the whole, go on considering the full Declaration, not yet adopted.

Yesterday, when they were considering the matter in a committee of the whole house, the votes of both Pennsylvania and Delaware were tied; some of each delegation voted for, and others against, the Lee resolution. Of the two Delaware Members present, George Read was against, and Thomas McKean for, Independence; Caesar Rodney, the other Delaware Member, has been away from Congress helping to quell a Loyalist uprising in Sussex. Then they put off the final vote till to-day.

Seeing how things were going, Thomas McKean sent Caesar Rodney an urgent message by express rider begging him to get to the city to-day without fail. All the Members, both those for and those against Independence, are in a tense state of mind.

And what like is the man they're anxiously expecting?

"Caesar Rodney is the oddest looking man in the world. he is tall, thin and slender as a reed, pale; his face is not bigger than a large apple, yet there is sense and fire, spirit, wit, and humour in his countenance."

Thus, in his *Diary,* John Adams has described Rodney more than a year before.

This afternoon, Rodney arrives just barely in time to give in his vote. Through the night he's ridden hard the 80 miles from Dover, in storm and rain, changing horses sundry times on the way. McKean's out waiting for him as he dismounts at the door of the State House, weak, weary and evidently suffering from his painful complaint. Booted and spurred, and all besplattered and caked with mud from head to foot, he enters the Chamber just as the roll's being called.

John Dickinson and Robert Morris are absenting themselves; that leaves a majority of Pennsylvania votes in favour of Independence. When Rodney's name is called for Delaware, he rises and says:

"As I believe the voice of my constituents and of all sensible and honest men is in favour of Independence and my own judgement concurs with them, I vote for Independence."

And so Lee's resolution is passed. The Declaration of Independence is made.

Now, all the Members in favour of the measure are jubilant. They feel a great decision has been reached at last. The die is cast; there's no turning back.

John Adams (he's been ardently advocating Independence all

along) fairly cackles with satisfaction. In the evening he writes
Mrs. Adams:

"The second day of July, 1776, will be the most memorable epocha
in the history of America. I am apt to believe that it will be celebrated by succeeding generations as the great anniversary Festival.
It ought to be commemorated, as the day of deliverance, by solemn acts of devotion to God Almighty. It ought to be solemnised
with pomp and parade, with shows, games, sports, guns, bells, bonfires, and illuminations, from one end of this continent to the
other, from this time forward, forevermore.
     You will think me transported with enthusiasm, but I am not.
I am well aware of the toil and bloodshed and treasure that it
will cost us to maintain this Declaration, and support and defend
these States. Yet through all the gloom I can see the rays of ravish-
ing light and glory. I can see that the end is more than worth all
the means; and that posterity will triumph in that day's transactions, even although we should rue it, which I trust in God we
shall not."

Letters of Members of the Continental Congress, E. C. Burnett, i, 524-526,
534; *Journals of Congress; The Continental Congress,* E. C. Burnett, 170-
183; *Autobiography* of John Adams, *Works,* iii, 54 *et seq.*

Thursday, July 4—This morning the Congress meet in the Assembly Chamber as usual, at 9 o'clock. After deciding to ask the Pennsylvania Committee of Safety for a supply of flints for the troops
at New York, and to urge Maryland and Delaware to hasten their
militia arrangements, they resolve themselves into a committee of
the whole to go on considering the full Declaration of Independence, on which they were debating nearly all of yesterday. Over
in the house where he lodges, at Seventh and Market Streets,
Thomas Jefferson's been busy on it, off and on, for near a month,
with some help from his Committee.

At to-day's session, the Congress finish discussing the Declaration and adopt it a little before adjourning time. It's really a fully
detailed justification in the eyes of the world for the Declaration
of Independence they made on Tuesday (the 2nd).

Right after adopting the full text of the Declaration as finally
amended, Congress give directions to have it printed and published. The Members don't sign it, but John Hancock's name and
Charles Thomson's—President and Secretary—authenticate it, by
order of Congress, for the handbills to be printed and for publication in the newspapers. All the affixing of Members' signatures

to the Declaration comes later—in August—on an engrossed copy. Only the names of John Hancock and Charles Thomson, as authenticators, appear at this time on the printed copies sent out for publication.

The Members of Congress don't stop to cackle after they've adopted the Declaration of Independence on July 4th. There isn't time. They take it in their stride as routine business; having disposed of it, they go right on with other accumulated affairs waiting their attention.

Just before they go home for the night, the Congress appoint John Adams, Doctor Franklin and Thomas Jefferson a Committee to get a design for a great seal and coat-of-arms for the United States of America.

The *Journals of Congress* for July 4th, after mentioning the deliberations of the Members as a committee of the whole, record that the President "resumed the chair." Then

"Mr. [Benjamin] Harrison reported, that the committee of the whole Congress have agreed to a Declaration, which he delivered.

"This Declaration being again read, was agreed to as follows:"

(Here follows the full text of the Declaration.) Immediately thereafter it is

"*Ordered,* That the declaration be authenticated and printed.

That the committee appointed to prepare the declaration, superintend and correct the press.

That copies of the declaration be sent to the several assemblies, conventions and committees, or councils of safety, and to the several commanding officers of the continental troops, that it be proclaimed in each of the United States, and at the head of the army."

July 4th sees the official *adoption* of the Declaration of Independence; also, there's an order for printing, publishing and proclaiming it. And a committee's named to procure the design for a seal and coat-of-arms. That is all!

Some will probably challenge this statement angrily. A widespread impression (indeed a *conviction*) got about at an early date, and obtained for many years, that the Declaration of Independence was *signed* on July 4th, with great jubilation immediately following. That conviction has become so fixed in popular acceptance that it's almost a matter of religious belief. There's neither space nor occasion to discuss the fallacy here; for a lucid and fully documented explanation of just what did take place in respect of signing, one cannot do better than consult E. C. Burnett's admirable *Continental Congress* (pp. 190-197).

As to the seal, all three members of the committee make suggestions for a design and they consult du Simitière about a draught. On August 20th they'll make a report.

July 5th and 6th, President Hancock's busy writing letters and transmitting printed copies of the Declaration to the various civil and military authorities throughout the Colonies so that there may be due proclamation at such times and places as the said several authorities may locally appoint. In Philadelphia, the *Pennsylvania Evening Post* prints the Declaration on Saturday, July 6th, without waiting for the official proclamation.

July 5th, Elbridge Gerry writes General Warren:

"A determined resolution of the Delegates from some of the Colonies to push the question of Independency has had a most happy effect, and after a day's debate, all the Colonies except New York, whose Delegates are not empowered to give either an affirmative or negative voice, united in a declaration long sought for, solicited, and necessary—the Declaration of Independency."

Letters of Members of the Continental Congress, E. C. Burnett, ii, 1, 49, 50; *Journals of Congress*; *The Continental Congress*, E. C. Burnett, 170-183, 190-197; *The Declaration of Independence*, Herbert Friedenwald, 121-151.

Monday, July 8—This morning's *Pennsylvania Packet* carries a notice in bold type at the top of its third page—"THIS DAY, AT TWELVE O'CLOCK, THE DECLARATION OF INDEPENDENCE WILL BE PROCLAIMED AT THE STATE HOUSE." Since the *Evening Post* printed the whole Declaration on Saturday (the 6th), everybody in the city knows about it and most are acquainted with its full purport; many of the people mistrust its wisdom, many others, like John Dickinson and Joseph Galloway (bitter opponents though they ordinarily be) definitely disapprove.

From 9 o'clock on, Congress are in session and absorbingly busy; too busy to pay much heed to anything else than the measures they're considering. Also, at 10 o'clock the polls open at the State House for an election that continues most of the day. It's the election likewise advertised in the morning's *Packet* on the same page with the proclamation notice—an "Election of Deputies for the city and county of Philadelphia, to attend the Provincial Convention," scheduled to meet in the city a week from to-day.

At noon, the members of the Committee of Safety and a representation from the Committee of Inspection and Observation come and listen to Colonel John Nixon read the Declaration from the Observatory platform in the State House Yard. Not a great many people are there, very few of the "better sort." There's some cheering when Colonel Nixon's finished.

Christopher Marshall and his fellow-members of the Committee of Inspection then go with some militia Associators, who've come to do a manual job, and pull down the Royal Arms in the Supreme Court Room. The Royal Arms the Associators are bidden to carry out to the Commons. The committeemen repair to nearby taverns for a drink, then go home to their middle-day dinners.

In the early evening, the Declaration's again read on the Commons at the head of each battalion of Associators. Follow bonfires and much bell-ringing, the State House bell giving tongue with the rest. In one of the bonfires on the Commons they burn up the Royal Arms the Committee of Inspection have taken down from the Supreme Court Room.

No tense, breathless crowds throng the street in front of the State House, waiting for the Declaration to be proclaimed and the "Liberty Bell" to peal forth in joyous clangour. There's none of the dramatic demonstration George Lippard so lavishly pourtrays more than two generations later. The actual proclamation of the Declaration goes off in a matter-of-fact, routine (almost perfunctory) way; there's no fanfare, no great public excitement, no spontaneous, overwhelming outburst of enthusiasm. Several days' previous knowledge of the *fait accompli* has dulled interest in the official announcement.

The minutes of the Committee of Safety, for Saturday July 6th, record:

"The President of the Congress this day sent the following Resolve of Congress which is directed to be entered on the Minutes of this Board:
  ' In Congress, 5th of July, 1776:
  Resolved, That Copies of the Declaration be sent to the several Assemblies, Conventions, and Councils of Safety, and to the several Commanding Officers of the Continental Troops, that it be proclaimed in each of the United States, and at the Head of the Army.
              By order of Congress,
                    sign'd John Hancock, Presid't '
In consequence of the above Resolve, Letters were wrote to the

Counties of Bucks, Chester, Northampton, Lancaster, and Berks, Inclosing Copy of the said Declaration, requesting the same to be published on Monday next, at the places where the Elections of Delegates are to be held."

(Although John Hancock's letter is dated July 5th, the "Resolve" he sends the Committee of Safety was actually passed July 4th, immediately after the Declaration of Independence itself was adopted.)

The minutes of the Committee of Safety continue without break:

"Adjourned to 5 o'clock; when the following Members Met:

George Clymer, Chairman

Samuel Howell	John Cadwalader
Owen Biddle	Joseph Parker
James Biddle	Thomas Wharton, Jun'r
John Nixon	

. . . .

Ordered, That the Sheriff of Philadelphia read, or Cause to be read and proclaimed at the State House, in the City of Philadelphia, on Monday, the Eighth day of July, instant, at 12 o'Clock at Noon of the same day, the Declaration of the Representatives of the United States of America, and that he cause all his Officers, and the Constables of the said City, to attend the reading thereof,

Ordered, That every Member of this Committee in or near the City, be ordered to meet at the Committee Chamber [in the Masonic Lodge building], before 12 o'Clock, on Monday, to proceed to the State House, where the Declaration of Independence is to be proclaimed.

The Committee of Inspection of the City and Liberties were requested to attend the Proclamation of Independence at the State House, on Monday next, at 12 o'Clock."

The Assembly are not sitting, and the Congress send that House no communication. It is the eight Members of the Committee of Safety, attending the 5 o'clock meeting on Saturday afternoon, who determine how, when, and where the Declaration of Independence is to be proclaimed. Obviously, the polling places on election day offer an advantage for immediate publicity.

Christopher Marshall, incessantly busy member of the Committee of Inspection, notes in his *Diary* for July 6th:

". . . Near eight, went to committee, Philosophical Hall . . . Agreed that the Declaration of Independence be declared at the State House next Second Day [Monday; Marshall is still a Quaker, though not in good standing because of his warlike activities] . . . At the same time, the King's arms there are to be taken down by nine Associators, here appointed, who are to convey it to a pile of casks erected upon the commons, for the purpose of a bonfire, and the arms placed on the top. This being Election, I opposed the motion, only by having this put off till next day, fearing it would interrupt the Election, but the motion was carried by a majority."

The Committee of Inspection, it seems, are responsible for taking down the Royal Arms and arranging the bonfire.

For July 8th, Marshall's *Diary* continues:

"Warm sunshine morning. At eleven, went and met Committee of Inspection at Philosophical Hall; went from there in a body to the lodge; joined the Committee of Safety (as called); went in a body to State House Yard, where, in the presence of a great concourse of people, the Declaration of Independence was read by John Nixon. The company declared their approbation by three repeated huzzas. The King's Arms were taken down in the Court Room, State House same time. From there, some of us went to B. Armitage's tavern; stayed till one. I went and dined at Paul Fooks's; lay down there after dinner till five. Then he and the French Engineer went with me on the commons, where the same was proclaimed at each of the five Battalions . . . This day, the eight members for this City, and the eight members for this County, were elected very quietly at the State House. Fine starlight, pleasant evening. There were bonfires, ringing bells, with other great demonstrations of joy upon the unanimity and agreement of the declaration."

John Adams, writing Samuel Chase July 9th, says:

". . . The Declaration was yesterday published and proclaimed from that awful stage in the State-house yard; by whom, do you think? By the Committee of Safety, the Committee of Inspection, and a great crowd of people. Three cheers rended the welkin. The battalions paraded on the Common, and gave us the *feu de joie,* notwithstanding the scarcity of powder. The bells rang all day and almost all night. Even the chimers chimed away. . . ."

The allusion to the "chimers" probably refers to the Christ Church bells. In the light of other contemporary statements, or statements of contemporary witnesses, and considering the widespread feelings of either mistrust or of outright disapprobation, which we know existed, it would seem not unreasonable to take with "several grains of salt" Marshall's and Adams's enthusiasm about the "great concourse of people," cheers that "rended the welkin" and the duration of bell-ringing. Both men were ardent advocates of Independence, immensely pleased that the step had finally been taken, and their very natural "wishful thinking" made the most of any incident indicative of public agreement with their views. As a matter of actual fact, the noonday proclamation appears to have caused comparatively little excitement; the real demonstrations to have occurred in the evening.

A few of the urgent matters that keep the Congress busily in session all day are consideration of a letter from General Washington; planning for supplies of powder and cartridge paper; perplexing finances; post-masters; means of recruiting soldiers; composing an awkward difference that's occurred between General Gates and General Schuyler; hospital supplies; arrangements about quartermasters—they're all set forth in the *Journals,* an appalling array of business. The letters of Adams's fellow-Members of Congress are curiously silent about the noonday proclamation if there was any noteworthy demonstration accompanying it.

Deborah Norris Logan, the little girl who perches on a fence to see and hear when the Declaration's first read, writes fifty years later with an aging woman's vivid recollection of events in her childhood. In her *Diary,* under date of July 9, 1826, she says: ". . . It is now a matter of doubt at what hour, or how, the Declaration was given to the people. perhaps few now remain that heard it read on that day. but of that few, I am one: — being in the lott adjoining to our old mansion house in Chesnut Street, that then extended to 5th Street, I distinctly heard the words of that Instrument read to the people (I believe from the State House steps, for I didn't see the reader, a low building being on 5th Street which prevented my sight.) [The "low building" was one of the wooden sheds put up as quarters for visiting Indians when their official delegations came to the city—quarters provided because the Indians were difficult guests, very dirty and stinking as they themselves admitted. Deborah couldn't see that it was Colonel Nixon and that he was reading from the Observatory platform in the Yard. Colonel Nixon's said to have had an exceptionally clear and resonant voice.], and I think it was Charles Thomson's voice. It took place a little after twelve at noon. . . . It was a time of fearful doubt and great anxiety with the people, many of whom were appalled at the boldness of the measure, and the first audience of the Declaration was neither very numerous, nor composed of the most respectable class of citizens: — though there is no mistake in saying that the Revolution itself was, (I believe,) in all the States, the work of the best informed and most efficient men: but then they only looked, in general, to their resistance to the Tyranny of the Government, inducing an abandonment of its obnoxious designs, as had been the case with the

Stamp Act — at first all disclaimed any wish to seperate; affection to the Mother Country was cherished as part of the Amor Patriae of every American. . . . "

In his *Autobiography,* Charles Biddle says:

"On the memorable 4th of July, 1776 [it was the *8th*], I was in the Old State House Yard when the Declaration of Independence was read. There were very few respectable [he uses "respectable" in the eighteenth-century sense] people present. General. . . spoke against it, and many of the citizens who were good Whigs were much opposed to it; however, they were soon reconciled to it."

In her book on Philadelphia and its people, Miss Repplier speaks of the proclamation

"to the few at least who gathered to hear it, and by whom it was received in serious and puzzled silence. . . . The dramatic side of this great historic event was not, as has often been observed, apparent to them. . . ."

Like many historic events, fraught with great import, the proclamation in the State House Yard seems to have had but a limited effect upon contemporary imagination. Its full dramatic force appears to have escaped most observers at the moment.

Letters of Members of the Continental Congress, E. C. Burnett, ii, 7; *Diary* of Christopher Marshall; *Diary* of Deborah Norris Logan, MS. in Collection of Historical Society of Pennsylvania; *Autobiography,* Charles Biddle, 86; *Pennsylvania Evening Post,* July 6, 1776; *Pennsylvania Packet,* July 8, 1776; *Pennsylvania Gazette,* July 10, 1776; *Journals of Congress; Colonial Records,* x, 633-635; *Philadelphia, the Place and the People,* Agnes Repplier, 112.

Thursday, July 11—A rumour's afloat that someone's trying to blow up the State House while Congress are in session. No one knows how the rumour started, but the Members have been talking about it; some of them are very worried.

Several days ago (July 8th) Joseph Hewes, of North Carolina, wrote:

"A paper has been privately laid on the Congress Table importing that some dark designs were forming for our destruction, and advising us to take care of ourselves. some were for examining the Cellars under the Room where we set."

Evidently they've in mind the "Gunpowder Plot" (of 1605) and the practice thereafter of searching the cellars of the Parliament Buildings for explosives. It's quite natural they should think of this; up till now, Guy Fawkes's Day (November 5th) has been regularly observed here (as it still is in England). Hewes's letter continues:

"I was against it and urged that we ought to treat such information with Contempt and not show any marks of fear or Jealousy. I told some of them I had almost as soon be blown up as to discover to the world that I thought myself in danger. no notice has been taken of this piece of information which I think is right. . . ."

Hewes may dismiss the matter lightly, but uneasiness persists and now the thing crops up again in open discussion at this day's session, when

"The President acquainted Congress, that last evening, information was given to him, of a conspiracy or plot carrying on for liberating the prisoners &c. in the gaol of Philadelphia, and other evil designs; Whereupon
Resolved, That a committee of five be appointed, and that they, together with the president, be directed to make strict enquiry into the truth of the matter; and, if they find the information well grounded, to take such steps as they shall judge prudent and effectual, for defeating the machinations of the conspiritors; and, in case of necessity, to call upon the brigadier general, or commanding officer of the associators, for the aid of the military."

Besides the President, Thomas Jefferson, Richard Stockton, Button Gwinnett, Robert Morris and James Wilson compose the committee.

Letters of Members of the Continental Congress, E. C. Burnett, ii, 5; *Journals of Congress.*

Monday, July 15—The State House is a busy place this livelong day. Congress, as usual, are sitting in the Assembly Chamber; that always means a lot of coming and going.

Besides that, across the hall in the Supreme Court Room, the Pennsylvania Constitutional Convention delegates, elected July 8th, gather for their first session—about ninety of them from all over the Province. They elect Doctor Franklin President, Colonel George Ross, from Lancaster, Vice-President.

Doctor Franklin, Colonel Ross, David Rittenhouse, George Clymer and a few others are the kind of people one's used to seeing in the State House—the same sort as the gentlemen in Congress. Barring these few, nearly all the rest are a grubby-looking lot of nobodies, people one's never heard of before; unkempt, back-country clodhoppers, very Whiggish and radical in appearance and behaviour. An hungry cannibal would probably prefer starvation to eating any of them. Perhaps the few that are still to come may be more intelligent-looking.

The Committee of Inspection's carefully-engineered preparatory Conference have met in Carpenters' Hall, June 18th to 25th, Thomas McKean President, Joseph Hart Vice-President. Colonel McKean and the handful of reasonable men in this assemblage are too few to be a brake on the rash folly of a substantial majority.

Without a shadow of legality to warrant their high-handed proceedings, with brazen effrontery the Conference arrogate to themselves all manner of powers never contemplated—at least, not openly admitted, whatever ambitions the sponsors may have cherished privately—when their local Committees of Inspection chose them. And the choosing was done in a manner not above question on either legal or constitutional grounds. They act as though they're a duly elected, fully empowered legislative, judicial and administrative body—the constitutional representatives of the whole population of the Province. Their minutes patronisingly mention their "constituents." Most of them seem to think they're already the *Convention,* the not-yet-existing body they intend shall abolish the old Provincial Assembly.

The Associators wholly dominate the Conference. And what like may the Associators be? Those most in evidence are too often insolent, officious, impatient of discipline or restraint of any kind, easily excited and swayed by crackpot enthusiasts and demagogues —in short, unstable and unpredictable. James Allen fondly hopes "discreet people mixing with them, may keep them in Order"; there are two few discreet people—they become fewer as time goes on.

Doctor Franklin, Colonel McKean, Doctor Rush and several others of high character and standing—all of them impatient advocates of *immediate* independence—have countenanced the Conference scheme; their names have saved it from "falling into discredit." Because of esteem for these gentlemen, and under pressure of circumstances, some have condoned the Committee of Inspection's attitude. The more moderate Whigs, both in Congress and out, have distrusted or openly condemned it. Charles Thomson and John Dickinson thoroughly disapprove. John Adams looks askance at the methods employed. As for James

Wilson, his outspoken opposition's provoked such virulent abuse and vilification from the "fiery Independents" that, June 20th, his fellow-Members of Congress—Hancock, Jefferson, the Adamses, Morris and others, about twenty in all—issue from "Congress Chambers" a "public defense" of his conduct.

The conferees have a definitely designated job—to set up election machinery for the Convention. This assignment they arbitrarily extend—they determine what voters may cast ballots; they bestow the right of suffrage broadcast on all whom they think will support them; at the same time, they ruthlessly disqualify the majority of the population—Quakers, non-Associators, "neutrals," all who have ever at any time incurred their displeasure or suspicion, or those likely to refuse a test they now devise for individual election inspectors to require at their own discretion. Great numbers of the people have strongly protested against the Convention and a new Constitution; the conferees ignore that. The extremists are in the saddle; nothing now shall stop them.

The test oath, or affirmation (an effective, handy means of disqualification), abjures the King and engages not to oppose "by any means, directly or indirectly, the establishment of a free government in this province by the convention now to be chosen." The conferees themselves may choose to consider declaration of independence a foregone conclusion; they've no right to impose on others the same assumption as prerequisite to the privilege of a vote. The Declaration of Independence has *not yet occurred*. It will not be made till July 2nd, nor adopted in full till July 4th. When the conferees put forth this test oath on June 20th, there's no *certainty* that either event will happen, or when. To prescribe such an oath beforehand is plainly a move to disqualify very numerous legitimate voters; not only Quakers and Moravians, but many more besides, will either have to lose their vote or else declare themselves in open rebellion against what are still (and may still be at election time) the lawfully constituted "powers that be," and this regardless of any conscientious or political scruples.

By one resolution, the conferees disqualify any

"person who has been published by any committee of inspection, or the committee of safety in this province as an enemy to the liberties of America; and has not been restored to the favour of his country."

This sounds all fine and patriotic; actually, it excludes a very considerable number of merchants and others who (though guilty of no real offense against either law or honest dealing) have at one time or another roused the ire of the hot-heads. The indictment's of elastic interpretation; the offense may have been merely a difference of political opinion. After an election thus hand-picked and "packed," one can readily imagine how representative will be the Convention.

On the 19th, the conferees "receive a petition" from the German Associators for the right to vote. Next day, sitting as a committee of the whole, they decree "every associator in the province" may vote if he's 21 years old, has lived in Pennsylvania a year, and has paid taxes or "shall have been rated or assessed towards the same." This appreciably broadens voting opportunity for the "well inclined." How the Associators will use their new enfranchisement one may conjecture from what Doctor Clitherall (an intelligent Whig onlooker from South Carolina) says in his *Diary:*

> ". . . the Committee of Privates (a body founded in faction and growing in insolence) became remarkable by their advice to Congress [He means the Assembly.] and indecent charge against that honourable body. . . signed by Simpson, a drunken shoemaker as chairman. I forgot to mention, that before the meeting of the conference every method was taken to force men into Independency by this body. They put the question to the City Battalions under arms, and any man who dared oppose their opinion was insulted and hushed by their interruptions, cheers [jeers?] and hissings. I do not mean by this that there was not a majority in their way of thinking, but to shew how unfair and partial their proceedings were."

Actually, the *numerical* majority of Pennsylvanians are *not* "in their way of thinking."

June 21st, the conferees entertain a memorial from the Patriotic Society, aimed at discrediting the Committee of Safety, whom the zealots think too conservative. Next day, they accept an Address from the Associator privates, and another Address and Petition from the captains of the row-galleys in the Delaware, who refuse to obey the Commodore the Committee of Safety have appointed. The conferees are quite ready to assert claims of jurisdiction against the Committee of Safety, as they did less than a year ago in the Kearsley affair, when (as the Committee of Inspection) Congress "put them in their place."

Sunday, the 23rd, the conferees have a busy day. They appoint a committee to prepare an Address "to the inhabitants of this province"; another committee to require of the Committee of Safety

"a copy of all orders given to Captain Samuel Davidson, since his appointment as principal commander of the navy of this province, to be laid before this conference."

As a matter of fact, "the captains of the thirteen gondolas" are insubordinate.

"On being suspected by the people of cowardice (excepting Huston and one or two more) they attempted to throw the blame on the Council [Committee] of Safety by accusing them of tardiness and negligence in not supplying them with sufficient ammunition. The Council [Committee] of Safety retorted and proved that they had sufficient ammunition, but were afraid of venturing too near the Roebuck and Liverpoole, and therefore wasted their supplies in ineffectual long shots . . . ."

This is Doctor Clitherall's concise statement; it's amply substantiated from other sources. The conferees' attempt to review and alter the Committee of Safety's decisions is impertinent interference without a scintilla of excuse. They've been called to create election machinery, not to direct naval or military affairs.

Sunday, too, they resolve to recommend "to the said convention to choose and appoint delegates or deputies to represent this province in the congress of the united colonies [Distinctly the office of Assembly, not of any convention!], and also a Council of Safety, to exercise the whole of the executive powers of government, so far as relates to the military defence and safety of the province . . ." All of this thoroughly irregular; they're plainly exceeding their instructions.

Same day, the conferees approve the Address "to the inhabitants." It begins,

"Friends and Countrymen"; continues, "In obedience to the power we derived from you [Imaginary power!], we have fixed upon a mode of electing a convention to form a government for the province of Pennsylvania under the *authority of the people*.

Divine Providence [It seems little short of blasphemy to saddle the Pennsylvania Constitution of 1776 on Providence!] is about to grant you a favour which few people have enjoyed before, the privilege of chusing deputies to form a government under which you are to live."

After more honeyed words (in which, doubtless, some of the better-minded conferees are really sincere), the "inhabitants" are enjoined to "chuse such persons. . . as are distinguished for wisdom" and integrity; to convey their "wishes and opinions. . . upon the subject of government" to their deputies; to show a "brotherly spirit" and to remember "that the present unsettled state of the province requires that you should shew forbearance—charity— and moderation to each other. . . ." A pity the conferees don't heed this last bit of advice themselves! If Doctor Rush, Colonel Hill (of "Madeira" fame) and Colonel Smith hadn't draughted this, one would more than suspect the authors of having their tongues in their cheeks.

At the end, the "inhabitants" are advised:

"The season of the year, and the exigencies of our colony require dispatch in the formation of a regular government. [The *majority* of the people think they have one.] You will not therefore be surprised at our fixing the day for the election of deputies so early as the 8th of next July."

The whole thing's been railroaded through in haste to forestall any possible action by the Assembly; also to minimise discussion by presenting a *fait accompli*. A *fait accompli* whitewashes many past irregularities.

The conferees reach the height of their magnificence Monday, the 24th. They condescend to assure Congress, after an imposing array of "Whereases," that

"We the Deputies of the people of Pennsylvania [Which they're *not!*], assembled in full Provincial Conference, do, in this public manner, in behalf of ourselves, and with the approbation, author- ity and consent of our constituents[!], unanimously declare our willingness to concur in a vote of the congress, declaring the united colonies free and independent states." However, there's a *proviso* attached—that "the forming the government, and the regulation of the internal police of this colony be always reserved to the people of the said colony."

This last touch is a back-handed compliment to the wisdom of Congress; in particular, it's a slap at John Adams, Charles Thom- son, James Wilson and several other level-headed Members of Congress whom they know have no use for their goings-on.

This production (11 days before July 4th) is probably respon- sible for the fallacious yarn one sometimes hears, that "the De- claration of Independence was *really* signed in Carpenters' Hall."

Patting themselves on the back, the conferees order

"That this declaration be signed at the table; and that the presi- dent deliver it in congress."

Colonel McKean must feel proud to deliver to Congress a docu-

ment some of whose signers can scarce write their own names!
McKean and the other "moderates" are hopelessly outnumbered;
it's impossible for them to restrain the madness of the rest,
prodded by Paine and Cannon. Doctor Franklin's just getting
over a fit of the gout and hasn't attended.

On Thursday, the 25th, the conferees take measures about raising Pennsylvania's militia quota; give orders about organisation
and the appointment of officers; and regulate pay and supplies.
By this time they're quite used to the usurpation of power. They
wind up their sessions with a dinner at the *Indian Queen* and
then—Thank Heaven!—go home.

The only possible shadow of excuse for their performances in
seizing control is the Assembly's moribund state. Decisions have
to be made and action taken; they're on the spot and brimful of
aggressive confidence. But don't forget the Committee of Safety
—whom Congress recognise, and whom they've just tried to override roughshod—are still functioning. And don't forget who are
largely to blame for the Assembly being impotent and moribund,
and minus a quorum day after day.

July 8th, while Congress are sitting and Colonel Nixon's proclaiming the Declaration of Independence in the Yard, the voters
(those still eligible) are giving in at the State House their ballots
for Convention delegates. In spite of the electioneering turmoil
the Tom Paines, Cannons, Matlacks, Youngses *et al.* keep up beforehand, the delegates elected—"very quietly," as Marshall assures
us—for both City and County are not all of them rabid, fire-eating
radicals. Some are "Moderate" Whigs; there's at least a leaven of
common-sense.

Not as much can be said for some of the other counties. In
Northampton, for instance, the "associators carry everything
before them." The Moravians and many others stay away from
the polls; "Five Germans and three Irish farmers" are returned.
This, in a county where May 1st—when the Assembly belatedly
increased representation—James Allen, who's opposed to Independence, was elected by 853 to 14. The same story's repeated
elsewhere. With the sundry disqualifications and the tests imposed, "the elections by no means represent the will of the legal
voters."

With the foregoing explanations of the personnel and behaviour of the June 18th-25th Conference, and the results of the July 8th elections, the proceedings of the Convention, called for July 15th, become intelligible.

When the Convention members meet in the Supreme Court Room, some of the best and more responsible element of the previous Conference aren't there; haven't been elected. Even more so than at the Conference, there are pitiably few to act "as a balance against the rash, the enthusiastic and the ignorant." Most of those who have acquaintance with constitutional questions

"have been left at home as suspected Tories, or for other reasons are not, unfortunately for the early history of the State, called to the task of preparing for it a frame of government."

There are only four lawyers amongst them all, of whom George Ross, of Lancaster, is the most eminent. Him they elect Vice-President; on him falls much of the duty of presiding, for Doctor Franklin (although President) is "frequently absent an account of his duties as a member of Congress." Graydon says Ross afterwards told him that Franklin

"not only devolved upon him [Ross] the whole business of the department, but even declined the trouble of thinking. As to the Constitution, whose provisions it was sometimes necessary to consider, it did not appear to him, that he [Franklin] had ever read it, or if he had, that he deemed it worth remembering."

In the rest of the membership, a scurvy lot of yeasty, and often ignorant, radicals preponderate. Ignorance is at a premium. One of the extreme "left" says

"men of education and learning should have no rule, in a democratic system; they always do mischief by introducing checks on the national impulses of the people."

James Cannon, renegade College tutor, a very "busy-bee" in the Convention (by no means ignorant himself, but obsessed with doctrinaire whimsies and infatuated with Turgot's teachings), says

"all learning is an artificial restraint on the human understanding." He's "done with it; and advises our sovereign lords, the people, to choose no *lawyers,* or other professional characters, called educated or learned; but to select men uneducated, with unsophisticated understandings."

A large percentage of the members fulfill these qualifications. Colonel Peter Grubb, of Lancaster, calls them "numsculs."

One of the comparatively few intelligent members of this choice assemblage writes that a "motion was made, without a blush, by a member, that whatever might require the consideration of the House might be printed before any resolve was passed upon it, for the use of members, as several of them could read *print* better than writing."

When the Convention have been sitting about three weeks, "Right Wing" Colonel Smith, one of the four lawyer members, writes General St. Clair:

"I believe we might have at least prevented ourselves from being ridiculous in the eyes of the world were it not for a few enthusiastic members who are totally unacquainted with the principles of government. It is not only that their notions are original, but they would go to the devil for popularity, and in order to acquire it, they have embraced levelling principles, which is a fine method of succeeding. Don't, therefore, be surprised if in the next letter I write to you, I should inform you that we had passed an Agrarian Law."

The rules of procedure adopted indicate that some of the members—enough of them to make very direct speaking necessary—not only are totally unacquainted with parliamentary methods but also labour under primitive conceptions of rudimentary decencies of behaviour. They're told they mustn't interrupt one another when speaking; they mustn't use

"indecent or reflecting language" [*i.e.* call one another names]; they mustn't "wilfully pervert the sense of what another member has said"; they mustn't pass between "the chair and a speaking member"; and the President has a right "to call to order, when a member may wander from the matter in debate." And, for the benefit of bores who love to hear themselves talk, "where any debate proves very tedious, and any *four* members rise and call for the question, the president shall put the same."

One wonders they're not told when to wipe their noses, or not to spit on the floor.

When the members get down to business, the precedent of usurpation, already successfully established by the June Conference, affords them heartening self-assurance. They assume

"all the powers of government, take all authority out of the hands of the old agents and carry on the executive and judicial as well as the legislative functions."

John Morton (signer of the Declaration of Independence) writes Anthony Wayne the Convention are doing

"some things which people did not Expect as it was given out at the time of Choice they were only to form a new Government."

They're really acting under false pretenses. By a degree of recognition, Congress bolster their position. Being met, President Hancock sends a communication across the hall asking them to

"take such measures as they may judge necessary and proper, for procuring as much lead, within that Colony, as can be obtained for the supply of the flying camp."

Consequently, Pennsylvania clock-weights are turned into bullets.

Saturday, July 20th, they elect by ballot a new Pennsylvania delegation to Congress; they carefully leave out John Dickinson and Thomas Willing. Years afterwards, John Dickinson writes:

"I had not been ten days in camp at Elizabethtown when I was by my persecutors turned out of Congress. While I was exposing my person to every hazard, and lodging every night within half a mile of the enemy, the members of the Convention at Philadelphia, resting in quiet and safety, ignominiously voted me, as unworthy of my seat, out of the National Senate."

A poor return, that, for all the services Colonel Dickinson's rendered his country for more than ten years past.

Tuesday, the 23rd, the Convention appoint a *Council* of Safety (recommended by the June Conference) to supersede the *Committee* of Safety. The old Committee of Safety consists of gentlemen. In that respect, the new Council starts off fairly well but, before long, comprises some gentlemen, some "gents," and some who can't claim even that dubious distinction. Christopher Marshall thinks they're "a poor lot for that important post at this time"; which means there are still too many gentlemen, and not enough "furious" radicals for Christopher, who's a member of the Whig Society and hand-in-glove with Paine, Cannon and Bryan.

Thursday, the 25th, they approve the Declaration of Independence and add Matlack, Cannon, Rittenhouse (all strenuous members of the Whig Society) and several more to the Committee (to make it more radical) already appointed to draught the new Constitution. This addition plainly shows the radicals are in complete control.

Friday, August 2nd, they resolve "That the future legislature of this state shall consist of one branch only, under proper restrictions." Friday, the 16th, they adopt a Declaration of Rights. That very day, Charles Thomson writes John Dickinson about the

"affairs of this state" thrown "into the hands of men totally unequal to them," and alludes to the "errors, which I fear those 'now bearing rule' will through ignorance—not intention—commit, in settling the form of government."

After much sitting "as a committee of the whole," at last on Thursday, September 5th, they order 400 copies of the new "Frame of Government" printed "for public consideration." Violent opposition immediately starts; dissensions and bitterness last well over a decade and, even after the Constitution of 1776 is replaced by a sane instrument, the rancours now hatched continue to poison the political atmosphere. In his excellent (and certainly not unfriendly) book, *The Pennsylvania Constitution of 1776,* Selsam says:

"The action of the Convention in submitting the Constitution to the people for 'consideration' can be looked upon as scarcely more than a gesture. It was not printed until the tenth, and did not appear in one of the leading newspapers until the eighteenth, while on the sixteenth the Convention 'resumed the consideration of the frame of government' [as they'd already definitely decided to do on the 5th, when they ordered the 400 copies printed] and adopted it on the twenty-eighth. The difficulties of travel and communication at that time made it impossible for many people to have learned anything about it. The members of the Convention may have been sincere in their motives, but who knows?"

Of resuming debate on the Constitution,

"Paine rather naïvely remarked that 'as the general opinion of the people in approbation of it was then known [How could it be, when many hadn't even heard of it?], the constitution was signed, sealed, and proclaimed on the authority of the people' "!

Considering the source, one can take this statement for what it's worth—with a liberal pinch of salt.

There are at least two members of the Convention who don't share "the general opinion of the people in approbation"—George Ross, the Vice-President, and George Clymer. On the 16th—the day set to "resume consideration"—Ross, seconded by Clymer, moves that the single-chamber feature be further debated and amended. They're answered by a resolution

"That the further debate on the second section is precluded, because it was fully debated and determined before, as appears by the minutes of the 1st and 2nd of August last."

—another evidence that sending out a few copies of the proposed Constitution "for public consideration" was nothing but a farce, mere "eye-wash."

Meanwhile, for a Saturday pastime on the 14th, the Convention blithely usurp another prerogative of a legally constituted legislature—they levy taxes. Deeply concerned about "the *associators* of this state" who "have freely and bravely gone into the field for the defence of the common liberties of America [Washington and some of the Continental Officers and recruiting agents would be a bit amazed at this blanket attribution of unselfish and spontaneous bravery.], while the non-associators remain at home in peace and security, without affording by personal service or otherwise, that just and necessary assistance they owe to the state for their protection," the Convention order that "every Non-Associator, between the ages of sixteen and fifty years, shall pay, for and during the time of his continuing a Non-Associator, at the rate of Twenty Shillings for each and every month," and "every Non-Associator above the age of twenty-one years, shall pay, in addition to the aforesaid fine, at the rate of Four Shillings in the Pound on the annual value of his estate."

That's a whack at the Quakers and "neutrals."

While framing the new Constitution, and incidentally making sundry excursions into the administrative, judicial and legislative fields, the Convention have unquestionably dawdled. They've been playing for time; they're counting on the newly-enfranchised Associators for votes, and they're afraid to risk an election with so many of those Associators absent "in the field." Popular dissatisfaction at the long delay, however, is steadily mounting until, as James Allen says,

"the Voice of the people, i.e. the Whiggist part, obliges them to frame a Government & dissolve themselves; having made it a necessary qualification for electors & elected to swear to preserve their frame."

Knowing their time's almost up, and that they've tried public patience to the limit, they declare the elections postponed till November 5th, and hope for success at the polls.

Proceedings of the Provincial Conference of Committees of the Province of Pennsylvania and *Minutes of the Proceedings of the Convention of the State of Pennsylvania . . . with the Constitution of the said State,* both published in vol i, *Journals of the Pennsylvania Assembly,* printed by John Dunlap, 1782; *Votes of Assembly; The Pennsylvania Constitution of 1776,* J. Paul Selsam, *passim; Journals of Congress; George Bryan and the Constitution of Pennsylvania,* Burton Alva Konkle, *passim; The Referendum in America,* Ellis Paxson Oberholtzer, *passim; Memoirs of a Life Chiefly Passed in Pennsylvania,* Alexander Graydon, *passim; Life and Letters of John Dickinson,* Charles J. Stillé, *passim; Colonial Records,* x, 582, 585, 603, 606-608, 615, 617, 618, 623-625; Christopher Marshall's *Diary, Diary of James Allen, Pennsylvania Magazine of History and Biography,* ix, 176, *et seq.,* 278 *et seq.,* 434 *et seq.;* Dr. Clitherall's *Diary, Pennsylvania Magazine of History and Biography,* xxii, 470; *True History of the American Revolution,* Sydney George Fisher, 165, 192; *Pennsylvania, Colony and Commonwealth,* Sydney George Fisher, 319-324, 389-391; Contemporary Newspapers.

Wednesday, July 24—The Council of Safety to-day order the Observatory in the Yard—the "Stage" as people have got into the habit of calling it—fitted up for the guard now stationed at the State House.

This is one of the first acts of the Council of Safety that has superseded the Committee of Safety under the new usurping Pennsylvania "Government." The new Council's just been appointed by the unconstitutional Pennsylvania Constitutional Convention now sitting.

It's been but little more than a fortnight (July 8th) since Colonel Nixon proclaimed the Declaration of Independence from this same "stage"—that is, the balcony of the Observatory.

The Minutes of the Council of Safety read:

"*Resolved*, That Captain Peters be authorised to have the Stage in the State House yard fitted up for the Accommodation of the Guard, And that he Provide a Sufficient number of Camp Kettles for their use."

"Light housekeeping" by the Guard's evidently in mind. "Captain Peters" is Richard, nephew of the Reverend Richard Peters; he's a member of the Board of War, a lawyer, and afterwards the distinguished Judge Peters, of Belmont.

Early in July, the Associators' officers asked the appointment of this City Guard. There are three patrols, a commissioned officer and four privates for each; each with a separate district assigned to it. They don't replace, but help and supplement the City Watch; it's their job to patrol the streets, from 11 at night until daybreak. Patrol duty's apportioned amongst the Associator companies of the city.

That their work's no sinecure we gather from Marshall's *Diary* for July 25th. He's been called to a committee meeting

"to consider what steps will be necessary to take in order to apprehend a company of negroes and whites, it's said to the number of thirty or forty, who meet in the night near one Clynn's in Camptown [part of Kensington], near the barracks. After some consideration, it's concluded that some persons in that neighbourhood keep watch, and when they are met, come and give information to Schriner or to Boehm, who are to go to the main guard at State House, for a file of their men, who have orders to attend when called upon such occasions."

The ever watchful—and suspicious—Committee of Inspection

envision the likelihood of some of the "disaffected" arming and instigating discontented blacks to make trouble.

Colonial Records, x, 653; Christopher Marshall's Diary; History of Philadelphia, Scharf & Westcott, i, 323; Portrait of a Colonial City, Eberlein and Hubbard, 254-264.

Friday, August 2—
   "The declaration of independence being engrossed and compared at the table was signed [by the members]."

   This entry in the *Journals* stands at the head of the day's minutes. The words in brackets were taken from the *Secret Journals* (not published until 1821) when Ford edited his many-volumed monumental set of the *Journals of the Continental Congress,* whose publication started in 1904 and ended in 1937.

   July 19th, four days after Congress have learned that New York has given her belated assent to the Declaration, Congress order the full Declaration adopted on July 4th

"fairly engrossed on parchment, with the title and style of 'The Unanimous Declaration of the Thirteen United States of America'; and that the same, when engrossed, be signed by every member of Congress."

   On examining a fac-simile of the engrossed and signed original, one will see a number of signatures subscribed by men who either are not Members of Congress on July 4th or who, if they are Members, for one cause or another are not present on that day. Samuel Chase, detained by urgency of affairs in Annapolis, writes John Adams July 5th:

"How shall I transmit to posterity that I gave my consent?"

July 9th, Adams replies:

"As soon as an American Seal is prepared, I conjecture the Declaration will be subscribed by all the members, which will give you the opportunity you wish for, of transmitting your name among the votaries of independence."

   Elbridge Gerry, who's left Philadelphia because of ill-health twelve days after the Declaration's adopted, July 21st from Kingsbridge, New York, writes John and Samuel Adams:

"Pray subscribe for me yᵉ Declaration of Independency if yᵉ same is to be signed as proposed. I think we ought to have yᵉ privilege, when necessarily absent, of voting and signing by proxy."

   Of Pennsylvania's roll of "Signers," Rush, Clymer, Ross, Smith and Taylor are not Members of Congress until July 20th. Charles Carroll of Carrollton, George Wythe and Richard Henry Lee are all absent from Philadelphia on July 4th. Obviously, there isn't any signing on July 4th save for authenticating a copy for the printer, subscribed by John Hancock and Charles Thomson, "by Order and in Behalf of the Congress." The authenticated copy's rushed right off to Dunlap, the printer, so printed copies can be despatched next day to the authorities in the several States.

Nor do all the "Signers," whose names appear on the document, sign it August 2nd, the day officially designated for signatures. Richard Henry Lee's still away from Philadelphia and doesn't get back to Congress until August 27th. George Wythe doesn't return until after mid-September. Elbridge Gerry, who's been so solicitous about signing, isn't in Philadelphia again until September 3rd; and Oliver Wolcott, who's been absent by reason of ill-health, doesn't return to Congress until about the end of September. Matthew Thornton isn't appointed a Member of Congress until September 2nd; doesn't take his seat until November 4th. Thomas McKean, away on military duty, according to his own statement doesn't sign the parchment at the designated date.

The skeptical or disquieted reader may find all the minutiae of this widely misunderstood incident of American history fully set forth in Friedenwald's *Declaration of Independence.*

Journals of Congress; The Continental Congress, E. C. Burnett, 170-183, 190-197; *The Declaration of Independence,* Herbert Friedenwald, 121-151; *Letters of Members of the Continental Congress,* E. C. Burnett, ii, 8, 20.

Thursday, August 20—
"The committee appointed [July 4th—Doctor Franklin, John Adams and Thomas Jefferson] to prepare a device for a great seal for the United States, brought in the same, with an explanation thereof. . . ."

The description and the "explanation thereof" take up more than two large pages of the *Journals* (mostly in small print). It was evidently the intent that the obverse of the Seal should be also the National Coat-of-Arms.

As described in the Committee's report, the device is a fearsome elaboration like nothing in "heaven above, or in the earth beneath, or in the waters under the earth." It's enough to make any

King-at-Arms in the College of Heralds howl with anguish—roses, thistles, harps, fleur-de-lys, black Imperial eagles, red Belgic lions, 13 scutcheons for the 13 States linked together by a chain with initial letters tacked on for identification, goddesses of Liberty and Justice tagged with appropriate emblems, Moses, the Children of Israel, the Red Sea, Pharaoh in a chariot, and sundry more features all in a bewildering jumble! Blasoned, it would look like "Joseph's Coat."

The weary Members have been wrestling most of the day with a thorny subject, the Articles of Confederation. Confronted by the Seal Committee with this paralysing production, they're amazed, stupefied. At the end of the verbose description, and of the symbolism intended, follows the laconic *Journals* entry:

"Ordered, To lie on the table."

How significant!

The Seal Committee have consulted M. du Simitière as an experienced draughtsman; this grotesque *mélange* is the result of their collaboration. It's hardly fair to blame du Simitière alone for devising this heraldic monstrosity; the Committee members have all tried to inject their individual ideas into the anomalous hodge-podge. Witness what John Adams has to say in a letter he's written Mrs. Adams on the 14th:

"... I am put upon a committee, to prepare... a device for a great seal, for the confederated States. There is a gentleman here of French extraction, whose name is Du Simitiere, a painter by profession, whose designs are very ingenious, and his drawings well executed. He has been applied to for his advice. I waited on him yesterday, and saw his sketches ... For the seal, he proposes, The arms of the several nations from whence America has been peopled, as English, Scotch, Irish, Dutch, German, etc., each in a shield. On each side of them, Liberty with her pileus, on the other, a rifler in his uniform, with his rifle gun in one hand, and his tomahawk in the other. ...

Doctor F. proposes a device for a seal. Moses lifting up his wand and dividing the red sea, and Pharaoh in his chariot overwhelmed with the waters. This motto. 'Rebellion to tyrants is obedience to God.'

Mr. Jefferson proposed, The children of Israel in the wilderness, led by a cloud by day, and a pillar of fire by night—and on the other side, Hengist and Horsa, the Saxon chiefs, from whom we claim the honor of being descended, and whose political principles and form of government we have assumed.

I proposed, The choice of Hercules, as engraved by Gribelin, in some editions of Lord Shaftesbury's works. The hero resting on his club, Virtue pointing to her rugged mountain on one hand, and persuading him to ascend. Sloth, glancing at her flowery paths of pleasure, wantonly reclining on the ground, displaying the charms both of her eloquence and person, to seduce him into vice. But this is too complicated for a seal or medal, and it is not original. . . ."

However much or little the several Members may know of the lore of seals or the science of heraldry—the general rules of heraldry some of them undoubtedly know—or however much or little taste in matters of design they may have, they show wisdom by not approving this incongruous fantasy and consigning it instead to "the Table."

Notwithstanding Silas Deane's complaint from France that Congress have no Seal, a suitable Seal design and a National Coat-of-Arms remain in abeyance until March, 1780, when James Lovell, John Morin Scott and William Churchill Houston become a committee to report on a Great Seal. They report May 10th, but their report meets the same fate as the first—the Table.

At last, in May, 1782, Congress appoint a third committee—Arthur Middleton, Elias Boudinot and Edward Rutledge—to design a Seal. The upshot of this attempt is that the Committee consult William Barton, of Philadelphia, son of "Priest Barton" and nephew of David Rittenhouse. Barton produces a design and then Charles Thomson's drawn into the discussion. Between them, Barton and Thomson evolve a design—for which they probably deserve equal credit. Congress adopt the Barton-Thomson design on June 20th, 1782. The device then approved remains the National Cognisance to-day.

Journals of Congress, v, 689-691, ed. Ford; *ibid., passim*; *Letters of Members of the Continental Congress*, E. C. Burnett, ii, 49, 50; *History of the Seal of the United States*, Gaillard Hunt, published by the Department of State, 1909.

Thursday, September 26—Here the Provincial Assembly have sat these forty years past. The State House, indeed, was primarily built for them to "meet and sit in." To-day that honourable body dies upstairs, and dies without a quorum present.

Forty years ago, as soon as the place was fit to sit in, they moved into the big Assembly Chamber downstairs, where the Congress are now sitting. When the Congress came, the Assembly moved over into the Supreme Court Room. Now the Pennsylvania Constitutional Convention are sitting there.

Not many Members are here at the last. Although there's no quorum, they order £1000 paid to Governour John Penn; settle the accounts of the Province for the past year, ordering the bills paid; and pass some resolutions against several orders the Constitutional Convention downstairs have issued.

Then they leave.

For more than a year the Province has been in ferment; the counties in the "back parts" have been clamouring for more representation; the people generally have been insistent about a new set of "Instructions" to the Pennsylvania Delegates in Congress, broader in scope than those of November 9th, 1775.

At last the Assembly yield and grant increased representation; the new Members, elected May 1st, take their seats. But reform's come too late to save the old order. Even before the May 20th Town Meeting in the Yard, demands for a new government to replace the old Assembly have grown louder and louder. After that meeting, hitherto unheard of indignities confront the Assembly. Besides the "Protest" from the Committee of Inspection, and incessant attacks from ultra-radicals, some of the military have sent highly insulting messages and refused to acknowledge the Assembly's authority.

From May 20th, when the Assembly convene with enlarged representation, the radical Members frequently absent themselves so as to cripple the House by preventing a quorum. At last, June 14th, when there *is* a quorum, the House give new "Instructions" to the Pennsylvania Delegates in Congress, leaving them free to vote for Independence. Then they adjourn till August 26th.

Thereafter there's never a quorum. With the Constitutional Convention now firmly in the saddle, nearly everybody—friend and foe alike—regards the Assembly as a defunct body. Virtually, it is. August 28th, the Members adjourn till September 23rd.

When they reassemble for this late September session, grant Governour Penn his £1000, and order all bills paid, there's no protest from their enemies—some of the moneys payable are due the radicals. After passing the accounts, a Member (name not recorded) rises and offers certain resolutions countermanding

ordinances unwarrantably passed by the usurping Constitutional
Convention. These resolutions pass.

"The House then rose." So ends the old Assembly record.

One of the countermanding resolutions is

"That the Convention have derived no Authority from the good
People of *Pennsylvania* to levy Taxes and dispose of their Property [which is true]; And, therefore, that the late Ordinance, imposing a Rate of *Twenty Shillings per* Month, and *Four Shillings*
in the Pound on the Estates of Non-associators, is illegal, and the
said Sums ought not to be paid."

Notwithstanding this parting shot from the forlorn, dying
Assembly, the fines are applied and the non-Associators (amongst
whom, of course, are counted the Quakers) have to pay, and continue to pay for a long period. The Quakers, on principle, *refuse*
to pay; consequently their goods are periodically levied upon by
distraint to cover the sums due.

October 5th, 1778, Sarah Logan Fisher notes in her *Diary*:

". . . just before Dinner Harding came for my Tommy's fine for
not Mustering, & took my best Andirons which cost me £ 6 for
£ 3. 10 fine." May 18th, 1779, she notes: ". . . drank Tea at Aunt
. . . . . . with Betsy S. . . . . & her Mother, she says most of their
Furniture have been taken for Fines, that they have not one
Table left."

Votes of Assembly; Diary of Sarah Logan Fisher.

Saturday, September 28—This autumn Saturday, a sinister episode
of Revolutionary story reaches its culminating act. In the Supreme Court Room, the new Pennsylvania State Constitution of
1776 is "unanimously" signed. In this room, just opposite the
Chamber where the Declaration of Independence has been
adopted less than three months ago, tragedy takes place.

No blood stains the floor. There's no scuffle, no weapons are
drawn, no blood's shed. Nevertheless, tragedy there is. The
State's bound and gagged. The *Body Politic's* put in fetters,
doomed to bitter years of dissension, disorder, shame and unhap-
piness. The instrument that works this humiliation? The Pennsylvania State Constitution of 1776!

The Convention *Proceedings* record:

"The frame or plan of government and preamble, being now
fairly engrossed, were deliberately read and compared at the table,

and being bound up with the declaration of rights, were passed
and confirmed unanimously."

The "unanimously" is grossly misleading. On this final day of
signing, 95 of the 96 Convention members are present. *Twenty-
three* do *not* sign! They refuse to put their names to such a document. Who they are, it's easy to divine. Owen Biddle, the
absentee, is busy elsewhere paying off the Conventionists. He's
favoured the idea of a new Constitution, but apparently disapproves the finished product; otherwise, he could doubtless find
an opportunity to sign. If the recorded "unanimously" is to be
accepted as true, then, as Selsam points out, it

> "must be that those who opposed the constitution withdrew, as
> was the practice then, before the final voting and signing took
> place."

Certain it is that a strongly dissenting party exists, and George
Clymer, George Ross, Colonel Thomas Smith and Thomas Mc-
Kean (who's presided over the June Conference) all appear subsequently as vigorous and outspoken opponents of this product of
consummate folly. Doctor Rush, who's sat in the Conference but
not in the Convention, is disgusted with the Constitution; he
writes Anthony Wayne,

> "it has substituted mob government for one of the happiest gov-
> ernments in the world . . . A single legislature is big with tyranny.
> I had rather live under the government of one man than seventy-
> two. . . . all governments are dangerous in proportion as they ap-
> proach to simplicity."

The new State Constitution's devised mainly by James Cannon
and George Bryan, who are constantly in cahoots with Tom Paine
(Bryan and Paine are not members of the Convention); it's signed
first by Doctor Franklin as President of the Convention. A few
days later, Franklin sails on his diplomatic mission to France;
takes a printed copy of the Constitution with him.

In fairness to the "Great Doctor's" memory, be it said that his
assent to the Constitution is not unqualified. Doctor Rush says:

> "in a letter to Wayne, & in conversation with Mr. John Morton,
> & myself, he [Franklin] strongly reprobated that part of the con-
> stitution which places the Supreme power of the state in the hands
> of a Single legislature."

In spite of sundry contemporary opinions quoted to the contrary,
Doctor Rush's direct and explicit testimony deserves major cre-

dence. In contradicting a prevalent rumour that named Franklin the author of the Constitution, John Adams writes:

"It was not Franklin, but Timothy Matlack, James Cannon, Thomas Young, and Thomas Paine, who were the authors of it."

In some pique at the French attribution of all the American constitutions to Franklin, Adams says, "He did not even make the constitution of Pennsylvania, bad as it is." Whatever may be said about Paine's connection with the Constitution, or his ignorance of it until it had been draughted, there can be little doubt that his influence plays a very appreciable part in its composition.

This sinister Constitution lets loose on Pennsylvania a poisonous torrent of social hates and inaugurates a class war; disrupts the course of justice; "splits the Whigs to pieces"; puts the power of political control into the hands of an ignorant, vindictive rabble; promotes oppression, confusion and anarchy that result in persecution, violence, and sometimes bloodshed; and sets up, as an head-piece with high-sounding title, the Supreme Executive Council [The name rather suggests Ku Klux Klan, with Serene Kleagles, Super Grand Dragons and all that stuff.] which the single-chamber legislature can keep under their thumb.

The several features of the Constitution that straightway become subjects of intense controversy—single-chamber legislature, weak executive, lack of checks and balances, annual elections, dependent judiciary, virtual impossibility of amendment—are too well known to warrant discussion here. But it's not irrelevant to advert to the franchise, its extension, and the immediately resultant troubles, recurrent with dramatic force.

In Sir William Keith's day, the rabble, sufficiently organised, can make plenty of trouble. Now, the proletariat's trouble-making capacity's infinitely increased. Hitherto, they've had no vote; property and financial requirements have denied ballots to the working classes and unpropertied freemen. Numerically the "lower orders" have multiplied rapidly. They afford richly-ready soil for the seeds of unrest. Besides this numerous disqualified element in the East, there are the equally numerous Scots-Irish settlers of the western and frontier counties—never noted for lamblike dispositions, and for years past restless under the East's repression, chafing at the neglect of their welfare or even adequate provision for their bodily safety. Some of these frontiersmen and their families are living in a state little better than animals or savages—witness missionaries' reports and letters. Truly, a powder magazine ready to blow up at the first fuse-spark!

It is, perhaps, the property of Divinity alone to be able to love the proletariat *en masse*. Towards the individuals, the just, humane man can quite readily and naturally feel and show pity, charity—love, in the Scriptural sense—admiration or even affection; and one would not willingly deprive another human being of the right to a voice respecting the conditions under which he lives. But the aggregate populace too often prompts the disdainful Horatian *"Odi profanum vulgus, et arceo."* Taken as a body, the mob is apt to inspire only hate and loathing, because a mob is always more bestial, more cruel, more criminal, more stupid— more everything objectionable—than any of the worst individuals composing it. The innate individualism that impels this attitude of revulsion—individualism to which nearly every human being is instinctively subject—is one of the limitations of humanity. Our Lord recognised that limitation. Unfortunately, the State cannot deal with the proletariat as individuals, but only *en masse*.

The crowning error of the Conventionists is that, ignoring the potency for mischief in the disfranchised "lower orders" *en masse*, they give them votes at a time when the State's least prepared to cope with the situation. They're "changing horses, crossing a stream." The untutored "rabble" fall a ready prey to the manipulation of unprincipled agitators and demagogues. Their subsequent behaviour shows that most of them are not yet ready to have the vote. To thrust the vote wholesale into the hands of a class totally unprepared to use it intelligently, is like putting a loaded gun into the hands of a five-year-old child. It's not a kindness.

It's not the fault of Pennsylvania's "lower orders" that they're ignorant and incapable of using the vote wisely. Blame, on that score, involves a long story that doesn't concern us here, but the unwisdom and wrong of the Convention's attempted remedy lie in the suddenness of the act, without any preparation for it. To shower political privileges suddenly on those unaccustomed to them, without any preparatory steps of education or probation, can tend only to demoralisation and levelling *down*. If given a fair chance, a modicum of political training, and left to themselves, large numbers of the so-called "lower orders" will do a vast deal of levelling *up* on their own responsibility, which is far better. "Fair chance" implies a gradually progressive dosage of privilege. Dealing with the proletariat *en masse,* in the precipitate way the Conventionists have done, has been a bad mistake. They've given the proletariat a fatal overdose of freedom.

Not all of the Constitution is inherently bad; it has certain good points or, at least, points of good intent. One of the best of these is the provision for religious liberty. In respect of tolerance, this makes Pennsylvania next best to what Maryland once was, under the early Proprietary Government, before the Puritans and then the Crown spoiled it all. On the whole, the Constitution might be workable with saints and angels to run the government; those who inaugurate it show no signs of either sprouting wings or bourgeoning aureoles.

One of the fundamental defects of the Constitution is that its prescribed pattern of government is too chameleon-like—too readily takes colour from the people administering it. Unfortunately for Pennsylvania, the Constitution is made, and the government for a long while administered, mainly by the wrong people. The few stable-minded men who have gone along with them, and tried to keep them within reason, have been outvoted and foiled in their endeavours, and will become their bitterest opponents. The rest have gone very wrong, too badly infected by the virus in that mixture of persuasively-phrased reasoning and inflammatory jargon spilling over from Tom Paine's rum bottle and inkpot. Would that he had stayed in England making corsets! We have Doctor Franklin to thank for sending him hither.

References on p. 192.

Thursday, December 5—The whole city's full of soldiers—some wounded, many more sick, ragged and forlorn; still more just passing through, either on their way to the army in the field, or else on their way home, their terms of enlistment expired.

Six or seven hundred of them are in the Yard, a sorry-looking lot; they've finished their terms of service and are eager to get home. The Maryland Delegates have come out into the Yard from the session of Congress; they and General Mifflin earnestly harangue these soldiers, plead with them, urge them to go back to service for a month—this, in view of Washington's pressing need of men. The Maryland Delegates and the General have some success in coaxing, but they have to offer substantial inducements.

Howe's army's moving rapidly across New Jersey. He's boasted he'd eat his Christmas dinner in Philadelphia; his advance seriously threatens the city. Congress are in direst anxiety about raising troops. Because of their short terms of enlistment, directly their time's up soldiers have "left the general in whole brigades," writes George Read, December 6th "—won't serve an hour longer, so that the city is filled with returning soldiers, though never more needed in the field."

Anent the efforts of General Mifflin and the Maryland Delegates, Read adds, "it is expected a great part [of the troops] will return for a month more in the army." Charles Carroll, writing Daniel of St. Thomas Jenifer next day, says:

"The Inactivity of the People Here was so Great and their Disinclination to stir to oppose the Enemy so apparent that we were forced to offer Clothing to some of our flying Camp Troops Here that will amount to about four Pounds per Man to Induce them to Return and Join the Army for one Month only . . . How many We may Get to return I Know not as from What they Have sufferd, they Do not seem to Have much appetite for the Service."

Letters of Members of the Continental Congress, E. C. Burnett, ii, 171, 172; *History of Philadelphia*, Ellis Paxson Oberholtzer, i, 254; *Journals of Congress*.

Monday, December 9—Congress sorely anxious and perplexed; worried chiefly about finances and the threatening military situation. The city's under martial law; the whole atmosphere's tense.

Congress ask the Pennsylvania Council of Safety to give all the help they can to the Continental officers and others busy removing the public stores from the city; they appoint Doctor Witherspoon, Richard Henry Lee and Samuel Adams a committee to draught an Address to the People of all the Colonies, including a recommendation to order in each Colony a day of "fasting, humiliation and prayer." Next, they resolve,

"That in case this Congress shall be under the necessity of removing from Philadelphia, it shall be adjourned to Baltimore."

Then they despatch express riders to the committees of Cecil, Baltimore, Harford and Frederick Counties in Maryland—committee in Delaware, likewise—imploring them to speed militia hither "for the defence of this city, and the reinforcement of General Washington's army." William Whipple, of New Hamp-

shire, intimates that near-panic has "seized the nerves of some
members of Congress." The more cool-headed are under no illu-
sion about the imminent danger confronting them.

The city's in complete hubbub, what with soldiers pouring in
and pouring out, troops drilling on the Commons and in every
place else available all day long, and many civilians in frantic
consternation. British scouting parties have been reported in
nearby Jersey towns—Burlington, Mount Holly and Moorestown;
Howe's army may fall on the city any moment. Christopher Marshall, bending all his energies to the housing and relief of sick
and wounded soldiers constantly arriving, takes time to enter in
his *Diary*:

"All shops ordered to be shut; the Militia to march into the
Jerseys; all in hurry and confusion; Gen. Howe is on his march."

Everybody knows the Council of Safety met four times yesterday
—most unusual for a Sunday—the first meeting, when they were
routed out of bed at 2 in the morning. Also, that they ordered
the Schuylkill ferrymen, and the guard detailed to help them, "to
give the utmost assistance to the Citizens, and others, who may
have occasion to pass and repass in this Time of danger." Further,
that later in the day they directed the commanding officer of
militia battalions "to impress Waggons to assist the Inhabitants of
the Country to remove their effects, if not to be had without."
This morning, they ordered the constables "to impress a Close
Carriage with Horses from James Pemberton, John Pemberton,
Israel Pemberton, or Sam'l Emlen, jun'r, to remove General
Roberdeau to Lancaster" to alarm the people in that part of the
State. That's making the "stiffest" of the Quakers help, willy-
nilly!

Ever since November 14th, the Council of Safety's orders have
really been danger signals; since the 27th, the newspapers have
suspended publication; for some days past, refugee removals have
clogged the roads north and west and impeded troop movements.
Only the Quakers keep a detached attitude of more or less calm.

Colonial Records, xi, 4-41; *Letters of Members of the Continental Congress*, E. C. Burnett, ii, 174, 176, 187; *Journals of Congress*.

Tuesday, December 10—Congress even more anxious and jumpy
than yesterday. They bid General Mifflin hasten into the neigh-

bouring counties and do his utmost to rouse and bring men in to defend the city; they ask the Assembly to send a committee to help the General. They direct General Putnam to parade recruits and other troops immediately; also, construct proper defenses for the city. And they beg the Council of Safety to give General Putnam all possible aid in defense work by "calling forth the inhabitants, and by any other means in their judgement proper."

They direct Mr. Hancock to write General Washington desiring him to despatch "a party to watch the roads leading from New Jersey to Philadelphia. . . and give Congress the earliest notice of the enemy's motions"—frayed nerves! Also, start a resolution about scouting parties to keep a lookout in Jersey—stop in the middle of it.

Yesterday afternoon, the Council of Safety ordered the money from the Treasury, with all the books and papers, taken to Lancaster. This morning they instruct the City Wardens

"to employ persons to Patrole the Streets, in order to prevent riots, burglarys, and other disorders, and that they be directed to pay particular attention to the security of the Inhabitants."

Violence and looting feared, in the city's distraught, turbulent state.

Panic's on, in good and earnest. Says Christopher Marshall, "Our people in confusion, of all ranks, sending all their goods out of town into the country." The roads are full of horses, waggons piled high with bedding, pots, pans, kettles, crockery—the most necessary items in the paraphernalia of living jumbled together with the most prized pieces of furniture and other household possessions; women, children, servants, some in carriages, some in carts, some on horseback, many trudging along a-foot, pushing barrows; squawking chickens in coops, in baskets, or with feet tied together and packed in wherever place can be found, while cows and other livestock are herded and prodded along—all in a mad, last-minute scramble to reach some place of safety. James Allen, coming into the city after this wholesale flight, finds it like Sunday in service-time. The Quakers are "almost the only people determined to remain."

In all this turmoil, there's only one trace of reassurance—the proclamation the three-member committee of Congress have drawn up and submit at to-day's session. While its main object is to stir up "immediate and spirited exertion in opposition to

the Army that now threaten to take possession of this city," it
takes care to explain that the British, during the whole campaign,
"have been checked in their progress, and have not till within
these two weeks ventured above ten miles from their shipping.
Their present advances are owing not to any capital defeat, or
want of valour in the Army that opposed them, but to a sudden
diminution of its numbers from the expiration of those short in-
listments which, to ease the people, were at first adopted . . ."
Then follow exhortations "to lay hold of the opportunity of destroying their principal Army, now removed from the ships of
war, in which their greatest strength lies." Then, a note of resignation—almost of despair about saving the city: "And though
(blessed be God) even the loss of Philadelphia would not be the
loss of the cause, yet while it can be saved," if men will only rally
quickly enough in sufficient force, "let us not, in the close of the
campaign, afford them such ground of triumph."

> Colonial Records, xi, 41, 42; James Allen's Diary, in Pennsylvania Magazine
> of History and Biography, ix, 176 et seq., 278 et seq., 424 et seq.; Journal
> of Henry Melchior Mühlenberg, Collections of the Historical Society of
> Pennsylvania i, 155; Journals of Congress.

Wednesday, December 11—Most Members of Congress plainly
have the jitters. The resolve started yesterday about scouting
parties, they finish to-day—small, well-led parties from the city are
to cross to Jersey, get all possible information about "motions and
situation of the enemy," and send "frequent daily intelligence"
through General Putnam to Congress "of the discoveries they be
able to make."

However, they feel bound to keep up appearances; very annoyed because "a false and malicious report hath been spread by
the enemies of America" that Congress are about to disperse.
Accordingly, they resolve

"That General Washington be desired to contradict the said
scandalous report in general orders, this Congress having a better
opinion of the spirit and vigour of the Army and the good people
of these states than to suppose it can be necessary to disperse. Nor
will they adjourn from the city of Philadelphia in the present
state of affairs, unless the last necessity shall direct it."

Whistling to keep up courage! The cooler-headed Members are
not yet convinced flight's inevitable. Samuel Chase writes, "The
Congress will not quit this City but in the last extremity"; Oliver
Wolcott writes, "If the Enemy should drive us out of this City

(which I do not expect) you will soon hear to what Place I shall go." Few Members are nearly so calm as Chase and Wolcott.

This afternoon, the Council of Safety decide Mr. Dunlap's press and types must be kept in town to issue bulletins; should they fall into British hands, the Council will reimburse Mr. Dunlap. They likewise order every able-bodied man to go out and labour on the earthworks north of the city,

"either by themselves or their Substitutes. . . the persons so employed to have the same pay and Rations as the Militia. . . and in case any person shall neglect to serve. . . the Commanding officer. . . is hereby authorised to Seize and make sale of the Goods and Chattels of. . . delinquents, to the amount of such Sum as shall induce another to perform the work. . . ."

Council and Assembly officially represent those who've espoused the cause of Independence; in ordering all available aid to General Putnam, Military Governour of the City, the Council are consistently doing a plain duty. Hitherto, they've been reasonably patient with "conscientious objectors"—in compulsory action, if not in words. Their present decision's a counsel of desperation.

Council's measures, albeit wise and timely, neither make for composure in Congress nor tend to allay public anxiety—that is, anxiety and fright amongst them that are neither Loyalists nor Quakers. Council's order for enforced labour definitely disquiets Loyalists and Quakers; indeed, it's aimed chiefly at them.

The Quakers (save a few Whig Quakers, like Christopher Marshall) have persisted in their attitude of neutrality, not a wholly benevolent neutrality. The Independence party—a well-organised, vocal, active minority—they honestly consider unjustified rebels against the lawful powers that be; any recognition of their claims, or any assistance given them, would be compounding rebellion. Besides their political convictions, to which they're certainly entitled, the Quakers' religious principles against war make their position doubly difficult. Council's order's a rude blow to their policy of inactive dissidence.

As to the panicky message Congress send General Washington, he very properly sees fit not to publish it in general orders. It's afterwards erased from the *Journals of Congress*.

Letters of Members of the Continental Congress, E. C. Burnett, ii, 174-176; *Colonial Records*, xi, 46; Christopher Marshall's *Diary*; *Journals of Congress*.

Thursday, *December 12*—Generals Mifflin and Putnam urge Congress to adjourn elsewhere because the Members can't give public business "quiet and uninterrupted attention," the city now being too near the seat of war. Giving some hurried, last-minute directions, Congress thereupon adjourn to meet in Baltimore on the 20th. They depute Mr. Wilson "to inform the assembly and council of safety of Pennsylvania" they've gone and whither. Robert Morris stays to attend the urgent business of Congress, after their flight to escape "the rude Disorder of Arms." He writes President Hancock, on the 16th:

> "The sudden departure of the Congress from this place seems to be a matter of much speculation and People who judge by events, think they have been too precipitate. . . things are thrown into great confusion by it."

Morris manages "continental business largely on his own responsibility but partly also as a member of certain committees" until, on the 21st, George Clymer and George Walton are appointed to help him.

The *Assembly* continue sitting at the State House. To-day, they offer the Associators a bounty to encourage them "to go out at this inclement season." Friday, they order the State's moneys, books and papers sent to "some safe. . . place in Lancaster or Chester counties." Under date of December 14th, Assembly minutes read:

> "From the 14th day of *December, 1776*, until the 13th day of January, 1777, a quorum of the members did not appear. . . occasioned by a number of the members being officers in the militia, who were under an obligation to attend in the army," or were busy recruiting, "although a number met" at the State House "and adjourned from day to day."

> *Letters of Members of the Continental Congress,* E. C. Burnett, ii, 175-177; *Journals of the Assembly; Colonial Records,* xi, 44-48; *Journals of Congress.*

Friday, December 20—Into the Council Chamber comes James Allen, under guard. The Council of Safety have had him arrested as a suspected "traitorous" person.

His father secured the land for the State House; his grandfather, Andrew Hamilton, designed and built it; his uncle, James Hamilton, and his brother-in-law, John Penn, have sat in this very Chamber as Governours of the Province; his father has sat here many years as Member of the Governour's Council, and down-stairs in the Supreme Court Room as Chief Justice of the Province; and he himself has sat downstairs as a Member of the Provincial Assembly. Hard for him, to be fetched here a prisoner!

"On Thursday 19 Decr 1776 at 7 o'clock A.M. my house [in Northampton County, at what is now Allentown] was surrounded by a Guard of Soldiers with fixed Bayonets; I got up & when I came down stairs the officer. . . produced a Warrant from the Council of Safety to seize me & bring me before them. I accordingly went to Philad^a & appeared before them, & opened the scene, by saying, that they had drawn me from my retirement unexpectedly; Mr. Owen Biddle then said, that they had received accounts of the unwillingness of the Militia of Northampton County to march, that they knew my influence and property there, & were afraid of my being the cause of it, and added that my brothers being gone over to the enemy the publick would expect that I should be put on my Parole & hoped I wou'd have no Objection to stay within six miles of Philad^a. Mr. Matlack said 'at least Mr. Allen may chuse his place of Residence.' "

So runs the *Diary* of James Allen, a "neutral"—friend of General Washington and of many of the American leaders. The *Diary* gives a picture of the abuses and disorders that followed in the wake of the Pennsylvania "Constitution of 1776"—a picture temperate, without exaggeration, saddened, but without the animus that might reasonably have been expected; therefore, the more credible. Abhorrence of Sulla's proscriptions is instilled into youthful students of Roman history; how many realise there was a parallel episode in Pennsylvania's "reign of terror"?

Upon the death of the old Provincial Assembly, Allen withdrew to his farm in Northampton County and tried to live in retirement, aloof from all part in the present political or military programme, which he conscientiously disapproves, though not a Quaker—wishes only to be let alone.

Upon Howe's expected arrival in Philadelphia, he says:

"a persecution of Tories (under which name, is included every one disinclined to Independence tho' ever so warm a friend of constitutional liberty and the old cause), begins; houses are broken open, people imprison'd without any colour of authority by private persons, & as is said a list of 200 disaffected persons made out, who were to be seized, imprisoned & sent off to North Carolina; in which list, it was said, our whole family was set down; . . . .

To describe the present state of the Province of Pennsylvania,

would require a Volume. It may be divided into 2 classes of
men, viz. Those that plunder and those that are plundered. No
Justice has been administered, no crimes punished for 9 months.
All Power is in the hands of the associators, who are under no
subordination to their officers. Not only a desire of exercising
power, in those possessed of it, sets them on, but they are supported & encouraged. To oppress one's countrymen is a love of
Liberty. Private friendships are broken off, & the most insignifi-
cant now lord it with impunity & without discretion over the
most respectable characters. . . This convulsion has indeed
brought all the dregs to the Top."

Continuing the account of his seance with the Council of Safety,
Allen says:

"I told them that my political principles were well known, to be
unfriendly to the present views of Independence, which I had
strenuously opposed before it was declared, that since, I had not
interfered in publick matters, further than in confidential con-
versations with my friends & I wished always to remain so during the present unhappy war. I then produced some certificates
which I had the precaution to procure, testifying the truth of the
above. I told them I would incline to go to dinner & wait on them
in the afternoon if they approved. They agreed & took my word
to return; . . ."

Before he goes away to dinner, Allen's told the Council his
brothers have taken refuge with Howe against his own advice, but
in trying to defend their conduct, he's drawn

"a picture of the state of the province, the military persecutions,
the invasions of private property, imprisonments & abuses, that
fell to the share of those whose consciences would not let them
join the present measures. I particularised two of their own Ordinances authorising field officers to invade & pillage our houses
& imprison our persons on mere suspicion & concluded by saying,
that I was almost frightened into a determination of seeking the
same protection, that my brothers had done. Mr. Biddle acknowledged the truth of what I said [This admission by a Member of
the Council is pretty convincing evidence.] & excused the necessity of the present arbitrary measures, by the divided state of
America. I told him conciliatory measures would make more
converts; that it was hard to forget we were once freemen, who
had lived under the happiest & freest Government on earth; &
I believed these violences inclined a majority of the people to
wish for Gen¹ Howe's arrival."

His very plain speaking does Allen no harm in the Council's
eyes. When he goes back in the afternoon,

"they produced a certificate, which they hoped I would not object to; wherein they set forth, my brothers' departure & the backwardness of our Militia as reasons for sending for me, that I had given them satisfaction respecting my prudent conduct, that my conduct did not appear unfriendly to the cause of Liberty, nor inconsistent with the character of a Gentleman; & I in return pledged my honour verbally not to say or do any thing injurious to the present cause of America. So we parted amicably & as we began, with great politeness on both sides."

"This disagreeable business over," Allen spends Christmas in the city with friends and gets back to Northampton County on the 28th. Notwithstanding the certificate given him, he soon meets with an incident of the very kind he's just complained of to the Council.

"Being ignorant that any of the Militia were in the Town [Allentown] Mrs. Allen with her daughter Peggy & Lyddy Duberry went to visit Mrs. Bond in the Chariot: entering the street a company of the Militia met them in front; Samson endeavoured to drive out of the Road, but was stopt by a hollow way. The soldiers beat him with their muskets, & pushed at him with their Bayonets, on which to defend himself he made use of his Whip. This so enraged them, that they pushed their Bayonets into the Chariot, broke the glass & pierced the chariot in 3 places; during the whole scene my wife begging to be let out & the children screaming; they also endeavoured to overset it, while they were within it. David Deshler [Commissioner of Army Supplies for Northampton County] happening to be present prevented it & led the horses on, by which means they escaped. Their design was to destroy the Chariot. I having walked across the field saw nothing of this till it was over & the company had marched on. Soon after the Major Boehm & Capt Buckhalter returned.—The former, a violent man, countenanced the attack, whereupon a rencounter ensued between him & me, in which he attempted to draw his swoard on me." Boehm afterwards goes to Allen's house "to assure me he was innocent of the attack on my chariot & and we buried the affair in Oblivion. He assured me that the soldiers were ripe for doing some violence to my house, which he with difficulty prevented, & upon the whole I had great good fortune to escape without some injury from a riotous incensed soldiery. . . ."

The incident's typical of conditions in Pennsylvania in the latter part of 1776 and for long afterwards.

Colonial Records, xi, 54, 57; Diary of James Allen, in Pennsylvania Magazine of History and Biography, ix, 176 et seq., 278 et seq., 434 et seq.

1777

Wednesday, March 5—At last the new State Government's got going. Yesterday the Assembly elected Thomas Wharton, junior, President of the Supreme Executive Council, George Bryan Vice-President.

This morning Mr. Wharton takes his oath of office before the Assembly, sitting in the Supreme Court Room, where the Provincial Constitutional Convention sat last summer. Then they all go upstairs to the Council Chamber and decide Mr. Wharton's title shall be "His Excellency"; most agree to this. (The President of the Council comes to be generally called "President of the State.")

Last December's unrest's all past and gone; confidence has returned; Congress are coming back from their sojourn in Baltimore; the new Assembly, under the "Constitution of 1776" have met and some Councillors have been returned; all in all, conditions are ripe for a bit of civic pageantry.

A procession forms at the State House, to go thence and, at noon, proclaim at the old Court House at Second and Market Streets the new President of the Commonwealth. On this "day of great pomp," the principal personages are on horseback; the order of march is:—

Constables with their staves

Sub-Sheriffs

High Sheriff and Coroner

The Honourable Speaker of the House—the Clerk of the House on his right hand

Members of the Assembly

The President and Vice-President

Members of the Supreme Executive Council

Gentlemen Members of the Council of Safety and Navy Board

Arrived at the Court House, the High Sheriff, William Masters, commands "silence, under pain of imprisonment." Then the "President and the Honourable Speaker of the House of Assembly" come forward on the balcony, the time-honoured proclamation place of Kings and Governours; the Clerk of the House publishes the election of the President and Vice-President, and proclaims, according to his "Stile and Title," "His Excellency

Thomas Wharton, Junior, Esquire, President of the Supreme Executive Council of the Commonwealth of Pennsylvania, Captain General and Commander-in-Chief in and over the same."

As the people applaud, thirteen brass cannon, from the Hessian field-pieces captured at Trenton, roar a salute and all the bells of the city ring out. Then the procession re-forms and they all move off down Second Street to the dinner the Assembly are giving at the City Tavern. Such Members of Congress as are returned also attend. At dinner, 17 toasts are drunk to the booming of cannon.

In her *Diary*, Sarah Logan Fisher gives a Quaker Loyalist account of the event.

". . . Tommy Wharton proclaimed President of the Council, or in other words Governour of this state, with some demonstrations of joy from the Mob, the Cannon fired & Bells rung, & an elegant entertainment was prepared for him & his Council at the City Tavern where they dined & in order to heighten the farce in the evening was fire rockets & Bonfires."

With dissension rife, Constitutionalists and anti-Constitutionalists at each others' throats, the choice of Wharton is fortunate. He's

"a conservative," and one whom "men of conflicting views will unite to support. Furthermore, he has wide executive experience as a member of the Committee of Safety from June 30, 1775, to March 13, 1777."

From a letter he wrote General St. Clair soon after its adoption, his opposition to the "Constitution of 1776" is evident. He says of it:

"True it is, there are many faults which I hope one day to see removed; but it is true that, if the Government should at this time be overset, it would be attended with the worst consequences, not only to this State, but to the whole continent in the opposition we are making to Great Britain. If a better frame of government should be adopted, such a one as would please a much greater majority than the present one, I should be very happy in seeing it brought about. . . ."

Colonial Records, xi, 173-174; Journals of Assembly; Pennsylvania Gazette, March 12, 1777; Pennsylvania Magazine of History and Biography, v, 436-438; The Pennsylvania Constitution of 1776, J. P. Selsam, 243-244; Sarah Logan Fisher's Diary; History of Philadelphia, Ellis Paxson Oberholtzer, i, 255.

Saturday, June 14—"Old Glory" is born to-day in the State House, in the very same Chamber in which the Declaration of Independence was adopted less than a year ago—signed later when it had been engrossed.

The *Journals of Congress* for June 14th say:

"*Resolved,* That the flag of the United States be thirteen stripes, alternate red and white; that the union be thirteen stars, white in a blue field, representing a new constellation."

That is all.

This resolve immediately follows directions to the Marine Committee about shipping in the Delaware. There's a tradition the design came from the Marine Committee. Aside from this tradition, we're in the dark. No record of any discussion prior to this official adoption; no mention of who proposed the resolve; no indication to show whether a committee or an individual suggested the design, or who made the first flag. We're left wholly to surmises—probabilities or, more likely, mere possibilities.

Before this definite appointment of the Congressional Flag, to be used in all thirteen States, by Navy and by Army, many different flags have been in use besides the Grand Union Flag General Washington first displayed at Cambridge, January 2, 1776. When the Grand Union becomes inappropriate after the Declaration of Independence, these other varied flags continue to be borne; indeed, even after Congress have constituted the recognised standard, the diversity does not wholly cease.

Between the "Stars and Stripes" that Congress now prescribe, and the Grand Union, the only difference is in the canton; the canton of the Grand Union shows the combined crosses of St. George and St. Andrew, on a blue field, while the canton of the Congressional Flag bears thirteen white stars, on a blue field.

The *stripes* are easily accounted for. Horizontal stripes of different colours are known on the Dutch and other standards. Alternate red and white stripes were on the old flag of the British East India Company as well as on the Grand Union that Washington unfurled at Cambridge. The immediate idea of *thirteen* stripes it seems highly likely his Excellency got from a flag he well knew, the flag of the Philadelphia City Troop, the first to ride with him after his appointment as Commander-in-Chief of the American armies, and his escort across the Jerseys on his way to Cambridge. The canton of that flag is "barry of thirteen alternate silver and blue stripes," and this device was chosen to represent the thirteen Colonies.

It's quite natural the canton of the Grand Union or Cambridge Flag should retain the combined St. George's and St. Andrew's crosses of Great Britain—when it's first hoisted, the Declaration of Independence is still more than six months in the future, and most Americans still cherish, or at least profess, loyalty to the British *Crown,* while they hate the British *Ministry* and willingly take up arms against it.

Whence come the *stars* it's impossible to say. Perhaps as good a guess as any is that they derive from the Rhode Island Flag.

Not until August do the newspapers print the resolve of Congress about the Flag. And not until September 3rd is the adoption of the Congressional Flag—the "Stars and Stripes"—officially published over the signature of the Secretary of Congress.

Journals of Congress; History of the Flag of the United States of America, Rear-Admiral George Henry Preble, 260 *et seq.; Book of the First Troop, Philadelphia City Cavalry, 1774-1914,* 243-248; *The Markoe Flag and Our National Emblem,* Fr. William Markoe, S.J., MS.; *The True Story of the American Flag,* John H. Fow; *National Geographic Magazine,* September, 1934.

Monday, July 28—A red-headed, impetuous, good-looking young Frenchman comes to the State House this morning; some of his French friends with him. They send in letters to Mr. Hancock, President of Congress, but are kept standing outside. The young man's scarce twenty, but seems the leader of his little party. He's the Marquis de la Fayette; he and his friends have come to fight in the American Army. Mr. Deane, in France, 'tis said, has promised them commissions as officers of high rank.

After a while Mr. Lovell, who's Chairman of the Foreign Affairs Committee and speaks French, comes out and tells them they're only a parcel of adventurers and there are already too many of their sort in Philadelphia; bids them be off. He's very short and savage about it. They can't speak enough English to answer him and seem dumbfounded as they leave. Surely, their letters can't have been read. They don't look like humbugs, especially the **red-headed lad.**

Silas Deane, while he's an American agent in France, unwittingly creates no end of trouble for the Continental Congress by commissioning, or promising commissions to, numerous French soldiers and others who, for one cause or another, wish to join the American Army. He's unquestionably imposed upon by many of them and, when they turn up on this side, Congress have to dispose of them, often in a summary manner; it's impossible to give them commissions or, indeed, to employ the majority of them in any capacity.

Consequently, as Trevelyan says of Deane's European recruits (except, of course, such men as du Portail):

> "These gentlemen, and their fellows, belonged to a species very easily recognised by students of the old Roman and the Elizabethan comedies. Pyrogopolineces and Thraso, Boabdil and Parolles, might be seen any fine afternoon of May or June, 1777, swaggering up and down Chestnut and Market Street in dingy white uniforms, amidst the growing aversion and indignation of Philadelphia. Almost all of them were loaded with debt, and some had left their own army in disgrace."

The general attitude of disgust—the feeling that these French commission-seekers are impostors or irresponsible adventurers with an axe to grind—appears in Charles Biddle's *Autobiography*. He happens to be nearby in South Carolina when la Fayette and his party have just come ashore from *La Victoire* (the ship la Fayette's bought and fitted out expressly for this expedition), and are staying at Major Benjamin Huger's house. Biddle says:

> "Morgan hearing that two French officers (La Fayette and de Kalb) had arrived, requested me, as I spoke a little French, to go with him and speak to them, but I had seen and heard so much of the French officers who came over to enter into the American service that I had conceived a very unfavourable opinion of them and told him that these were only barbers or tailors and would not go with him."

After barking at la Fayette and his companions, the next day (the 29th) Lovell writes William Whipple:

> ". . . In addition to the perplexities which I have before mentioned to you about French treaties made by Deane we have a fresh quantity from the arrival of 2 Major Generals (La Fayette and de Kalb) 2 Brigadiers, etc. . . ."

Since Deane's exceeded his instructions in promising commissions, almost promiscuously, one can readily understand Lovell's irritation, while regretting his outburst of ill-humour at la Fayette. When Lovell stages his hostile reception, it would seem that la Fayette's credentials have been "laid on the Table" unconsidered;

in any event, the Committee of Foreign Affairs can scarcely yet have seen Franklin's letter from France, in which he writes:

"The Marquis de la Fayette, a young nobleman of great family connections here and great wealth, is gone to America in a ship of his own, accompanied by some officers of distinction, in order to serve in our armies. He is exceedingly beloved, and everybody's good wishes attend him. We cannot but hope he may meet with such a reception as will make the country and his expedition agreeable to him. Those who censure it as imprudent in him, do, nevertheless, applaud his spirit; and we are satisfied that the civilities and respect that may be shown him will be serviceable to our affairs here, as pleasing not only to his powerful relations and the Court but to the whole French nation. He has left a beautiful young wife and for her sake, particularly, we hope that his bravery and ardent desire to distinguish himself will be a little restrained by the General's prudence, so as not to permit his being hazarded much, except on some important occasion."

La Fayette's not to be rebuffed by the hostile reception at the State House and by the lack of "civilities and respect" shown him. He at once addresses a communication to Congress in which he says:

"After the sacrifice I have made, I have the right to exact two favours: One is to serve at my own expense, the other is to serve at first as volunteer."

On the receipt of this, Congress have probably read la Fayette's credentials and also become aware of Franklin's letter.

Letters of Members of the Continental Congress, E. C. Burnett, ii, 430; Autobiography, Charles Biddle, 148.

Thursday, July 31—The young red-headed Marquis has had a turn of luck since his rude reception and dismissal last Monday. To-day, the wind's blowing from a different quarter. Congress make him a major-general; an unusual distinction for a mere boy. He won't be twenty till September.

The Journals of Congress record:

"Whereas, the marquis de la Fayette, out of his great zeal to the cause of liberty, in which the United States are engaged, has left his family and connexions, and, at his own expence, come over to offer his service to the United States, without pension or particular allowance, and is anxious to risque his life in our cause:

Resolved, That his service be accepted, and that, in consideration of his zeal, illustrious family and connexions, he have the rank and commission of major general in the army of the United States."

It would have caused a serious set-back to Franklin's diplomatic efforts in France if Congress hadn't done this.

Journals of Congress.

Sunday, August 24—About 10 o'clock this hot August morning the State House windows look down on a military parade that breaks Philadelphia's wonted Sunday calm and quiet. The Continental Army's on its way southward through the city; a few days hence will fight the Battle of the Brandywine. From their overnight camp near Nicetown the troops march down Front Street and continue up Chestnut to the Commons; thence they'll cross the Schuylkill by the floating bridge at the Middle Ferry.

All told, they're a sorry-looking lot, but evidently determined; they're "putting their best foot forward" to make as imposing a show as possible. Alexander Graydon—captured at Fort Washington and, after near a year's captivity in New York, allowed to come back and live at home on parole—stands at the Coffee House to watch the troops pass down Front Street, Washington and la Fayette at their head. Only a short time before, on his way through Morristown, he's said:

"I had been extremely anxious to see our army. Here it was, but I could see nothing which deserved the name." The sight recalls to him that "it had been humorously stated in the English prints, that upon a gentleman, who had been in America and seen our troops, being asked what was their uniform, he replied, 'In general it is blue and buff, but by this time it must be all buff!' The period for this unity of colour, however, had not yet arrived; though, from the motley shabby covering of the men, it was to be inferred that it was rapidly approaching. Even in General Wayne himself there was, in this particular, a considerable falling off. His quondam regimental, as colonel of the 4th battalion, was, I think, blue and white, in which he had been accustomed to appear with exemplary neatness; whereas he was now dressed in character for Macheath or Captain Gibbet, in a dingy red coat, with a black rusty cravat, and tarnished laced hat."

Now, as he sees the same army going through the city, Graydon thinks the impression made on the onlookers is presumably

"rather favourable than otherwise, . . . But it was very disproportioned to the zeal for liberty, which had been manifested the year before." But the troops, "though indifferently dressed, held well burnished arms, and carried them like soldiers, and looked, in short, as if they might have faced an equal number with a reasonable prospect of success."

La Fayette's comment on the shabby, nondescript aspect of the Continental Army's illuminating, but not more favourable:

"Eleven thousand men, but tolerably armed, and still worse clad, presented a singular spectacle. In this parti-coloured and often-naked state, the best dresses were hunting-shirts of brown linen. Their tactics were equally irregular. They were arranged without regard to size, except that the smallest men were in the front rank. With all this, there were good-looking soldiers conducted by zealous officers."

General Washington has a very definite purpose in marching the army through the city—to impress the citizens. On Saturday (the 23rd) from the Neshaminy camp, he's written John Hancock, President of Congress:

"I beg leave to inform you, that the army marched early this morning, and I expect, will encamp this Evening within Five or Six miles of Philadelphia. To-morrow morning it will move again, and I think to march It thro' the City, but without halting. I am induced to do this, from the opinion of Several of my officers and many Friends, in Philadelphia, that it may have some influence on the minds of the disaffected there, and those who are Dupes of their artifices and opinions." He says the army will enter the city "about seven o'Clock."

Saturday night Washington makes Stenton his headquarters and dines "on a Sheep they got of the Tenant & killed after they got there." The troops encamped near Stenton do "abundance of damage to the Tenant in the Night, destroyd his Corn, Potatoes &c."

The general orders for Sunday direct:

". . . The army is to march in one column through the city . . . going in at and marching down Front Street to Chestnut, and up Chestnut to the Common. A small halt is to be made about a mile this side of the city until the rear is clear up and the line in proper order."

General orders show what pains Washington's taking to have this display make a telling impression on the civilian mind. After directions about the exact order of the several divisions and their distances apart, the "ranks six paces asunder," the officers are

"strongly and earnestly enjoined. . . to see that the men carry their arms well and are made to appear as decent as circumstances will admit. It is expected that each officer, without exception, will keep his post in passing through the city, and under no pretense to leave it. And if any soldier shall dare quit his ranks, he shall receive thirty-nine lashes at the next halting-place afterwards. The field-officers of the day will prevent any of the men who are allotted to attend the waggons from slipping into the city. As the baggage will be but a little separated from the column, very few men will be sufficient to guard it, and the General wishes to have as many of them as are able to appear in the ranks in the line of march. The drums and fifes of each brigade are to be collected in the centre of it, and a time for the quick step played, but with such moderation that the men may step to it with ease, without dancing along or totally disregarding the music, which has been too often the case. The men are to be excused from carrying their camp-kettles. . . ."

To give this motley host "something of a uniform appearance," they wear "sprigs of green in their hats."

Memoirs of a Life, Chiefly Passed in Pennsylvania, Alexander Graydon (Edinburgh, 1822) 293, 294, 308; *Diary*, Sarah Logan Fisher; *Pennsylvania Gazette*, August 27, 1777; *Pennsylvania Evening Post*, August 28, 1777; *Itinerary of General Washington*, etc., William S. Baker, 84, 85; *Life of George Washington*, Washington Irving, iii, 138; *History of Philadelphia*, Ellis Paxson Oberholtzer, i, 261; *History of Philadelphia*, Scharf & Westcott, i, 343, 344.

Thursday, August 28—Congress in a stewing dither. Been struggling for weeks over Articles of Confederation; badly harassed about finances; and vastly uneasy about the British Army being in Maryland and marching towards Philadelphia. Besides, there's the agitation about "disaffected people"; on Tuesday, they've recommended the Supreme Executive Council to arrest all "suspected persons" and search all houses in the city for arms.

Now, this morning comes a letter from General Sullivan that's upset them still more. The General's letter, from Hanover in New Jersey, has enclosures of disquieting tenour; the one that raises all the storm, a trumped-up "plant" taken in captured baggage August 22nd, purporting to be a communication of August 19th from "Spanktown Yearly Meeting"—"Spanktown, a place scarcely known even as an inferior part of Rahway, which is a remote town on the east side of New Jersey"—where there's never been a Yearly Meeting!

Were the "Spanktown" paper genuine, it would be incriminating. General Sullivan fails to see he's being humbugged by a spurious document, contrived and planted by a trouble-maker;

sends it post-haste to Congress; Congress in alarm, already be-devilled by serious major worries, swallow "bait, hook and sinker" and resort to Proscription!

They have John Adams, William Duane and Richard Henry Lee draw up resolutions dealing with this newest headache. At 5, this troubled Thursday afternoon, Congress adopt the morning's resolutions and thereby *proscribe by name* some of Philadelphia's most respectable citizens.

Thus begins that episode known as the banishment of the "Virginia Exiles." In its long history as a legislative meeting-place, the Assembly Chamber—that Chamber in which the Declaration of Independence has been adopted and signed—has witnessed many foolish enactments prompted by political obduracy, jealousies and animosities, as well as many enactments inspired by wisdom and worthy motives. This act of proscription's one of the worst blunders ever committed within the State House, a deplorable folly that reflects no credit upon Congress, a blunder committed under stress of overwrought nerves and failure to comprehend the victims' attitude.

Wednesday, the 27th, in compliance with Tuesday's "recommendation" by Congress, the Supreme Executive Council ordered a search for arms in

"the Houses of all such of the 'inhabitants of the City of Philadelphia, who have not manifested their attachment to the American cause'"

by becoming Associators. They referred "to further consideration" Tuesday's "recommendation" to arrest "notoriously disaffected" persons and hold them secured

"till such time as the State shall think they may be released without injury to the common cause."

To-day's frenzied communication from Congress gets no mention in the Council minutes until Sunday, August 31st.

On Sunday morning, (the 31st) the Supreme Executive Council, sitting in the Council Chamber at the State House, act on the Thursday message "earnestly" recommending the Council

(1) "forthwith to apprehend and secure the persons of Joshua Fisher, Abel James, James Pemberton, Henry Drinker, Israel Pemberton, John James, Samuel Pleasants, Thomas Wharton, Sen., ~~Joseph Pemberton, James Fisher~~, Thomas Fisher, son of Joshua, ~~Henry Lisle~~ and Samuel Fisher, son of Joshua, together with such papers in their possession as may be of a political nature." And

because they fear these persons may "maintain correspondence and connection highly prejudicial to the public safety, not only in this State but in the respective states of America," Congress urge the Council (2) to arrest all persons of generally unfriendly conduct, "Quakers and others," to be "confined in such places and treated in such manner, as shall be consistent with their respective characters and the security of their persons."

This is outright, arbitrary Proscription. The justification for it? *Suspicion!*

To their Sunday morning session, Council have summoned David Rittenhouse, Colonel William Bradford, Colonel Sharp Delany and Captain Charles Willson Peale. To them, in confidence, Council show Thursday's Congressional resolutions; ask their help in making "a List of persons dangerous to the State, & who ought to be arrested"; also, "a list of Gentlemen proper" to make the arrests.

In view of the "menace" to the State from Quakers, in view also of the threatened invasion of the city by the British Army, Council then resolve,

"That a suitable number of the friends to the Public cause be authorised to seize & Secure the Persons of" all those previously named by Congress, and also thirty-one others—both Quakers and non-Quakers—among them Doctor Adam Kuhn, Phineas Bond, junior, Provost Smith, the Reverend Thomas Coombe and Thomas Pike, the dancing master. Since the Council "wish to treat Men of reputation with as much tenderness as the Security of the Persons & Papers will admit," they "desire that if the persons whose names in the list are marked with a Cross x thus, offer to you, by promise in writing, to remain in their Dwellings, ready to appear on the demand of Council, & meanwhile to refrain from doing any thing injurious to the United Free States of North America, by Speaking, Writing or otherwise, & from giving intelligence to the Commander in Chief of the British Forces, or any other Person whatever, concerning public Affairs, you dismiss from further confinement of their Persons"; refusers, "together with the others to whose names the said mark is not prefixed," are to be confined "in some convenient place under a Guard with which the Town Major, Colo. Nichola, will supply you. The Free Masons' Lodge may be perhaps procured. It would serve as well as any other place for this purpose. You may perceive that Council would not without necessity commit many of the persons to the Common Gaol, nor even to the State Prison."

Although Thomas Wharton, junior, President of the Council, is present at this Sunday session, George Bryan, Vice-President,

signs the order of proscription and arrest. One can easily understand Thomas Wharton's reluctance to sign an order for the
seizure of his cousin, Thomas Wharton, senior (only a few years
older than himself), several kinsmen, and a number of friends and
acquaintance. George Bryan has no such qualms. He's an Irish
Presbyterian and cordially dislikes the Quakers. David Rittenhouse and Charles Willson Peale have helped make the list, and
it's not unreasonable to infer that Timothy Matlack, Secretary of
the Council, has also had something to say; he's not noted for
holding his peace on such occasions.

The proscription list rather noticeably includes the names of
those who've been outspoken in condemning the State "Constitution of 1776"—such men as Provost Smith. Two of the "proscrib-
ers," David Rittenhouse and Charles Willson Peale—three, if we
count Timothy Matlack—are exigent members of that "Whig
Society" that figured so conspicuously, a little over a year ago, in
engineering and forcing through that iniquitous instrument;
they've been ardent "Constitutionalists" ever since. And George
Bryan, though not a member of the 1776 Constitutional Convention, is credited with being the chief author. Under the circumstances, one's inclined to suspect that political rancour and
personal animosity were not altogether set aside in making the
list. In this period of high feeling and tense nerves, there's little
doubt that acts ascribed to impetuous "patriotism" sometimes
mask personal grudges gratified with impunity.

Congress, deceived and alarmed by the "Spanktown" hoax, and
most of them totally ignorant of Quaker psychology, are scarcely
to blame for what is in reality an ill-advised act done in the heat
of harrowing anxiety and excitement.

Quakers, as well as any else, are entitled to their political convictions. On July 6th, 1775, Congress declared to the people:
"Our forefathers, inhabitants of Great Britain, left their native
land to seek on these shores a residence for civil and religious freedom, at the expense of their blood, at the hazard of their fortunes,
without the least charge to the country from whence they removed.
Lest this declaration should disquiet the minds of our friends
and fellow subjects in any part of the empire, we assure them that
we mean not to dissolve that union which has so long and so happily subsisted between us, and which we sincerely wish to see restored." Two days afterwards, Congress thus addressed the King:
"Attached to your Majesty's person, family, and government, with

all the devotion that principle and affection can inspire, connected with Great Britain by the strongest ties that can unite societies, and deploring every event that tends in any degree to weaken them, we solemnly assure your Majesty that we not only most ardently desire the former harmony between her and these Colonies may be restored, but that a concord may be established between them upon so firm a basis as to perpetuate its blessings uninterrupted by any future dissensions, to succeeding generations in both countries. . . ."

With these declarations the Quakers are in full accord. They're quite ready to resist strenuously the objectionable measures of the British Ministry. If others, in resisting, wish to bear arms, Quakers will not oppose them beyond "bearing testimony" against force; their own resistance must needs be passive. Still abiding in the spirit of the foregoing declarations, now that the conflict has passed beyond reconciliation into irrevocable revolution, the Quakers cannot conscientiously approve the concept that a *de facto* régime may ultimately become a *de jure* régime; or, at any rate, they're not yet convinced that such a point of justification has actually been reached in the course of events. They consequently wish to draw into their shells and keep clear of all external concern; their "testimonies" all enjoin Friends to keep aloof from the contest. They're non-combatants on religious principle; politically they've been neutralised. This attitude Congress, as a body, can't understand.

Tuesday, September 2nd, the Council's "proper persons" visit the proscribed; some accept the "stay-at-home-and-shut-up" conditions offered, but most of the Quakers, standing on their legal rights, refuse and are marched off to confinement in the Masonic Lodge. Some of the arresting parties are polite to the accused; some are rough and abusive. Charles Willson Peale and his "file of musketeers" seize John Pemberton, break into his desk and rifle it of "as many papers as could be found relative to the Quaker meetings." No warrants are shown; those thrust into confinement are not told of any specific "crime" with which they're charged.

Three of the "culprits" escape imprisonment till Wednesday—Israel Pemberton, John Hunt and Samuel Pleasants. Then a detail of soldiers appears at Israel's home in Germantown. To their bewilderment, Israel declares he's a

"free man and will not submit to arrest without being shown a warrant prescribing it. The perplexed soldiers retire apologetically to return later with a warrant, just as Samuel Pleasants and John Hunt enter the house exclaiming that soldiers have entered the latter's house and broken into his desk. This is just what Israel needs to strengthen his next move as he summarily proceeds to lecture the now thoroughly intimidated soldiers on the rights of freemen. He then tells them that he will insist upon keeping the warrant, and in the midst of their confusion, he advises them to consult upon the matter, whereupon they sheepishly withdraw."

Straightway Pemberton, Hunt and Pleasants draught a remonstrance to the Council, declaring their arrest arbitrary and unconstitutional. Accompanied by a lawyer, they go to the State House and send in their paper to the Council; the Council accept it, but refuse to let them into the Council Chamber or give them a hearing. Instead, they're seized and sent off to the Masonic Lodge with the rest.

Meanwhile, the prisoners in the Lodge have already sent a spirited remonstrance to the Council, and a like one to Congress, at the same time warning that august body that the "Liberty, Property, and Character, of every Freeman in *America,* is, or may be endangered" by such procedure; they add, they can't understand why Congress haven't prescribed a hearing, "especially inasmuch as few of them know any of the victims of their resolutions." Furthermore, they say Congress have acted on the "reports of personal and old political enemies," availing themselves of a chance for revenge. Israel Pemberton writes several Members of Congress asking them to intercede in behalf of the proscribed, and reverse the decision to pack them all off to Virginia.

Thereupon, Congress debate the matter again, much to the irritation of Henry Laurens and those who, like him, don't understand the Quakers. On September 5th, Laurens writes about the waste of

"five hours debating one silly point whether certain persons chiefly Quakers . . . should have a hearing in their own defence. the hearing which they aim at is not intended, but a hearing *they may have,* if they will accept the mode prescribed. Congress have recommended to the Executive Council to hear what they have to allege *'for removing Suspicion that they are Enemies to the Independence of the United States.'* "

When Congress make this recommendation, the Council say they've "not time to attend to that business"; they intimate the job's up to Congress. Congress answer

"That it would be improper for Congress to enter into any hearing of the Remonstrants or other Prisoners in the Masons' Lodge, they being inhabitants of Pennsylvania, and therefore, as the Council decline giving them a hearing. . ." it is recommended "to said Council, to order the immediate departure of such of the said Prisoners as yet refuse to swear or affirm allegiance to the State of Pennsylvania, to Stanton in Virginia."

After Congress and Council thus mutually "pass the buck," Council order the prisoners sent to Virginia and say their own action in arresting them

"upon suspicions arising from their general behaviour," and expelling them from the State, "may be abundantly justified by the conduct of the freest Nations & the authority of most judicious Civilians."

This admission of *arrest on suspicion* buttresses Pemberton's charge that the Quakers' imprisonment is inspired by "resolutions of our personal enemies."

Besides the communications addressed to Congress and Council, the proscribed prisoners in the Masonic Lodge have a vigorous protest to the citizens printed and distributed throughout the city. As might be expected, this creates a sensation (even amidst the confusion of imminent invasion) and enlists public sympathy for the persecuted. "Many of the warmest Whigs think this [the arrest and banishment] an instance of unjustifiable oppression."

Those about to be exiled are given one day at home to settle their affairs; then, on September 11th, they leave for Virginia, many riding in their own carriages. Because of the British forces to the south, they have to take a roundabout course, going out the Ridge to Pottstown and Reading. As they depart, they can hear the distant sound of cannon at the Battle of the Brandywine. They drive

"through third street to the upper part of the city and from thence to the falls of the Schuylkill, a spectacle to the people; who by their countenances sufficiently tho' silently expressed the grief they felt on this extraordinary occasion, nor were any marks of approbation of our hard sentence & suffering given except by a very few of the lower class, until we had crossed Vine Street, where a rabble, consisting for the most part of boys. . . threw stones at one or two of the hindermost carriages."

Before leaving the city, Israel Pemberton and eight others apply to Chief Justice McKean for writs of *habeas corpus*. The Chief Justice issues the writs and sends them to the prisoners at Pottsgrove (now Pottstown). The rest of the exiles apply for writs when they reach Reading. The same day, one of the officers in charge of them sets off for Philadelphia "to enquire whether or not they should respect the writs or other acts by the Chief Justice"! At this, the Assembly prevent release under bail and a legal hearing "by a law to suspend the Habeas Corpus act; thereby making a law, *ex post facto* & *pendente lite;* the very extreme of Tyranny."

It soon becomes evident to Congress and the rest of the "powers that be" that the banishment—quite apart from being ill-advised and legally unjustifiable—has been useless. It's served no particular purpose (save momentary gratification of spite and waspish vindictiveness) and has engendered much needless bitterness. It certainly hasn't helped to conciliate the very numerous "neutrals" and other "disaffected" portions of the population—surely a desideratum in the precarious state of the military outlook.

After several months' sojourn at Winchester, during which two of the party die, the "Virginia Exiles" are allowed to come home, with the full approbation of Washington and the wiser heads; they re-enter the city during the British Occupation. The story (a long one) after the beginning of their banishment has no connection with the State House; up to that point, however, the record of this tragic blunder's intimately associated with State House annals and must be included in that venerable building's story.

By way of sequel to the exile incident, it may add a touch of human interest to mention an encounter, nearly two years later (March 6th, 1779, to be exact), between one of the persecutors of 1777 and one of the "Exiles"—Timothy Matlack and "Tho's Fisher, son of Joshua." Timothy, though reared a Quaker, finds Friends' discipline irksome and has been read out of Meeting; too "fond of convivial company" and sporting life, the Quakers have disowned him in 1765 for "frequenting company in such manner as to neglect business whereby he contracted debts, failed and was unable to satisfy the claims of his creditors." (It's said that when Timothy's in gaol for debt, either Israel Pemberton, or some other nameless benefactor comes to his rescue with the sum necessary to liberate him.) However, notwithstanding Timothy's "disownment" by Friends, Mrs. Matlack and young Timothy have been in good odour in Meeting until now, when Timothy *fils* has incurred censure for "departure from Friends' principles." Perhaps it's carrying a sword, like *père;* dereliction not specified. At any rate, Timothy *fils* becomes the subject of a "concern."

Here Sarah Logan Fisher's *Diary* takes up the story:

". . . upon coming Home found my Tommy unwell, & he informed me that John James & him by appointment of the Monthly Meeting had been to wait on Timothy Matlocks Son to deal with him for his departure from Friends principles, & upon his Fathers entering the Room he appeared to be in a passion, & enquired their Business. He insulted them by calling them names and ordered them to leave the House, which they did, but he stepping out quick before them into the Entry, struck my Tommy with a large Hicory Stick on his head, then followed them out of the House, repeating his Blows with all his might for a considerable distance. My dear Tommy was favoured with great calmness that he bore this cruel insult with all the meekness of a true Christian, pitying the Man who had a Heart capable of such an action—after bathing my dear creatures bruises with Tutlingtons Balsam & Brandy, he was Bled, & seemed brave considering, & in a very sweet calm state of mind, being made willing in a great degree to suffer for the cause & Testimony of Truth. . . ."

One can well understand T.M. *père* appearing "to be in a passion" at having his house invaded by an officious "concern" poking their noses into what he considers "none of their damned business." At the same time, one can't help regretting that "Tho's Fisher, son of Joshua," after showing a proper measure of true Christian "meekness," doesn't suddenly face round and soundly wallop T.M. A good trouncing would doubtless benefit T.M's spiritual attitude and might, perhaps, improve his manners.

Journals of Congress; Colonial Records, xi, 279-300; *Exiles in Virginia,* Thomas Gilpin, *passim; Israel Pemberton, King of the Quakers,* Theodore Thayer, 214-223; *Letters of Members of the Continental Congress,* E. C. Burnett, ii, 476, 477, 486, 487; *Pemberton Papers,* xxi, xxx, in *MS.S Collection,* Historical Society of Pennsylvania; *Diary* of Sarah Logan Fisher; *Dictionary of American Biography; Diary* of James Allen, in *Pennsylvania Magazine of History and Biography,* ix, 292, 293; *Pennsylvania Archives,* 1st Series, iv, 554, 555, 593, 596; *Pennsylvania Gazette,* September 10, 1777.

Friday; September 19—Last night Congress adjourned to 10 o'clock this morning. This morning only empty chairs in the Chamber; Congress fled during the night!

Sunday, the 14th, Congress resolved,

"That if Congress shall be obliged to remove from Philadelphia, Lancaster shall be the place at which they shall meet."

The same day John Adams writes Mrs. Adams:

"Mr. Howe's army is at Chester, about fifteen miles from this town . . . How much longer Congress will stay is uncertain. I hope we shall not move until the last necessity, that is, until. . . certain Mr. Howe will get the city."

Though the city's likely to fall to Howe at any moment, Congress stick doggedly to their job (that is, a good many of them do), hoping "this plaguy fellow of an How does not disturb us," and intent on "Confederation and finances." Eliphalet Dyer adds, "we are now very Sulky and determined not to move for him if we can help it. . . you know we Scorn to fly."

The 16th, Henry Laurens writes:

"Congress. . . think it necessary to prepare for adjourning to Lancaster about 66 Miles West. perhaps before sunrise tomorrow I shall be on my journey some of us are already gone. I will continue here as long as most of the Company, but. . . will not stay the very last man." The 18th, still in Philadelphia, he writes: "fright has driven some great Men to do precipitantly what I strongly urged as necessary to do cooly and deliberately as soon as we learned of Mr. Howe's landing at Elk . . . Some who smiled at the proposition are gone in a hurry, embarrassed—others are now on the wing. we keep enough to make a Congress and thats all. . . . I sent my baggage forward, some days ago and can easily transport myself."

For September 19th, John Adams's *Diary* says:

"At three this morning, was waked by Mr. Lovel, and told . . . the members of Congress were gone, some of them, a little after midnight; that there was a letter from Mr. Hamilton, aid-de-camp to the General, informing that the enemy were in possession of the ford and the boats, and had it in their power to be in Philadelphia before morning, and that, if Congress was not removed, they had not a moment to lose. Mr. Marchant and myself arose, sent for our horses, and, after collecting our things, rode off after the others. Breakfasted at Bristol. . . ."

Sarah Logan Fisher's *Diary*, for September 21st, gives the civilian and Loyalist side of the picture:

". . . two Nights ago the City was alarmed about two oClock, with a great knocking at peoples Doors & desiring them to get up, that the English had crossed the Swedes ford at 11 oClock & would presently be in the City. Had I not had my Spirit too much depressed with the absence of my dear Companion [her husband's one of the "Virginia Exiles"], the scene would really have diverted me, Waggons rattling, Horses Galoping. Women running, Children Crying, Delagates flying, & all together the greatest consternation fright & terror that can be imagined, some of our Neighbours took their flight before Day & I belive all the Congress mov'd off before 5 oClock, but behold when Morning came, it prov'd a false alarm. . . thus the guilty fly when none pursue."

Not all Members of Congress "mov'd off before 5 oClock" or, if they did, didn't stay. September 23rd, James Lovell (the same that barked at la Fayette in July) writes from Philadelphia:

"I was averse to going at first and after breakfasting at Bristol, Curiosity and some Interest brought me back to dine the same day." Lovell's "Curiosity and Interest" keep him even longer in the city; October 5th, he writes from York, "the Congress left Philada. the 19th, at 2 oClock A.M. I returned from Bristol to the Capital to dine, and tarried till the 25th; when, the Enemy being within a mile and without any opposing Troops in the City, I slipt into the Jersies. It was lucky I had a young Lady to gallant thither; for 3 or 4 Officers who left Philada. before me were taken in the Franckfort Road."

Journals of Congress; Letters of Members of the Continental Congress, E. C. Burnett, ii, 485, 492, 495, 497, 498, 500, 508; Sarah Logan Fisher's *Diary.*

Tuesday, October 7—Since the Battle of Germantown last Saturday, the British have used the State House as an hospital. They laid the wounded American prisoners on the floor. Some had terrible bayonet wounds. Naturally, they had to wait for treatment until the British surgeons had dressed their own wounded. The floors badly blood-stained; the place kept none too clean.

Soon after the wounded Americans were brought in,

"the streets were filled with the women of the city carrying up every kind of refreshments. . . with lint and linen and lights" for them. "A British officer stopped one of these women. . . and not ill-naturedly. . . reproved her for so amply supplying the rebels, whilst nothing was carried to the British hospitals. 'Oh, sir,' replied she, 'it is in your power fully to provide for them; but we cannot see our poor countrymen suffer, and not do something for them.'"

To-day, the British make the State House a gaol as well as an hospital. Some captured American officers, not wounded, they put in the rooms upstairs, closely guarded. These new arrivals are crowded and uncomfortable; nor have they enough to eat.

Colonel Persifor Frazer (afterwards General Frazer) is one of the officers now confined at the State House along with others taken either at the Battle of Germantown, or previously. Colonel Frazer's been taken September 16th while on scouting duty after the Battle of the Brandywine. Sunday, September 28th, he signs his parole at Germantown; then he's brought to the city. His own account, from the day of his capture, says:

"During the. . . march from the White Horse to Germantown, we were exposed to the insults of the army twice a day. In the morning the prisoners were drawn up near the road on which the troops were to march," remained till all had passed, "and then fell in to the rear. In the evening we passed from the rear to the headquarters, near the front, at which times every kind of abusive language was made use of by the troops as we passed, without the least check from the officers.

It had been frequently said by an officer of the first rank that when we came to the City we should be admitted to our parole. On our arrival there on the 30th of September I was informed by the Provost Marshall that we were to go to such quarters as he chose, and remain there till further orders, our parole having been previously signed at Germantown.

Thus we remained till the 7th of October, when the Commissioner of Prisoners . . . informed us. . . he had orders to take us to the State House. . . to be kept in close confinement. The reason given us for this was that, there being so large a number of prisoners, it might be prejudicial to their interests to have us at liberty.

Many of us were six days without having any provisions sent to us, and for many weeks after our allowance did not exceed from four to six ounces of salt pork and about half a pound of ordinary biscuit per day. Had it not been for the supplies sent by the citizens we must have perished. We remonstrated, but were told we had the same allowance as their own troops when on board transports. We were told to purchase what we had need of in the City. Upon Mr. Ferguson [the husband of Elizabeth Graeme, of Graeme Park] being appointed Commissary, our allowance was honestly dealt out for a considerable time. . . .

At the first of our confinement our acquaintance were suffered to visit us, but that and every other privilege was, under various pretexts, withheld from us except in some instances where particular officers of more humanity than the rest had the guard.

. . . Sentries were placed in each of the rooms, who often picked our pockets and stole our clothes while we slept. Letters sent to us were withheld, and often considerable sums of money.

The persons who brought us our victuals were treated with abusive language and women with indecent behaviour, and kept waiting at the outside door for a long time in bad weather. . . . The soldiers also stole food and clothing they were entrusted with to deliver.

We were refused the liberty of going from one room to another. The windows were nailed down, though the smoke from a stove below stairs in the guard room, owing to the badness of the chimneys, has, for many days, been almost intolerable.

There were forty of us in the two upper rooms in the State House, which served for every purpose of kitchen and bedchamber. . . ."

Colonel Frazer finally escapes, but not without an exciting experience. His narrative continues:

"About the latter part of December we were informed that we were about to be removed to the new gaol [at Sixth and Walnut Streets]. As we had been told by the physician who attended the prisoners that a very malignant fever raged among them, and as we frequently saw six or eight bodies taken out to be buried in a day [from the south windows of the State House they could plainly see the Gaol and the Potters' Field—now Washington Square], we thought it our duty to complain to General Howe of this inhuman order. We were answered that the General intended. . . to put us in a more comfortable situation. . . and. . . would order the physician to examine the state of the gaol and report theron.

The doctor reported. . . no infectious disorder existed there, and consequently we were desired to hold ourselves in readiness for removal, with promises that the rooms. . . should be cleansed in the best manner, and everything made as agreeable. . . as possible, which was neglected in almost every particular. One hundred and eighty of the private soldiers were sick when we were sent to this place, which, together with the cause, occasioned such a. . . ."

Thus abruptly ends the narrative—possibly a rough draught of what he writes as justification of his escape. Colonel Frazer afterwards successfully maintains before a Court of Enquiry that the British administration—by confining officers in gaol—has itself violated parole terms, and thereby absolves imprisoned officers from parole obligations. This decision the British admit.

Complaints of insufficient food generally date from the period while the Delaware's still blocked to British shipping and the whole British Army's on uncomfortably short rations. That the private soldiers imprisoned under the inhuman Provost Marshal Cunningham are cruelly treated and starved, there can be no doubt—testimony's too abundant and damning. Several of them that die in the State House Yard have

"pieces of Bark, Wood, Clay & Stones in their mouths, which the ravings of hunger had caused them to take in for food in the last Agonies of Life!" and "one of these poor unhappy men, drove to the last extreem by the rage of hunger, eat his own fingers up to the first joint from the hand, before he died." Others perish "with grass in their mouths."

Amongst the manifold associations that throng the State House and State House Yard, hovering like a grisly shadow in the background will always be the memory of starving men's anguish and despair.

Returning to Colonel Frazer—his granddaughter relates that "during the winter of 1777-78, gaol-fever broke out among the American prisoners, and the prisoners were taken out of the gaol and lodged in different parts of the City. Colonel Frazer, Major Harper and Colonel Hannum. . . were lodged at the Golden Swan tavern . . . Notwithstanding they had given their parole, the doors of their sitting-room and bedrooms were kept locked, their windows barred, and a guard was placed over them. They considered. . . these restrictions. . . indefensible by military law, and felt themselves. . . at liberty to escape if they could. On St. Patrick's Day . . . when the Guard who were Irishmen got patriotically drunk, they escaped from their rooms, and clambering over a stone wall in the rear of the house went, some to the house of Mr. Frazer, . . . a distant relative of Colonel Frazer, . . . and other to the house of Mr. Blackstone, who lived in the same neighbourhood.

Vigorous efforts were made to find the escaped prisoners; all the avenues leading from the City were closely watched, and many of the houses searched." Once, "when some of the party were hidden in a deep closet behind shelves, on which china was so arranged as to conceal them, the house was entered and the closet searched without discovering the fugitives.

Their escape was aided by the indiscretion of some young British officers, who, calling on a lady of their acquaintance immediately after the gaol delivery, told them of it, which news they received with apparent surprise. The officers said . . . the prisoners . . . could not get out of the City, and proceeded to speak of the plans for their recapture. Being encouraged, they talked freely, and as the escaped prisoners knew what traps were set for them, they took good care not to spring them.

They remained in the City . . . till the ardour of the chase had somewhat abated, when Mr. Blackstone procured a boat on which they crossed the Delaware, passing through the British fleet, and landed in New Jersey, and in a short time rejoined the army."

History of Philadelphia, Thompson Westcott, ch. cclvi; *Pennsylvania Magazine of History and Biography*, xxxi, 131; xxi, 309; xxii, 502; *The Collateral Ancestry of Stephen Harris and of Marianna Smith*, Joseph S.

Harris, privately printed at Philadelphia, 1908, pp. 44 *et seq.; General Persifor Frazer; A Memoir Compiled Principally from his own Papers,* by his great-grandson, Persifor Frazer, Philadelphia, 1907, pp. 162 *et seq.*

Thursday, October 9—So far, the British gaolers at the State House occasionally let relatives and friends of the imprisoned officers come to see them. If their friends weren't allowed to bring them food, the officers would have little enough to eat, and that little in bad condition. The bread's mouldy and disgusting—not fit to touch, let alone eat.

To-day, Mrs. Frazer comes to see the Colonel. Yesterday she rode in from their home at Thornbury, in Chester County. A friend and neighbour, Mrs. Gibbons, came with her, their horses laden with as much food as they could carry in saddlebags and sundry parcels fastened to the saddles. Mrs. Frazer had a pass from General Washington; that let them through the American lines. The British were glad enough to see food from any source coming into the city—the "starving time," before British shipping can reach Philadelphia's wharves, is serious.

Through the kindness of a nameless friend—Mrs. Frazer never does discover to whom she's indebted—and after anxious waiting, she's permitted to see her husband in the State House. Colonel Frazer's written General Washington a letter about the treatment the American officers suffer, calling especial attention to the bad and insufficient food.

Mrs. Frazer's own account (dictated to her granddaughter) tells the rest:

"Your Grandfather asked me if I could take a paper. . . addressed to General Washington and signed by the officers (and men, too, I believe) describing their condition; and some of the bread. . . given them; and have them both shown to General Washington. . . then. . . at White Marsh. This I undertook to do.

In the morning after seeing Colonel Frazer we mounted and turned our horses' heads towards home. At the Ferry there were persons. . . to search all those who left the City by that road, and Mrs. Gibbons and I were shown into a room where two women came forward to undress us.

She [Mrs. Gibbons] gave full employment to them both, declaring . . . they should not touch her. I had ripped the quilting of my petticoat, putting in the paper between the lining and outside, and had sewed pieces of the bread all round inside the hem, and did not feel very comfortable at the thought of undergoing a search.

Mrs. Gibbons kicked and slapped, and fought and scolded, giving them a great deal of trouble, and making them believe she had something to fight for tho' she had nothing. They took off her shoes and stockings and undressed her entirely, greatly provoked that they had their trouble for their pains. I was very quiet. When they turned to me they performed their office slightly saying this one has nothing to be afraid of or she would not take it so quietly. After examining our saddles we were allowed to go on our way.

Tho' I had kept my composure I was very far from feeling unconcerned. I tho't of my little children at home without Father or Mother if I should be detained, I thought of the business at home with no one to attend to it, and what would become of our living, but most of all I thought of the poor prisoners if their efforts for relief should be discovered and frustrated: . . . I took a very long breath when we were safely over the River.

It was afternoon before I reached home; I had something to eat, changed my dress, had a fresh horse saddled and set out for White Marsh. It was dark and raining when I came to the Swedes' Ford [the crossing at what is now Norristown]. . . .

There was a large house not far from the ford. . . I rode up to it to ask for some one to go with me across the River . . . It seemed to be full of Soldiers drinking and swearing, and carousing, and I was afraid to call, and rode down again to the River; here all was dark, and raining, and blowing, the River rushing and rising, and I was afraid to venture through a Ford I was not used to. After sitting awhile. . . I determined to return to the house. The Soldiers were some of our own, and seeing a man at the door I asked him if he would request the commanding officer. . . to come to me. This he did and when the Officer came he proved to be a gentleman I knew. He ordered his horse to be saddled and crossed the river with me keeping hold of my rein; the current was very strong, the River rising and the water above the saddle girth.

I saw General Washington. . . next morning. . . I gave him the paper and the bread; he seemed much moved at the condition of the prisoners, and after asking some questions. . . He sent a gentleman with me to see me safely across the River.

General Washington immediately had communication with Howe respecting the treatment of American prisoners in Philadelphia and their condition was improved, tho' it never was what it ought to have been."

Colonel Frazer's letter to Washington occasions a re-opening of negotiations with Howe, ultimately successful

"in renewing the cartel for the exchange of prisoners, and in effecting the release of Gen. Charles Lee on whose account ex-

changes had been abruptly stopped for nearly a year, *i.e.* since
Gen. Howe, upon Lee's capture at Basking Ridge, Dec. 13, 1776,
had refused to exchange him on the ground that he was a deserter."

Pennsylvania Magazine of History and Biography, xxxi, 131; *The Collateral
Ancestry of Stephen Harris and of Marianna Smith*, Joseph S. Harris,
privately printed at Philadelphia, 1908; *General Persifor Frazer; A Memoir
Compiled Principally from his own Papers*, by his great-grandson, Persi-
for Frazer, Philadelphia, 1907; *Portrait of a Colonial City*, Eberlein and
Hubbard, 197-199.

1778

Thursday, June 18—This morning the last of the British troops leave the city. Almost treading on their heels, the Americans come in and take possession again. The city's physically in a deplorable condition; damage and dirt everywhere. The whole State House and its surroundings are in a filthy, sorry mess. It will take time and a lot of hard work to set things to rights again.

Civilians who've stayed in the city throughout the British Army's sojourn, view the evacuation with varied feelings. Some are jubilant; some are regretful, like Sarah Logan Fisher, who writes in her *Diary*:

"This morning about 6 the Grenadiers & Light Infantry left us, & in less than a Quarter of an Hour the Americans were in the City. Judge O any impartial person, what were my feelings at this time."

For most of the Quakers and for "neutrals" of Loyalist convictions, the return of the radical or "furious" Whigs means a renewal of vexations and persecutions.

John Maxwell Nesbitt, a Philadelphia shipping-merchant, Treasurer of the Pennsylvania Council of Safety and active collaborator with Robert Morris, writes a friend on July 4th:

"Mr. Morris & myself wth some other of our acquaintance got in here the 18th of June a few hours after the Enemy left this place ... my house I found in a wretch'd Condition—not fit to live in & am getting it cleaned &ca.

The Stores back are in a great measure destroy'd & everything left in & about the House gone, a few chairs & a couple of Tables excepted ...

The Town exceedingly Dirty & disagreeable, stinks Intolerably, I hope it will soon be clean'd; I shall be absent ten days by the time I return I hope it will be better, it's by no means agreeable at present & I can assure you, you are at no loss by being absent."

A little later, Josiah Bartlett, of New Hampshire, writes that "some of the genteel Houses were used for Stables and Holes cut in the Parlor floors & their Dung shoveled into the Cellars"; he deplores the shocking plight of the State House, "the inside torn much to pieces," making it an unfit place for Congress to meet in on their return from York.

Nesbitt Letter, MS.S Collection, Historical Society of Pennsylvania; *Dic-*

tionary of American Biography; Letters of Members of the Continental Congress, E. C. Burnett, iii, 329, 340; *Diary* of Sarah Logan Fisher.

Thursday, July 2—Although Congress are expected to assemble to-day at the State House for their first meeting since the adjournment from York, comparatively few of the Members have returned to the city. Henry Laurens, the President, and a handful of Members attend at the hour appointed but soon go away. There aren't enough to make a quorum.

Thomas McKean's one of those who turn up and, in a letter several days later, mentions what appears to be the only official recognition of the reassembling of Congress. He says:

"On Thursday last [July 2nd] Congress met at the State House, when 13 cannon were discharged on Market street wharff . . ."

The State House is still in "a most filthy and sordid situation," and the process of "Cleansing & repairing" hasn't advanced very far.

Letters of Members of the Continental Congress, E. C. Burnett, iii, 321, 329, 340; *Journals of Congress.*

Saturday, July 4—To-day, just as they did yesterday, the President of Congress and a few Members attend at the State House, but stay only a little while; still no quorum.

In spite of the generally disorganised condition of the city since the recent British evacuation, there's some disposition to celebrate the second anniversary of the adoption of the Declaration of Independence. However, there's little official encouragement to indulge in festivity. In the morning, the *Pennsylvania Packet* publishes a notice saying Congress don't expect the people to illuminate their houses in the evening. The Executive Council also publish a communication of like purport; they give as reasons the excessive heat of the weather and the present scarcity of candles.

All the same, the Members of Congress who are in town, bored with waiting for a quorum, have themselves a bit of jollification in the shape of a dinner. In a letter, the following week, Thomas McKean says:

"Saturday the Anniversary of Independence was celebrated at the new Tavern, where there was an elegant entertainment, and a fine band of musick, the firing of a vast number of cannon proved that there was no want of powder . . ."

And Samuel Holten records in his *Diary*:

"It being the anniversary of Independence, the Congress dined together at the City tavern and a number of the Council of this State, several Gen. officers and other Gentlemen of Distinction and while we were dining there was an Agreeable band of Musick and we had a very elegant dinner."

> *Letters of Members of the Continental Congress*, E. C. Burnett, iii, 320, 321; *Pennsylvania Packet*, July 4, 1778; also July 6th Supplement to the *Pennsylvania Packet*.

Thursday, July 9—Ever since last Thursday (the 2nd), Mr. Laurens and a few Members of Congress have been coming to the State House, then going away as soon as they could. No quorum, most of the time, and the State House not a pleasant place to be in just now. Day before yesterday there was a quorum, but the Members stayed only long enough to transact the most pressing business, holding their noses and brushing away swarms of flies. Yesterday and to-day conditions have been even more revolting, were that possible—the stench hellish, the flies innumerable.

To-day, the urgent matter that compels Congress to stick it out —as long as they can stand the almost insupportable atmosphere— is signing the Articles of Confederation. The *Journals* record:

"The ratification of the articles of confederation, engrossed on a roll of parchment, being laid before Congress, was examined, and . . . ~~the states called upon to sign, beginning with New Hampshire, and~~ the same was signed, on the part and in behalf of their respective states, by all the delegates present, except the delegates from the states of New Jersey, Delaware and Maryland, who informed Congress they were not authorised to sign."

At the end of the day's minutes is the brief entry:

"Adjourned to 9 o'clock to Morrow to meet in the College Hall." Congress are being literally stunk out of the State House!

Festering garbage, dead human bodies and the carcasses of several horses, all thrown together into an open pit, under a blistering July sun do not exhale "odours of Araby the blest." The appalling stench therefrom is one of the "exigencies" that have occasionally compelled Congress to meet elsewhere than at the State House. If the *Journals* are silent about the cause of removal to College Hall, Henry Laurens is not. In a letter to Rawlins Lowndes (July 15th), Laurens writes of "the offensiveness of the air in and around the State House, which the Enemy had made an Hospital and left it in a condition disgraceful to the Character of civility. Particularly they had opened a large square pit near the House, a receptacle for filth, into which they had also cast dead horses and the bodies of men who by the mercy of death had escaped from their further cruelties. I cannot proceed to a new subject before I add a curse on their savage practices."

In the same Independence Chamber of the State House, the Articles of Confederation were first reported by a Committee, July 12th, 1776. Since then, they've been frequently under debate— a polite way of saying they've been the subject of prolonged bitter and stubborn wrangling. Now, at last, after two years lacking three days, ten States have ratified and signed them. By an hair's breadth they've missed being signed in the College Hall instead of at the State House, their birthplace.

When Maryland completes the ratification in March, 1781, these Articles represent "the entire progress of the country towards a solid union during the five years of experience of war and weakness and inefficiency of the government." Small wonder the need of a stronger union is more and more keenly felt until the framing of the Federal Constitution in 1787!

Letters of Members of the Continental Congress, E. C. Burnett, iii, 332; History of the Celebration of the One Hundredth Anniversary of the Promulgation of the Constitution of the United States, ed. Hampton L. Carson, i, 13; Journals of Congress.

Thursday, August 6—Well before noonday there's bustle and excitement all round the State House. At noon, Congress give their official audience to Le Sieur Gérard, Minister Plenipotentiary to the United States from His Most Christian Majesty, the King of France.

The State House has now been cleaned, repaired, the stench quelled, and everything's in thorough order for this notable diplomatic function (postponed, indeed, until the State House could be made ready). Everybody's dressed in his very best clothes—an impressive array of brocade waistcoats, lawn ruffles and silk stockings—even Sam Adams is neat and spruce.

A few minutes past 12, the Minister arrives in a coach and six (furnished by Congress), attended by Richard Henry Lee and the ubiquitous Sam Adams. When they all get into the Assembly

Chamber [Independence Chamber], there's much bowing, getting up and sitting down, speech-making, and then more rising and bowing. After that, the Messers Lee and Adams escort the Sieur Gérard home again in the coach and six, the Minister's own chariot following with his Secretary in it.

Right after this function, Congress give a grand dinner for the Minister at the City Tavern. To the Audience at the State House, and to the dinner afterwards, Congress have invited the Pennsylvania Executive Council, the Speaker and Assembly and a number of distinguished guests. During the toasts after dinner there's a great firing of salutes.

On July 12th, Henry Laurens has written the President of New Hampshire:

> "I expect Monsr. Gérard in the Character of Plenepotentiary from the Court of Versailles, in Philadelphia early this Morning, a Novelty in these Infant States which cannot but occasion some uncommon and extraordinary movements among those whose proper business it is to pay due attention to the first European Ambassador to Congress."

To meet and welcome the Minister on his arrival, Congress have appointed a committee to go down to Chester and escort him to the city. Elias Boudinot, one of the committee, writes Mrs. Boudinot:

> "On their Arrival a Barge with 12 Oarsmen dressed in Scarlet trimmed with Silver were ready to receive them [the Committee from Congress]. When the Barge was half way to the Ship, she lay on her Oars and fifteen Guns were fired. When they came to the Ship her Sides were Manned and our Committee were received on the Deck by the Marines with rested Arms. At the Gang way they met the Plenipotentiary etc. etc., and were conducted into the great Cabbin where the Compliments of Congratulation being given they returned to the Shore in the same Manner and with the same Ceremony, accompanied by Le Sieur Gérard, Mr. Deane etc., etc. here were four Coaches with four Horses our Committee had prepard, in which they returned to this City, when they were saluted with 15 Guns . . ."

Richard Henry Lee, Gouverneur Morris and Samuel Adams have been the committee charged with arranging protocol for the Audience; the first time such a task has confronted the representatives of "these Infant States." July 17th, they submitted an elaborate report, in Gouverneur Morris's handwriting. Monday following, Congress debated and settled the procedure, and delegated Messers Lee and Adams to fetch the Minister and usher him into the Assembly Chamber.

Elias Boudinot, in another letter to Mrs. Boudinot, describes the Audience ceremony, the settling of which has caused so much discussion:

> "Our President [Henry Laurens] was seated in a Mahogany armed chair on a platform raised about two feet, with a large table covered with green cloth and the secretary along side of him. The Members were all seated round within the Bar and a large armed chair in the middle opposite the President for the Plenipo. At Twelve Oc. our State Coach and Six waited on the Minister at his quarters. He was preceded by his own Chariot and two with his Secretaries. The Minister was attended by two Members [Lee sits on the back seat at the Minister's left, Adams on the front seat opposite] who introduced him thro' the crowd and seated him in the chair; He then sent to the President (by his Secretary) the Letters from the King of France to Congress, which was opened and read aloud first in French and then in English. It was then announced to the house by the waiting Member, that the stranger introduced was the Minister Plenepotentiary from His Most Christian Majesty, upon which the Minister arose and bowed to the President and then to the House, and the House rising returned the Compliment. The Minister then addressed the Congress and was answered by the President, on which, the bowing again took place and the whole concluded. A public Dinner succeeded at which was a band of musick and the firing of Cannon. The whole was plain, grand and decent. The Minister was much pleased as well as the Audience."

Boudinot says of the Sieur Gérard:

> "He is about 50 Years of Age, appears to be a Modest, Grave, decent, cheerfull Man—highly pleased with our Country and the Struggles we have made for Liberty."

(Charles Willson Peale, at the order of Congress, afterwards painted a full-length portrait of Gérard wearing a full suit of red velvet, with white silk stockings. This portrait now hangs on a landing of the stair in the State House.)

Although neither Boudinot nor the other contemporary letter-writers and newspapers say where the dinner takes place, it's at the City Tavern, as we learn from the French diplomatic account (Doniol, iii, 311-313):

> "Le Congrès donna ce jour là un grand repas au ministre pleni-potentiaire à la taverne de la Cité. . . . Le ministre. . . fut placé par le comité du repas à la droite du président et le Chef de l'État à sa gauche.

Les 21 toasts furent but au bruit du canon. On but à la santé du roi, de la reine, du roi d'Espagne, à la perpétuité de l'Union entre la France at l'Amérique, au succès des armes combinées," etc.

Even though the State House has been all "freshly swept and garnished" for the occasion, Philadelphia's still far from its wonted condition. In a letter of September 3rd, Doctor Rush says:

"Our city has undergone some purification, but it still resembles too much the ark which preserved not only the clean but unclean animals. . . ."

Journals of Congress; Letters of Members of the Continental Congress, E. C. Burnett, iii, 325, 329, 363; *Pennsylvania Packet,* August 11, 1778.

Monday, November 2—Into the Council Chamber to-day come the weeping wives and children of the two Quakers, John Roberts and Abraham Carlisle. Along come also their relatives, and many petitioners besides, all begging the Supreme Executive Council's mercy for the condemned men. Tragedy impends over this harrowing scene.

John Roberts, a miller of Lower Merion Township, "being nearly sixty years of age," has "from his youth up lived not only irreproachably but spent his whole Life in the performance of the Duties of a tender Parent, a Faithful Friend, kind Neighbour & useful Citizen. To the Poor, the Stranger, and the Orphan his hospitable House" has "ever been open, his liberal Hand most Cheerfully extended."

Some of his "ultra-American" neighbours have accused him of being a Tory and have threatened his life. Terrified, he flees to Philadelphia when General Howe's army are occupying the city.

May 8th, 1778, Pennsylvania's Executive Council publish a proclamation ordering John Roberts (along with many others named in the list) to surrender himself under pain of being attainted of high treason. Thereupon, he leaves Philadelphia, surrenders himself, subscribes an affirmation of allegiance, and gives bail to appear for trial.

He's tried on the charge that he "did falsly and traiterously prepare, order, wage and levy a public and cruel war against this Commonwealth, then and there committing and perpetrating a miserable and Cruel slaughter of and amongst the faithful and Liege subjects and inhabitants thereof"!

All this charged against a man who "wouldn't hurt a flea," as everyone who knows him agrees!

Abraham Carlisle, an house carpenter by trade and a native
Philadelphian, has kept one of the city gates at a northern redoubt
during the British occupation. Sundry venomous charges have
been trumped up against him, too, and he's been arraigned for
high treason with the same pomposity of (misspelled) legal verbiage.

Pennsylvania Magazine of History and Biography, xxv, 21 *et seq.; History
of Philadelphia*, Thompson Westcott, ch. cclxiv; *Colonial Records*, xi, 613.

Tuesday, November 3—The Supreme Executive Council, sitting
in the Council Chamber—the same seven as yesterday—again consider the cases of John Roberts and Abraham Carlisle; they decide
to turn a deaf ear to all appeals for mercy. They doom these
unfortunate men to be hanged for treason. A strong feeling's
abroad that the Council think these harmless old men must be
sacrificed to the blood-lust of the mob. Their views of "expediency" recall the attitude of Pontius Pilate.

The hanging of the two "Quaker Martyrs" is one of the disgraceful acts of Philadelphia's "Reign of Terror." Technically,
as Chief Justice McKean has pointed out in delivering his sentence, they are guilty. Actually, they're the victims of extenuating
circumstances; considerations of equity give them claim to more
merciful judgement. Otherwise, there would not be the many
urgent appeals for a reprieve. Chief Justice McKean himself
recommends a reprieve. General Joseph Reed, one of the prosecuting attorneys (soon to be elected President of the State) writes
the Vice-President of the Council (there's been no President since
Thomas Wharton, junior's, death) to the same effect.

Of the jury that condemned Roberts, ten

"were in favour of acquittal, but yielded to the argument that it
was necessary for the State to secure a conviction, but that the
jury would all join in a petition for a pardon so that his life
would be spared."

And the jury does petition as follows:

"That it appears to us that the said John Roberts was under the
influence of fear, when" he came to "reside among the enemy,
while they had possession of this City. That, altho' by the oath
we have taken, we found ourselves obliged to *pronounce him
Guilty*, yet knowing that *Juries* are but *fallible Men*, and reflecting that the evidence before us was of a very complicated nature,

and some parts of it not reconcileable with his general conduct, and other evidence of his good offices to many persons who were prisoners among the enemy. . . .

That, altho' general Laws cannot be framed with an eye of compassion to guilt, yet it is the glory of every wise State, that the doors of mercy should be kept open, and ours has made ample provision in this case. In compassion, therefore," the jurors pray "that the penal part of the said John Roberts's sentence may be suspended till the Assembly can take his Case into consideration, for the exercise of that mercy which the Constitution hath lodged in their power."

The clergy of Philadelphia (among them Provost Smith and Doctor William White, afterwards Bishop) petition the Council, saying:

"Deeply sympathising with their distrest wives, children and relatives; earnestly desiring that the Mercy and Forgiveness which we preach, through Christ, may be accepted and copied among men; and hoping that, if possible, the Foundation of our civil Liberty may be firmly established without the Blood of Fellow-citizens, Do, therefore, Pray that the lives of the said Abraham Carlisle and John Roberts, who are now far advanced in years, may be spared, & such measures of mercy and forgiveness extended to them as may be thought consistent with the public safety."

The intimation's plain that the petitioners are quite aware of the "political expediency" pretext for the extreme penalty!

Petitions from sundry Continental soldiers, who'd been taken prisoner, declare their lives have

"been saved by the kindness of John Roberts, when they were confined in the British gaol, and that he had procured the release of some and had gone bail for others."

There are petitions "from over one thousand of the best men of the State, forty-two military officers among them," praying for a reprieve until the Assembly, who alone have power to pardon, can "take these cases into consideration." Likewise, twelve of the Grand Jurors petition the Council for this act of mercy.

The twelve jurors "who found Carlisle guilty asked that leniency and a reprieve should be extended to that unhappy prisoner." The defense has urged that Carlisle took

"the office to protect the inhabitants as far as he could; that he had been liberal in granting passes; and that he had been kind to various women, who had testified in his behalf. Many of these witnesses were the wives of soldiers and officers whom Carlisle knew were in the American army."

Besides the foregoing petitions, three others on behalf of Carlisle, with hundreds of signatures, are presented from Philadelphia.

These appeals for clemency addressed to the Supreme Executive Council are not the outpourings of sentimental hysteria (such as we too often have nowadays in the case of convicted murderers); they embody the sober, considered judgement of responsible people, not a few of whom have borne, and will later bear, a significant part in the direction of our national life. James Wilson, a signer of the Declaration of Independence, and Elias Boudinot, who will become a President of the Continental Congress, have been counsel for the defense. Amongst the petitioners are such men as Doctor Rush, Lewis Morris (both "Signers" of the Declaration of Independence), General John Cadwalader, Colonel Sharp Delany, Blair McClenachan and many others, some of them reputed such "good Whigs" that their names ought surely to carry weight with the Council.

George Bryan, the Vice-President, and the six other Members sitting with him, are fully competent to stay execution of the sentence and grant a reprieve until the Assembly convene and a plea can be laid before them.

Bryan and his associates obstinately choose to ignore the appeals and enact in the Council Chamber an ignominious rôle in this tragedy. "Expediency" that the State shall "secure a conviction" and payment of the death penalty is only another term for political cowardice in the face of an irresponsible mob clamouring for victims. The Jacobinism of a blood-thirsty, vindictive, rancorous rabble, "(who have submitted to the exactions of the British Army without a whimper), has grown so intense that nothing but blood, shed without any risk to themselves, can satisfy their fury." Roberts and Carlisle are the victims of "necessary example."

They are hanged November 4th.

Pennsylvania Magazine of History and Biography, xxv, 21 *et seq.; History of Philadelphia,* Thompson Westcott, ch. cclxiv; *Colonial Records,* xi, 614.

1779

Tuesday, February 23—The red-hot Whig "Constitutionalists" have been stewing a long time about the College. They're down on it because they say it's run by Tories. To-day the College comes up for attack in the Assembly. They decide to investigate. The day's minutes say:

"*Ordered,* That Mr. Clymer, Mr. Mark Bird, Mr. Hoge, Mr. Gardiner, and Mr. Knox, be a Committee to enquire into the present state of the College and Academy of Philadelphia, its rise, funds, etc., and report thereon to the House, and that they be empowered to send for persons and papers."

March 16th, a Committee of the Board of Trustees of the College deliver to the Assembly Committee a detailed report that Provost Smith has prepared. The report gives a complete history of the College and fully meets every objection raised by ill-disposed persons. There seems to be no record of the Assembly Committee making a report; the matter's allowed to sleep for the time being.

Journals of Assembly; Life of Dr. William Smith, Provost C. J. Stillé; Life and Correspondence of the Reverend William Smith, D.D., Horace Wemyss Smith, ii, 21.

Tuesday, May 25—At 4 this afternoon, crowding round the Observatory "staging" in the Yard, mills an uneasy, sullen Town Meeting. "High costs of living," and especially food prices, have caused loud clamour. Puzzled, indignant and not too orderly folk stand right under the windows of the Assembly Chamber where Congress are sitting. If any Members are listening, they may catch pointed remarks about repeated emissions of paper currency and inflation. For this meeting, General Roberdeau's "in the chair." Next day's *Gazette* says,

"several judicious and spirited Resolves were entered into for reducing the Prices of Goods and Provisions, supporting the Currency, and reforming Abuses."

The "judicious and spirited Resolves" (drawn up last Friday night by the Constitutional Society) are more spirited than judicious; economic ills can never be cured by invective, explosive denunciation nor arbitrary measures of control proposed by quacks and empirics. Whilst approving sundry ways to stem the tidal wave of inflation threatening the State, the Resolutions denounce "profiteering" and declare

"the public have a right to enquire into the causes of such extraordinary abuses and prevent them."

Then the Resolutions aim a shaft directly at Robert Morris—

"whereas, since the last importation of a cargo of goods, said to have been purchased [by] or consigned to the management of Mr. Robert Morris, Merchant, or others, the prices of all kinds of dry goods have been greatly advanced, to the injury of the public, and the great detriment of trade,

Resolved, That this meeting, justifying their conduct on the necessity of the measure, and being deeply affected and injured by these increasing evils, will appoint a Committee to enquire of Mr. Robert Morris, or others, what part he or they have acted respecting the said cargo, and to require from him or them their answers in writing to such questions as the Committee may find it necessary to put. . . ."

This direct thrust at Morris is the *immediate* outcome of the *Victorious* incident, the *Victorious* being laden partly with flour. That story's too long even to recapitulate here; any good U.S. History gives the facts. Suffice it to say that Holker (the French Consul), the French Minister (the Sieur Gérard), and other personages of proved integrity are all involved in the odium now focussed on Morris as the chief and most vulnerable target.

Contributory to this malicious, vindictive outburst are several factors. First, honestly alarmed at the menace of inflation (caused by repeated issues of "printing-press money" sanctioned by Congress), the Constitutional Society promoters of the Town-Meeting fondly think to stop it by fiat fixing retail prices; few, even of the responsible and intelligent citizens, have more than a superficial grasp of the principles of economics, and the masses of plain people now protesting so loudly are victims of delusion; they don't understand that where State decree can simultaneously regulate *both* distribution and sources of production, a certain measure of control may succeed for a while, but that to control distribution prices *alone* and thus try to stop inflation—in an advanced stage, at that—is naught but economic quackery and sheer madness. By gossip, by cleverly planted innuendo and by open accusation, the crowd have been led to think Morris is at the bottom of their ills.

Second, the unpleasant Deane-Beaumarchais-Lee row has greatly perturbed and embarrassed Congress, precipitated a "delicate" and troublesome Franco-American tension, caused the French Minister deep anxiety and put his adroit diplomacy to the test. It's also cost Tom Paine his job as secretary to the Congressional Committee of Foreign Affairs, whereupon the Sieur Gérard's employed him as a sort of hack-secretary, hoping to use his pen to still some of the storm it's helped to raise. This job doesn't last and Paine, once more cast upon the resources of meddlesome freelancing, finds outlet for his spleen in the doings of the Constitutional Society, which pretty accurately reflect his own festering resentments.

Third, and by no means least, Morris is an outspoken anti-Constitutionalist and, therefore, anathema to the Constitutionalist radicals now in full political control of the State. Here's a chance to "get" him and make him a scapegoat for some of their rancorous spite. Altogether, this afternoon's episode, though not besmirched by any open riotous outbreak, is an ugly evidence of the class war the "Constitution of 1776" has let loose as part of Pennsylvania's "Reign of Terror."

Timothy Matlack, Charles Willson Peale and Tom Paine (all ardent members of the Constitutional Society) are three of the

"Gentlemen. . . appointed on the Committee to enquire respecting the cargo lately arrived, and said to be purchased by or consigned to the management of Mr. Robert Morris, or others. . . ."

The record of their enquiry and ensuing correspondence—a tedious, sordid chronicle—is fully available to any with the patience to dig into it. The investigation's upshot? The hostile examiners unwillingly have to admit their "witch-hunt's" led them off on a false scent—the reprehensible Morris isn't guilty of the iniquities they'd hoped to prove. Even the Supreme Executive Council (more than suspected of covertly encouraging the Constitutional Society agitators) are obliged, however grudgingly, to exonerate Morris and apologise to the French Consul.

Another of this Town Meeting's resolutions appoints a committee to consider support of the currency and, at a future Town Meeting, report what programme they've devised to compass equilibrium for public finances. To-day's sullen assemblage in the Yard, its truculent anger only waiting to be fanned into flames of open disorder, is but the ominous, growling forerunner of a later gathering, which a disgraceful outburst of violence and persecution will precede, and savage, lawless turbulence follow. That the temper of to-day's crowd is none too docile, Christopher Marshall (member of the Constitutional Society) implies in his *Diary*—it's "all as peaceable as could be expected."

Pennsylvania Gazette, May 26, June 2, 1779; Christopher Marshall's *Diary;* *History of Philadelphia*, Ellis Paxson Oberholtzer, i, 288; *History of Philadelphia*, Scharf & Westcott, i, 398; *Deane Papers*, iv, 4-34, *Collections of New York Historical Society*, 1889; *Conrad Alexandre Gérard*, J. J. Meng, 750, 753-758, 829n, 832; *Colonial Records*, xii, 46, 47, 56, 59, 60, 61, 63, 66, 68, 69; *Journals of Congress; Papers of the Continental Congress*, in MS.S Division of Congressional Library.

Monday, July 26—Another Town Meeting this afternoon in the Yard—the people still all wrought up about food-prices and inflation. This is the meeting they decided to call when they adjourned May 25th. General Roberdeau's again chairman.

Wednesday (the 28th) the *Gazette* reports:

"In General Town-Meeting. . . the plan for stopping emissions and raising a revenue by subscription was unanimously approved of and agreed to, and a Committee appointed thereon.

The association for regulating prices was likewise agreed to with only a few, it is thought not more than four, dissenting voices.

The remainder of the business, on account of the change of weather [Likely a drenching rainstorm; cold water's wonderful in quelling disorder!]," was postponed and "the meeting was adjourned to the next day, Tuesday, and to meet in the State-House Yard at nine o'clock."

Anyone reading this matter-of-fact newspaper account might imagine an orderly gathering of well-behaved citizens under tolerably peaceful conditions. Such is not at all the case. There's a seething unrest. The mass mood's just so much tinder ready for the first spark to send off an explosion. "Change of weather" averts the explosion this afternoon, but anything might have happened with public temper unsettled and excited since Saturday's mob violence and outrage blackened the city's annals.

Let Silas Deane tell *that* story. He's in the city, well aware what's happening. Writing his brother, Simeon Deane (July 27th) he says:

"We are here in the greatest Anarchy & Confusion. On Saturday Night the House of Mr. Humphreys a respectable Citizen, & as True, & brave a Whig, as any in the State was forced by the

Rabble, excited, & led on, by Two of the Committee, He was from Home, but returned, just after they had entered in search of him. They had knocked down, and Wounded his Sister a Young Lady in the House, and were retiring just as He made his Way thro' them into his House; he armed himself, and stood on his defence, whilst they insulted and Abused him, and to intimidate Him, led up a File of Soldiers armed. but He bravely defied them all Unitedly, and without Assistance from the Authority of the City or his Neighbours, dispersed them. This daring outrage, tho' not the greatest that has been committed here, has alarmed the Citizens, & yesterday [the 26th] there was a Town Meeting, at which the Committee found themselves greatly embarrass'd and were severly censured; M^r R Morriss was acquitted of every Charge, and greatly applauded, this indeed looks favourable, but the Meeting stands adjourned until this Morning, & the proceedings of this Day will shew what will probably be the Event, the Contest is between the Respectable Citizens, of Fortune & Character, opposed to the Constitution ["Constitution of 1776"] of this State, and People in lower Circumstances, & Reputation, headed by Leaders well qualified for their Business, & supposed to be secretly supported by the Pres^t & Council However Things may End, It may at this Instant be truely said, there are few unhappier Cities, on the Globe than Philad^a, the reverse of its Name, is its present Character, which I hope will not be its situation for any Time."

The truthfulness of this picture's amply confirmed by other contemporary sources. Rampant rowdyism's abroad, winked at or covertly approved by those in highest executive office. The Committee of Inspection (in great measure identical in membership with the Constitutional Society) act as self-appointed judges of who, amongst their fellow-citizens, are friends or enemies to the American cause, and take advantage of their arrogated authority to gratify personal spites against defenseless neighbours. The city's become a very welter of hates, suspicions, envyings, irresponsible tattlings, espionage, lies, injustice and violence; "totalitarian" prying and dictation have become the order of the day, with mob rule and all the bitterness of class war unleashed. Captain Graydon, who's home on parole from his British captivity in New York, says the zealous so-called "patriots"

"rivet themselves with all their might in an anti-patrician spirit of perverseness to every thing candid, or noble, or honourable. Nothing is republican with them, but as it is crawling and mean, and candied over with a fulsome and hypocritical love for the people. . . all who are less violent and bigotted than themselves, are branded as Tories."

There are too many "stay-at-home" militiamen—a scurvy, insolent crew—too brainless to think for themselves but ever ready
to do the behests of rabble-rousing demagogues (*cf*. instance noted
in Deane's letter), the kind of soldiers Graydon deplores when he
writes,

> "captains, majors, and colonels, had become 'dog-cheap' in the
> land. But, unfortunately, these war-functionaries were not found
> at the head of their men. They, more generally, figured as bar-
> keepers, condescendingly serving out small measures of liquor to
> their less dignified customers. Some were brimful of patriotism,
> the prevailing feature of which was, to be no less ardent in their
> pursuit, than fervent in their hatred of Tories . . . Power, to use
> a language which had already ceased to be orthodox, and could
> therefore only be whispered, had fallen into low hands."

With the city in such sorry plight, anyone who presumes to dis-
agree with the "furious" Whigs or Constitutionalist radicals is,
ipso facto, a Tory and fair game for vilification and persecution.
And that's why the rabble attacked Whitehead Humphreys's house
Saturday night. Humphreys had dared to criticise Tom Paine;
he must be punished. The outrage by a band of hoodlums—the
"File of Soldiers armed," playing "supers"—is the mark of political disfavour. When Deane says the rabble were "led on, by
Two of the Committee," he names no names, but it needs no
exceptional imagination to guess who inspired—perhaps directly
instigated—the show.

And how came this acute variance between Humphreys and
Paine? The protagonists of the anti-Constitutionalists or Republican Society, on the one side, and the rabid "Constitutionalist"
partisans, on the other, both indulge extensively in the practice of
talking *at* their political adversaries through anonymous or pseu-
donymous "communications" to the newspapers—most are much
too verbose to call "letters." Whitehead Humphreys, thoroughly
disgusted and indignant at Paine's performances, especially with
reference to the Deane-Beaumarchais affair, speaks out in newspaper print with some deserved strictures on Paine's conduct.
The reply? Vitriolic abuse in the newspapers, climaxed by Saturday night's raid on Humphreys's house.

As a respectable, responsible and courageous citizen—"no Tory,
but a man who had accompanied your arms to battle," says
"Junius," who champions him in the *Pennsylvania Packet* (August
3rd)—Humphreys has both a right and a duty to protest against

what he believes harmful to the Country and City, and to say openly of Paine in his public capacity "what Congress, many eminent citizens, &c., had long since thought him, viz., a disturber of the public peace, a spreader of falsehoods, and a sower of dissension among the people." Even the usually temperate Oberholtzer calls Paine the "most mischievous of the mob leaders."

Pennsylvania Gazette, July 7, 28, 1779; *Pennsylvania Packet*, July 7, 28, 1779; *Pennsylvania Magazine of History and Biography*, xvii, 348; *Memoirs of a Life, Chiefly Passed in Pennsylvania*, Alexander Graydon, *passim; History of Philadelphia*, Ellis Paxson Oberholtzer, i, 288; *Deane Papers*, iv, 4-34, *Collections of New York Historical Society, 1889; Conrad Alexandre Gérard*, J. J. Meng, 750, 753-758, 829n, 832; *Journals of Congress; Papers of the Continental Congress*, in MS.S Division of Congressional Library.

Tuesday, July 27—In the Yard, at 9 this morning, a continuation of yesterday's Town-Meeting. Dreadful hubbub part of the time, regular pandemonium let loose. General Cadwalader and all the respectable people leave and go to the College Yard, where they hold an orderly meeting; the disorderly faction stay at the State House Yard and finish their business in their own way. All this rumpus goes on right under the windows of the Assembly Chamber; must greatly disturb Congress.

Silas Deane's letter to his brother misses the post, so he adds a postscript about to-day's doings in the State House Yard.

". . . will now add briefly, the transactions of the Day [Tuesday, 27th]. At Nine oClock Two or Three Hundred Men of the lower Orders of the People armed with large Staves or Bludgeons with Drum & Fife entered the State House Yard, and Stationed themselves Near The Hustings [the Observatory platform], soon after a large Number of Citizens of the first Character entered. A few Resolutions passed, when Gen[ll] Cadwallader [*sic*] offering to Speak, the Phalanx prepared for the purpose raised such a Noise that he could not be heard, the Chairman call'd to Order and put the Question if He should be heard, a very great Majority declared for the hearing of him. But the Moment He began, He was interrupted by the same party, with their Shouts, striking, & cracking of their Sticks against each other &c, on this He with His Friends amounting to near Three fourths present, to prevent the most fatal as well as disgraceful Consequences retired in a Body to the College where they formed a Meeting & went on with their Business, & appointing a Comm. to protest against the proceedings of the other party, they came to several Resolutions and Adjourned. The party left in the State House Yard also went on, & passed a Number of Resolutions, such as might be expected from them, & then broke up. Thus the Two Parties are pitted against each other. . . meantime the Minister [the Sieur Gérard] has taken up the Insult offered to Mr Holker, & thro' him, to his Most Christian Majesty by the late Committee. . . & demanded satisfaction; This will I hope bring some of these Leaders to their Senses, but some of them I have no doubt have their Views, & their Interest so strongly & deeply fixed in promoting Anarchy & Confusion, That Nothing will call them off the desperate Course they are pursuing."

The *Pennsylvania Gazette* (July 28th) carries two accounts of the split meeting; one evidently written by a "Constitutionalist" sympathiser, the other a dignified statement from the group in the College Yard. As near as can be gathered by comparing all accounts, the trouble appears to start when the Chairman puts the question whether it's

"the sense of this meeting that the present committee have discharged their duty with honour?"

General Cadwalader rises to speak in vindication of Robert Morris (who's been getting abundant vilipending and calumnious attention from Paine in the public press), whereupon the callythumpian concert strikes up. After the Chairman's repeated efforts to preserve order, and after General Cadwalader's repeated attempts to speak, only to be drowned out each time by the rabble's hellish din—the clack seem to have come with their officers, so they presumably act with military precision—the respectable citizens move over to the College Yard, put Robert Morris in the chair, and proceed to business.

They resolve that

"the interruption given to John Cadwalader, Esq: in his attempt to address his fellow citizens. . . was a violation of the LIBERTY OF SPEECH, and dangerous to the liberties of the people." Also, they "protest against the said proceeding, and against all such proceedings of the Committee, and of such of our fellow-citizens as remained with them in the State-House yard, as were carried on after we left them, and that we do not consider ourselves bound by them."

They agree to vote for a committee of 120 citizens who are to consider measures for dealing with the present economic troubles. Then they resolve that

"Mr. Holker has acted in the most unexceptionable manner." Likewise "That Robert Morris, Esq; has fully acquitted himself, in his late publication, of all the charges brought against him; and we do approve of his conduct in all the transactions mentioned in the report of the Committee." [That Committee consisted mainly of "Constitutionalists," including Timothy Matlack and Tom Paine.]

Finally, they resolve

"That the following Gentlemen, viz. Messieurs Andrew Caldwell, James Wilson, Sharp Delaney, Whitehead Humphries, Benjamin Rush, Major David Lenox and Major Benjamin Eyre, be a Committee to publish an account of the above proceedings."

Two of the resolutions "unanimously" passed by the rabble rump left in the State House Yard, "such as might be expected from them," are

"That Mr. Thomas Paine is considered by this meeting as a friend to the American cause, and therefore

That we will support and defend him, so long as his conduct shall continue to prove him to be a friend to this country."

Of this "most mischievous of the mob leaders," Oberholtzer observes,

"his name . . . was one to be conjured with by the Constitutionalists . . . Whoever proposed to touch this palladium of the people's liberties was looked upon as a Tory, or something near akin."

Pennsylvania Gazette, July 7, 28, 1779; Pennsylvania Packet, July 7, 28, 1779; Pennsylvania Magazine of History and Biography, xvii, 348; History of Philadelphia, Ellis Paxson Oberholtzer, i, 288; Deane Papers, iv, 4-34, Collections of New York Historical Society, 1889; Conrad Alexandre Gérard, J. J. Meng, 750, 753-758, 829n, 832; Journals of Congress; Papers of the Continental Congress, MS.S Division of Congressional Library.

Thursday, September 9—The State House has been the birthplace of many great institutions. It now comes nigh to being the death place of one. The College is in for trouble. President Reed's out for somebody's scalp in that nest of Tories, as he considers it. Today, in his speech to the new Assembly, he doesn't mince words in showing his dislike for the College and those charged with its conduct. Politics and party hates are at the bottom of it all. The red-hot Whigs are having their hey-day under the aegis of the Pennsylvania "State Constitution of 1776."

As President of the Supreme Executive Council of Pennsylvania, it's General Joseph Reed's prerogative to point out, in his opening Message to a new Assembly, such matters as he deems meet for legislative attention during their term of service. In addressing the House, he speaks thus of the College:

"The principal institution of learning in this State, founded on the most free and catholic principles, raised and cherished by the hand of public bounty, appears by its Charter to have allied itself so closely to the Government of Britain by making the allegiance of its Governours to that State a pre-requisite to any official act, that it might well have been presumed they would have sought the aid of Government for an establishment consistent with the Revolution, and conformable to the great changes of policy and government. But whatever may have been the motives, we cannot think the good people of this State can, or ought to, rest satisfied, or the protection of Government be extended to an Institution framed with such manifest attachment to the British Government and conducted with a general inattention to the authority of the State. How far there has been any deviation from the liberal ground of its first establishment, and a pre-eminence given to some societies in prejudice to others equally meritorious, the former enquiries of your Honourable House will enable you to determine."

Though there's been some previous hostile agitation, this is really the opening gun of a dastardly campaign to gratify personal animosity at the expense of an innocent institution of learning. It suits President Reed's purpose to brand his political opponents as Tories and to misrepresent facts about the conduct of the College.

His election as President of the Supreme Executive Council, in December, 1778, has made General Reed virtually Dictator of Pennsylvania, a post whose powers he's apparently nothing loath to exercise to the uttermost.

The President's broadside at the College prompts the Assembly to appoint a committee of five to investigate. Three members of this investigating committee are "yes-men" whose report—which is accepted—is but an echo of the President's speech. The House refuse to consider the minority report of the two members who say that

"no evidence has arisen during the enquiry to support the same, but that much the contrary has appeared."

Life and Correspondence of Joseph Reed, William B. Reed, ii, 37-39; *Journals of Assembly; Colonial Records,* xii, 98; *Life and Correspondence of the Reverend William Smith, D.D.,* Horace Wemyss Smith, ii, 22, 23.

*Monday, October 4—*A sorely uneasy day, not only at the State House but throughout the city. President Reed, the Vice-President and a few Members of the Council meet in the Council Chamber, but only in the morning and don't stay long. All seem oppressed with some foreboding and anxious to get away. President Reed's evidently unwell; seems badly worried.

The Assembly meet in the morning, but hardly any come back for afternoon session; there's no quorum, so they adjourn till 7 P.M., when there's still no quorum. All day long Assemblymen are visibly disturbed and excited.

Congress meet, not many of them; they, too, behave uneasily.

From 2 o'clock on, there's turmoil all round about the State House—people running hither and thither, drums beating, shooting heard nearby; shouts, clamour everywhere. The mob's broke loose, and there's bloodshed ere the day's over.

From daybreak this memorable Monday the city's all agog. A surge of unrest—one's felt it for days past—breaks forth in open violence in early afternoon. The mob marches from the Commons and attacks James Wilson's house, at Third and Walnut Streets, almost under the shadow of the State House. This, the mob's respect for a signer of the Declaration of Independence! Henceforth the house will be called "Fort Wilson."

Wilson, a Scot and a Presbyterian, like most of the Presbyterian Scots, has been a staunch advocate of independence from the outset. His *Considerations on the Nature and Extent of the Legislative Authority of the British Parliament*—an exceptionally able discussion of constitutional questions—has created a deep impression both in England and throughout the Colonies. It's "one of the ablest arguments for what the Britannic Commonwealth of Nations has become"; its prophetic statement that "all the different members of the British Empire are Distinct States, Independent of Each Other, But Connected Together Under the Same Sovereign" foreshadows the Statute of Westminster.

Wilson's present odium with the mob is largely because of his outspoken opposition to the "Pennsylvania State Constitution of 1776"; he's called it "the most detestable that ever was formed." It was "this opposition to George Bryan and his party that made Wilson's place in Congress increasingly precarious" until the Pennsylvania politicians ousted him in September, 1777.

Amidst the futile efforts to stem alarming depreciation of the currency, and the swelling tide of popular indignation about prices of goods and provisions, the ignorant masses—egged on and inflamed by that pestilent jingo Tom Paine and his coterie of rabid "Constitutionalists",—have blamed Robert Morris, the French Consul-General Holker, and the merchants generally for the financial disorder that's made the labouring part of the city "desperate from the high price of the necessaries of life."

Although the Supreme Executive Council (overwhelmingly "Constitutionalist" as they are) have exonerated Morris and Holker from all the charges brought against them, this the mob choose to ignore; they blindly persist in associating high prices with anti-Constitution sentiment. Paine and his rancorous "Constitutionalists" seem ready to go any length to injure all who oppose their lop-sided Constitution; they know that no one's more stoutly fought that mischievous production than James Wilson. Morris, too, they know is an anti-Constitutionalist.

Furthermore, the radical Whigs have fanned animosity to white heat against the Quakers, Loyalists and "neutrals"; to them, along with the anti-Constitutionalists, they lay the blame for present money ills. The mob are aware, too, that Wilson was one of the counsel defending Roberts and Carlisle.

To bring matters to a head, the militia—most of them privates —have suddenly taken things into their own hands. Not satisfied with the speed of the "proscription" committee, sitting at the State House "to consider measures for ascertaining whether persons inimical to the United States remain in the city," the militiamen have formed a committee of their own, one man from each company, "to effect the arrest of British sympathisers." Rumours have been rife in the city—encouraged and spread by the militiamen themselves—of the dire things about to befall the proscribed. In their eyes, Wilson's stand against their beloved Constitution's enough to damn him; but their bitterness towards him's still further fired because—quite justifiably—he "exercised his professional duty as a lawyer in behalf of certain persons. . . prosecuted for treason." The militiamen have determined "The punishment for his crimes is banishment to the enemy, yet in New York." And they plan still further mischief.

Charles Willson Peale, a zealous "Constitutionalist" but, nevertheless, capable of some restraint and of "keeping his feet on the ground," gives a lucid account of the day's doings; likewise, of what happens immediately before. In this statement, *apologia*, or whatever you choose to call it (in which he speaks of himself in the third person), he's apparently intent on dissociating himself from the day's excesses. The account's verbose; boiled down, it amounts to this: The militiamen, "a number of those active Whigs whose zeal would carry them any length in their favourite cause," some time ago meet at Burns's tavern on the Commons (at about 10th and Vine Streets). They adopt a resolution "more passionate than judicious, that of sending away the wives and children of those men who had gone with the British, or were within the British lines." Then they send for Captain Peale to come and take command of them.

Peale meets them; disapproves their plan. The venture, he points out, would be dangerous; driving women and children from their homes would cause unbounded grief; their fellow-citizens would stir up intense opposition; the attempt would surely fail. The militiamen are deaf to reason; with a *determined* band, they see no difficulties. Peale says their leader would be in imminent danger, in case of failure. General Washington had to take risks, they answer; they're ready to stake their lives to carry their point. Peale flatly refuses. The excuse? He expects to be a candidate, next election, for General Assembly. He leaves them.

He hears nothing more till last Thursday. Then the militiamen send for him, Major Boyd, Doctor Hutchinson and Colonel Bull to meet them at Burns's tavern Monday morning. The four gentlemen thus invited go into a huddle; decide they'd better be there Monday and make one last effort to dissuade the rowdies from their riotous scheme. Monday morning, Colonel Bull's ill, doesn't go; the three others exhaust their powers of persuasion in fruitless pleas to the men to disband and go home. "They only looked straight forward, regardless of consequences." The tavern's supplied them with enough "Dutch courage" to make them totally reckless.

Peale goes home, but bethinks him he'd better warn President Reed; which he goes and does. Having done so,

"Captain Peale immediately returned to his home, where he had not long been before he heard the firing of small arms. He then began to think that he ought to prepare himself by getting his fire-arms in order, in case he should be under the necessity of making use of them; for no man could know where the affair would end; and finding his wife and family very uneasy, he determined to stay within his own doors for the present time."

This morning, proscription placards are up all over the city. Amongst the proscribed victims devoted to the mob's rage are Robert Morris, Blair McClenachan and James Wilson. Even without the menacing posters, everybody knows serious trouble's brewing. Morris, McClenachan and Wilson know full well they can expect no protection from the civil authorities. The hellish, venomous hates of class war are unleashed; there's strong suspicion —to say the least—this poisonous spirit has the sympathy of some of the present State administration.

Wilson, Morris and a number of their friends, "between twenty and forty" in all, meet at the City Tavern in Second Street to consider what they'd best do. These friends are by no means all of the same political stripe—some are "Constitutionalists"—but they've rallied to defend Morris and Wilson because they know the mob's wrath will be focussed on them.

Meanwhile, the City Troop have gathered at their stable, horses saddled, ready to mount at a moment's notice. Despite ominous rumours all morning, there's been no open turbulence. Deceived by the morning's calm, the Troopers go home to their middle-day dinners.

Near 2 o'clock the mob starts from Burns's tavern. In the meantime, they've captured Buckridge Sims, Matthew Johns, Thomas Story and John Drinker—nabbed the last leaving Friends' Meeting —and held them at the tavern. Leaving the Commons, the armed militiamen about 200 strong and dragging two field-pieces—drums beating, fifes tootling, a crowd of boys tagging at their heels—come down Arch Street to Front, down Front to Chestnut and up Chestnut to Second, where they halt and give three cheers. A few of Wilson's friends, still at the City Tavern, now hasten down Second Street and up Walnut to Wilson's house. When the mob reach the City Tavern, they give three cheers again; finding their quarry gone, they move on to Second and Walnut.

Amongst others in his house with Wilson are Robert Morris, George Clymer (all three Signers of the Declaration of Independence), Colonel Chambers (a Member of the Supreme Executive Council), General Mifflin and General Thompson. All in the house are armed, but they have no ammunition until Major Nichols and Daniel Clymer—at the last minute, while the mob are drawing near—dash over to the arsenal at Carpenters' Hall, cram their pockets full of cartridges, and rush back, just in the nick of time.

Captain Allen M'Lane's standing on his front steps (Walnut Street above Third) when Colonel Grayson beckons him over to the War Office (north side of Walnut above Third) and tells him he's afraid "several of our most respectable citizens, now. . . at Mr. Wilson's house, will be massacred, as they're determined to defend themselves against the armed mob." The front of the mob's now near Dock Street. Grayson asks M'Lane if he can recognise the leaders; M'Lane thinks "Captain Faulkner, a militia officer" is leading. Grayson suggests they both go and try to "persuade them to turn up Dock to Third Street." Their attempt to head off the mob fails.

M'Lane's account continues:

"I introduced Colonel Grayson to Captain Faulkner, as a member of the Board of War. Grayson. . . expressed his fears as to the consequences of attacking Mr. Wilson in his house." Faulkner says "'they have no intention to meddle with Mr. Wilson or his house, their object is to support the constitution, the laws, and the Committee of Trade. The labouring part of the City has become desperate . .'"

The halt in front brings a great press from the rear; two men, Pickering and Bonham, run up armed with muskets and bayonets fixed, and enquire the cause of the halt, at the same time order Faulkner to move up Walnut Street.

"Grayson addressed Bonham," says M'Lane, "and I addressed Pickering, who answered me with the threat of a bayonet, sometimes bringing himself in the attitude of a charge from trailed arms."

Faulkner and a bystander interpose to pacify Pickering and Bonham. Then the order's given to pass up Walnut Street.

By this time the press of the mob's so great that

"it was difficult to keep our feet, and we were crowded among the citizen prisoners, which they had taken into custody in their march through the City. Colonel Grayson and myself linked arms, and determined to clear ourselves from the press when we reached the War Office. As we passed my house, I saw my wife and Mrs. Forrest at the window of the second storey; the moment she saw me in the crowd she screamed out and fainted; it was impossible then to escape; we were then within pistol shot of Wilson's house: I saw Captain Campbell, of Colonel Hazen's regiment of the Continental Army, at one of the upper windows . . .; heard him distinctly call out to those in arms to pass on."

Straightway there's musketry fire from street and from house. The mob scatter in all directions and leave Grayson and M'Lane

"under the eaves of the house in Third Street, exposed to the fire of those in the street at a distance. We concluded we would run into Wilson's garden, but there," M'Lane goes on, "we found ourselves exposed to the fire of both the mob in the neighbours' yards, as well as those of Wilson's friends in the house. In a few minutes we were discovered by General Mifflin, who. . . ordered one of the doors of the back building to be opened; at this moment several persons in the house became much alarmed and jumped out of the second storey windows."

Grayson and M'Lane go in the back door; Generals Mifflin and Thompson meet them and take them upstairs.

"When I reached the third storey," says M'Lane, "I looked out of one of the windows on Third Street, looked up Third Street, could see no person in the street nearer than Dock Street, where the mob had dragged a field-piece. I looked down Third Street, and saw a number of desperate-looking men in their shirt sleeves, coming out of Pear Street. . . armed with bars of iron and large hammers."

These men batter in one of the doors on Third Street; as they push in, shots from the stairs and cellar windows drop several of them. The rest run, leaving their wounded in the house. Then the defenders barricade the doors with tables and chairs.

So much for Captain M'Lane's story. Some further details emerge from the account of another eye-witness, Philip Hagner, who gets dragged into the *mêlée* because curiosity's impelled him to follow the mob. He says that while the mob march up Walnut Street,

"Captain Campbell, who has but one arm, shakes his pistol, and discharges it from the third storey window; the party in the street. . . opens a brisk fire into the house, and Campbell falls mortally wounded."

Hagner's standing at the northeast corner of the streets when some of the mob come round into Third Street and start firing from there.

"During the heat of the firing, General Mifflin. . . opens a window in the second storey, and attempts to harangue them."

Hagner then crosses to the southeast corner. While Mifflin's trying to make himself heard, a man near Hagner fires at the General; the bullet misses, strikes the sash near Mifflin and breaks it.

"The General immediately discharges both his pistols into the street. Upon my asking the man if he knows whom he's fired at, he replies 'he supposes it's some damned Tory,' and when I inform him it's General Mifflin, he expresses surprise and regret."

Hagner knows one of the men breaking in the Third Street door, goes over to coax him off—but too late. As the door crashes in, two assailants enter. Colonel Chambers fires at them from the stair, wounds one in the arm. Both rush "forward and pull Chambers by the hair downstairs, and wound him with bayonets." Hagner joins in and succeeds in pulling them off Chambers. (This, a slight variation from M'Lane's story.) He tries to carry Chambers off, but he's too heavy; "old Colonel Mifflin" comes to help; together they bear him "nearly to Mr. Willing's house" (less than half a square away).

While all this is happening in far less time than it takes to tell it, the commotion's brought the City Troop together again in wild haste; now they appear on the scene. Leaving Colonel Chambers to Colonel Mifflin's care, Hagner's turning back to "Fort Wilson" when he sees President Reed on horseback dashing down Third Street, waving his pistol—"his knee-buttons being unfastened, and his boots down, as if he had just risen from bed" [which is the fact]. Two horsemen "in white uniforms" [from Captain Baylor's Continental Horse] follow him. Just as President Reed appears, the Troopers arrive "in three detachments, from different points." The President and his two mounted followers "join them [the Troopers] on Third Street and all charge the mob simultaneously."

"The Horse! The Horse!" cry the mob and scramble to give way. The "sword is freely used" and the rioters scatter right and left; "not, however, before a considerable number of them are wounded, two or three of whom die of their wounds, and many others are taken prisoners and handed over to the civil authorities."

On his way to the point of riot, President Reed's met General Arnold driving thither in his coach and has ordered him to turn back and go home; he knows Arnold's unpopularity with the crowd, fears his presence will only add fuel to the fire. Arnold, nevertheless, gets to "Fort Wilson" just as the fighting's ceased, the rioters in full flight, President Reed gone. As they help him out of his coach (Arnold's lame), he says, "Your President has raised a mob, and now he can't quell it!"

Samuel Rowland Fisher sees some of the disturbance from the windows of the old gaol at Third and Market Streets; he records in his *Diary* that twenty-seven men during the afternoon are put into gaol in the room beneath him; also "The 27 men under us continued very noisy all night." Into Samuel Fisher's room are put John Drinker, Buckridge Sims, Matthew Johns and Thomas Story (the mob's former prisoners) "under 'protective arrest' to keep them from the rage of the mob."

Stay-at-home, peaceful citizens are pretty thoroughly terrified by the day's disorder. The Thomas Fishers live in Second Street below Walnut, quite within earshot of "Fort Wilson." Sarah Logan Fisher, for October 5th, notes in her *Diary:*

"Yesterday a Day of great confusion the Militia assembled in a large Body, with a design of taking up the Tories, the Merchants & House of Assembly joined to oppose them & in Walnut Street they met & fought which was terrible to hear. . . ."

The sullen mob broods over defeat; the fire's not quenched, but smouldering and ready to break out afresh at the first opportunity. The City Troopers patrol the streets during the night.

Life and Correspondence of Joseph Reed, William B. Reed, ii, 149-154, 423-432; *Book of the First Troop, Philadelphia City Cavalry, 1774-1914,* 28, 29; *Colonial Records,* xii, 121; *Journals of Assembly; Journals of Congress; Diary* of Allen M'Lane, *New York Historical Society,* quoted by Reed, *op. cit.,* ii, 150-152; *Letters of Members of the Continental Congress,* E. C. Burnett, iv, 468, 469; *Pennsylvania Magazine of History and Biography,* xvii, 348-350; *History of Philadelphia,* Thompson Westcott, ch. cclxx; *History of Philadelphia,* Ellis Paxson Oberholtzer, i, 289-291; *Diary* of Sarah Logan Fisher; *Diary* of Samuel Rowland Fisher, in *Pennsylvania Magazine of History and Biography,* xli, 145 *et seq.,* 274, *et seq.,* 390, *et seq.; Portrait of a Colonial City,* Eberlein and Hubbard, 459.

Tuesday, October 5—Turmoil at the State House, continuous turmoil throughout the city. Nobody knows what's going to happen or what to expect next. Wild confusion, excitement, visible alarm reign in the Supreme Court Room where President Reed's called a citizens' meeting. Most of the clergy and the principal people of the city are there, as well as some of the "lower orders," all bewildered, all talking and gesticulating at once. They quiet down only when President Reed comes in and harangues them. He, too, is excited and upset; evidently much worn out. When he's finished talking, the people go away, but are certainly not calm.

The calmest people in the State House appear to be the Congress. The Executive Council meet in the Council Chamber, but do nothing in particular; stay only a short time. The general atmosphere's not conducive to calm or the despatch of business; noise and suspense on every hand but, fortunately, no shooting, as there was yesterday.

Last night, "the citizens turned out and placed a guard at the powder magazine and the arsenal." This, and the City Troop's patrol of the streets, seem to have kept the mob in hand within the city; but in Germantown they attempted another outrage.

David Lenox, one of the City Troop, the mob had "particularly marked out for destruction." He's living in Grumblethorpe. After the day's turbulence had somewhat abated, he went home. "The mob followed and surrounded" the house "during the night, and prepared to force an entrance. Anxious to gain time, he pledged his honour that he would open the door as soon as daylight appeared." In the meantime, while he was parleying with the rabble of attackers from the balcony (that used to be) over the front door of Grumblethorpe, his intrepid cousin slipped out the back door and made her way to the city on foot to give the alarm and ask help. "A party of the City Troop arrived in time to protect their comrade; but he was compelled to return to town for safety."

Scattered by the Troopers and balked of their victim, these disorderly militiamen march in from Germantown this morning and first engage President Reed's attention. He manages to prevail on them not to keep on into the city and increase the disorder. While he's endeavouring to pacify this contingent, there's more trouble a-foot around the Court House and the old gaol nearby, where the 27 rioters arrested yesterday were confined, and kept Samuel Fisher and his friends awake most of the night.

Aware of this second threat of an outbreak, President Reed's sent thither Timothy Matlack, Secretary of the Council (whether with or without sword is not recorded), to keep the militia officers, and others there gathered, from making a disturbance until he himself can come and reason with them. Matlack finds the militia officers

"exceedingly warm, and full of resentment that any of the militia [yesterday's rioters] should be kept in durance in the gaol; they appear to be ripe for undertaking the release of the prisoners, and all Mr. Matlack's arguments, perhaps, will be insufficient to keep them much longer from being active."

Charles Willson Peale's turned up and sees the situation's getting out of hand. Some of the magistrates are there and Peale whispers Matlack, Wouldn't it

"be prudent to propose the taking bail for the persons, and let them be released by the magistrates then present?" Matlack agrees to this "as the most certain means to prevent disorder, and perhaps a further shedding of blood." This suggestion the militia officers accept; "they further enter security for the personal appearance of the militia then confined, at any future time for trial, and, in consequence, the prisoners are released by the magistrates' orders."

According to Samuel Fisher,

"The 27 Men. . . were let out about noon by order from Reed & his Companions, who began to be alarmed for their own safety, as I was informed, for many in the City spoke very free against him & 'twas said threatened to shoot him.

The 27 Men as soon as they got into the Street drew up in a line, gave three very loud Huzzas & then walked home. . . ."

By Charles Willson Peale's account, President Reed, on arriving at the scene, is

"not a little mortified to find Mr. Matlack could not do as he had ordered." After the public meeting at the State House, "amongst a number of the officers and his particular acquaintance, he is blaming Mr. Matlack for not doing as he had requested him." Peale then tells Reed that Matlack "ought not to suffer blame"; he [Peale] was the "unlucky person who had proposed that measure, which he then conceived was the best expedient, as it had the appearance of being a judicial act."

President Reed's not a physical coward. Samuel Fisher, who intensely dislikes him, admits that much—yesterday "with much difficulty Reed, Matlack, Claypoole & Kelly [two of the constables], with sundry assistants, forced the Militia into Gaol, not without many strokes of their swords." But Reed, as Chief Executive, ought to have shown more moral backbone by taking strong measures in advance to prevent the disorder being planned (of which he must have known), whether such action offended his "Constitutionalist" partisans or not. Samuel Fisher says many are

"speaking very free against Joseph Reed for his Conduct towards the Militia, so called, whom it seems most probable & I have no reason to doubt Reed had encouraged to take up friends & tories not expecting any opposition, . . . & when it did break out, those called the Militia having mixed in their list of friends [Friends] or others called Tories some of the Republican Society [the anti-Constitutionalists], so called, who would not be taken caused this disturbance."

Notwithstanding this pointed insinuation by a bitterly hostile Quaker, who has very wide-open ears and exceptional aptitude for getting all the news, whether he's in gaol or not, there's no sufficient reason to think Reed deliberately encouraged the plotting. But, if he'd been alert enough at the right time, he might have forestalled an outbreak.

The Evil Genius is out of the bottle and Reed's having a bad time getting him back, in spite of all the morning's efforts, winding up with the State House meeting, after which

"Jos. Reed with several of his partizans & some Presbyterean preachers, in very mild and humble terms" is haranguing "them in order to pacify them & remove the great uneasiness which spread amongst them."

This last, from Samuel Fisher's *Diary*, seems to point to an outdoors sequel to the State House meeting, Reed still endeavouring to mollify the wrought-up passions of the Associators and their adherents.

Last night at 10 o'clock, at Reed's instance—he was exhausted, besides quite unwell and "taking the Bark"—Matlack wrote Chief Justice McKean (who's in Lancaster on circuit) begging him to come straightway back and help to restore order. (McKean replies he feels the trouble will soon blow over, and continues on circuit.)

The "great uneasiness" isn't to be so quickly allayed. For some days ominous rumblings carry menace of renewed mob violence. Threatened by sullen "Constitutionalists," and friends of the militia, for their part in quelling Monday's riot, the City Troopers

"find it necessary. . . to keep themselves together." Also, "the gentlemen who had comprised the garrison [at "Fort Wilson"] were advised to leave the city, where their lives were endangered. General Mifflin and about thirty others accordingly met at Mr. Gray's house below Gray's Ferry, where it was resolved to return to town without any appearance of intimidation. But it was deemed expedient that Mr. Wilson should absent himself for a time."

Wednesday (the 6th) President Reed's sufficiently recovered to preside in Council. By Council's order he signs a proclamation anent the riot, covertly blaming the anti-Constitutionalists for "the undue Countenance and Encouragement which has been shewn to persons disaffected to the Liberty and Independence of America, by some, whose rank and character in other respects gave weight to their conduct. . ."; also for "the unwearied opposition and the contempt manifested, in many instances, to the Laws and Publick authority of the State."

At the same time, the proclamation "whitewashes" the rioters—"some licentious and unworthy characters, taking advantage of the unhappy tumult . . . have led many innocent and otherwise well-disposed persons, into outrages and insults, which it is hoped, on cool reflection, they will condemn." It then goes on to "declare that all those who were immediately Concerned in the Unhappy Transaction of the Fourth Instant, without distinction, shall, as far as is possible, be amenable to Justice," and requires "all those who Marched down from the Commons, in Hostile array, to the House of James Wilson, Esquire, and also all those who had previously assembled in the said House, with Arms or otherwise, immediately to surrender themselves to the Sheriff of the City and County of Philadelphia, or to some Justice of the peace, who is directed to commit them to prison, there to remain until Examination can be had, and they be delivered in due course of Law."

After this feeble fulmination from the Council Chamber, Council minutes for some days subsequently note the posting of bail by "Fort Wilson's" defenders. The real culprits, on one pretext or another, get off scot free. Eventually, an "obsequious legislature" passes an "act of oblivion for the protection of the mob who have caused the riot."

On the very day Council are wielding the whitewash brush upstairs in the Council Chamber, downstairs there's a lively exchange of letters between Congress and General Benedict Arnold (Military Governour of the City)—all indicative of the still menacing atmosphere. In the first letter, addressed to "His Excellency Samuel Huntington Esqr Presidt. Congress," Arnold writes:

"*Sir*

A Mob of Lawless Ruffians have Attack'd me in the Streets and threaten my life now I am in my Own House, for defending myself when attacked. As there is no protection to be expected from the authority of the State for an honest Man, I am now under the Necessity of requesting Congress to Order me a Guard of Continental Troops. This request I presume will not be denied to a Man who has so often fought and bled in Defence of the

Liberties of his Country. I have the honor to be with great respect Sir,

Your most obedt. Hble, Servt.
B. Arnold

N.B. I believe 20 Men with a good officer sufficient."

Journals of Congress record:

"A letter of this day, from Major General Arnold was read:

On motion of Mr. G[ouverneur] Morris, seconded by Mr. [Elbridge] Gerry,

Ordered, That the President inform General Arnold that his application ought to be made to the executive authority of the State of Pennsylvania, in whose disposition to protect every honest citizen Congress have full confidence, and highly disapprove the insinuations of every individual to the contrary."

Burnett observes the "refusal of Congress to order the guard was probably as much because of Arnold's insinuations against the Pennsylvania authorities as for any other reason." Congress are hesitant about trenching on State prerogatives.

On this negative communication from Congress, Arnold sends off another letter to the State House:

"*Sir,*

This Instant I have the honor of receiving your Letter and the Resolution of Congress of the Present date. I am extremely sorry Congress should have misunderstood my meaning when I said, 'There was no protection to be expected from the Authority of the State for an honest Man,' their Disposition to protect the honest Citizens I did not Doubt, their Abilities I doubted and still have reason to doubt," from the consequences of Monday's commotions. Pointing out that some citizens had asked protection, but to no avail, he continues: "Agreeable to the Sense of Congress I shall immediately make application to the Executive Authority of this State for Protection. I must beg leave at the same time to observe, I think it will be ineffectual, as I do not believe it is in their Power to Protect every honest Citizen who is in danger from a Mad Ignorant and deluded Rabble, from whose Brutality I have every thing to fear and reason to think my life in danger. And must again beg leave to renew my request to Congress for a Guard. . . . If I am not happy enough to obtain one, and am again Attack'd, Self Preservation will Induce me to defend myself to the last Extremity, and I hope the Hon'ble Congress will not think me Chargible for the Consequences."

Whatever Arnold may or may not be, he's neither a coward nor an alarmist. Unless there were real danger, he wouldn't ask for a guard. He either doesn't apply to the Council, knowing it will be useless or, if he does, Council minutes don't mention it.

Arnold's an especially likely object of attack by the "Mad Ignorant and deluded Rabble" because they well know the bitter
enmity between him and Reed.

The threat of arrest and imprisonment in Council's proclamation seems to have some deterrent effect on the mob. After simmering and nursing their wrath for several days, they finally
subside into ill-natured quiet.

Pennsylvania Archives, 1st Series, vii, 732; *Life and Correspondence of
Joseph Reed*, William B. Reed, ii, 149-154, 423-428; *Book of the First
Troop, Philadelphia City Cavalry, 1774-1914*, 28, 29; *Colonial Records*, xii,
121, 122 *et seq., passim; Journals of Assembly; Journals of Congress; Letters of Members of the Continental Congress*, E. C. Burnett, iv, 408, 409,
476, 477; *Diary* of Samuel Rowland Fisher, in *Pennsylvania Magazine of
History and Biography*, xli, 145 *et seq.*, 274 *et seq.*, 399 *et seq.*; Sarah
Logan Fisher's *Diary; Portrait of a Colonial City*, Eberlein and Hubbard,
459.

Saturday, November 27—A disgraceful travesty on honest legisla-
tion by the radical Assembly. They annul the College Charter;
they dissolve the Board of Trustees; and they confiscate the College estates with which, over a period of years, benefactors have
endowed it.

By the same Act, the Assembly establish a new college controlled by the political party that now rules Pennsylvania; they
create a new board of trustees in whom they vest the college
temporalities. The new college they call "The University of the
State of Pennsylvania"; the law passed to-day puts it completely
under the thumb of the Supreme Executive Council and Assembly. From the proceeds of the confiscated estates, they grant this
new seat of learning £1500 a year!

The Act's preamble starts off with pious platitudes anent blessings conferred on the State by institutions of learning. The
"cloven hoof," the Act's real intent, however, soon appears— "semi-
naries of learning. . . when in the hands of dangerous and disaffected men. . . have troubled the peace of society, shaken the
government, and often caused tumult, sedition and bloodshed."

Since a preamble's purpose is to declare the *raison d'être* of an
Act of Legislature, the foregoing obviously implies that Robert
Morris, Provost Smith, Francis Hopkinson, Edward Biddle, Alexander Wilcocks, James Wilson, General John Cadwalader and
others of their stamp are "dangerous and disaffected men," who

must be restrained by Act of Assembly from causing "tumult, sedition and bloodshed"!

This unwarrantable Act of November 27th annulling the College Charter is the direct result of President Reed's instigating Message to Assembly on September 9th.

The other excuse the preamble offers for the Act is that the "trustees. . . by a vote or by-law [June 14, 1764] have departed from the plan of the original founders and narrowed the foundation of the said institution." If one wishes to be polite, they can call this assertion a "misrepresentation"; preferring to "call a spade a spade," it's a willful, bare-faced lie.

The said "vote or by-law" reads:

"The trustees. . . have taken the above letter [a joint letter from the Archbishop of Canterbury, Thomas and Richard Penn, and the Reverend Samuel Chandler, a dissenting minister—all of them instrumental in securing contributions in England for the College] into their serious consideration, and perfectly approving the sentiments therein contained, do order the same to be inserted in their books, that it may remain perpetually declaratory of the present wide and excellent plan of this institution . . . They further declare that they will keep this plan closely in their view, and use their utmost endeavours that the same be not narrowed, nor the members of the Church of England, or those dissenting from them (in any future election to the principal offices mentioned in the aforesaid letter) be put on any worse footing in this seminary, than they were at the time of obtaining the royal brief. They subscribe this with their names, and ordain that the same be read and subscribed by every new trustee that shall hereafter be elected, before he takes his seat at the board."

The "above letter," after congratulating the Trustees on Provost Smith's success in collecting subscriptions in England for the College, amongst the "sentiments therein contained," has noted

"That the institution was originally founded and carried on for the benefit of a mixed body of pupils—that on the King's brief [Royal license to solicit subscriptions] it is represented as a seminary that would be of great use for securing capable instructors and teachers, as well for the service of the society for propagating the gospel in foreign parts, as for other protestant denominations in the colonies . . . That at the time of making the collection, the provost was a clergyman of the Church of England—the vice-provost a Presbyterian—a principal professor a Baptist, with other useful professors and tutors all carrying on the education of youth with great harmony, and people of various denominations have heretofore contributed liberally and fully . . . That jealousies had arisen lest the foundation should be narrowed, and some party exclude the rest."

The letter therefore recommended that the Trustees "make a fundamental rule or declaration to prevent inconvenience of this kind."

It was in full and voluntary compliance with the letter's rec·ommendation in this particular that the Trustees, June 14th, 1764, registered the "vote or by-law" already quoted, to which they've steadily adhered ever since; the very same "vote or by-law" to which President Reed took exception in his September Message to the Assembly; the very same "vote or by-law" the preamble to the November 27th Act assigns as justification for annulling the College Charter!

Says the author of the "History of the University" printed in the presently current catalogues of the University of Pennsylvania,

"Perhaps no more striking instance could be given of the distortion to which men's minds were subject in those days of political commotion, than the fact that in 1779 this resolution was construed by the State Legislature into a 'narrowing of the foundation,' and seized upon as a pretext for confiscating all the rights and properties of the Trustees."

That's a very mild and charitable way of putting it.

This act of confiscation's expressly forbidden by an article of the "Pennsylvania State Constitution of 1776," an article incorporated at Benjamin Franklin's instance, while the Constitutional Convention was elaborating the new Frame of Government. That article, respecting property held for the use of churches, colleges and hospitals, provides that no misconduct of a trustee can work a forfeiture of the trust, and that alleged infractions of a charter are to be determined by *judicial proceedings*, and not by the *Legislature*.

The November 27th Act's a flagrant usurpation of powers the Legislature does not possess, as the Act of a subsequent Assembly (March 6th, 1789), which reinstates the College Charter, plainly admits. The preamble of the March, 1789, Act says the Act of 1779 is

"repugnant to justice, a violation of the Constitution of this Commonwealth, and dangerous in its precedent to all incorporated bodies, and to the rights and franchises thereof."

(In 1791 the old College, reinstated in 1789, and the new "University of the State of Pennsylvania"—created by the 1779 Assembly—are combined as one institution, the University of Pennsylvania.)

The Trustees the 1779 Assembly appoint for the new institution are the same as those on the Board of the old College (except former Chief Justice Allen and Richard Penn), with sundry additions of political henchmen and radical partisans. The same faculty and teaching staff continue. *The one person eliminated is Provost Smith.* The Provost is, and always has been, outspoken in opposing the "Constitution of 1776"; his "misconduct" that makes him a "dangerous and disaffected man," to be restrained from causing "tumult, sedition and bloodshed," consists in this opposition. President Reed's his political and personal enemy. The Provost's devotion to the College, his many years of able administration, count for naught. He's sacrificed to the political intolerance and rancour of the bitterly proscriptive Jacobin régime, of which President Reed and George Bryan are the official heads. If charity's to temper judgement of Reed's despicable conduct, it can only be because he labours under the warping, two-fold handicap of ill-health and congenital Calvinism.

Journals of Assembly; Life and Correspondence of Joseph Reed, William B. Reed, ii, *passim; Life and Correspondence of the Reverend William Smith, D.D.,* Horace Wemyss Smith, ii, 480-482; *History of Philadelphia,* Thompson Westcott, ch. cclxxii.

1781

Thursday, August 30—About 1 o'clock in the afternoon, on the outskirts of town, the City Troop meet
> "his Excellency the Commander-in-chief of the American armies, accompanied by the Generals Rochambeau and Chastellux, with their respective Suites,"

and escort them into the city.

The General goes first to the City Tavern, where he knows many of the principal citizens are gathered to meet him. After a few minutes there, he goes on to Robert Morris's house in Front Street, where he stays during the several days he's in the city.

Robert Morris notes in his *Diary* that besides General Washington, there dine with him the President of Congress (Chief Justice McKean), the Comte de Rochambeau, the Marquis de Chastellux, Generals Knox, Moultrie and several others. While they're drinking toasts in ripe old Madeira—"The United States," "His Most Christian Majesty," "His Most Catholic Majesty," "The United Provinces," "The Allied Armies" and "Comte de Grasse's Speedy Arrival"—the ships in the Delaware fire salutes. Comte de Grasse's "speedy arrival" they're all anxious about; thereon hangs the chance of dealing successfully with Cornwallis in the South.

About 3 in the afternoon, General Washington goes to the State House and pays his respects to Congress in the Assembly Chamber. President McKean and all the Members rise and greet him cordially. He and the French generals are on their way South, hoping to attack Lord Cornwallis's army near Yorktown, in Virginia. The American and French troops are on their way from the North, expected to go through the city in a day or two.

In the evening, the city's illuminated and his Excellency walks
> "through some of the principal streets, attended by a numerous concourse of people, eagerly pressing to see their beloved General."

The people are so "eagerly pressing" that some windows get smashed. Samuel Rowland Fisher, at long last released from gaol —the Executive Council, worn down by his determined refusal either to plead or give bail, have finally opened the gaol doors and begged him to leave—is coming
> "home from Jersey on 30th of 8 mo: & from Wm. Cooper's ferry

opposite the City," he observes "the City to be noisy, many houses illuminated, & the Bells ringing. on account of Washington's coming to Town . . . Upon my landing in the City with my Sister," he continues, "the Streets were so amazingly thronged we could hardly get home, & there being but two houses between my father's & R. Morris's where Washington resided—*I saw this Man.* . . several times walking the Street, attended by a concourse of Men, Women & Boys, who Huzza'd him, & broke some of my father's Windows & some near us. . . ."

Pennsylvania Packet, September 1, 1781; *The Diaries of George Washington, 1748-1799,* ed. by John C. Fitzpatrick, ii, 258-259; *Itinerary of General Washington,* W. S. Baker, 235-237; *Diary* of Robert Morris; *Diary* of Samuel Rowland Fisher, in *Pennsylvania Magazine of History and Biography,* xli, 455-456.

Tuesday, September 4—In a black velvet suit with a sword at his side, Chief Justice McKean, President of Congress, stands on the State House steps to take the Royal Salute from the French troops as they march past. At his right, stands the Chevalier de la Luzerne, French Minister, uncovered; on his left, stand General Washington and the Comte de Rochambeau, also uncovered. Behind them are the Honourable Members of Congress and other dignitaries.

The crack regiment, the Soissonnais, present a dashing spectacle —all metal accoutrements polished and glittering, white uniforms with rose-coloured facings, white and rose-coloured feathers in their grenadier caps, "which strike the beauties of the city with astonishment." Rochambeau, with his staff, has preceded them and stopped to join the reviewing party on the State House steps.

As the troops approach, "with their respective commanders at their head," President McKean turns to Rochambeau and asks "whether he ought to salute or not." Rochambeau tells him the King's orders are that the troops shall pay full Royal Salute to the President and Congress, as the heads of a sovereign state. He adds, "when the troops pass before the King, his Majesty kindly condescends to salute them." So, every time the colours dip and the officers in the line salute, the President of Congress takes off his hat with stately flourish and bows. Of the Members of Congress sharing the Royal Salute, standing behind and at the sides, Guillaume de Deux-Ponts quaintly says, "the thirteen members. . . took off their thirteen hats at every salutation by a flag or an officer." Ezra L'Hommedieu writes Governour Clinton:

"Count de Rochambeau ordered his whole Army to march by the City Hall [State House] and to salute Congress as a crowned head, and the President as the first prince of the blood. How do you think friend Thomas [McKean] felt?"

"Friend Thomas" doesn't say.

That same afternoon, however, "friend Thomas" does "transmit the Count Rochambeau the following letter," in accordance with a resolution of Congress:

"Sir,

I have the honour to express to your Excellency the satisfaction of Congress ~~at the tribute of respect~~ in the compliment which has been paid to them as the sovereign power of these United States by the troops of ~~our great and good ally~~ his Most Christian Majesty under your command. The brilliant appearance and exact discipline of the several corps do the highest honour to their gallant officers and afford a happy presage of the most distinguished services in a cause which they have so zealously espoused, ~~and cannot fail to endear to every American the Prince who gives such proof of his friendship and affection to his allies.~~"

On Sunday, the 2nd, a large part of the American Army passes through Philadelphia, marching south to fight Cornwallis in Virginia. Monday and to-day, the French troops follow—also bound towards Yorktown. Monday, the first division of the French forces marches from the *Red Lion* on the Bristol Road, reaches the city about 11 o'clock, comes down Front Street, or Second, and up Chestnut past the State House. This morning, the rest of the French contingent reaches the city about the same hour. Their progress elicits exuberant applause and the wide-eyed admiration of the citizens. Windows and balconies are full of enthusiastic ladies; cheering crowds of men, women and children throng the pavements. These troops of Louis XVI, after marching past the State House, encamp on the Commons west of the city.

One and all, the people praise their immaculate appearance and precise discipline. Even Samuel Rowland Fisher, still at heart a staunch Loyalist, admits their evident excellence, though he can't refrain from commenting,

"They are said & I suppose with truth to have behaved much better on their march than either Brittish or Washington's Soldiers— This I conclude cannot be supposed to arise from the general principles & morals of the French being better than those of the Inhabitants of the Brittish Dominions in Europe & America." And he can't help adding that he opines their exemplary behaviour is "merely from a peice of French policy to gain the good opinion of the people of America, that they may thereby effect their purposes the better, for can any man that has the use of his faculties, or is not deluded beleive that they have meddled as it were in a Quarrell between Members of the same family, Religion & Language, upon any other motive than to serve their own purposes, which they study to keep covered till a suitable time may arrive to discover the cloven foot."

The old Provincial bugaboo—suspicion and dread of the French as scheming Papists!

In his extreme Quaker and Loyalist intransigeance, Samuel's an exception. Most of the Quakers, Loyalists and "neutrals" have reconciled themselves to the existing state of severance from the Mother Country by this time. If withholding entire approbation, they at least accept conditions with philosophic realism; in any event, they're able to regard the French troops with commendation of their manifest qualities.

(From letters and other contemporary accounts, it seems impossible to determine whether there were reviews on both Monday and Tuesday, or a review on Tuesday only; all things considered, it appears more likely there was only one review—Tuesday, the 4th.)

While one could wish President McKean had recorded his own personal impressions of the reviewing function, we're indebted to him for a diverting bit of news in a letter he writes Arthur Lee, this same day. Of Henry Laurens's recent return from France, he says:

"The King has written a very friendly letter to Congress, and presented their special Minister Colo. Laurens with an elegant gold box, having his picture in the lid, ornamented with diamonds, etc., nearly resembling the one you had the honour of receiving."

After the review, General Washington, "the chief officers of Congress" and the principal French officers dine with the Chevalier de la Luzerne at his house on Chestnut Street in the square above the State House. The Chevalier's just got word of Comte de Grasse's arrival in the Chesapeake. This agreeable news he tells his guests. Rumour soon spreads; crowds seek the French Minister's house to learn whether the report be true. Assured it is, they break forth with cheers and shouts of "Long live Louis the Sixteenth!" The Abbé Robin says,

"Some merry fellows mount on scaffolds and stages, pronounce funeral orations for Cornwallis, and utter laments upon the grief and distress of the Tories."

While they're in the city, President McKean, too, entertains the French generals and their aides-de-camp. In his *Journal,* Cromot du Bourg tells with relish of the "English dinner" at the McKeans':

"There was a turtle that I considered perfect, and which might weigh from sixty to eighty pounds. At dessert they drank all possible toasts."

Du Bourg also mentions Mr. Benezet as the

"most zealous Quaker in Philadelphia." Talking with him, Benezet seems to du Bourg "permeated with the excellence of his morality; he is little, old and ugly, but he is truly a worthy man, and his face bears the stamp of a tranquil and a calm conscience."

On Wednesday, the rose-and-white Soissonnais are drilled on the Commons "in the presence of Congress, the French Minister, and the Generals." There are about 20,000 spectators; they're warned not to bring their horses too close, unless they're trained to stand under fire.

The entry in Washington's *Diary* for Wednesday, the 5th, is:

"The rear of the French Army having reached Philadelphia and the American's having passed it. The Stores having got up and everything in a tolerable train here: I left this City for the head of Elk to hasten the Embarkation at that place and on my way (at Chester) received the agreeable news of the safe arrival of the Count de Grasse in the Bay of Chesapeake. . . ."

Whatever report he may have heard at the French Minister's yesterday, this is his first direct and full communication from de Grasse. It overwhelms him, and we see Washington in an exceptional mood. Fairly bursting with joy, he runs "to greet Rochambeau, calling the news, and waving his hat." Deux-Ponts says:

"The French officers were as much surprised as they were touched by the joy very true and very pure of General Washington. . . . Naturally cold and of a demeanour grave and noble. . . his features, his expression, his whole carriage were changed in an instant. He cast off the quality of the arbiter of North America and was content for a moment with that of a citizen happy in the welfare of his country: a child whose every wish had been granted, could not have revealed a livelier emotion."

Lauzun says, "I have never seen a man moved by a greater or sincerer joy."

Journals of Congress; Letters of Members of the Continental Congress, E. C. Burnett, vi, 206, 212; *Itinerary of General Washington,* W. S. Baker, 235-237; *The Diaries of George Washington, 1748-1799,* ed. by John C.

Fitzpatrick, ii, 258-259; *Pennsylvania Packet,* September 8, 1781; *The French in America,* Thomas Balch, i, 173; *History of Philadelphia,* Thompson Westcott, ch. cclxxviii; *Diary* of Samuel Rowland Fisher, in *Pennsylvania Magazine of History and Biography,* xli, 456.

Wednesday, October 24—To-day there's great *official* rejoicing over Lord Cornwallis's surrender at Yorktown. Ever since Monday, when the first news came, there's been general joy and preparation. Now, since Colonel Tilghman got here about 2 this morning with Washington's official despatch, public celebration begins.

The ceremonies centre in the State House. At 11 o'clock, Vice-President Moore and the Members of the Executive Council go downstairs from the Council Chamber and wait upon the President and Congress and the French Minister in the Assembly Chamber, to congratulate them on the good news. At noon, the State standard's hoisted, an artillery company with four cannon begin firing salutes in the Yard, and all the bells in the city ring out joyfully. All the ships in the harbour, too, fire their guns and run up their colours.

At 2 o'clock, Congress leave the State House in a body and attend a solemn Thanksgiving in the German Lutheran Church; the Reverend Mr. Duffield, one of the Chaplains of Congress, conducts the service.

At 6 o'clock, illuminations begin throughout the city, and there's a lot of window-smashing—the windows of Loyalists who don't put candles in their windows.

Because of the weather, fireworks, "new and excellent in their kind," are postponed till to-morrow evening. Then, too, Mr. Peale lights up ingeniously-contrived transparencies.

News of victory reaches Philadelphia in two installments. About 3 o'clock Monday morning (the 22nd), an express-rider dashes into town and enquires of the watchmen the way to Chief Justice McKean's house. An old German night-watchman, whose name's said to be Hurry, leads him thither. Banging at the Chief Justice's door, waking the household and all the neighbours, the rider delivers his message; then disappears from public view. The news soon spreads; lights begin to twinkle in house after house.

The *Freeman's Journal* of the 24th prints an anecdote going the rounds:

"A Watchman of this City, after having conducted the express rider to the door of his excellency the president of congress, on Monday morning last, the honest old German continued the duties of his function, calling out, 'Basht dree o'—glock, und Gornwul—lis isht da—ken!' "

The old watchman's gratuitous addition to the hour of the night isn't needed to rouse the citizens. According to all tradition, tidings have gone like wildfire, people pour into the streets and there's little sleep the rest of the night.

At 8 o'clock Monday morning, Elias Boudinot adds a postscript to a letter he's written Mrs. Boudinot Sunday:

"At three oClock this Morning an Express arrived with the glorious News of the Surrender of Lord Cornwallis with his whole Army. God be praised. It was on Wednesday last. I congratulate you and all our Friends."

In a letter of the 23rd to Lewis Pintard, he says:

"Our official letters are not yet arrived and are not expected till tomorrow Evening. The News is announced in a Letter from Comte De Grasse. . . ."

De Grasse's letter, dated the 18th, is read in Congress Monday morning. Well may the *Gazette* say, "We impatiently wait the arrival of his Excellency General Washington's dispatches." Everyone's on the *qui vive* but, pending the receipt of General Washington's own announcement, there are no orders for a public celebration. Official confirmation being expected, there's time for the authorities to plan the celebration with orderly schedule; time, too, for Mr. Peale to paint his transparencies.

In the small hours of Wednesday morning, October 24th, a weary horseman's battering at Chief Justice McKean's door, and a night-watchman's about to arrest him for disturbing the peace. He doesn't know it's Lieutenant-Colonel Tench Tilghman, aide-de-camp to General Washington, bearing the official despatches from Yorktown for which the whole city's been anxiously and impatiently waiting since early Monday morning. Colonel Tilghman hasn't had to ask the way; he knows quite well the President of Congress lives in the Duché house at Third and Pine Streets, cater-cornered from St. Peter's, assigned to him as the official residence of the Chief Justice when the State was confiscating Loyalist property in 1778.

Not only is the Chief Justice roused but the whole neighbourhood's soon agog, soon the whole city, and an impromptu celebration begins. By daybreak everyone knows confirmation's come. The *Freeman's Journal* comes out later in the morning with a big display head in a "box" on its front page:

"Be it remembered! That on the 17th Day of October, 1781, Lieut. Gen. Charles Earl Cornwallis, with above 5000 British troops, surrendered themselves prisoners of war to his Excellency Gen. George Washington, commander in chief of the allied forces of France and America. LAUS DEO."

(Preliminary negotiations began the 17th; actual final surrender did not take place till the 19th.)

Just what part Colonel Tilghman takes in all the public jubilation's not recorded. He probably goes to bed right away, utterly worn out—as he himself admits—with exposure and fatigue after his arduous journey from Yorktown. He writes General Washington on Saturday, the 27th:

"Sir:

I arrived at this place early Wednesday morning. Although I lost one whole night's run by the stupidity of the skipper, who got over on Tangier shoals, and was a whole day crossing, in a calm, from Annapolis to Rock Hall. The wind left us entirely on Sunday evening, thirty miles below Annapolis. I found that a letter from Count De Grasse to Governour Lee, dated the 18th, had gone forward to Congress, in which the Count informed the Governour that Cornwallis had surrendered. This made me the more anxious to reach Philadelphia, as I knew both Congress and the public would be uneasy at not receiving dispatches from you; I was not wrong in my conjecture, for some really began to doubt the matter.

The fatigue of the journey brought back my intermittent fever, with which I have been confined almost ever since I came to town. I shall set out, as soon as I am well enough, for Chestertown. I beg you to be assured that I am with the utmost sincerity your excellency's

Obedient servant,
Tench Tilghman."

Colonel Tilghman makes the journey from Yorktown to Rock Hall in an open boat; from Rock Hall, in Kent County, he has a full hundred-mile ride to Philadelphia. To-day, with good roads all the way and all modern motoring advantages, it's a full day's run from Philadelphia to Yorktown, without wasting any time *en route*. Considering the means of travel in Colonel Tilghman's time, the state of the roads, and the uncertainty of wind and weather once you're in the Bay, his journey's remarkably quick. With all due respect to Mr. Clinton Scollard's enthusiasm and keen dramatic sense, one feels it would have been thoroughly distasteful to Tench Tilghman—it is certainly so to present members of his family—to be pictured as a kind of whooping, hallooing Paul Revere, dashing through the country, shouting the glad tidings at the top of his lungs, and winding up with a thunderous tattoo on the Chief Justice's front door.

In his report of the 27th to General Washington, Colonel Tilghman says:

"A Committee consisting of Mr. Randolph, Mr. Carrol and Mr. Boudinot, were appointed to inquire of me the several matters of a particular kind which were not included in your dispatches. They not only went into these, but into the motives which led to the several Articles of the Capitulation, and I have the pleasure to inform you, that they were perfectly satisfied with the propriety and expediency of every step which was taken. . . . Upon the whole, Sir, you may be assured, that the Capitulation is considered, by every unbiassed person. . . as highly honourable to the Arms and beneficial to the interests of both Nations. . . ."

On the very day of receiving the official confirmation, Congress resolve,

"That it be an instruction to the said committee [Edmund Randolph, Elias Boudinot, James Mitchell Varnum and Daniel Carroll], to report what in their opinion, will be the most proper mode of communicating the thanks of the United States in Congress assembled, to General Washington, Count de Rochambeau and Count De Grasse, for their effectual exertions in accomplishing this illustrious work; and of paying respect to the merit of Lieutenant Colonel Tilghman, aid-de-camp of General Washington, and the bearer of his dispatches announcing this happy event."

Pursuant to the latter part of this resolution, the following Monday Congress direct the Board of War to present Lieutenant-Colonel Tilghman with

"a horse properly caparisoned, and an elegant sword, in testimony of their high opinion of his merit and ability."

On this eventful Wednesday (24th), the minutes of the Supreme Executive Council, in recording the orders for city illumination in the evening, add

"that it be recommended to the Justices of the Peace to take necessary measures for preserving good order and decorum in the city during the evening."

This injunction for maintaining order's more honoured in the breach than in the observance. The "Constitutionalist" mob have it in for anti-Constitutionalists, Quakers and Loyalists alike; also those whom they're pleased merely to suspect of being in any one of those categories. This is an excellent chance to have their innings; they have it. Witness one of the Rawle letters, written Thursday, October 25th:

"I suppose, dear Mammy, thee would not have imagined this house to be illuminated, last night, but it was. A mob surrounded it, broke the shutters and the glass of the windows, and were coming in, none but forlorn women here. We for a time listened for their attacks in fear and trembling till, finding them grow more loud and violent, not knowing what to do, we ran into the yard. Warm Whigs of one side, and Hartley's of the other (who were treated worse than we), rendered it impossible for us to escape that way. We had not been there many minutes before we were drove back by the sight of two men climbing the fence. We thought the mob were coming in thro' there, but it proved to be Coburn and Bob Shewell, who called to us not to be frightened, and fixed lights up at the windows, which pacified the mob, and after three huzzas they moved off. A number of men came in afterwards to see us. French and J.B. nailed boards up at the broken panels, or it would not have been safe to have gone to bed. Coburn and Shewell were really very kind; had it not been for them I really believe the house would have been pulled down. Even the firm of Uncle Fisher was obliged to have his windows illuminated, for they had pickaxes and iron bars with which they had done considerable injury to his house. In short it was the most alarming scene I ever remember. For two hours we had the disagreeable noise of stones banging about, glass crashing, and the tumultuous voices of a large body of men, as they were a long time at the different houses in the neighbourhood. At last they were victorious, and it was one general illumination throughout the town. As we had not the pleasure of seeing any of the gentlemen in the house, nor the furniture cut up, and goods stolen, nor been beat, nor pistols pointed at our breasts, we may count our sufferings light compared to many others. Mr. Gibbs was obliged to make his escape over a fence, and while his wife was endeavouring to shield him from the rage of one of the men, she received a violent bruise in the breast, and a blow in the face which made her nose bleed. Ben. Shoemaker was here this morning; tho' exceedingly threatened he says he came off with the loss of four panes of glass. Some Whig friends put candles in the windows which made his peace with the mob, and they retired. John Drinker has lost half the goods out of his shop and been beat by them; in short the sufferings of those they pleased to style Tories would fill a volume and shake the credulity of those who were not here on that memorable night, and to-day Philadelphia makes an uncommon appearance, which ought to cover the Whigs with eternal confusion . . . J. Head has nothing left whole in his parlour. Uncle Penington lost a good deal of window glass . . . The Drinkers and Walns make heavy complaints of the Carolinians in their neighbourhood. Walns' pickles were thrown about the streets and barrells of sugar stolen. . . ."

Shoemaker Papers; Letters & Diaries of a Loyalist Family of Philadelphia, in *Pennsylvania Magazine of History and Biography,* xxxv, 385 *et seq.; Journals of Congress; Colonial Records,* xiii, 94; *History of Philadelphia,* Thompson Westcott, ch. cclxxviii; *History of Talbot County,* Oswald Tilghman, i, 24, 25, ii, 129; *Pennsylvania Packet,* October 23, 25, November 1, 1781; *Pennsylvania Gazette,* October 24, 1781; *Freeman's Journal,* October 24, 31, 1781; *Pennsylvania Journal & Weekly Advertiser,* October 24, 31, 1781; *Letters of Members of the Continental Congress,* E. C. Burnett, vi, 246-251.

Saturday, November 3—Escorted by the City Troop and a band of music, Colonel Humphry, aide-de-camp to General Washington, comes late this afternoon to the State House. He brings and lays before Congress the flags taken from Cornwallis's Army at Yorktown. Colonel Humphry brings also Washington's report of the prisoners-of-war, the arms, and the stores taken at the same time. Some of the captured colours are very handsome. Attracted by the parade and common report bruited by word of mouth, a crowd of cheering citizens has gathered outside the State House.

The *Journals of Congress*—never vouchsafing any hint of the dramatic aspect of incidents chronicled—upon Colonel Humphry's arrival laconically record:

"*Resolved,* That the several matters now before Congress be referred over" until "Monday next.

Advice being received that a messenger was arrived from head quarters with despatches, the President resumed the chair, and Colonel Humphry, one of the General's aids, was introduced, and delivered a letter from the General. . . containing returns of prisoners, artillery, arms, ordnance and other stores, surrendered by the enemy. . .; he also laid before Congress 24 standards taken at the same time. . . ."

From other sources, however, comes a far livelier picture. Between 3 and 4 o'clock this late autumn afternoon, the City Troop meet Colonel Humphry and his party at the Middle Ferry over Schuylkill (where is now the Market Street Bridge). Contemporary newspapers put the meeting of Colonel Humphry at the Ferry, a usual place for an escort of honour to welcome distinguished arrivals; the Troop Annals record the meeting "upon the

Commons," where the colours are "given in charge to the Troop." Whether the exact spot be the Ferry or the Commons is immaterial; the main thing is there's an imposing parade.

Of the flags captured at Yorktown there are

"eighteen German and six British regimental colours, with four British Union and seventy-three German and British Camp Colours"—a very respectable sheaf of trophies. The standards of the German Regiments are "four feet square. . . all made of doubled white damask embroidered in gold bullion and silver thread, on both sides with crowns and other devices, as mottoes, dates and monograms, and with silver bullion tassels suspended by silver cords."

The Troopers, on well-groomed and spirited horses, are, as always, "spick and span"—very smart-looking in their uniforms of

"dark blue short Coat, faced with red and lined with white; white Vest and Breeches; high topped Boots; round black Hat, bound with silver cord," embellished with a buck's tail, and "white Belts for the sword and carbine." The arms they carry— "A Carbine, a pair of Pistols and Holsters, . . .; a horseman's Sword."

The Troop have "procured a full band of music." Led by the Troop colour-guard, with the well-known Troop standard (its canton barry of thirteen alternate silver and blue stripes), the music heads the procession. Follows a detachment of the Troop with the flags of the United States and France displayed; behind them come the captured standards, also displayed. Another detachment of the Troop brings up the rear, their swords glittering in the fading light. Thus they proceed through the principal streets of the city.

In the gathering dusk the Yorktown trophies are borne into the State House and carried into the Assembly Chamber, where the Declaration of Independence was adopted five years ago. There, in the glow of the candles, the British and German colours are laid before President McKean and the Members of Congress, amidst the echoing shouts of the "numerous concourse of spectators" outside.

One of the inevitable newspaper "poets" breaks forth into exultation with some very questionable verse—

> ". . . . .
> Taken's your Earl, soldiers and plunder.
> Huzza! what colours of the bloody foe!
> Twenty-four in number at the State House door!

Look! they are British standards, how they fall
At the President's feet, Congress and all!"

*Journals of Congress; Book of the First Troop, Philadelphia City Cavalry,
1774-1914, 4, 43; Pennsylvania Magazine of History and Biography, xxxi,
498; Letters of Members of the Continental Congress, E. C. Burnett, vi,
257; Colonial Records, xiii, 102; Pennsylvania Packet, November 10, 1781;
Pennsylvania Journal, November 7, 1781; Freeman's Journal, November 7,
1781.*

Monday, November 5—This morning the first Congress elected
under the Articles of Confederation assemble in the State House.
"Their credentials being read," say the *Journals,* "Congress proceeded to the election of a President; and the ballots being taken,
the hon^ble John Hanson was elected."

When Maryland ratifies and signs the Articles of Confederation, March 1, 1781, those articles become operative. What have
hitherto been 13 disunited States aiming at confederation, now
become "United"—at least in name.

Samuel Huntington is President of Congress in March, 1781,
and serves until July 6, when Thomas McKean succeeds him.
McKean wishes to relinquish the post in October. Doctor Witherspoon thereupon reminds Congress that the Articles of Confederation

"had provided for a federal year to begin on the first Monday in
November, and that to abide by that provision a new president
should then be elected. He accordingly moved that Mr. McKean
be requested to continue in the chair until that time. The motion was unanimously adopted, Mr. McKean continued to preside through Saturday, November 3. . . ."

Both Samuel Huntington and Thomas McKean preside over
Congress under the Articles of Confederation; John Hanson is
the first President of the "United States in Congress assembled,"
elected in conformity with the provisions of these Articles.

Journals of Congress; The Continental Congress, E. C. Burnett, 524.

Wednesday, November 28—At 1 o'clock to-day Congress give General Washington an "audience of ceremony." Two Members meet
and escort him into the Assembly Chamber where President Hanson, rising, addresses him:
"Sir:
Congress, at all times happy in seeing your Excellency, feel

particular pleasure in your presence at this time, after the glorious success of the allied arms in Virginia."

The rest of President Hanson's speech is an expression of earnest desire that the Commander-in-Chief remain long enough in Philadelphia to advise about further prosecution of the war.

Although Secretary Thomson's letter to the General, acquainting him of the hour of audience, says it is "to give you a further testimony of the high esteem they have" for his person and extraordinary services, the official thanks of Congress, and their congratulations for the victory at Yorktown, were embodied in their Resolution of October 29th. This explains why President Hanson's address deals chiefly with future plans rather than past achievement.

When His Excellency and Mrs. Washington arrived on Monday afternoon, the City Troop, commanded by Captain Morris, met and escorted them; in the evening "the Bells were rung, and other Demonstrations of Joy were shewn by People of all Ranks." On Tuesday evening, Mr. Peale didn't miss the opportunity to exhibit his "Transparent scenes" depicting the "glorious events" of the Revolution.

Journals of Congress; Letters of Members of the Continental Congress, E. C. Burnett, vi, 269; *Book of the First Troop, Philadelphia City Cavalry,* 44; *Pennsylvania Packet,* November 27, 1781; *Pennsylvania Gazette,* November 28, 1781.

Doorway from Hall into Independence Chamber (Old Provincial Assembly Chamber).

Photograph by C. V. D. Hubbard

Banquetting Hall or Long Gallery, Upper Floor, looking West.

The Liberty Bell, Ground Floor of Tower.

Arch from Main Hall to Tower and Stair.

The Liberty Bell, looking from Main Hall into Tower.

Photograph by C. V. D. Hubbard

Hall and North Door.

Photograph by C. V. D. Hubbard

Supreme Court Room, looking across Hall to Independence Chamber.

U. S. Senate Chamber, Congress Hall, Upper Floor.

Visitors' Gallery, U. S. Senate Chamber, Upper Floor, Congress Hall.

Photograph by C. V. D. Hubbard

Independence Chamber (Old Provincial Assembly Chamber), East Room, Ground Floor.

Photograph by C. V. D. Hubbard

State House Group from the South.

House of Representatives. Congress Hall. Inside the Bar.

Congress Hall, West Unit of State House Group.

Speaker's Chair, Desk and Inkstand, Independence Chamber.

The Mayor's Court Room, Old City Hall, Fifth and Chestnut Streets.

North Front of State House Group, from Northeast.

Upper Stage of Tower and Steeple.

Doorway of Independence Chamber.

Photograph by C. V. D. Hubbard

State House Group from Southwest; Hall of American Philosophical
Society at Right.

Photograph by C. V. D. Hubbard

State House Group, from Southeast.

1782

Monday, May 13—At noon to-day to the State House comes the Chevalier de la Luzerne, the French Minister, to be received in ceremonious audience by Congress assembled. The object of his visit? To announce the birth of the Dauphin and deliver a letter from His Most Christian Majesty anent that joyous event.

From his house in the next square above the State House, escorted by the City Troop under Captain Morris, the Chevalier arrives in his coach. Two Members await him at the foot of the State House steps and attend him into the Assembly Chamber. President Hanson, the other Members, and the distinguished guests rise. They're all uncovered save President Hanson, who keeps his hat on until the Minister bows; then he takes it off, returns the bow, and puts it on again. Being seated, the King's letter's read in French and in English; the President makes a speech; there's more concerted rising and bowing; the two Members escort the Minister again to the foot of the steps; and he re-enters his coach amid the din of cannon and a *feu de joie* fired by the Continental troops stationed in the State House Yard.

Then off they all go to a banquet at the City Tavern tendered the Chevalier by Congress. Toasts, more artillery salvos and, in the evening, fireworks, bell-ringing and all the customary hubbub of joy.

When Robert R. Livingston, Secretary for Foreign Affairs, on May 2nd makes known the Chevalier's desire for an audience, Congress appoint John Rutledge, Elias Boudinot and James Madison a committee to determine protocol—which they do, down to the last detail of green cloth covers for the tables, seating, and the appropriate bowing and hat-ritual for President Hanson. James Madison writes May 14th:

"It was deemed politic at this crisis to display every proper evidence of attachment to our Ally."

Journals of Congress; Book of the First Troop, Philadelphia City Cavalry, 45; The Continental Congress, E. C. Burnett, 547; Letters of Members of the Continental Congress, E. C. Burnett, vi, 343, 346, footnotes 346, 347, 351; Pennsylvania Packet, May 14, 1782; Pennsylvania Journal, May 15, 1782.

Monday, July 15—The common people are crawling all over the State House most all day and evening. They climb up on the roof in crowds. They sit on the balustrades; they perch on the chimney tops. They're all keen to see what's going on up the street in the big garden of Joshua Carpenter's old house; this house the Chevalier de la Luzerne's leased for his official residence as French Minister. From the State House roof one can see plainly everything inside the garden; it's as good as a grand-stand whence the common people can watch the Chevalier's respectable visitors.

In the eighteenth century, "respectable" people are people of consequence or prominence. The term has definitely positive significance—not negative, as now, when it's generally used merely to mean "not disreputable." Newspapers and people in general are not squeamish about quite plainly calling the rank and file "common people," as distinguished from "respectable" or noteworthy members of the community.

St. Swithin's propitious to-day; not the least sign of rain. It's as clear as a bell. Wonderful weather for the Chevalier to have his great fête to celebrate the Dauphin's birth. M. L'Enfant, one of the young French officers who came to serve in the American army, has been superintending the arbours and pavilions he's designed for this festivity. He's given free rein to his fancy; the Chevalier's depending on him to make this party outdo anything of the kind Philadelphia's ever seen.

More than 1500 people have been invited, all of them distinguished or important folk. Judging by the crowds flocking in as evening comes on, and the streams of carriages drawing up, it looks as though they've all accepted. General Washington and the Comte de Rochambeau are there, besides the President of Congress, the President of the State of Pennsylvania, the Presidents of Delaware and New Jersey, and hosts of lesser notabilities.

The Chevalier's celebration begins at 9 in the morning with a service of thanksgiving, when a solemn "Te Deum" is sung. General Washington and the Comte de Rochambeau attend; all the important French people in town besides. Since then, there've been visits of congratulation throughout the day. And now, at evening, it all winds up with music, fireworks, feast and ball.

For weeks past, L'Enfant's been completely transforming the garden with his ingenious creation of "occasional architecture." It's probably the most extensive and elaborate composition of "occasional architecture" that's ever yet been attempted in Amer-

ica. Besides the banquetting hall, and ample provision for the
concert and dancing, there are arbours, colonnades, *tempietti*,
domes and all the pretty conceits the young Frenchman's fertile
genius can devise.

L'Enfant's designed all his structures in Classic manner and
embellished them with the graceful *motifs* appropriate thereto,
not forgetting to introduce, in addition, many emblems and devices allusive to the Dauphin's birth and to the happy Franco-
American *entente*. The ceilings are enriched with symbolic
paintings, and there are brilliant illuminations throughout the
garden. The newspaper writers are so chock full of enthusiastic
admiration, and so bent on describing all the architectural
minutiae, that their effusions suggest the authors must have swal-
lowed several architectural encyclopaedias whole.

Inside the garden, a detail of French soldiers do guard duty;
outside, American soldiers guard the entrance and also act as
traffic police.

A concert begins the evening. The programme's well chosen
and the performers carefully selected; the Chevalier himself is an
accomplished musician, as is also his Secretary, Captain Otto.
While the Chevalier's taken the Carpenter house as his town residence, he's rented Laurel Hill for his country place. There, he
and Captain Otto often play for the pleasure of their friends as
well as their own diversion.

"While they lived at Laurel Hill in summer, the sound of the
harp and violin often floated from the windows over the Schuylkill." As the Chevalier "was so lavish in his entertainment, we
may well believe that Laurel Hill during his occupancy was the
scene of much social gaiety. It was certainly the scene of much
good dining. The Chevalier, of course, had his French cook and
the French cook, to be sure, had his truffle-dog, and the truffle-dog
was fain to follow the occupation for which he had been bred.
That sagacious animal, to his everlasting credit be it said, did
what no botanist had ever done before or has ever succeeded in
doing since. He dug for truffles on the lawn of Laurel Hill and
found them!"

The concert's over at 9. After that, there's a display of fireworks
on the open ground across Chestnut Street, opposite the Chevalier's house. Philadelphians dote on fireworks, and the variety of
pyrotechnical effects contrived by the manufacturers deserve the
admiration they command. Dancing starts directly the fireworks
are finished. Ladies of "stiff" Quaker convictions, with qualms

about appearing in the same room with the dancers, nevertheless have their curiosity gratified by a place whence they can look on without being seen themselves—they sit behind a thin gauze curtain. (Rather suggests the latticed gallery of an harem!) About midnight there's a bountiful supper; the dishes are excellent and varied as the Chevalier's versatile French cooks can make them. It's said he's impressed cooks from the French war ships to help. (It's sometimes said ice-cream made its first appearance in America on this occasion. That is incorrect. Ice-cream was known in England at least as early as the reign of Charles II and, in 1769, a cookery book was published in London giving the recipe for making real ice-cream, properly made—not merely frozen custard. And whatever London had, was sure to be found in colonial Philadelphia. In the library of the Historical Society of Pennsylvania there's a copy of this cookery book [1787 edition] and the delicacy was known and relished in Philadelphia before the Chevalier's party. In his *Diary*, 1744, William Black mentions having ice-cream at the Governour's house in Annapolis.)

After supper, dancing continues till long after 2 in the morning. The elegant raiment of the ladies comes in for due newspaper comment, and we're assured that "joy did not cease to sparkle in the eyes of every one present." We're told also that

"An Indian Chief, devoted to France and the United States, had. . . arrived in Philadelphia to attend the entertainment. He was apparelled and adorned in the fashion of his country, and he did not fail to express in three languages which he spoke well, the sincere part he and his countrymen took in the event that was then celebrated. The singularity of his mien and behaviour contrasted perfectly well with that of the other guests."

In one of his letters, Doctor Rush gives a description of the ball and incidentally observes that all the guests—in spite of their varying shades of political opinion, and some bitter political enmities—bottle up their animosities for the nonce and behave with exemplary politeness to each other.

Republican America, rejoicing in her newly-acquired republicanism and severance from all ties with royalty, is celebrating with tremendous fervour the birth of an heir to His Majesty, the Most Christian King!

Pennsylvania Packet, July 18, 1782; *Pennsylvania Journal,* July 17, 1782; *Freeman's Journal,* July 31, 1782; *Philadelphia, the Place and the People,* Agnes Repplier, 260-263; *Portrait of a Colonial City,* Eberlein and Hubbard, 299.

1783

Saturday, June 21—A mob of mutinous soldiers, led by some sergeants, have surrounded the State House, are pointing their bayonets at the windows, muttering threats, and are plainly in an ugly mood—made worse by the whisky the rabble give them. They send in an impertinent message to President John Dickinson and the Pennsylvania Council; give them twenty minutes to send out a "satisfactory" answer. If President and Council don't answer within that time, the mutineers threaten riot and dire vengeance.

Some Members of Congress are sitting and are greatly perturbed. One of them, very frightened, advises

"his fellow-members to think of eternity, for he confidently believes that in the space of an hour not an individual of their body will be left alive."

Finally, about 3 o'clock they're allowed to escape from the State House with only rude epithets cast at them.

The soldiers causing the disturbance are men of the Pennsylvania Line who've marched down from Lancaster to demand their back pay. Other soldiers from the Barracks join them and altogether there are 300 to 500 exasperated soldiery surrounding the State House. The impertinent threatening message they send in is meant solely for President Dickinson and the Council, but the Members of Congress feel they're being menaced as well, and they're outraged that the dignity of Congress is being insulted.

Since the malcontents marched down from Lancaster in an orderly manner and have behaved quietly till this morning, neither the State nor City authorities have taken any measures to prevent disorder. Both Congress and Council, however, have been forewarned of trouble brewing and General St. Clair's been sent for. Being present, he tries to pacify the mutineers; eventually, they go back to the Barracks without committing any actual violence.

About 4 in the afternoon, when Congress are safely out of the immediate neighbourhood, President Boudinot writes General Washington:

"Dear Sir,
I am greatly mortified that our circumstances here oblige me to trouble your Excellency with a detail highly disagreeable and

perplexing. I presume your Excellency has recd. copies of letters from Colo. Butler and Mr. Henry in Lancaster, forwarded a few days ago. All endeavours to oblige the Men to return to Lancaster proved ineffectual. They entered this City yesterday morning. . . matters seemed tolerably easy till this morning, when they positively refused all obedience to their Officers and seemed forming a design to be troublesome by evening. Congress being adjourned till Monday, I thought proper to call them together at One O'Clock. Six States had got together, when the Mutineers. . . appeared before and surrounded, the State House . . ." In their message, the mutineers demanded "of the President and Council to authorise them to choose their own Officers (being deserted by their former Officers as they alledged) in order to represent their grievances." After 20 minutes, "if nothing was then done, they would turn in an enraged Soldiery on the Council, who would do themselves Justice, and the Council must abide the consequences. . . . Neither Congress [n]or the Council, would take any measures while they were so menaced, and matters continued thus till half past 3 O'Clock" when the mutineers were prevailed on to return to the Barracks. "They have secured the public Magazine, and I am of opinion that the worst is not yet come. Tho' no Congress was regularly formed, for want of one Member present, yet the Members present, unanimously directed me to inform your Excellency of this unjustifiable movement. The Militia of the City I suppose will be called out but there are some suspicions, that the Mutineers value themselves on their interest with the Inhabitants. It is therefore the wish of the Members who were assembled, that your Excellency would direct a movement of some of your best troops, on whom you can depend, under these Circumstances, towards this City; as it will be of the most dangerous consequence, if a measure of this kind is to be put up with, and no one can tell where it will end. . . .

I forgot to inform your Excellency that the month's pay for January has been ordered to these Men and three months' pay etc. in Notes. They complain heavily of their accounts yet remaining unsettled. It is to be wished the Pay Master could arrange matters so as to close the Accounts of the Soldiery with more expedition."

The same evening President Boudinot calls an emergency session of Congress in Carpenters' Hall to take action on the day's events. At 11 that night he writes Washington another letter:
"*Dear Sir,*

. . . .
I thought proper to call Congress together this evening since writing by the Express. . . to deliberate. . . in consequence of the unpardonable insult of the day.
I have the honour to enclose your Excellency the result of

our deliberations on the subject. These resolutions are to be kept a secret till we see what the issue of the conference with the Supreme Executive Council will produce. By the last Resolve your Excellency will perceive, that the request of the Members present this morning is confirmed, as it has become absolutely necessary that this wound to the dignity of the Foederal Government should not go unpunished."

The indignant temper of Congress fully appears in the resolutions adopted (recorded for June 21st, in the *Journals*):

"*Resolved,* That the president and supreme executive council of Pennsylvania, be informed that the authority of the United States having been this day grossly insulted. . . it is, in the opinion of Congress, necessary that effectual measures be immediately taken for supporting the public authority.

Resolved, That the committee. . . be directed to confer. . . with the supreme executive council of Pennsylvania, on the practicability of carrying the preceding resolution into effect: and that in case it shall appear to the committee that there is not a satisfactory ground for expecting adequate and prompt exertions of this State for supporting the dignity of the federal government, the President on the advice of the committee be authorised to summon the members of Congress to meet on Thursday next at Trenton or Princeton, in New Jersey, in order that further and more effectual measures may be taken for suppressing the present revolt, and maintaining the dignity and authority of the United States.

Resolved, That the Secretary at War be directed to communicate with the Commander-in-Chief, the state and disposition of the said troops, in order that he may take immediate measures to despatch to this city such force as he may judge expedient for suppressing any disturbance that may ensue."

President Dickinson calls a meeting of the Council at his house next morning (Sunday) to consider the communication from Congress. Alexander Hamilton, Judge Peters and Oliver Ellsworth—the Committee from Congress—are there, too. It's the sense of the Council that it will be unwise to call out the militia; that not enough of them will respond to cope with any widespread turbulence, and that any move to raise the militia "might provoke the soldiery to excesses" they would not otherwise commit; last of all, that the citizens in general are inclined to regard the mutineers rather as objects of pity than of resentment.

Monday, the Council meet again with the Committee from Congress. After making many enquiries of militia officers and citizens in the meantime, Council's opinion remains unchanged; consequently, there's no military provision by the State to "protect" Congress and punish Saturday's insult to their dignity.

Tuesday (the 24th), President Boudinot issues a proclamation (printed on handbills and distributed through the city) summoning Congress to convene on Thursday (the 26th) at Princeton. This, along with several other factors, apparently quells any remaining unruliness at the Barracks.

For some time prior to this episode, Congress have been losing popular respect. Weakened by short-sighted "isolationism" and jealousies on the part of the several States; hampered by irregular attendance of Delegates—oftentimes there are States without *any* Delegates to represent them; and impotent to deal with many of the most urgent problems, because the "toothless" Articles of Confederation give them no power to enforce decisions, the contempt that weakness engenders in the public mind meets their best endeavours. As their strength wanes, jealousy for their corporate dignity increases.

A common attitude towards Congress appears in a letter Major John Armstrong, jr. (he of the "Newburgh Addresses" fame), writes General Gates from Philadelphia (June 26th) about the mutiny:

> "It has now ended. Peace has return'd. Order is again visible in our streets, and the Wheel of Government once more goes round. A consequence however it has had, not unacceptable to many here. The grand Sanhedrim of the Nation, with all their solemnity and emptiness, have removed to Princeton, and left a state, where their wisdom has been long question'd, their virtue suspected, and their dignity a jest."

Armstrong's a Carlisle man; at this time Secretary of the Supreme Executive Council.

How a Philadelphian feels about the whole affair a letter (August 2nd), from Doctor Rush to President Boudinot, shows:

> "I do not mean to defend the conduct of our counsel [Council] or of the citizens of Philad[a]:—I should wish they were a thousand times more criminal in the eyes of the world, provided their infamy would justify the Congress. Indeed my friend the states deceive you in their pretended sympathy . . . Strangers from Europe as well as every state in the Union condemn you. You are called the *little* Congress, & in many companies no *Congress at all*. Our *whole* state have taken part with the counsel [Council] & the city of Philad[a]:, and I have no doubt but some measures will be adopted when the assembly meets (unless your

By His EXCELLENCY

Elias Boudinot, Esquire,

President of the United States in Congress Assembled.

A PROCLAMATION.

WHEREAS a body of armed Soldiers in the service of the United States, and quartered in the Barracks of this City, having mutinously renounced their obedience to their Officers, did, on Saturday the Twenty-First Day of this instant, proceed, under the direction of their Serjeants, in a hostile and threatning manner, to the Place in which Congress were assembled, and did surround the same with Guards: And whereas Congress in consequence thereof, did on the same Day, resolve, " That the President and Supreme Executive Council of this State " should be informed, that the authority of the United States having been, that Day, grossly insulted by the " disorderly and menacing appearance of a body of armed Soldiers, about the Place within which Congress were assem- " bled; and that the Peace of this City being endangered by the mutinous Disposition of the said Troops then in the " Barracks; it was, in the Opinion of Congress, necessary, that effectual Measures should be immediately taken for " supporting the public Authority:" And also whereas Congress did at the same Time appoint a Committee to con- fer with the said President and Supreme Executive Council on the practicability of carrying the said Resolution in o due effect: And also whereas the said Committee have reported to me, that they have not received satisfactory Assurances for expecting adequate and prompt exertions of this State for supporting the Dignity of the fœderal Government: And also whereas the said Soldiers still continue in a state of open Mutiny and Revolt, so that the Dignity and Authority of the United States would be constantly exposed to a repetition of Insult, while Congress shall continue to sit in this City, I do therefore, by and with the Advice of the said Committee, and according to the Powers and Authorities in me vest- ed for this Purpose, hereby summon the honourable the Delegates composing the Congress of the United States, and every of them, to meet in Congress on Thursday the Twenty Sixth Day of June instant, at Princeton, in the state of New-Jersey, in order that further and more effectual Measures may be taken for suppressing the present Revolt, and maintaining the Dignity and Authority of the United States, of which all Officers of the United States, civil and military, and all others whom it may concern, are desired to take Notice and govern themselves accordingly.

GIVEN under my Hand and Seal at Philadelphia, in the state of Pennsylvania, this Twenty-Fourth Day of June, in the Year of Our Lord One Thousand Seven Hundred and Eighty-Three, and of the Sovereignty and Inde-pendence of the United States the seventh

ELIAS BOUDINOT.

Attest.

SAMUEL STERETT, *Private Secretary.*

Handbill Issued by Elias Boudinot, President of Congress, June 24, 1783.

return to Philad[a]: prevents them) that will seperate us for ever. Madness you know begets madness.—The first act will probably be to put a stop to our taxes being paid into the foederal treasury. The report of this, has already affected M[r] Morris's notes. You have no time to loose. For God's sake—be wise—& let not those words *dignity of Congress* produce the same fatal effects upon our Union, that *Supremacy of parliament* has produced upon the British Empire. . . . We do not want you back again for our *own* sakes. We know full well how much of the 150,000 [per] annum you spend among us comes out of the Pennsylvania treasury. You cannot hurt us by your absence. . . . I solemnly declare that I view thier [Congress] sullen—pettish—puerile absence from our city in so alarming a light to our Union, & future consequence as a Nation, that I would willingly give 1000 Guineas to bring them back again (if it is only for one month) to Philadelphia. I protest no defeat or catastrophe that happened to us during the war distressed me half so much as your present Conduct. 'The Congress is *angry*—The Sovereigns of the new world are in a passion—at what—Has England broken her late treaty—? Is all Europe in arms ag[st] her?—no—Sergeant Nogel [Nagel] called them rascals— and a few drunken soldiers insulted them as they walked the streets.—Oh! no this is not all—M[r] Dickinson looked crolly [*sic*] on, and tho' called upon over and over would not run the dogs thro' the body.' This is the daily language my friend of every table & of every company in our city. I am distressed to hear such things. Dearly as I love my native state, I could cheerfully sacrifice a great part of her honor to save the honor—I almost hate the word—it smells of *dignity*—I ought to have written CHARACTER of Congress.

With love to all the family I am D[r] Sir in great sincerity yours

Benj[n] Rush

PS: Three wrongs will not make one right. The soldiers did wrong in revolting—The Counsel [Council] did wrong in not calling out the militia—& the Congress are doing wrong in *remaining* at Princeton.—The two former have come *right*—Congress alone persevere in the *wrong*.—If you fled for safety—come back—the Mutiny is quieted—If you fled 'till a power could be collected to protect you, come back—here are 1500 of your troops devoted to your wills. . . . I honour your Authority—I am zealous above all things for our Union. . . ."

Albeit there's a general feeling the hasty action of Congress was neither prudent nor necessary—that it was

"the result of too high a degree of pride, and a disposition to construe an undesigned affront into a wanton insult," or else the "consequence of a pusillanimous fear that was unjustified by the succession of events."

—over and above all that, responsible people in Philadelphia, and throughout Pennsylvania, feel very much as does Doctor Rush. They opine concessions should be made and inducements offered to coax the offended Delegates back. They think it a real misfortune for Congress to leave Philadelphia.

John Montgomery, another Carlisle man and himself one of the Pennsylvania Delegates to Congress (he can hardly be held a special advocate of Philadelphia's interests), naïvely sets forth his sentiments in a letter to Doctor Rush when he says:

"Will you proud Philadelphians Condesend to invite them to return or will you rather say they went without our Knowladge and they may return without an invetation?" He thinks an "happey Effect" would follow an invitation. And if the State and Council will "Disscovere a Conceliating Dissposition" towards the Delegates, "mens tempers will Cool and thire fears Subside and Congress will strut on the pavements of the grand metroplaiss and talk those woundefull things over and Congratulate Each other on the mervelous Esscape we made and the great Wisdom and prudence in Conducting affair[s] to a happey Esue."

An appropriate invitation, with many signatures, does go to Congress. Congress, however, choose to nurse their wounded dignity "to keep it warm" and decline.

When General Washington investigates the mutiny, he finds the offenders that started all the trouble are "Recruits and Soldiers of a day"; they've not "born[e] the heat and burden of the War," nor "suffered and bled without a murmur"; they've not "patiently endured hunger, nakedness, and cold," but have actually "very few hardships to complain of." John Montgomery pours out his scorn on these same fellows who have received £9 bounty, "a suit of clothes, and their arms, most of whom had been in service not more than five months and had never been in action." He calls them "the offscourings and filth of the earth."

Call this episode "tempest in a teapot," "ham drama," or what you will, when the Congress in high dudgeon shake the dust of Philadelphia from their feet, they go away never to return until they come back a transformed and revivified body under the new Federal Constitution.

Letters of Members of the Continental Congress, E. C. Burnett, vii, 193, 194, 199, 200, 216; *Pennsylvania Magazine of History and Biography*, lxx, 94-96; *Colonial Records*, xiii, 606-614; *The Continental Congress*, E. C. Burnett, 578 *et seq.*; *Journals of Congress; History of Philadelphia*, Thompson Westcott, ch. cclxxxvii.

1785

Saturday, October 29—Monday morning, October 31st, the *Pennsylvania Packet* briefly tells its readers,

"Saturday last the council and general assembly of this state met in the assembly room [of the State House], for the purpose of choosing a president and vice-president for the ensuing year; when his excellency BENJAMIN FRANKLIN, esquire, was chosen president, and the honourable CHARLES BIDDLE, esquire, vice-president of this commonwealth. After which, proclamation of the election was made at the court-house, amidst a great concourse of people, who expressed their satisfaction by repeated shouts."

This perfunctory notice certainly isn't conducive to visualising a notable ceremony.

Doctor Franklin came back to Philadelphia in September, after his long absence in France, and had a tremendous welcome. The October elections made him a Member of the Supreme Executive Council, and it's been a foregone conclusion his fellow-Councillors and the Assembly would elect him President this morning.

Alone, of all the Philadelphia newspapers, the *Pennsylvania Journal* (issued only on Wednesdays) the following Wednesday (November 2nd) informs us that after the election

"at the State House, where all the officers of government were assembled . . . the whole proceeded to the Court-House in the following order;—

Constables with their Staves,
Sub-sheriffs with their Wands,
High Sheriff and Coroner with their Wands;
Judges of the Supreme Court, and Judges of the High Court
of Errors and Appeals.
Attorney General and Prothonotary of the Supreme Court.
Marshal of the Admiralty.
Judges and Register of the Admiralty.
Wardens of the Port of Philadelphia.
Collector of Customs.
Naval Officer.
Treasurer and Comptroller General.
Secretary of the Land Office.
Receiver General and Surveyor General.
Justices of the Peace.
Prothonotary of the Court of Common Pleas and Clerk
of the Court of Quarter Sessions.

Clerk of the City Court.
Master of the Rolls and Register of Wills.
Secretary of the Council.
His Excellency the PRESIDENT, and Honourable the
VICE-PRESIDENT.
Members of the Council, two and two.
Doorkeeper of the Council.
Serjeant at Arms with the Mace.
Honourable the Speaker of the General Assembly.
Members of the General Assembly, two and two.
Doorkeeper of the General Assembly.
Provost and Faculty of the University.
Officers of the Militia.
Citizens."

The *Journal* further vouchsafes the information that after the proclamation at the Court House, "the procession returned to the State-House, in the order above mentioned."

The *Journal*'s exceptional "fulness" of account leaves much for the imagination to fill in. It doesn't tell us what like are the wands the High Sheriff and the Coroner carry; nor does it say whether Chief Justice McKean and his Associate Justices wear their powdered wigs and scarlet silk robes. (We know they wear them when on the Bench in the Supreme Court Room.) Neither does the *Journal* enlighten us about the Militia Officers' uniforms, nor about the Mace the Serjeant-at-Arms, with due pomp, bears before General Mifflin, "Honourable the Speaker of the General Assembly," followed by the Members of Assembly, "two and two." Repeated emphasis on the "two and two" feature of the procession recalls Noah's Ark with "the elephant and the kangaroo." As to the Mace, we know only that the ultra-radicals are wont to denounce it (with true Cromwellian spleen) as a senseless "bauble" that ought to be abandoned.

At Thomas Wharton's Proclamation as President of the State, little more than eight years ago, the chief personages in the procession were mounted; at the Court House, there was much roaring of cannon and clangour of bells; afterwards, there was the big dinner the Assembly gave at the City Tavern, the toasts accompanied by the banging of field-pieces; and, to top off the day, in the evening bonfires and fireworks.

By comparison, although there's a more numerous muster of civil officers and legislators, to-day's function seems unimposing. The procession's wholly pedestrian, the cannon are silent, and there's no civic dinner to mark the inauguration with creature cheer. Had the Doctor elected to ride in his sedan-chair to-day, it would have given the proccssion a novel focus of interest; besides, he himself would have been more comfortable. Instead, "well stricken in years, quite corpulent and heavy in his motions," he leans dependently on Charles Biddle's arm and admits his complaint, the stone, is giving him "uncommon pain." The proclamation over, they walk back to the State House and have "to wait until the Council and House of Representatives" have congratulated them. The Doctor's then "very much rejoiced when he reaches his own house" again.

Pennsylvania Packet, October 31, 1785; Pennsylvania Gazette, November 2, 1785; Freeman's Journal, November 2, 1785; Pennsylvania Mercury, November 4, 1785; Pennsylvania Journal, November 2, 1785; History of Philadelphia, Ellis Paxson Oberholtzer, i, 321; Autobiography, Charles Biddle, 198; Philadelphia Public Ledger, October 9, 1849; Pennsylvania Magazine of History and Biography, xxiii, 123.

1787

Monday, May 14—In the Assembly Chamber to-day come together the Delegates from two States for the Convention called to draught a Constitution for the whole country. And where are the others? Washington's *Diary* notes:

"This being the day appointed for the Convention to meet, such members as were in town assembled at the State Ho. but only two States being represented, viz. Virginia and Pennsylvania, agreed to attend at the same place to-morrow at 11 Oclock. . . ."

Besides Washington, the other Members from Virginia are John Blair, James Madison, jr., Edmund Randolph and George Mason. The Pennsylvania Members are Benjamin Franklin, Thomas Mifflin, Robert Morris, George Clymer, Thomas FitzSimons, Jared Ingersoll, James Wilson and Gouverneur Morris. The gentlemen talk for a while in the Assembly Chamber; then go away hoping that by 11 to-morrow morning the Delegates from the other States will have come.

General Washington got to Philadelphia yesterday; he's staying with Mr. and Mrs. Robert Morris.

"At Gray's Ferry the city light horse [the City Troop], commanded by Colo. Miles, met me and escorted me in by the artillery officers who stood arranged and saluted as I passed. Alighted through a crowd at Mrs. House's [her boarding-house is at Fifth and Market Streets]; but being again warmly and kindly pressed by Mr. and Mrs. Robt Morris to lodge with them, I did so, and had my baggage removed thither.

Waited on the President, Doctor Franklin, as soon as I got to Town. On my arrival, all the Bells were chimed."

So reads Washington's *Diary* for Sunday, May 13th. It's Friday, May 25th, before he can record that a "Delegate coming in from Jersey gave it representation & made a quorum." Up to this time the Members have been "cooling their heels," so to speak. However, though they couldn't officially settle down to business, they've been doing a vast deal of talking and discussing. Discussion has helped in some measure to clarify the complex issues to be dealt with when the Convention really gets going.

It's July before all twelve States are represented (Rhode Island's under control of anti-federal radicals and will have nothing to do with the Convention). The apparent reluctance or indifference in some States about sending representatives, and the dilatory arrivals of their several Delegates, recall that line of a hymn,

"Our feet, how heavily they go to seek eternal joys."

Here's a Convention called for the general salvation of all the States, yet in more than one case the response (to put it mildly) is discouragingly half-hearted. The Articles of Confederation are toothless, the Congress virtually impotent. Sectional interests and jealousies are endangering such union as the Revolutionary War achieved. Danger of defeat removed by the Peace of 1783, each State's sought its own interests, regardless of all the others. It's rapidly becoming "every man for himself, and the devil take the hindmost."

More than a year ago, the wisest heads saw that commercial relations alone were threatening the whole national fabric; unless something were soon done to regulate both inter-State and international trade, and secure some unity of action in matters affecting the common welfare, the ship of state would surely drift on the rocks. When the Annapolis Convention recommended a Convention to draught a National Constitution, it opened the way to one of the most momentous events in American history, an event that has inevitably influenced the life of every American since the ratification of that Constitution, framed by what is well called "one of the greatest sessions of wise men in the history of the world," sitting in the Independence Chamber of Philadelphia's State House.

As soon as there's a quorum, on May 25th, the Members unanimously elect General Washington President of the Convention; Major William Jackson's appointed Secretary. The "wise men" are oftener in disagreement than in agreement. Once, when there's an absolute impasse, Doctor Franklin suggests they seek Divine guidance and have a parson open each day's session with prayer. One conflict that threatens to disrupt the Convention's a battle between the large and small States over representation in Congress. Out of this conflict comes the Great Compromise of July 16th—each State to have equal representation in the Senate; representation in the Lower House to be based on population.

The Convention summer's not a period of constant, unremitting toil for the Members, unrelieved by *any* relaxation or brief intervals of heed for social amenities. For instance, we know that on June 8th the Governour and "Citizens" of the "State in Schuyl-kill" decide to entertain General Washington and other notable guests at their "Castle" (generally known as the "Fish House") on Thursday the 14th. There's no further record of the event, but there's a credible tradition that Washington and some of his fel-low-Members partake of the "State in Schuylkill's" hospitality on that date and regale themselves with the deservedly celebrated Fish House Punch. Again, on Friday, July 27th, the Members adjourn until Monday, August 6th, to give a committee time to prepare a special report. Washington improves this opportunity to go a-fishing twice. Once, he and Gouverneur Morris go up the Schuylkill and stay several days at Moore Hall, the former home of doughty old Judge Moore; while Gouverneur Morris is fishing, Washington revisits Valley Forge and goes carefully over all the ground of the encampment in that grievous winter of 1777-78.

The second fishing trip, Washington and Gouverneur Morris take with Mr. and Mrs. Robert Morris into Jersey.

The Diaries of George Washington, 1748-1799, ed. John C. Fitzpatrick, iii, 214-238; *The Story of the Constitution,* Sol Bloom, *passim.*

Monday, September 17—The Constitution of the United States is signed to-day in the Independence Chamber.

After four months of hard work through summer's sweltering heat, the gentlemen from the different States, who came to Phila-delphia to draw up a Constitution for the whole country, finally set their names to the document this morning—that is, all do ex-cept Mr. Randolph and Mr. Mason from Virginia, and Mr. Gerry from Massachusetts. Now, they're sending the Constitution draught off to the Congress in New York.

Except Sundays, they've sat in the Independence Chamber from five to seven hours nearly every day, sometimes till 6 in the evening.

Their work's finished, they're tired; they're going home.

Washington's *Diary* for Saturday, September 15th, records:
"Concluded the business of Convention all to signing the pro-ceedings; to effect which the House sat till 6 o'clock; and ad-journed till Monday that the Constitution which it was proposed to offer to the People might be engrossed, and a number of printed copies struck off."

Sunday, the 16th, Washington writes "many letters in the fore-noon. Dined with Mr. and Mrs. Morris at the Hills [now Lemon Hill, in Fairmount Park] and returned to town in the Eveng."

Monday, the 17th, the *Diary* reads:

"Met in Convention, when the Constitution received the unani-mous consent of 11 States and Colo. Hamilton from New York (the only delegate from thence in Convention), and was subscribed by every Member present except Govr. Randolph and Colo. Mason from Virginia, and Mr. Gerry from Massachusetts.

The business being thus closed, the Members adjourned to the City Tavern, dined together and took a cordial leave of each other; after which I returned to my lodgings [at Robert Morris's], did some business with, and received the papers from the Secre-tary of the Convention, and retired to meditate on the momentous w[or]k which had been executed, after not less than five, for a large part of the time Six, and sometimes 7 hours sitting every day, except Sundays and the ten days adjournment to give a comee. opportunity and time to arrange the business, for more than four months."

Tuesday, the 18th, Washington dines early (about 1 o'clock) at the Morris's; then Robert Morris and Gouverneur Morris speed him on his way as far as Gray's Ferry. He's giving John Blair a lift in his carriage as far as Mount Vernon.

In all known history, there's probably never been a like number of finer or more able men gathered together and entrusted with the performance of so tremendously momentous a task—an achievement whose significance far transcends the comprehension of most men of their day and generation. Well may Washington "retire to meditate on the momentous work which has been executed." It's the means by which the thirteen jarring and mutually mistrustful States are to be welded into effective union; the ladder by which the old (and often squabbling) Colonies of British America are to ascend to strong nationhood, capable of both cohesion and healthy growth. It's said that Doctor Franklin, at the end of the Convention, pointing at the carved and gilt sun on the high back of the Speaker's Chair, observes that he's often wondered whether it's a rising or a setting sun. Now, he says with prophetic sense, he's convinced it's a *rising* sun.

The "unanimous consent of 11 States and Colo. Hamilton from New York" indicates a compromise that induces sundry Members to sign, who are unwilling to subscribe to "unanimous consent of all the Members." They're ready to certify the draught's received the votes of all the *States*, but not that it necessarily has their personal approval. "Most truly has the Constitution been called a 'bundle of compromises. . . a mosaic of second choices accepted in the interest of union.' "

The Signers for the several States are as follows: *Delaware,* George Read, Gunning Bedford, jr., John Dickinson, Richard Bassett, Jacob Broom; *Maryland,* James McHenry, Daniel of St. Thomas Jenifer, Daniel Carroll; *Virginia,* John Blair, James Madison, jr., and, of course, General Washington, President of the Convention; *North Carolina,* William Blount, Richard Dobbs Spaight, Hugh Williamson; *South Carolina,* John Rutledge, Charles Cotesworth Pinckney, Charles Pinckney, Pierce Butler; *Georgia,* William Few, Abr. Baldwin; *New Hampshire,* John Langdon, Nicholas Gilman; and *Massachusetts,* Nathaniel Gorham, Rufus King. The Pennsylvania Signers are those Delegates already named.

On that eventful Monday of the signing, before they send the Constitution off to Congress in New York, the Convention pass a resolution

> "That the preceding Constitution be laid before the United States in Congress assembled, and that it is the Opinion of this Convention, that it should afterwards be submitted to a Convention of Delegates, chosen in each State by the People thereof, under the Recommendation of its Legislature, for their Assent and Ratification; and that each Convention assenting to, and ratifying the Same, should give Notice thereof to the United States in Congress assembled."

They also pass another resolution, saying it's the opinion of the Convention, that

> "as soon as the Conventions of nine States shall have ratified this Constitution, the United States in Congress assembled should fix a Day on which the Electors shall assemble to vote for the President, and the Time and Place for commencing Proceedings under this Constitution without delay."

These resolutions, attached to the draught of the Constitution, are signed

> "By the Unanimous Order of the Convention, September 17th
> W. Jackson, *Secretary*   G⁰. Washington, Presidᵗ"

The Diaries of George Washington, 1748-1799, ed. by John C. Fitzpatrick, iii, 214-238; *History of the Constitution,* George Bancroft, *passim; The Story of the Constitution,* Sol Bloom, *passim; Journals of Congress.*

Saturday, September 29—A lively scuffle at the State House this morning. Some much riled citizens (led by that doughty Irishman, Commodore John Barry) raided the lodgings of two anti-Federal "Constitutionalist" Assemblymen, dragged them enraged and protesting to the State House, their clothes all awry and torn, and thrust them into the Chamber where the Assembly were in session and needing the two recalcitrants to make a quorum. In this very same Chamber, only twelve days ago, the Federal Constitution was signed!

Yesterday the Assembly had a bad day with a die-hard minority of anti-Federal "Constitutionalist" democrats—direct successors of the "furious" radicals who foisted the imbecile State "Constitution of 1776" on Pennsylvania, thanks to the machinations of political polecat Tom Paine and the votes of a packed majority of ignorant "hicks" and "hill-billies." These same democrats have been confident the question of a State Convention to ratify the recently-draughted Federal Constitution would lie over until the new Assembly's elected in October; hoping enough of their own stripe would be then returned to defeat ratification. Assemblyman George Clymer (who signed both the Declaration of Independence and the Federal Constitution) non-plussed them at the morning session—stole a march on them and offered a resolution to call a State Convention straightway; the Delegates to this Convention to be of like number with the Members of Assembly, apportioned in the same ratio to City and Counties, and to be returned by the same electorate as the Members of Assembly.

The anti-Federal Members from the interior and western Counties immediately balked. Although everyone already knows the nature of the proposed Federal Constitution, that the Continental Congress (now sitting in New York) are going to recommend the several States to call State Conventions to ratify it, and that many petitions have been sent to the Pennsylvania Assembly praying a Convention be called forthwith, the "Constitutionalists" urged "the impropriety of adopting" Clymer's resolution "till the Federal Constitution should be forwarded to the house by Congress." However, in spite of the obstructionists, the first part of the resolution passed by a vote of 43 to 19. The House then adjourned until 4 o'clock in the afternoon.

At 4 o'clock, when General Mifflin took the chair, there was no quorum; the 19 opposition Members had stayed away on purpose

to block further action. By unanimous consent of the Members
present, the Speaker sent the Serjeant-at-Arms to summon the
seceders to attend. The Serjeant found most of the dissidents at
Major Boyd's house, seemingly the malcontents' "hang-out," where
some of them also lodged. When he came back and reported the
19 absentees refused to heed his summons, the House could do
nothing but adjourn till 9.30 on Saturday. And when the House
rises this last Saturday in September, the present Legislature dies.

Comes this morning at 9.30. By now everybody in town's heard
about the mulish behaviour of the 19. A good many also know
that at 3 A.M. has arrived an express rider from New York bringing
Speaker Mifflin yesterday's resolution of Congress bidding the
States summon Conventions to ratify the Federal Constitution.

As General Mifflin takes the chair, the roll-call shows 44 Members present—two short of a quorum. Again the Serjeant-at-Arms
is sent to summon the dissidents; the Assistant Clerk goes along to
note their answers. Around the State House and in the lobby
there's a waiting crowd of orderly but highly indignant citizens,
thoroughly incensed at the seceding minority. When the Serjeant
and the Assistant Clerk report they've seen McCalmont, of Franklin County, and Miley, of Dauphin County, at Major Boyd's, and
that they both flatly refuse to attend; that others, evidently ap-
prised of the Serjeant's approach, have suddenly disappeared,
dodging out back doors or otherwise; and that still others, seeing
the Assembly's officers coming, have scuttled down back alleys and
escaped, like stray curs fleeing before the dog-catcher—then the
crowd at the State House lose all patience and determine on direct
action.

Off they go at Commodore Barry's heels to remedy the Assembly's embarrassment by rough and ready means. Some nameless
satirist recounts the comedy in the *Pittsburgh Gazette;* the *Pennsylvania Gazette* reprints the flight and capture:

> "They ran off headlong hurry scurry;
> Some ran to cellars, or absconded
> In kitchens, and were there impounded.
> . . . .
> It seems to me I yet see B[arr]y
> Drag out McC[a]lm[o]nt . . . . .
> . . . . and also Mil[e]y
> Was taken from an outhouse slyly,
> To constitute with him a quorum,
> For he it seems was unus horum."

Jacob Hiltzheimer, a kindly but understandably vexed Assembly-man, says with considerable restraint,

"... the spectators, being much displeased that a matter of so much consequence should be left undone for want of two members, they hunted up two—Claymont [*sic*] and Miley—and brought them to the house ..."

Though the "bringing" is none too gentle, and vigorously resisted by the "brought," and though McCalmont and Miley are dishev-elled and white with rage as they're hustled into the Assembly Chamber—"in appearance greatly agitated," the *Pennsylvania Gazette* observes—the *Minutes of Assembly* laconically record,

"Mr. McCalmont and Mr. Miley appeared in the Assembly Chamber, and, there being a quorum, the House resumed the consideration of the matter postponed yesterday."

After this spectacular entrance, we hear no more of Miley. McCalmont is both bellicose and vocal. He rises and tells the Speaker that

'certain persons, whom he could not at that time ascertain, had forcibly intruded upon his lodgings, and brought him to the house by compulsion.'

Since his attendance is involuntary, he seeks permission to leave, but is aware he must abide by the rules of the House. Told that permission to leave involves a fine of 5/-, he tenders 5/- at the Table, only to learn that Mr. Barr, the sole person officially competent to receive such fines, is one of the absentees. Therefore, the fine can't be paid and permission to leave is refused. In a fuming temper, McCalmont starts to stamp out of the House willy-nilly, only to be greeted from every side by shouts of "Stop him, Stop him!" alike from the other Members and the crowd who've fetched him hither. Barry's biographer adds:

"As Captain Barry had 'dragged' him to the place, it is likely he remained to see the result of his course, and so to have been chief among those preventing McCalmont's exit."

And doubtless McCalmont doesn't relish the immediate prospect of further man-handling. All escape barred, the session continues.

All the resolutions are passed at this morning's sitting; the election for Delegates to a State Convention is set for November 6th, and the Delegates are to meet at the State House on November 21st. McCalmont and Miley have to content themselves with casting negative votes. The *Pennsylvania Journal* says,

"In consequence of the arrival of the unanimous resolution of

Congress, and the adoption of it by our Assembly, the bells of Christ Church rang during the greatest part of Saturday."

Smarting under the ignominy of his forced appearance in the House, McCalmont seeks legal redress for his kidnapping, but without result.

Pennsylvania Journal, September 29, October 3, 1787; *Pennsylvania Mercury,* October 5, 1787; *Pennsylvania Gazette,* October 3, 1787; *Pittsburgh Gazette,* November 3, 1787; *Pennsylvania Packet,* October 1, 1787; *History of Philadelphia,* Scharf & Westcott, i, 446; *History of Philadelphia,* Ellis Paxson Oberholtzer, i, 333; *Commodore John Barry, Father of the American Navy,* Joseph Gurn, 207-208; *Commodore John Barry,* Martin I. J. Griffin, 274; *Diary,* Jacob Hiltzheimer; *Journals of the Assembly of Pennsylvania.*

1788

Friday, July 4—Philadelphians have always loved parades and pageantry, bell-ringing, gun-firing and feasting. To-day, they've all these things a-plenty, all day long.

New Hampshire, the ninth State to ratify the new Constitution, has notified Congress on June 21st; that definitely assures the Union. Thereupon, all the Federalists in the city decide to have a grand public rejoicing on the 4th of July to celebrate the Constitution's adoption.

Festivities begin at sunrise. Christ Church bells are set a-pealing, the State House bell replies and the other bells in town swell the chorus of bell music. All the ships in the river roar salutes with their guns. At 9.30 an elaborate procession starts; after parading through the city, it winds up at Bush Hill, where William Hamilton's "kindly offered the spacious lawn before his house. . . for the purposes of the day."

Two outstanding features of the parade—objects of much civic pride—are the Federal Ship *Union* and the Federal Edifice. These ingenious creations are drawn on ten-horse floats. When the parade's over, and the celebration at Bush Hill finished, they're brought back and left at the State House, where the public can inspect them to their hearts' content.

Francis Hopkinson's Chairman of the Arrangement Committee. They all have a flair for pageantry; to-day, they've let their imaginations run riot. Right afterwards, Francis Hopkinson publishes a full detailed description of the parade, with an account of the day's doings—a memorial of this hitherto unparalleled spectacle.

Nine gentlemen—General Mifflin, General Stewart and Major Lenox amongst them—with white plumes in their hats and speaking-trumpets, act as marshals. In the procession come 12 axemen, in white frocks with black girdles—the City Troop in resplendent uniforms, commanded by Captain Miles—Colonel John Nixon on horseback, bearing the staff and cap of liberty—artillery—symbolising the French alliance, Thomas FitzSimons riding a horse that formerly belonged to Rochambeau—George Clymer bearing a staff with olive and laurel to represent the Treaty of Peace with England—Colonel John Shee with a blue flag bearing the legend

"Washington, the friend of his country"—Captain William Bingham and Major William Jackson with their Light Dragoons—Richard Bache mounted, "as a herald, attended by a trumpet, proclaiming a new era"—and, to commemorate the Constitutional Convention, the Honourable Peter Mühlenberg, mounted, bearing a blue flag with "Seventeenth of September, 1787" in silver letters. Detachments of infantry fill the intervals between the mounted gentlemen taking part in the display of symbolism.

And now comes "a band of music performing a grand march, composed by Mr. Alexander Reinagle for the occasion," a fitting feature to precede the symbol of the Constitution. That symbol's "a lofty ornamented car, in the form of a large eagle, drawn by six horses." The car's so lofty that it takes a ladder to get into it. In it sit Chief Justice McKean, in his scarlet silk judge's robe, with powdered wig, along with his Associate Justices Atlee and Rush, also in their scarlet silk robes. Rising from the car's a standard "crowned with the cap of liberty. . . bearing the Constitution framed and fixed" on the staff, "the words 'The People' in gold letters on the staff, immediately under the Constitution."

Following more infantry are "ten gentlemen, representing the States that have ratified the Federal Constitution, each bearing a flag with the name of the State he represents, in gold letters, and walking arm in arm, emblematical of the Union."

Captain James Morris and his Montgomery Troop of Light Horse come next and precede an ornamented car, drawn by four horses, containing the Ministers and Consuls of foreign States in alliance with America. The Honourable Francis Hopkinson, Judge of Admiralty, follows,

> "wearing in his hat a gold anchor, pendant on a green ribbon, preceded by the register's clerk carrying a green bag filled with rolls of parchment."

Every civic organisation, all the tradesmen and artisans—cordwainers, brick-makers, ship-chandlers, cabinet and chair-makers, rope-makers, ship-carpenters, coach-painters and endless more, many with floats exhibiting their crafts in operation—and the several professions are all suitably represented in this pageant.

But the two features of prime interest and pride to the citizens are the Federal Ship *Union* and the Grand Federal Edifice. The *Union* is

> "thirty-three feet in length. . . her bottom is the barge of the ship 'Alliance,' and the same barge which formerly belonged to the

'Serapis,' and was taken in the memorable engagement of Capt. Paul Jones of the 'Bon Homme Richard' with the 'Serapis.'

The 'Union' is a masterpiece of elegant workmanship, perfectly proportioned and complete throughout, decorated with emblematical carvings . . . And what is truly astonishing, she was begun and completed in less than four days [Who says Philadelphia's slow?]. . . . The workmanship and appearance of this beautiful object command universal admiration and applause, and do high honour to the artists of Philadelphia who were concerned in her construction."

The Grand Federal Edifice appears

"on a carriage drawn by ten white horses; the dome supported by thirteen Corinthian columns. . . the frieze decorated with thirteen stars; ten of the columns complete [Virginia's the tenth State to ratify, and does so before this festival.] and three left unfinished. On the pedestals of the columns are inscribed. . . the initial of the thirteen American States. On top of the dome a handsome cupola, surmounted by a figure of Plenty . . . On the floor of the Grand Edifice are placed ten chairs for the accommodation of ten gentlemen," among them John Wharton, John Nesbitt, Samuel Morris and Tench Francis. "These gentlemen sat as representatives of the citizens at large, to whom the Federal Constitution was committed previous to the ratification." When the Grand Edifice arrives at Bush Hill, "these gentlemen give up their seats to the representatives of the States enumerated. . . who enter the temple and hang their flags on the Corinthian columns to which they respectively belong."

Arriving at Bush Hill about 12.30, the paraders find

"a very large circular range of tables, covered with canvas awnings, and plentifully spread with a cold collation . . . In the centre of this spacious circle the Grand Edifice is placed, and the ship 'Union' moored. The flags of the consuls and other standards are planted round the Edifice.

As soon as the rear of the line has arrived, James Wilson, Esq. addresses the people from the Federal Edifice in an eloquent oration." The military then fire a *"feu de joie* of three rounds, also three volleys," and then the company attack the refreshments. "No spirit nor wines of any kind are introduced. American porter, beer and cider are the only liquors."

The green's entirely cleared by 6 o'clock, and the ship *Union* and the Grand Federal Edifice begin their journey back to town. They're cherished toys of the public; people are loath to part with them and it's a gratification to have them placed at the State House where everybody can look at and enjoy them a while longer.

Full text of Hopkinson's memorial description printed in *The History of Philadelphia*, Scharf & Westcott, i, 447-452.

1789

Friday, October 2—The General Convention of the Episcopal Church are meeting to-day in the State House. Since the United States are now a Nation independent of the Mother Country, and since the Anglican Church in America, therefore, can no longer be considered a part of the Diocese of London and under the control of the Established Church of England, there must be constitutional adjustments for the governance of the American child of the British parent. One of the most important items of business before the Convention is the amendment and ratification of the Constitution, proposed and tentatively adopted some time previously at Christ Church.

The General Convention of 1789, upon first assembling, have sat in Christ Church but, on October 1st, the minutes record:

> "The meeting in Christ Church being found inconvenient to the members in several respects, it was resolved that the Rev. Dr. William Smith and the Hon. Mr. Secretary [Francis] Hopkinson be appointed to wait upon his Excellency Thomas Mifflin, Esquire, the President of the State, and request leave for the Convention to hold their meeting in some convenient apartment in the State House."

Later in the day there's an entry:

> "The Rev. Dr. William Smith and Hon. Mr. Hopkinson reported that the President of the State had very politely given permission to the Convention to hold their meetings at the State House in the apartments *of the General Assembly* until they shall be wanted for the public service.
>
> Adjourned to meet at the State House to-morrow morning."

Saturday, October 3rd, the Convention ratify the proposed amendment to the Constitution by virtue of which the governing body is henceforth divided into an Upper and Lower House, the two sitting separately—the House of Bishops and the House of Clerical and Lay Deputies. The Lower House sit in the Independence Chamber; the House of Bishops sit upstairs in the Council Chamber.

Only two Bishops are present at this meeting of the House of Bishops—Bishop White, of Pennsylvania, and Bishop Seabury, of Connecticut. Bishop Provoost, of New York—the only other

Bishop in the American Church—has seen fit to stay away, presumably because of his feeling against Bishop Seabury on the ground of the Connecticut prelate's consecration by the Scottish Bishops instead of in England.

The House of Clerical and Lay Deputies immediately elect Doctor William Smith their President and the Provost thereupon takes his seat in the Speaker's Chair, the chair occupied in 1787 by General Washington when he presided over the Constitutional Convention.

As he presides over the Lower House, Doctor Smith can scarcely fail to recall how, thirty-one years ago, the Assembly in their malice haled him before them in this very room; how he denied their right to try him and appealed to the Crown; and how, thereupon, the gathered gentry of Philadelphia clapped and shouted.

The General Convention continue to sit in the State House until Saturday, October 10th. On the 12th they continue their sessions at the College.

Life and Correspondence of the Reverend William Smith, D.D., Horace Wemyss Smith, ii, 283 *et seq.; Minutes of the General Convention.*

1790

Monday, December 6—In Congress Hall this morning, the Senate and the House of Representatives of the United States assemble for the third session of the First Congress. With this meeting of the National Legislature, Philadelphia's ten-year period as the National Capital is in full course.

The Lower House sit in the large chamber on the ground floor; the Senate sit in the chamber upstairs right above the Lower House.

Against the coming of Congress, the Philadelphia County Commissioners have made sundry furnishing preparations. Whatever unrecorded appointments they may have provided, we know they've seen to the hanging of

"6 Venetian Blinds. . . with plain fronts in Senate Chamber and Committee Rooms. . . at £ 4. 10 each—9 do. for Arch windows down stairs in the House of Representatives of U.S. at £ 6 each." The Commissioners are billed also for "Lengthening 5 Blinds, 3 tossils etc. £ 2. 50 spitting boxes for Congress, £ 6. 5."

How the "spitting boxes," at 2/6 apiece, are apportioned between the Senate and House of Representatives, we're not told.

In the Senate Chamber upstairs, the big bay-window towards the south overlooks the State House Yard. Sitting with his back to this window,

"in a very plain chair, without canopy, and a small mahogany table before him, festooned at the sides and front with green silk, Mr. Adams, the vice-president, presided as president of the Senate, facing north."

Conspicuously hung are two portraits, one of King Louis XVI, the other of his royal consort, Marie Antoinette. The King of France has sent these portraits in answer to the urgent request (June 15, 1779) of a Congress grateful for the French alliance and assured financial, military and naval aid in the Revolutionary struggle—

". . . we entreat you to be persuaded that the permanence and stability of our friendship will be equal to the magnanimity of that conduct, and the importance of those good offices by which it was created.

Permit us to request the favour of your majesty to oblige us with portraits of yourself and royal consort, that, by being placed in our council chamber, the representatives of these states may

daily have before their eyes the first royal friends and patrons
of their cause.

We beseech the Supreme Dispenser of events to keep you both
in his holy protection, and long to continue to France the blessings resulting from the administration of a prince who nobly
asserts the rights of mankind."

Amongst the Senators great decorum and dignity prevail at their
proceedings. "They all appear every morning full powdered and
dressed as age or fancy may suggest in the richest materials." If
conversation ever rises above a subdued note, three gentle raps
on the table with Mr. Adams's silver pencil-case restore the wonted
quiet.

By the end of 1792 the Members of the Lower House have
appreciably increased in number and it's become plainly (and
inconveniently) evident that Congress Hall's now not large enough
to accommodate the legislative branch of the National Government.

Hence, in March, 1793, the State Legislature consider a bill and,
on April 11th, pass an "Act to Provide for the Accommodation
of the Congress of the United States."

"Whereas," says the preamble, "it is found that the building at
present occupied by the congress of the United States will not
be sufficiently large for their accommodation, in consequence of
the representation from the different states having become enlarged by the late enumeration of the said states,"

the Pennsylvania Legislature grant the County Commissioners the
sum of "six thousand, six hundred and sixty-six dollars and sixty-
seven cents. . . for the purpose of enlarging the building." And
the Act further prescribes

"that so much of the ground of the State house square, as may be
requisite for this purpose, be granted to the said commissioners
for the purpose aforesaid; provided the quantity do not exceed
forty feet in depth on Sixth street, commensurate with the width
of the said building."

Since popular sentiment's increasingly clamorous for the public's
admittance to the Senate's debates, the Legislature tack on another
proviso (both a broad hint and a pious hope)

"that the commissioners. . . shall prepare in the room of the
senate. . . a gallery calculated for the admission of the citizens. . .
to hear the debates of that house, whenever the senate of the
United States may agree to open the doors of the senate chamber
for that purpose."

The 40-foot extension of Congress Hall southward seems to have been completed early in 1794 for, on February 8th, committees from the State Legislature are appointed

"to examine the building. . . and report whether the said building is improved agreeably to the law passed April the eleventh last [1793]."

February 19th, the joint committees report "the said law has been complied with," except for building a visitors' gallery in the Senate Chamber; that work

"has not been carried into full effect, by reason of the late prevailing sickness [the Yellow Fever Visitation of 1793], and the insufficiency of the sum appropriated."

The Legislature appropriate $1000 and the Senate Chamber gallery's finished in 1795.

If anyone wishes to know what Congress Hall looked like before the 1793 enlargement, they have only to look at the Supreme Court House (Old City Hall) at the other end of the square. Long before either building was erected, it was well understood that both were to be exactly alike so that the whole State House Group should be perfectly balanced and symmetrical. Congress Hall's enlargement—a makeshift attempt to squeeze as much as possible into the least space, and provide a large enough chamber for the Lower House—messed up a dignified structure with a noble stair, and substituted a miserably "scrunched up" stair with a cruel gradient, about as comfortable to ascend as a step-ladder.

Theophilus Bradley, a Massachusetts Member of the House, writes his daughter (evidently soon after the enlargement) a description of both Congressional chambers. In the House of Representatives, the Speaker sits

"in a large arm chair with a table before him like a toilette, covered with green cloth, fringed. The Speaker's seat is elevated about 2 feet and is on the west side of the hall. The members' seats are 3 rows of desks, rising one above the other in the form of a semi-circle, opposite the Speaker; these are writing desks with large armed chairs with leather bottoms. There is a lock and key to each desk and places on the desks for ink, pens, sand and a plentiful supply of paper. There are two fireplaces on each side of the hall with stoves."

One of the stoves, at least, is a large pyramidal affair. The Member from Massachusetts might have added that the Speaker's great leather-covered armchair is garnished with brass-headed tacks, and has no canopy above it; also, that the Clerk's table's on the floor

of the House in front of the Speaker's dais, and to the left of the
Speaker are four desks for the stenographers. Outside the "Bar
of the House," there's an open space or lobby where Members
may talk with their visitors, and there's a visitors' gallery at the
north end of the chamber.

At the south end of the hall, on each side of the bay, a small
door opens directly into the Yard, which the *Columbian Magazine,*
of January, 1790, describes as

> "a beautiful lawn, interspersed with little knobs or tufts of flower-
> ing shrubs and clumps of trees well disposed. Through the mid-
> dle of the gardens runs a spacious gravel walk lined with double
> rows of thriving elms and communicating with serpentine walks
> which encompass the whole area. These surrounding walks are
> not uniformly on a level with the lawn, the margin of which
> being in some parts a little higher forms a bank which, in fine
> weather, affords pleasant seats."

The *Columbian Magazine* writer pictures the State House Yard
as an idyllic spot wherein Congressmen may meditate, walk, talk
and "hold sweet converse together"—or argue and squabble.

The first Speaker of the House to occupy the spacious brass-
studded chair is Frederick Augustus Mühlenberg who,

> "by his portly person and handsome rotundity, literally filled the
> chair. His rubicund complexion and oval face, hair full pow-
> dered, tambored satin vest of ample dimensions, dark blue coat
> with gilt buttons, and a sonorous voice. . . all corresponding in
> appearance and sound with his magnificent name,"

combine to make a profound impression on Members and visitors
alike. By way of sharp contrast, the next succeeding Speaker's
gaunt Jonathan Dayton, of New Jersey,

> "a very tall, rawboned figure of a gentleman, with terrific aspect,
> and, when excited, a voice of thunder," whose "slender, bony
> figure filled only the centre of the chair."

When "babbling politicians" in the lobby make too much noise,
Mr. "Jupiter" Dayton starts to his feet, looks fiercely around the
hall and roars, "Order, order, without the bar!" in such appalling
tones that

> "as though a cannon had been fired under the windows. . . the
> deepest silence in one moment prevailed, but for a very short
> time."

Of the Senate Chamber upstairs, Theophilus Bradley says,

> "the Vice-President's chair is in an area (like the altar in a
> church) at the south end. The Senators' seats, two rows of desks

and chairs, in a semi-circle, but not raised from the floor. The floors of both halls are covered with woolen carpets."

At each side of the passage leading to the Senate Chamber are Committee Rooms; to these—since the enlargement—in their "elegantly carved and gilt" frames, have been relegated the portraits of Louis XVI and Marie Antoinette. It looks as though the guillotine's severed not only the royal head (January 21, 1793) but also any lingering ties of erstwhile gratitude.

The Senate Chamber's "furnished and fitted up in a much superior style to that of the lower House." The American Eagle, with thunderbolts in his talons, is painted in the cove of the ceiling directly above the President's chair. A grapevine, with 13 stars enclosed by its tendrils, surrounds the rayed oval in the plaster decoration of the ceiling from which hangs the chandelier.

Congress continue to sit in this building until May 14, 1800. It's well to remember that, while they sit here, the Federal Constitution's "practically put in running order"; that the Army and Navy are placed on a creditable footing; the United States Mint is established; "Jay's Treaty," the Treaty of Commerce with England, is debated and ratified; the Bank of the United States is instituted; the States of Vermont, Kentucky and Tennessee are admitted to the Union; the Government successfully withstands two great insurrections that threaten its overthrow—"Shays's Rebellion" in Massachusetts and "The Whisky Insurrection" in Pennsylvania; during the Indian War, "St. Clair's Defeat" and "Wayne's Success" become conspicuous events in American history; and, notwithstanding the disloyalties and bitter animosities engendered, involvement in the wars of the French Revolution is avoided.

Congress Hall, Honourable Samuel W. Pennypacker; The Old State House of Pennsylvania, Frank M. Etting, 140, 141; Columbian Magazine, January, 1790; Pennsylvania Magazine of History and Biography, xxvii, 51; ibid., viii, 226; Journals of Congress; Journals of the Senate of the Commonwealth of Pennsylvania; Statutes at Large of Pennsylvania, xiv, 431.

1793

Monday, March 4—At noon the Senate Chamber in Congress Hall's packed to its utmost capacity for President Washington's inauguration to his second term. The Senate, the House of Representatives and the diplomatic circle fill most of the small space (the 40-foot southward extension of the building hasn't yet been made), so comparatively few besides them can squeeze in for the ceremony. However, the throng in the street get a good sight of the President coming and going.

The President's the most punctual of men. Just a few minutes before noon, the waiting crowd outside Congress Hall opens and gives room for his Excellency's white coach, drawn by six superb white horses, to pull up at the kerb. The coach panels are embellished with paintings of the Four Seasons by Cipriani, coachman and footmen wear white liveries turned up with red.

As the coach stops, two ushers with long white wands step out and open a way for the President from the kerb to the steps of the Hall. On the top step, his Excellency pauses and turns to look at a carriage following his own. He's dressed in a full suit of black velvet, with black silk stockings, diamond knee-buckles, shoes "brightly japanned," with large square silver buckles; his carefully dressed hair's fully powdered and gathered behind in a black silk bag with a bow of black ribbon. He carries a cocked hat, with the American cockade. At his side's a light dress sword in a green shagreen scabbard; the hilt's richly ornamented.

As his Excellency enters the Hall, the ushers with their wands precede him and, with some difficulty, open a way through the press to the stair. On the President's entrance, everyone in the Senate Chamber rises.

At the head of the Senate stands Thomas Jefferson. A small boy's edged his way through the crowd and somehow managed to wriggle into the Senate Chamber unobserved. Years afterwards, with vivid recollection, he describes Jefferson's appearance "in a blue coat, single-breasted, with large bright basket-buttons—his waistcoat and small clothes of crimson." He remembers "being struck with his animated countenance of a brick-red hue, his bright eye and foxy hair, as well as by his tall, gaunt, ungainly form and square shoulders. A perfect contrast was presented by the pale reflective face and figure of James Madison; and, above

all, by the short, burly, bustling form of General Knox, with
ruddy cheek" and prominent eye.

Vice-President Adams, as usual, wears a light drab suit, with white
silk stockings.

Observant Edward Thornton, Secretary to the British Minister,
writing home next day to the Under Secretary of State for Foreign
Affairs, mentions a curious circumstance at the inauguration:

"The portraits of the King and Queen of France, which were presented, I believe, during the war, were covered with a curtain,
a circumstance which was not the case most certainly when I have
been there on former occasions. Alas! poor Louis!
        'Deserted at his utmost need
        By those his former bounty fed!' "

This childish, picayune blocking-out of royalty, of former benefactors, is apparently a sop to the present rabid pro-French-Revolu-
tionary sentiment that's causing the President and the Federal
Party so much embarrassment and trouble. Who's responsible for
this insulting gesture, one can readily guess. It's certainly *not* the
President. As a matter of fact, it's a subtle slap at him.

The ceremony's brief; over in a few minutes. Before he takes
the oath of office, the President makes a short speech expressing
"his sense of the high honour conferred on him by his re-election."
Then Mr. Justice Cushing, of the United States Supreme Court,
in full-bottomed judge's wig, administers the oath. After that,
the President departs in stately dignity, as he's entered. As he gets
into his coach, the crowds in the street cheer loudly.

Dunlap's American Daily Advertiser, March 5, 1793; *Recollections and
Anecdotes of the Presidents of the United States*, Arthur J. Stansbury;
The Republican Court, Rufus Wilmot Griswold, 367-368; *History of Phila-
delphia*, Thompson Westcott, ch. cccxiv; *Letter from Edward Thornton,
Esq.* to Sir James Bland Burges, Bart., in *Pennsylvania Magazine of His-
tory and Biography*, ix, 220; *Dictionary of American Biography*.

Thursday, May 16—Rabid pro-French citizens hold an evening
meeting at the State House; it's about the arrival to-day of the
new French Minister, called "Citizen" Genêt, whom the French
Revolutionists have sent to the United States since they beheaded
King Louis XVI. The Philadelphia "Gallic" party are bent on
furthering Genêt's aggressive designs.

Edmond Charles Genêt (the final "t" is pronounced), well-
born, of a family long connected with the government of France;

of marked ability and exceptionally well educated; and employed for some time past in the French diplomatic service, has joined the revolutionary party. When Louis XVI is beheaded, he represents France at the Russian Court and is obliged to leave St. Petersburg as *persona non grata*. The revolutionaries think he'll be useful to them in America and send him hither. He lands in Charleston and, by his very undiplomatic behaviour, creates commotion all the way thence to Philadelphia.

To-day, a "great concourse of citizens" meet him at Gray's Ferry and escort him into the city "with loud acclamations." Those who stage this demonstration are the bitter anti-Federalists—former ultra-Whig Pennsylvania "Constitutionalists," most of them—infected with what their fellow-citizens call the "Gallic madness." They're violently opposed to Washington's policy of neutrality and wise determination not to be drawn into a war by the wiles of the French Revolutionists.

These Philadelphia radicals have caused the President no end of trouble and anxiety; they've carped at him for his courtly manners and his proper insistence on maintaining a dignity befitting his high office. They've even descended to the most petty and venomous personalities, in both speech and print. However, on this very day of Genêt's arrival in Philadelphia, 300 of the most reputable and representative citizens have addressed the President and assured him of their whole-hearted support.

This gesture, of course, doesn't lessen the animosity of the pro-French enthusiasts—many of them, indeed, only a short time before, have been lauding the King of France to the skies and celebrating his birthday as though it were a national American holiday. They're inexcusably fickle—both in their present abuse and vilification of Washington (whom only a little while ago they professed to adore) and in their loud-mouthed acclaim of those bloody-handed revolutionaries who've just beheaded their erstwhile idol.

At the State House meeting this mid-May evening, Charles Biddle's in the chair; Robert Henry Dunkin acts as secretary. A committee—David Rittenhouse, Alexander James Dallas, Doctor James Hutchinson, Peter Stephen Duponceau, Jonathan Dickinson Sergeant, George Fox and William Barton—draught an address of welcome to the new "representative of French republicanism." The address, a fulsome adulatory composition, is adopted. The

"Gallic" partisans then form themselves "in sections of three abreast, and, with Charles Biddle at the head of the line, walk to the City Tavern," followed by a crowd of people. There are sundry introductions and they read the address to Genêt. The adulation and flattery he gets, both now and later, only increase his effrontery to Washington, the whole Federal Party, and the National and State Governments.

A few days after this, there's a "grand civic feast" at Oellers's Hotel, on Chestnut Street, just above Sixth—only a stone's throw from Congress Hall, and doubtless planned to be held "right under the nose" of Congress. It's also planned to be as conspicuous as possible. From early morning, American and French flags are hung out from the hotel. Genêt's the guest of honour, officers from *L'Ambuscade* (now moored in the Delaware) attend, "and officers of the Federal and State Governments." One can readily guess *which* Government officers.

At this function, Charles Biddle presides; Doctor Hutchinson acts as vice-president. The table decorations include American and French flags, liberty trees and liberty caps. There are 15 toasts, and an artillery company stationed outside booms a salvo for each. The seventh toast is, "In complaining of the temporary evils of revolution, may we never forget that the greater evils of monarchy and aristocracy are perpetual." This is a direct dig at Washington, whom they accuse of monarchical tendencies. Genêt sings the *"Marseillaise,"* the company join in the chorus, the last stanza standing. After the toasts, the *bonnet rouge* is placed on Genêt's head (by whom's not recorded), "from thence is placed successively on the heads of all present"!

Is it any wonder that some of the Federalists, "as a set-off to these furious proceedings," celebrate the Birthday of George III (June 4th) at a public dinner, with toasts to the King, Queen Charlotte, the Prince of Wales and George Washington?

The 4th of July this year seems more a French than an American festival. Societies are being formed

"in imitation of the Jacobin clubs; everything that is respectable in society is condemned as aristocratic; politeness is looked upon as a sort of *lèse républicanisme;* the common forms of expression in use by the *sans culottes* are adopted by their American disciples; the title citizen becomes as common in Philadelphia as in Paris, and in the newspapers it is the fashion to announce marriages as partnerships between citizen Brown, Smith or Jones, and the *citesse* who has been wooed to such an association."

One of the pro-French taverns hangs out a revolting sign, picturing the bloody, mutilated corpse of Marie Antoinette.

On July 14th, to celebrate the fall of the Bastille, the 2nd Regiment of Militia hold a dinner. Citizen Genêt's the guest of honour. Governour Mifflin's there, along with a number of others, too, who ought to have been more prudent, considering the excesses to which the pro-Gallicans are letting their frenzy carry them. At this dinner a roasted pig is named for Louis XVI,

"and the head, severed from the body, is carried round to each of the guests, who, after placing the liberty cap on his own head, pronounces the word 'Tyrant!' and proceeds to mangle with his knife that of the luckless creature doomed to be served for so unworthy a company."

Puerile and disgusting!

If all this affectation of Gallicism were but a kind of simian mimicry, it would be silly but not particularly harmful. It's worse than that. That such as those already mentioned—men of good birth and background and, under ordinary circumstances, punctilious about the decencies of conduct—should so far disregard the traditions of their upbringing as to praise and emulate Robespierre and his foul crew, can be laid only to a species of daemonic possession, operating through a wave of mass hysteria. Mere political rancour can scarcely account for it.

History of Philadelphia, Thompson Westcott, ch. cccxiv; *The Republican Court,* Rufus Wilmot Griswold, 349-351; Contemporary Newspapers.

Thursday, August 29—The Assembly meet to-day and Governour Mifflin reads his Speech to the State Senate and House at 1 o'clock. Then they adjourn till next Monday; all the Assemblymen very jittery because of the yellow fever. There's a young man named Fry lying dead of it on the pavement just beyond the west end of the building. Young Fry's very, very dead; the Assemblymen very, very scared. Jacob Hiltzheimer, himself a Member of Assembly, tells us this.

August 22nd, the epidemic's first officially noticed. From his office in City Hall Mayor Clarkson issues

"most peremptory orders, to have the streets properly cleansed and purified by the scavengers, and all the filth immediately hawled away."

He has to repeat these orders insistently on the 27th. It may give some of us now, 154 years later, a ray of consolation to know that Philadelphia streets were offensively dirty then, too, and that street cleaners showed the same reluctance to do a thorough job.

August 30th, Hiltzheimer notes in his *Diary:*

"A small cannon was hauled through the streets and constantly discharged, as the flashing of gunpowder is thought will prevent the spreading of the disorder. This is being done by order of Governour Mifflin and Mayor Clarkson."

Those who can, have already begun to flee the stricken city. Mathew Carey writes:

"The removals from Philadelphia began about the 25th or 26th of this month: and so great was the general terror, that, for some weeks, carts, waggons, coaches, and chairs [chaises], were almost constantly transporting families and furniture to the country in every direction."

Marks are set on the doors or windows of houses where there be folk sick of the plague. At the instance of the College of Physicians, all tolling of bells is stopped. People are counselled "to bury those who die of the disorder in carriages, and as privately as possible." The medical faculty ridicule the notion that bonfires at street corners will stay the sickness. In their consternation, the citizens grasp at all manner of fancied preventives—carry pieces of tarred rope, tie camphor bags around their necks, chew garlic or put garlic in their pockets or shoes, or perpetually smoke strong cigars. Even young women and children are seen puffing at cheroots. All the newspapers save one (the *Federal Gazette*) suspend publication.

Carey paints a picture of well-nigh universal panic, a "total dissolution of the bonds of society."

"The corpses of the most respectable citizens, even of those who do not die of the epidemic, are carried to the grave, on the shafts of a chair, the horse driven by a negro, unattended by a friend or relative, and without any sort of ceremony."

Near Ricketts's Circus at 12th and Market Streets, a man, suddenly stricken, has fallen down, shunned by all till death ends his misery. His body lies rotting in the heat for 48 hours; everyone's afraid to go near him. At last a man's found to undertake the task of burial. Alone, he can't lift the body into the rude coffin. A passing servant girl offers to help him, if he won't tell her employers. Together, they manage to get into the box what's left of the body, now little more than a mass of stinking putrescence crawling with maggots.

Jacob Hiltzheimer's *Diary; A Short Account of the Malignant Fever Lately Prevalent in Philadelphia,* Mathew Carey, 1794, *passim.*

Thursday, September 5—After a short, hurried session, the Assembly adjourn and forsake the State House. Yellow fever's scared the Members nearly out of their wits; nothing under the sun will induce them to stay in the city any longer.

"The disorder is not abating, but appearing in every part of the city. . . . Very few people are seen on the streets, and they keep at a safe distance from each other, and if it is known that you have sickness in your family or among your neighbours you are avoided."

The few who are abroad take to the middle of the street to keep well away from houses where there may be a fever patient and to avoid contact with other foot passengers. Anyone with the least sign of mourning is "shunned like a viper."

Samuel Breck's in the city part of the time and gives a gloomy picture. At first,

"no hospitals or hospital supplies are in readiness to alleviate the sufferings of the poor. For a long time nothing can be done other than to furnish coffins for the dead and men to bury them." The calamity's come so suddenly that it's "terrified the physicians, and led them into contradictory modes of treatment." Oftentimes the disorder's course is so swift that the stricken victim seems doomed from the outset—"stupor, delirium, yellowness, the black vomit, and death rapidly succeeding each other." Now and again, "burning fever occasioned paroxysms of rage which drove the patient naked from his bed to the street, and in some instances to the river, where he was drowned. Insanity was often the last stage of its horrors."

As grim pestilence stalks the streets, conditions in many a visited house are appalling. Carey asks,

"Who, without horror, can reflect on a husband, married perhaps for twenty years, deserting his wife in the last agony—a wife, unfeelingly, abandoning her husband on his death bed—parents forsaking their only children—children ungratefully flying from their parents, and resigning them to chance, often without an enquiry after their health or safety—masters hurrying off their faithful servants to Bush-hill, even on suspicion of the fever, and that at a time, when, like Tartarus, it was open to every visitant, but never returned any—servants abandoning tender and humane masters, who only wanted a little care to restore them to health and usefulness—who, I say, can think of these things, without horror?"

Panic fear's banished or paralysed natural affections.

Sometimes, when fever strikes, all other occupants of an house flee in terror, leave the helpless victim to suffer and die alone; days afterwards, the body's found in advanced decay. Sometimes the inspectors find houses where four or five dead bodies have lain until the stench prompts investigation.

Jacob Hiltzheimer's *Diary; Recollections of Samuel Breck*, ed., H. E. Scudder, 194; *A Short Account of the Malignant Fever Lately Prevalent in Philadelphia*, Mathew Carey, 1794, p. 24.

Friday, September 13—To the State House the people—those of them that are still in the city—are bringing old shirts, shifts and any other old linen they can spare, and leaving it for use in the yellow fever hospital. This in response to Mayor Clarkson's appeal several days ago.

It's not a pleasant sight, but by now one's got used to seeing the coffin-sellers standing on the pavement of City Hall (the easternmost building of the State House Group, at the southwest corner of Fifth and Chestnut Streets). When they're not bargaining about burial jobs, they're feeding their horses oats out of the rough pine coffins they've brought ready for use.

Yesterday, at the citizens' meeting in the Mayor's Office, ten gentlemen volunteered to help the guardians of the poor; a committee, also, was appointed to report on Bush Hill. They've turned Bush Hill into a pest-house; poor people, who can't be properly cared for at home, are sent thither. Hiltzheimer says he's "observed a one-horse covered cart with a bed in it, which is used to convey the sick to Bush Hill Hospital."

The Hamiltons are away from Bush Hill, the place in charge of a caretaker. When a committee of citizens go to requisition the barn and outbuildings for an emergency hospital, the caretaker's so reluctant to co-operate that the committee seize the house itself and hastily prepare it to receive fever victims.

Through haste and lack of proper organisation, the arrangements at first are extremely bad. The investigating committee appointed yesterday report intolerable abuses.

"A profligate, abandoned set of nurses and attendants (hardly

any of good character could at that time be procured), rioted on
the provisions and comforts prepared for the sick, who (unless at
the hours when the doctors attended) were left almost entirely
destitute of every assistance. The sick, the dying, and the dead
were indiscriminately mingled together. The ordure and other
evacuations of the sick, were allowed to remain in the most offensive state imaginable. . . . It was, in fact, a great human slaugh-
ter-house, where numerous victims were immolated at the altar of
riot and intemperance. . . . At length, the poor were so much
afraid of being sent to Bush-hill, that they would not acknowledge
their illness, until it was no longer possible to conceal it."

Of the coffin-sellers or "attendants on the dead," with their stock
of hastily knocked-together cheap coffins on City Hall pavement,
Breck says:

"These speculators were useful, and, albeit with little show of
feeling, contributed greatly to lessen, by competition, the charges
of interment."

About this time, Hiltzheimer writes:

"Called at Matthew Clarkson's on Arch Street, and observed a
hearse with a blind horse in the Friends' graveyard. Was informed
that it was stationed there daily to receive the corpses of those
who belong to the Society: that carriers were not allowed to
handle the coffins, owing to the infection."

Again, he writes:

"By request of Mayor Clarkson the water engines [a more accurate
term than *fire*-engines] began sprinkling the streets of the city, as
it is said a moist atmosphere will add to the general health."

This possibly *adds* to the trouble; Philadelphia water at this time,
from the city pumps and wells, is almost pure sewage.

Recollections of Samuel Breck, ed. H. E. Scudder, *passim;* Jacob Hiltzheimer's *Diary; A Short Account of the Malignant Fever Lately Prevalent in
Philadelphia,* Mathew Carey, 1794, 31.

Saturday, September 14—At noon there's another citizens' meeting
at the Mayor's Office in City Hall; called to concert further measures for dealing with the general distress.

Fortunately, there are a good many representative citizens
who've kept cool heads, have refused to run away with the panicky
part of the population, and are determined to do all they can to
fight the pestilence and give public relief. Some of them—Carey
gives many of their names—display the utmost heroism and devotion. In the discharge of their self-imposed duties, more than one,

including several doctors, fall victims to the plague. It's no unusual thing for these volunteers to give eight hours or more daily to relief work.

The report on conditions at Bush Hill's outraged the meeting at the Mayor's Office. The following day (Sunday) Stephen Girard and Peter Helm offer their services and take charge of Bush Hill. Girard assumes responsibility for everything inside the building, Helm for everything outside. They soon bring order out of the disgraceful chaos.

> "Stephen Girard, whose office was in the interior part of the hospital, has had to encourage and comfort the sick—to hand them necessaries and medicines—to wipe the sweat off their brows—and to perform many disgusting offices of kindness for them, which nothing could render tolerable but the most exalted motives that impelled him to this heroic conduct."

In other words, besides being superintendent, he's often nurse and orderly as well. More than once, without stopping to remove the black vomit voided on his clothing by a dying patient, he hastens on to minister to another. There's a long and honourable roster of those who unselfishly give their services and substance, and sometimes their lives, in manifold works of mercy and relief during this period of dire need.

Exaggerated reports cause the utmost apprehension outside of Philadelphia. People in other cities and towns refuse to let anyone from Philadelphia come near them. It's said the people of Easton (in Maryland) have burned a waggon-load of goods coming from Philadelphia; also, that they've tarred and feathered a woman who accompanied the waggon.

> "Some of the postmasters, in the different states, use the precaution to dip Philadelphia letters into vinegar with a pair of tongs, before they handle them. Several of the subscribers for Philadelphia papers, make their servants sprinkle them with vinegar, and dry them at the fire, before they venture to touch them."

What befalls wayfarers suddenly attacked by the fever, whether they be from Philadelphia or not, Carey tells:

> "A poor man was taken sick on the road at a village not far from Philadelphia. He lay calling for water, a considerable time in vain. At length, an old woman brought him a pitcher full, and not daring to approach him, she laid it at a distance, desiring him to crawl to it, which he did. After lying there about 48 hours, he died; and the body lay in a state of putrefaction for some time, until the neighbours hired two black butchers to bury him for

twenty-four dollars. They dug a pit to windward—with a fork, hooked a rope about his neck—dragged him into it—and, at as great a distance as possible, cast earth into the pit to cover him."

A Short Account of the Malignant Fever Lately Prevalent in Philadelphia, Mathew Carey, 1794, 35, 84; Jacob Hiltzheimer's *Diary; Recollections of Samuel Breck,* ed. H. E. Scudder, *passim.*

1796

Wednesday, December 7—Exactly on the stroke of noon, President Washington enters the House of Representatives. Both Senate and Lower House are there to hear his Excellency's last stated Message to Congress before he retires from office. Because of the last paragraph's valedictory tone, this speech is often confused with the "Farewell Address."

The "Farewell Address to the People of the United States" was never *orally* delivered, nor was it intended to be. *Claypoole's American Daily Advertiser's* already published it (Monday, September 19th) while Congress are in recess. Claypoole's printed it from Washington's own manuscript (sent him by the President, and the proof corrected by his Excellency); the other newspapers throughout the country have reprinted it. A major purpose of its printed circulation, before election time, has been to acquaint the nation fully that the President absolutely declines candidacy for a third term in office.

When Congress assemble for their winter session (Monday, December 5th), there's no quorum in the Senate till Tuesday. Then, a joint committee (from Senate and House) wait on the President to say they're met and "ready to receive any communication he may be pleased to make to them." The President replies he'll meet the two Houses "to-morrow [Wednesday] at twelve o'clock in the House of Representatives."

Senate and House attending as appointed, the President, "delivered the following address," most of which is the routine "report on the State of the nation," but, at the close, he says:

"The situation in which I now stand, for the last time, in the midst of the Representatives of the People of the United States, naturally recals the period when the administration of the present form of Government commenced; and I cannot omit the occasion to congratulate you, and my country, on the success of the experiment; nor to repeat my fervent supplications to the Supreme Ruler of the Universe and sovereign Arbiter of Nations, that his providential care may still be extended to the United States; that the virtue and happiness of the people may be preserved; and that the government, which they have instituted for the protection of their Liberties, may be perpetual."

Directly he's finished, the President presents "a copy of it [the address] to the President of the Senate [Vice-President Adams], and another copy to the Speaker of the House of Representatives [Frederick Augustus Mühlenberg]." The President and the Senate then withdraw; portly Mr. Speaker Mühlenberg resumes his chair.

Realising the national import of the sentiments expressed, doubtless many people in the Hall are deeply affected. The national election's result's not yet known; to the intense bitterness of political animosities between Federalists and Democrats are added uncertainty and anxiety as to where power will reside in the immediate future.

In 1859, an elderly lady, quoted in George Washington Parke Custis's *Recollections of Washington* (source of many unprovable anecdotes about *"Pater Patriae")*, recalls the scene at what she mistakenly terms the delivery of the "Farewell Address," when she was an impressionable girl of twenty:

"... Mr. Adams covered his face with both his hands; the sleeves of his coat, and his hands, were covered with tears. Every now and then there was a suppressed sob. I cannot describe Washington's appearance as I felt it—perfectly composed and self-possessed, till the close of his address: Then, when strong nervous sobs broke loose, when tears covered the faces, the great man was shaken. ... Large drops came from his eyes. ..."

Even allowing for lapses of memory after sixty-three years, and some inexactitude about details, this account probably reflects pretty well the Federalist and, indeed, general sentiment of the moment.

The Aurora—as might be expected—comes out in the next few days with its usual pestilential crop of waspish attacks and spiteful innuendoes, but the majority of the President's political enemies and detractors, blinded though they be by their insensate adulation of Revolutionary France, have the decency (or discretion) to keep reasonably silent. On this occasion, few are as rancorously outspoken as a former Pennsylvania anti-Federalist Senator who, at some previous juncture when the President had stirred his ire, is recorded to have said, "Would to God this same General Washington were in Heaven!"

Claypoole's American Daily Advertiser, September 19; December 6, 7, 8, 9, 1796; *History of Philadelphia*, Scharf & Westcott, i, 483-484; *The Aurora*, December, 1796, *passim; Recollections of Washington*, George Washington Parke Custis, 434; *Congress Hall*, Honourable Samuel W. Pennypacker.

1797

Wednesday, February 22—This is his last birthday General Washington will spend in Philadelphia as President of the United States. Christ Church bells ring to mark the event. In the forenoon, most of the Members of Congress, along with the Governour and State Legislature, go in a body from the State House around to Market Street to congratulate his Excellency at his house. The military officers and the Society of the Cincinnati soon follow them. At noon, all the guns roar a Federal Salute, and there are military evolutions.

At night, there's a great Birthday Ball at Ricketts's Circus, just across Sixth Street from Congress Hall, by its position almost a part of the State House Group. The President's many devoted friends and admirers in the city are giving this ball as a testimonial of their esteem. It's a brilliant function, "which for Splendour, Taste and Elegance, was, perhaps, never excelled by any similar Entertainment in the United States," according to next day's newspapers. James Iredell writes Mrs. Iredell:

"At the Amphitheatre. . . it is supposed there was at least 1200 persons. The show was a very brilliant one, but such scrambling to go to supper that there was some danger of being squeezed to death. The Vice President handed in Mrs. Washington, and the President immediately followed. The applause with which they were received is indescribable. The same was shown on their return from supper. The music added greatly to the interest of the scene. The President staid till between 12 and 1."

Ricketts's Circus has become a favourite place of entertainment, in much demand for public dinners, balls and other gatherings that require ample space; the wealth and fashion of the city give generous patronage. John Bill Ricketts, to whose enterprise the city owes this popular place of amusement, is an expert equestrian and celebrated riding master. He comes to Philadelphia from London—probably a Scot by birth—where he's been a pupil of Hughes, of the Blackfriars' Bridge Circus. A "circus" in the eighteenth century's literally a circle or ring for exhibiting equestrian feats. It also serves as a riding-school and a circus proprietor generally teaches riding.

In 1792, Ricketts opened a circus at 12th and Market Streets.

Besides equestrian feats, he gradually introduced other attractions —tightrope walking, clowns, pantomimes, slack-rope dancing, acrobats—thus starting the evolution of the modern circus. Matthew Sully, father of Thomas Sully, the painter, made his first Philadelphia appearance as "funny-man" in Ricketts's employ. Ricketts immediately endeared himself to the people by giving benefit performances to buy fuel for the poor. The Board of City Trusts still administers a charitable fund he created in 1796 for the relief of the city's poor.

In 1795, his success warrants a more ambitious establishment than the circus at 12th and Market Streets. October 19th (1795) he opens his new Circus at the southwest corner of Sixth and Chestnut Streets; it's the most elaborate thing of the kind America's yet seen. Washington, expert horseman as he is, enjoys going there to see the shows Ricketts puts on. This new building's 97 feet in diameter, seats 1214 persons, is lighted with "patent lights," and has a coffee-room at one side that communicates with pit and boxes. There's also a stage. A figure of the Flying Mercury tops the conical roof.

Claypoole's American Daily Advertiser, February 23, 1797; *Encyclopaedia of Philadelphia,* Joseph Jackson, ii, 455-458; *Washington after the Revolution,* W. S. Baker, 341.

Saturday, March 4—In the House of Representatives at noon the Honourable John Adams takes the oath of office as the second President of the United States. Chief Justice Oliver Ellsworth administers the oath.

Besides the Senate and House of Representatives, the foreign Ministers and Consuls attend; the ladies, dressed in their best, crowd the gallery. Let's hope the "spitting-boxes" have been removed for this State occasion.

As the President enters, "as well as on the entrance of the late President, and of Thomas Jefferson, the Vice President," the hall resounds with "loud and reiterated applause." President Adams takes

"his seat on the elevated Chair of the Speaker of the House of Representatives, the Vice President, the late President and the Secretary of the Senate on his right, the Speaker and the Clerk of the House of Representatives on his left, and the Chief-Justice of the United States and the Associate Judges at a table in the centre."

In places of honour are "all the Foreign Ministers and Ambassa-
dors," the Heads of Departments and General Wilkinson, Commander-in-Chief of the Army.

President Adams, as usual, wears a light drab cloth suit with
lash sleeves, wrist ruffles, and white silk stockings; his hair well
powdered and tied behind in a rose and bag, like Washington's.
Jefferson has on a long, blue, single-breasted coat; his hair slightly
powdered and tied in a queue with a black ribbon. The most
gorgeous personage is the Spanish Minister, the Marquess d'Yrujo,
in full diplomatic array—

> "of middle size, of round person, florid complexion, and hair
> powdered like a snowball; dark striped silk coat, lined with satin;
> white waistcoat, black silk breeches, white silk stockings, shoes
> and buckles. . . by his side an elegant hilted small sword, and his
> chapeau, tipped with white feathers, under his arm."

The inauguration ceremony's brief, with the usual risings,
bowings and sittings-down. As the new President departs,

> "Washington and Jefferson remain standing together, and the
> bulk of the audience watching their movements in curious silence.
> Presently, with a graceful motion of the hand, Washington invites
> the Vice-President, Jefferson, to pass on before him, which is de-
> clined by Mr. Jefferson. After a pause, an invitation to proceed is
> repeated by Washington, when the Vice-President passes on to-
> wards the door and Washington after him."

The day's final event's a great public dinner the City Mer-
chants give General Washington, at Ricketts's Circus, "in testi-
mony of their approbation of his conduct as President." Thomas
Willing and Thomas FitzSimons preside. The city's most repre-
sentative gentlemen attend; also, all the foreign Ministers, many
Members of Congress, and the Governour of the State. Meeting at
Oellers's Hotel next door, they march thence together into
Ricketts's.

"On their entering the Circus, *Washington's march* resounds
through the place, and a curtain draws up which presents to view"
a transparency—a full-length figure of Washington, Fame crowning him with a laurel wreath as he takes leave after handing her
a copy of his farewell address as General of the American Armies.
A female figure holds a Cap of Liberty, before her an altar inscribed "Public Gratitude"; sundry appropriate devices and emblems accompany this composition, and there's a distant view of
Mount Vernon.

Richardet, the caterer, has excelled himself in serving a "sumptuous entertainment"; the best of food and drink in abundance. Numerous toasts follow. The "remains of the festival" are sent to the Hospital and the prisoners in the Gaol.

Claypoole's American Daily Advertiser, March 6, 1797; *Poulson's Advertiser,* March 6, 1797; *History of Philadelphia,* Thompson Westcott, ch. cccxv.

1798

Tuesday, January 30—Disgraceful rumpus in the House of Representatives in Congress Hall. The House in session (but in an interval while ballots are being counted and Members out of their places, walking about and talking), Vermont's Matthew Lyon in blatant manner disparages Connecticut's people, in particular asperses Connecticut's Representatives. Connecticut's Roger Griswold retorts by alluding to Lyon's "wooden sword"—the wooden sword a court-martial compelled Lyon to wear when they cashiered him for cowardice in the field during the Revolution.

Lyon's face works convulsively; then he spits a stream of tobacco-juice square in Griswold's face. Childish and disgusting!

Griswold hauls off, about to punch Lyon's head. Then, "from respect to the house, and being instantly cautioned by some of his friends," he refrains and wipes his face.

The House called to order, Samuel Sewall, of Massachusetts, moves to expel Lyon for his "violent attack and gross indecency." The House appoint a "Committee of Privileges" to investigate. After endless depositions, on *February 12th* the Committee report in favor of expulsion. The resolution to expel Lyon gets a majority of votes but fails of the requisite two-thirds! Of course, Federalist and anti-Federalist bitterness underlies the whole affair.

Abigail Adams, writing her sister February 14th, says:

". . . You will see much to your mortification, that Congress have been fitting [fighting], not the French, but Lyon, not the Noble British Lyon, but but [*sic*] the beastly transported Lyon [For spitting proficiency he might be named *Llama*.]. . . What a picture will these 14teen days make upon our Journals?! Yet are the supporters of Lyon to blame: *the Gentlemen* the real federilist would have expeld him instantly, and if it were possible a federilist could be found thus to have degraded himself, he would not have cost the country 14 days debate, besides the infamy and disgrace of sitting again there. . . . The Brute has not been in the house for several days, but he is unfealing enough to go again, and if he does, I have my apprehensions of something still more unpleasant."

Journal of the House of Representatives of the United States, iii, 145, 178; *New Letters of Abigail Adams, 1786-1801,* Stewart Mitchell, 132-133; *House of Wisdom in a Bustle,* William Cobbett, 1798; Contemporary Newspapers, Jan. 30—Feb. 14, 1798.

Thursday, February 15—Another shindy in Congress Hall, after prayers but before the Speaker calls the House to order. Griswold and Lyon at it again.

Lyon's writing at his desk; Griswold comes up and whangs him over the head and shoulders with a hickory stick. Lyon grabs a pair of tongs from the stove. Then they lambaste each other like savages. Griswold gets Lyon down and pummels him. At risk of broken heads in the *mêlée,* other Members manage to separate them. Two anti-Federalists drag Griswold off by the legs. Mr. Speaker objects—they should have taken him by the shoulders.

Not much dignity in the House; some Members—part of the scum cast up by the Revolution—wear their cocked hats during debates, throw their legs across desks, and habitually spew into the "spitting boxes" provided. Sharp contrast to the decorum upstairs in the Senate Chamber!

Cobbett's *House of Wisdom in a Bustle*—one of the versified satires on the Griswold-Lyon fracas—besides describing the fight, pictures the lousy behaviour of the "indecorous House":

"The clock had just struck; the doors were extended;
The Priest to his pulpit had gravely ascended.
Devoutly he prayed, for devoutly he should
Solicit for wicked as well as for good.

. . . .

This duty performed, without hesitation,
He left to their wisdom the charge of the nation.
When the parson retired, some members sat musing,
Whilst others were letters and papers perusing.
Some apples were munching; some laughing and joking;
Some snuffing, some chewing, but none were a-smoking;
Some warming their faces—others back s——s indulging,
Whilst they to their Colleagues were secrets divulging. . . ."

It's just at this point the row occurs. When order's restored, the Speaker exacts a pledge from Griswold and Lyon to let each other alone for the rest of the term.

Journal of the House of Representatives of the United States, iii, 185-202, 484, 487; *House of Wisdom in a Bustle,* William Cobbett, 1798; Contemporary Newspapers, especially *The Aurora, Porcupine's Gazette, Gazette of the United States,* and *Claypoole's American Daily Advertiser,* January 31-February 20, 1798.

1802

Wednesday, March 17—Charles Willson Peale's long been trying to lodge his Museum in the State House. Since 1794 he's had it in the Philosophical Society's building; kept some of his live animals and birds in cages in the State House Yard. Now, he says he needs more room.

There've been all sorts of people in the State House in years past; all manner of things have happened within its walls; never before has it been overrun by stuffed birds and fishes.

St. Patrick's Day, 1802, the State Legislature give Mr. Peale leave to use the east room—the Assembly or Independence Chamber—downstairs, and all of upstairs. The Philosophical Society have memorialised the Legislature in his favour; City Councils have endorsed his application. The only conditions specified are that elections shall continue to be held at the State House; that Mr. Peale take care of the State House Yard; and that he

"open the doors in the hall and permit citizens to walk in the yard for recreation, and to pass and repass at reasonable hours as heretofore."

The room in which Washington was commissioned Commander-in-Chief of the American Forces, the room in which the Declaration of Independence was Adopted and Signed, the room in which the Federal Constitution was Framed—now becomes the repository of reptiles, skeletons, wax figures and freaks! Mr. Peale wields considerable political influence.

One suspects the Philosophical Society are rather relieved and thankful to have their building to themselves. Their amiability in offering it to Mr. Peale in 1794—and the sequel—recall the old story of the camel and the tent.

Mr. Peale's a thorough-going expansionist—not only adds constantly to his collections and contrives new conceits to divert the curious and conjure admission fees from their pockets but, in 1811, when the wings (formerly called the "Offices") of the State House are about to be rebuilt, he wishes to spread his Museum into their upper floors, too. This privilege isn't granted.

In 1816, when the City buys the State House and State House Yard from the State, City Councils tell Mr. Peale he'll have to pay rent—$400 a year. In 1818, Councils raise the rent to $1200 and require Mr. Peale to vacate the ground floor, which they let to the County Courts for $2400 yearly. In 1821, Councils reduce Museum rent to $600.

Until 1806 the Museum's open only in daytime; then Mr. Peale decides to keep open two evenings a week, lighting by "patent lamps and candles." To popularise this venture, special attractions appear—lectures by Mr. Peale, members of his talented family, and others; spectacular experiments in chemistry or exhibitions of electrical phenomena; magic-lantern shows and the like.

For a time, the Museum's open Sundays. A placard at the entrance says:

"Here the wonderful works of the Divinity may be contemplated with pleasure and advantage. Let no one enter with any other view."

For them that prefer "sermons in stones" to being bored by long-winded homilies from the pulpit, this is a rare break. How long Sunday-opening continues isn't recorded; it arouses strong opposition.

In 1809, Mr. Peale puts on a show (or side-show) of stuffed monkeys! Dressed up like people, they represent various human occupations and trades. Another grotesquerie, in 1820, is the "Pandean Band." Mr. Peale's persuaded an hapless Italian performer to make an hellish din at regular intervals by working five musical (?) instruments simultaneously.

"By using his hands, elbows, and knees, he manages to play on the Italian viola, the Turkish cymbals, and the tenor drum, while he blows into a set of pandean pipes thrust into his waistcoat, and by wagging his head tinkles the Chinese bells fixed thereon as a sort of helmet"!

It's said this "musical" prodigy "draws well."

Mr. Peale's many portraits of Revolutionary worthies naturally fill an important place in the Museum. Incongruously jumbled with stuffed alligators and dodos, they're nevertheless dignified paintings of real excellence. Their presence is the sole justification for the Museum ever being allowed in the State House.

In 1828, the Museum moves to the new Arcade, in the next square above the State House. While in the State House, Mr. Peale's annual "take" is estimated at $7000 to $10,000.

Phenomenally versatile and enterprising, Mr. Peale's also amazingly ingenious and tirelessly industrious. With the psychology of a good showman and a capable artist's talent, he's very wide awake himself and has vision; he sponsors the infancy of many worthwhile movements destined later to reach dignified fulfillment. His presence and varied activities stimulate the people of his own day and generation.

History of Philadelphia, Scharf & Westcott, *passim; History of Philadelphia*, Ellis Paxson Oberholtzer, *passim;* Advertisements in Contemporary Newspapers; *Journals of Pennsylvania Assembly*.

1805

Friday, June 21—The Pennsylvania Academy of the Fine Arts, Charles Willson Peale's brain-child, is born in the Independence Chamber.

Poulson's American Daily Advertiser printed yesterday a notice with a pointing hand:

> "The members of the association for promoting the Fine Arts in the city of Philadelphia, are requested to meet at Mr. Rembrandt Peale's painting room, in the east room of the State-house, to-morrow morning at 9 o'clock, to choose a president and directors for the ensuing year."

This morning's paper has a like notice.

About 70 have associated and subscribed; they elect as President the now venerable George Clymer, who signed both the Declaration of Independence and the Federal Constitution in this very room. The 12 Directors elected are William Tilghman—soon to become Pennsylvania's Chief Justice—William Rawle, Moses Levy, Joseph Hopkinson, of "Hail Columbia!" and legal fame, Joseph B. McKean, William Meredith, sculptor William Rush, Doctor John Redman Coxe, John Dorsey, William Poyntell, Doctor Thomas Chalkley James and Charles Willson Peale. The majority are lawyers; Peale and Rush the only artists.

After to-day's meeting (elated at progress of his long-cherished scheme) Peale writes from the "Museum" (State House) to Benjamin Henry Latrobe in Wilmington:

> "I wish you had been here while an association was forming for the advancement of the Fine Arts. We have upwards of $2400 subscribed, a constitution formed; President and 12 Directors chosen to-day. Shall probably purchase bills on to-morrow for the purchase of plaster figures, which will be sent by a vessel to sail on Sunday next.
>
> We ought to have a building to put the figures in when they arrive; you know the disadvantage of subjecting them to removals. . . ."

Monday following, he writes son Rubens the Directors have allotted "$600 to purchase casts of statues. . . ."

Mr. Peale's a good "pudding-stick"; he's at last succeeded in convincing enough representative and public-spirited citizens that it's both timely and feasible to establish a gallery of painting and

sculpture, and combine with it a school for training art students.
Keen to see Philadelphia "the seat of arts and sciences in America," he's made two previous essays to found an academy—in 1789,
and again in 1794. Both attempts came to naught. Now, when
he's 64, success rewards his perseverance.

The preparatory agitation before the State House meeting appears from several of Peale's letters. He's written son Raphaelle,
June 6th:

". . . We have begun again an attempt to form an Institution for
the encouragement of the fine arts. You may remember to have
heard that Mr. Hopkinson had said that he would get the Lawers
[sic] to undertake to make a subscription—A Mr. Li [illegible]
or some such name (a Hollander who has a collection of fine
paintings) called on Rembrandt. . . they asked me to meet them
one evening and. . . we proposed to get a meeting of Mr. Hopkinson, Mr. Rawle Mr. Sansom Doct^r Coxe and Mr. Meredith—I
invited them to my House, we have had several meetings—
and each have aided to obtain subscribers. we have over 1600$
subscribed and expect 2000 will be made up soon . . . The pro-
posial [sic] is to import casts and begin a Gallery of figures and
Paintings; . . . out of this will arise the Academy of drawing
from the Models and afterwards from the life—Rembrandt is
preparing a general sketch to be considered at our next meeting—
so that the whole of the business will be ready cut and dryed
before a general meeting is called. This you know is a prudent
procedure, as large bodies can never do business well, it must
always be well prepaired [sic] for them and they will have nothing
to do but give their assent . . ."

June 9th, Peale's written daughter Angelica:

". . . a few gentlemen meet [sic] at my House. . . and have formed
a Plan which cannot fail of success. . . . The Lawyers appear to be
most active in this undertaking."

Amongst the lawyers who do yeoman service, in favourably disposing the public and securing subscriptions, are young Horace
Binney (aged 26) and Joseph Hopkinson, whose influence "appears on the surface and confers the executive and cementing
strength."

Peale's written Thomas Jefferson, June 13th:

". . . A handsome subscription is already made by very respectable characters, and we hope soon to begin a building." He intimates further that Benjamin West (with whom there's already
been communication anent sending certain of his own and other
paintings) highly favours the enterprise and "thinks our Legislature will make appropriations. . . and might be induced to pur-

chase the paintings as models of colouring, composition, &c. If he knew the constitution of our Country better," continues Peale ruefully, "he would loose [sic] all hopes from that quarter . . ."

Following the State House meeting, the Directors lose no time in planning for a building. July 8th, at Judge Hopkinson's house, they authorise a building committee to proceed immediately. They secure a lot on Chestnut Street; John Dorsey "gives the plan." Lacking explicit documentary evidence, we know not precisely who does what in erecting an exquisite little "Regency" building. What seems most likely is that John Dorsey, gifted amateur and (as one of the Directors) fully cognisant of the proposed structure's requirements, produces a sketch which, approved by the committee, is put into workable form in Latrobe's office, in all likelihood by young Robert Mills. Of one thing we may be certain—Latrobe's influence determines the type of architecture; he's the apostle and first exponent of the Regency manner (otherwise known as "Federal") in America. September 7th, Peale writes, "the building is begun." The Academy's incorporation by Act of Legislature is "approved by the Governour, the 28th day of March, 1806."

Barring the *contretemps* of some unforeseen building costs, the Academy starts its career under happy auspices. Aware of the value of well-known names in the roll of persons supporting such an undertaking, the Directors elect as honorary members Benjamin West, now Court Painter to George III and President of the Royal Academy; Robert Fulton, whose fame in developing steam navigation is international; and Judge Bushrod Washington.

By gift or loan, the Directors secure a creditable show of paintings. In this, both West and Fulton help materially. Both of them are native Pennsylvanians; in their early days, both painted in Philadelphia. Young Nicholas Biddle—"a handsome, graceful youth," now a secretary in the American Legation at Paris, where he attends Napoleon's coronation, is presented at Court, dances with the Emperor's sisters, and is very much *persona grata* with the Imperial Family—uses "his influence to get from the Emperor a series of plaster casts from the antiques in the Louvre." These (paid for by the Academy) afford a seemly show of sculpture. Visitors resort to the Academy in encouraging numbers; admission fees soon amount to $100 a month.

The prevalent prudery—prudery that banishes arms and legs,

especially legs, from polite conversation and substitutes "limbs"—
causes Peale misgivings about exhibiting the plaster casts. In 1807,
he writes Fulton, "I long very much to hear what will be said by
the Friends and other denominations of Xans." Public opinion
decrees it's not proper for ladies with male escort to look at such
naked things as the Laocoön or the Apollo Belvedere. If they wish
to behold such indecent nudity without blushing, they can slip
into the sculpture gallery surreptitiously on Mondays, when male
visitors are excluded.

This absurd inhibition lasts a long time. When Mrs. Trollope
comes to Philadelphia, she writes:

"We visited the nineteenth annual exhibition . . . One of the
rooms. . . has inscribed over its door,

ANTIQUE STATUE GALLERY

The door was open, but just within it was a screen, which prevented any objects in the room being seen from without. . . .
pausing to read this inscription, an old woman. . . guardian of
the gallery, bustled up, and. . . said 'Now, ma'am, now: this is
just the time for you—nobody can see you—make haste.' " Mrs.
Trollope amazed, asks what she means. " 'Only, ma'am, that the
ladies like to go into that room by themselves, when there be no
gentlemen watching them.'

On entering this mysterious apartment, the first thing I remarked, was a written paper, deprecating the disgusting depravity
which had led some of the visitors to mark and deface the casts in
a most indecent and shameless manner. This abomination has unquestionably been occasioned by the coarse-minded custom which
sends alternate groups of males and females into the room. Were
the antique gallery thrown open to mixed parties of ladies and
gentlemen, it would soon cease . . ."

Mrs. Trollope doesn't deserve all the indignant damnation usually
meted out to her.

Poulson's American Daily Advertiser, June 20, 1805; *History of Philadelphia,* Ellis Paxson Oberholtzer, i, 433-4; *Pennsylvania Magazine of History
and Biography,* ix, 121 *et seq.; ibid.,* xiii, 482; "The First American Art
Academy," in *Lippincotts' Magazine,* February & March, 1872; *The Port
Folio,* 1809; *Domestic Manners of the Americans,* Mrs. Trollope, ch. xxv;
Portrait of a Colonial City, H. D. Eberlein & C. V. D. Hubbard, 428, 544-
546; *Letter Books of Charles Willson Peale,* Library of American Philosophical Society.

1809

Tuesday, January 31—Diabolical bedlam in the Yard this morning; politics the cause of it all. Nobody gets killed nor, indeed, badly hurt; but there's rampant ruffianism, and a worse din one never heard. The Republicans try to break up a Federalist town-meeting—fetch in a lot of rowdies from the Northern Liberties and Southwark; when they find they can't budge the Federalists, they set up an infernal pandemonium and try to drown out the speakers' voices.

Jefferson's Embargo's immensely unpopular with Federalists throughout the country. It's especially odious to Philadelphia's shipping and mercantile interests; it's brought real suffering to all the sailor folk. The political situation's caused intense excitement, bitterness and not a little disorder.

January 23rd, the Republicans (the democratic party, successors of the ultra-Whigs) meet in the State House Yard, make speeches, call the Federalists all manner of unpleasant names—they can think of plenty—and adopt resolutions supporting the Embargo policy.

The Federalists, thereupon, in the name of "friends of the Constitution, Union and Commerce," call another town-meeting in the Yard for January 31st. The newspapers carry advertisements of it every day from the preceding Thursday. This "gets under the skin" of the Republicans. Think of Federalists calling themselves "friends of the Constitution"! Everybody knows they're going to break up the Federalist meeting if they can; they've held Republican ward meetings, pasted up abusive handbills and filled "the papers of two *foreign* printers with inflammatory paragraphs."

Comes January 31st. The Federalists have taken the precaution to bring a goodly number of the aggrieved sailors, whose cause they've espoused. They organise their meeting with Commodore Truxtun, Chairman; George Clymer, Secretary. On the platform with Truxtun and Clymer are such men as Commodore Richard Dale, a lieutenant under John Paul Jones; Colonel James Read and General Francis Gurney, of Revolutionary fame; Captain John Dunlap and Samuel Wheeler, members of the City Troop

348

when it "distinguished itself at the capture of the Hessians at Trenton"; Thomas FitzSimons, Revolutionary officer, Member of the old Congress, of the Convention that framed the Federal Constitution, and of the first Congress under the Constitution; Joseph Hopkinson, eminent lawyer and author of "Hail Columbia!"; Joshua Humphreys, "commissioned to fit out the fleet of vessels which sailed from Philadelphia in 1776," "the first officially appointed naval constructor of the United States," who built the *United States* at Philadelphia, furnished the designs for the other warships built at the same time, and revolutionised the science of naval construction; and that estimable gentleman, Robert Wharton, whom the scurrilous *Aurora* slightingly alludes to as "late mayor of this city, and persons of that cast." George Clymer, it seems scarce necessary to recall, was one of the "Signers" of the Declaration of Independence and a Member of the Constitutional Convention in 1787. All the people at the forefront of this meeting are mature, reputable, representative citizens, patriots of unquestionable record—in short, at least tolerably "respectable"! The *United States Gazette* quite justifiably displays the headline "SPIRIT OF '76" for the column giving the names of "the numerous revolutionary characters who appeared at the town meeting."

Just as the Federalists begin their meeting, the Republicans push into the Yard, drums beating, colours flying, and try to capture the speakers' stand; they're going to attend the Federalist meeting and shout out "their approbation of the late measure of the Government" [the Embargo "Enforcing Act"]. At this mob attempt, the Federalists' sailor supporters "act summarily" with the disturbers—"summarily" meaning nose-punching, shin-kicking, pate-whacking and like tokens of vigorous physical resentment.

Finding they can't take the stand, nor disrupt the meeting, the Republicans get as near as they can come on the sidelines and keep up an incessant concert of hoots, yells, howls, whistles, catcalls and hisses, with a thunderous drum *obbligato*. In spite of this hellish deafening din, the Federalists pass resolutions denouncing the Embargo in all its bearings; appoint a committee to draught a memorial to Congress; and take up a collection of $700 to help needy sailors out of work. (The same evening there's a "benefit" ball for the seamen's relief fund.)

Then, according to *Poulson's Daily Advertiser*,

"at the close of the meeting. . . a large concourse of grateful seamen [the *United States Gazette* says "about a thousand grateful tars"] crowded around their beloved Truxtun; took the chair from the stage; placed the Commodore in it, and carried him from the State House to the Coffee House; accompanied by a very extensive procession of applauding Citizens. From the balcony of the Coffee House, the Commodore addressed the meeting in a short speech, upon which the assembled Citizens made the air resound with acclamations, and then retired to their respective homes." (The "Coffee House" here mentioned is the City Tavern.)

Back at the State House, the Republicans have pressed into the Yard on the very heels of the departing Federalists, pelting them with snowballs. Then they stage an impromptu meeting at which Alexander James Dallas and John Barker, the Mayor, hurl anathemas at the Federalists. Leaving the Yard, they then form a procession and march through the streets—with music, we're told. Let's hope it's less raucous than the noise they've just been making. As a gentle, polite attention, they march down to the Coffee House (City Tavern), let out insulting yells, then disperse.

The Aurora gives a misleading account—represents the Federalists as disorderly intruders who've tried to seize the Yard when the Republicans had called a meeting (!); sneeringly terms the Coffee House the "British" Coffee House; and pictures the Republicans as vanquishing the Federalists and driving them ignominiously from the field! But, then, that's what one expects from Mr. Duane's paper; never any qualms about "arrangin' de trufe" to suit its own ends.

United States Gazette, January 26-31, 1809; *Poulson's American Daily Advertiser*, January 26-February 2, 1809; *The Aurora*, January 26-February 3, 1809; *History of Philadelphia*, Ellis Paxson Oberholtzer, ii, 10; *History of Philadelphia*, Scharf & Westcott, i, 538-539.

1814

Friday, August 26—At 10 o'clock this morning the Yard's full of frightened, anxious people, old and young—from the City, from the Northern Liberties, from Southwark—people of all classes and of all political parties.

Yesterday evening, the *United States Gazette* printed notice of a "TOWN MEETING," addressed *"To the Citizens of Philadelphia, Northern Liberties and Southwark."* It said:

"The times require the most prompt and energetick exertions—they require union and organisation for your own defence—for the defence of your families, and the preservation of your rights as citizens of a free Nation.

You are therefore called upon to assemble in the State House Yard at 10 o'clock to-morrow morning to make arrangements for combining with effect the services of all the citizens in defence of a cause that is common to all without distinction."

This morning's papers carry the same notice.

The morning's prevalent alarm increases when the evening paper comes out with an account of how the British have burnt the President's "Palace" and the Capitol in Washington City. It's generally expected they'll take Baltimore next, then make for Philadelphia.

Though ignorant as yet of this humiliating disaster, but impelled by a sense of impending danger, the people throng the Yard long before the hour appointed. At 10 o'clock, when he calls the meeting to order, former Governour McKean—he's now eighty—tells the gathering, "This is not a time for speaking, but a time for action." Dispensing with oratory, the meeting gets right down to business. Joseph Reed, General Joseph Reed's son, is secretary. They appoint a Committee of Defense with Charles Biddle at the head. The Committee are to meet in the evening at 7 o'clock in the Mayor's Court Room.

Lack of popular enthusiasm for the War of 1812; lack of unity in supporting it; strong opposition to it in many quarters; failure to be adequately prepared to resist invasion—all derive from the bitter political animosities that have rent the country. Perpetual fighting between Federalists and Republicans has not only kept the people in a turmoil but has also engendered sharp personal enmities. For the economic ills and unrest that have beset the land and, finally, for the break with England, the Federalists blame the policies of the National Government; the Republicans, say they, have caused the war—now let them get the country out of the mess they've put it in!

In Pennsylvania, with its heritage of tempestuous politics, even the Republicans are at loggerheads amongst themselves. Whatever the *moderate* Republicans do is wrong in the eyes of the still radically-Whiggish heirs of the Pennsylvania State "Constitutionalists of 1776," and comes in for venomous attacks from *The Aurora*.

With City and State thus three-ways divided, nothing more clearly reflects the disunity of sentiment about the war and defense than this excerpt from a Federalist paper on September 8th:

> "Binns [one of the *moderate* Republican democratic leaders] tells the president and governours to go on executing their *war authorities,* and the republicans and federalists will support them— This is not true—the federalists will defend their homes from an invading enemy, although we know this calamity has been brought upon us by the wickedness and folly of our administration, but beyond this they will give no support to this accursed war or those who made it."

Samuel Breck, a Federalist, cries out,

> "O Democracy! to what have you brought us! O Madison, Armstrong, and your conceited, ignorant and improvident cabinet! how guilty are you toward this dishonoured, unhappy nation!" Then, apostrophising Pennsylvania's Governour, "And Snyder, thou governour by appellation! Thou goader of this war! thou Democratic feeble disorganiser! say what hath thy imbecility, thy guilty incompetency, to answer for? Is Philadelphia safe, I ask, even against four thousand men? I shall be answered by thee, 'I know not,' and perhaps, thou phlegmatic chief, thou wilt add, 'I care not.'"

However bitter they may feel about the war, and who's to blame for it, now, in the face of imminent danger, people thrust aside party dissensions and rancours—enough, at least, to unite in common measures of defense against invasion of the city. Of this, the Committee of Defense membership is proof; Federalists and Republicans of all shades serve together with a will.

'They agree on alarm signals, and points of rendezvous. Volunteer militia drill in the State House Yard and in other available open spaces. At the enemy's approach, horses, cattle and vehicles are to be sent into the interior; provisions are to be removed or destroyed. Some of the more timid are already fleeing with their money and valuables. Stephen Girard's sent to Reading ten Conestoga waggons filled with silver, nankeen and silks. Most people, however, stand their ground; the newspaper advertisements indicate "business as usual."

The most important defense measure is the construction of earthworks southwest of the city, beyond the Schuylkill. Throughout September, citizens of "all ranks," high and low, rich and poor, young and old, go out and give a day's labour with pick and shovel. Lawyers, doctors, artists, counting-house clerks work side by side with bricklayers, cobblers, carpenters and all sorts of artisans—"silk stockings" and "leather-aprons" in common effort. Various trades band together to contribute to this volunteer free labour supply. On September 7th, the *United States Gazette* carries a notice:

"To the Printers. You will parade, provided with one day's rations, in the State House Yard on Friday morning the 9th inst. at 5 o'clock, thence to proceed to the ground west of Schuylkill to assist on the works erecting for the defence of the city."

Many more such notices appear from day to day. Cordwainers, victuallers, hatters, "sons of Erin, citizens of the United States," all bear their corporate share in the work. On Thursday evening, September 8th, the *United States Gazette* announces,

"As the hands employed in this office will to-morrow be engaged upon the public works west of Schuylkill, the next number of this Gazette will not appear till Saturday."

The working parties all start off between 5 and 6 in the morning. Nearly every party tramps westward to the sound of fife and drum. James MacAlpin, a braw Highlander in tartan and kilt, skirling the bagpipes, leads about thirty other Scots to the task. If James plays the pipes now and again during the day, his party— if they be true Scots—will do twice the work any like number of other men will do.

On the scene of labour, at 10 o'clock the drum beats for grog; enough is dealt the captain of each corps for his party. Dinner at 12; more grog. Drums and grog again at 3 and 5. What with the food each worker carries with him, and the spirituous comfort of the periodic grog, the day's digging has somewhat the character of a picnic. Whoever's responsible for the grog ration is something of a psychologist. At 6, beat of drum sounds "retreat" to go home. General Orders say, "For the honour of the cause we are engaged in, it is hoped that every man will retire sober."

United States Gazette, August 25-September 25, 1814; *Poulson's Daily American Advertiser,* August 25-September 25, 1814; *The Aurora,* August 25-September 25, 1814; *Recollections of Samuel Breck,* ed. H. E. Scudder, 253-255; *History of Chestnut Street,* Souder, ch. xxxvi; *History of Philadelphia,* Ellis Paxson Oberholtzer, ii, 17; *History of Philadelphia,* Scharf & Westcott, i, 571-574.

1820

Tuesday, October 10—All day and all evening, until 10 o'clock, an election's going on for the Governourship of Pennsylvania; the State House is the focus of excitement and turmoil. Chestnut Street in front of the State House is jammed with milling crowds of people, often behaving like so many Kilkenny cats. For weeks past, the Federalists and old-school Democrats (formerly called Republicans) on one side, and the new-school Democrats (radicals) on the other, have been calling each other names in the newspapers, indulging in all manner of abuse and invective. To-day, the political kettle's fairly boiled over and the partisans have been pushing and pulling each other about till it's a wonder more people haven't been hurt. There's been a-plenty of torn clothes; tomorrow morning there'll be sore heads and black eyes.

The 1820 election campaign's been exceptionally hot and bitter; acrimonious charges and counter-charges have been bandied from mouth to mouth as well as filling the party newspapers. Federalists and old-school Democrats have united to support Joseph Hiester for Governour; the new-school Democrats are trying to keep Governour Findlay in office.

Wooden platforms are built under the State House windows; voters mount the platforms and hand their ballots through the windows to the tellers inside. Different windows are assigned to different wards. From about 4 o'clock on, when labourers and artisans—who've been at work all day—come to vote, the crowd in Chestnut Street gets especially dense and noisy, also rough.

Scrimmage and hubbub are the order of the day at this tumultuous election. Pie-men, oyster-men, hot-chestnut men, "cheesemongers, beer men, hot-muffin men, cake women and other venders all bawling their wares" make a deafening din. Buglers, fifers, drummers, in the banner- and placard-covered waggons (sent about to beat up negligent voters), swell the uproar. The heavy bourdon of the State House bell, rung at intervals of three to five minutes to call dilatory citizens to their suffrage duty, punctuates the shrill cacophony. Added to it all's the surging swell and ebb of massed human voices, angry or excited.

Flags fly, streamers and banners float from the various party headquarters at neighbouring taverns; handbills, tickets and papers litter the street and pavements. "All sorts and conditions of men" jostle, shove, push and tread one on another's toes in this rough hurly-burly. Political clubs, marching to the polls in a body, augment the congested confusion. The taverns nearby, filled with knots of political henchmen and "heelers," dispense potables in amazing quantities. Amos Holahan, the Irish boniface who keeps the inn opposite the State House, in blue coat and brass buttons, serves his thirsty customers with "beer in pewter mugs," brought up separately from the cellar, fresh and foaming, instead of pouring it from pitchers that have been standing in the barroom, as is usual elsewhere.

A few invalids drive to the State House to cast their ballots and are helped up on the platforms before the windows. Now and again, carriages arrive, sent out by the different party headquarters to fetch and take home again voters too indifferent to walk to the polls. On the whole, it's a rowdy throng. The sceptre's passed to a new species of citizen. Gone are "the substantial Quaker merchant of colonial times, the zealous Whig of the Revolutionary day, the dignified Federalist or the restless Jeffersonian of the Washington administration." All have "given way in favour of loungers and brawlers."

As darkness falls, transparencies at party headquarters are lighted, torches and lanterns help the feeble glow of the street lamps. The crowd grows rougher, the noise more raucous. Here and there, arguments end in free fights, head-punching and bloody noses. Sometimes a group of "plug-uglies" deliberately crowds up and blocks a window to keep legitimate voters from getting near. As the human mass sways and surges, men climb on the shoulders of those along side them and struggle across the heads of their fellow-citizens to reach the voting platforms. In the general *mêlée*, hats are lost and trampled under foot, shirts rent and coats torn to tatters.

Long before the returns are announced, bonfires flare up in a dozen places. Whatever's combustible and movable, the mob seizes on to feed the flames. The votes are not all counted till near midnight, though the polls close at ten. When the election officers give out the result, Hiester's won, Governour Findlay's out.

Contemporary Newspapers; *History of Philadelphia*, Ellis Paxson Oberholtzer, ii, 79-81; *History of Philadelphia*, Thompson Westcott, ch. dcii.

1824

Tuesday, September 28—About 5 this afternoon comes Marie Joseph Paul Yves Gilbert du Motier, Marquis de la Fayette. He arrives in a barouche drawn by six cream-coloured horses, liveried outriders also on cream-coloured horses; Judge Peters sits beside him. Throngs of notables attend him, both those in the long escorting procession, and those waiting at the State House to receive him.

As the Marquis alights, "a fine band of music plays the appropriate air 'See, the Conquering Hero Comes.'" The attending gentlemen take him first into the Court Room for a few minutes, then lead him across the hall to the Independence Chamber; there Mayor Watson and the Corporation, the Judges, and sundry committees await him. They make an address of welcome; the Marquis replies in a short but eloquent speech. The poor gentleman must be completely tuckered out with all the reviewing and speech-making he's had to undergo to-day; from the perpetual bowing he must be well-nigh seasick.

For weeks past, they've been making all sorts of preparations around the State House. They've painted the Independence Chamber stone colour, hung up curtains of scarlet and blue powdered with gold stars, placed star-spangled draperies behind Rush's statue of Washington, and put in lots of extra furniture and portraits.

Outside, in Chestnut Street, they've built a big triumphal arch about thirty feet high, made of framework and covered with canvas painted to look like stone. Mr. Strickland designed it, 'tis said after the Arch of Septimius Severus at Rome; 45 feet front and 12 feet deep. The Arms of the City, on top, Mr. Sully painted. The scene-painters from the New Theatre (Messrs. Darley, Warren and Jefferson) did the rest of the painting. Two sculptures by Rush, *Fame* and *Justice,* stand in niches at the sides of the arch.

At the welcome in Independence Chamber, the Judges and other dignitaries have been "all seated on superb sofas"! Perhaps the sofas are upholstered in material like that of the new curtains —scarlet and blue, spangled with gold stars; that might account for their "superbity." At any rate, no effort's been spared to make the occasion properly gorgeous, with blaring band and burst of colour. In the evening, there are brilliant illuminations throughout the city—both public buildings and private houses.

What a contrast between the Marquis's coming to the State House to-day and his first appearance there more than forty-seven years ago! Then, unknown and coldly rebuffed, he hangs about in the heat of July for several days, impatient and anxious about his letter to Congress, until the Members, with some misgivings, at last decide to commission him a major-general. To-day, no one can do enough to welcome him as the Nation's guest.

Before he reaches the State House, the Marquis has a gruelling day of it. Leaving Frankford at 9 o'clock, near Kensington he reviews the Militia under General Thomas Cadwalader, along with a contingent of New Jersey soldiery. Then the procession forms and leaves the reviewing field at 12 o'clock.

The procession,

"which consisted of several thousand citizens, some on foot and others mounted, divided into their various trades & occupations, with appropriate banners and devices," and a "few patriots of 'seventy-six, in three handsome cars [floats] with suitable mottos," comprises (besides numerous interspersed detachments of cavalry, infantry, artillery and military bands, all duly beflagged) the Governours of Pennsylvania and New Jersey in four-horse coaches, "cars decorated with evergreens, flags, and emblematical inscriptions," and "a large car, containing a body of printers, and also the various articles belonging to a printing office. The compositors and pressmen were at work, and the latter distributed from the press an ode, prepared for the occasion, by Alderman Barker." Cordwainers, weavers, rope-makers, ship-builders, as well as "700 mechanics of different branches" all take part in this marching spectacle. "150 coopers, preceded by a car containing a cooper's shop, with workmen fitting staves, driving hoops &c." vie for attention with "150 butchers, well mounted, and handsomely dressed. . . in blue pants, white frocks with blue sashes, black revolutionary cockades and Lafayette badges." The 29th division of the parade's a "body of about 300 farmers, from the neighbouring country," who bring up the rear.

Truly, Philadelphia's laid herself out to do her most impressive best in honour of the old General.

The parade's line of march is down Fourth Street to Arch, to Eleventh, to Chestnut, to Eighth, to Spruce, to Second, to Chestnut, and "up Chestnut to the grand civic arch in front of the State House." Altogether, including that at the State House, there are thirteen triumphal arches at various points. Doors, windows, and stands built for the occasion at every point of vantage along the route, are all crowded with cheering spectators. The descriptions of the evening's "chaste illuminations"—transparencies, lamps, candles set amidst alabaster vases of flowers, *et al.*—reach their high point with the Bank of the United States which "was a perfect anomaly [!] in illumination. The lights were so arranged [behind the columns] as not to be seen, and the doors being thrown open, so as to disclose the interior, the whole building presented the appearance of a palace of transparent marble," or, as another eye-witness puts it, "it reminded the beholder of those alabaster palaces which are described in fairy tales." (Trust the Federal Era writers for spilling "genteel diction" about, with plenty of "elegance" and "sentiment.")

The official welcome in Independence Chamber ended, the Marquis walks through the Yard to Walnut Street and gets into his barouche to drive to the Mansion House. Thither the City Troop and other military escort attend him. After all the day's dizzy bedazzlement and his subsequent escape to the Mansion House (where, let's hope, he has some brief rest and a little refreshment), the Marquis finds time to call on Mrs. Robert Morris, and later attends at Washington Hall a "grand banquet given in his honour by about seventy gentlemen, which was kept up to a late hour." Poor Marquis!

Notes on p. 363.

Wednesday, September 29—About noon General la Fayette comes to the State House again to hold a levee. Before he leaves at 3, he must have shaken hands with thousands of people. At 5, he's expected to dine with Mayor Watson and the Corporation. Afterwards, he intends a short visit to the Provost of the University; at 10, he's to go to General Cadwalader's. General Cadwalader's invited a number of distinguished persons to meet him, chiefly military officers.

At his State House levee, General la Fayette
"received no less than fourteen addresses, from the aged Soldiers; the Clergy, presented by Bishop White; the Philosophical and Bible Societies; the University; the Chamber of Commerce; the Bar; the Young Men; the French Citizens; the Washington greys; the La Fayette Association; the Revolutionary Officers; and the

Young Ladies of the several schools. His answer to each was peculiarly pertinent."

Besides these classified bodies of admirers who come to pay their respects to the great man and shake his hand, the rank and file of citizens have their innings, too. Levasseur, la Fayette's secretary, says:

> "Mechanics with their hardened hands and uprolled sleeves, advanced to La Fayette; the magistrate and the plain-clad farmer stood together; the clergyman and the players moved side to side, and the children. . . marched boldly along before soldiers and sailors."

Had zoot-suits then existed, there would doubtless have been zoot-suiters, too, in this motley gathering.

At the Mayor's and Corporation's 5 o'clock dinner at "Mr. Kid's saloon, next the Mansion House," Mayor Watson presides; Bishop White says grace.

Thursday, the 30th, the General escapes functions. 'Tis said the party last night at General Cadwalader's didn't break up till midnight or later. After a strenuous Wednesday, a free day's welcome. They say the Marquis dines privately at his hotel to-day and goes afterwards to a concert in Masonic Hall.

Amidst the whirl of activities arranged for him, Levasseur says,

> "all the time that General La Fayette could withhold from the kindness of his numerous friends and the people of Philadelphia [which couldn't have been much], was spent in visiting the humane and public institutions, which are exceedingly multiplied in this vast city. . . ."

We know that he does manage to see, amongst other places, the Fairmount Water Works, recently completed and reckoned an outstanding "sight." We know also that he finds time to go with Judge Tilghman and Nicholas Biddle to call on

> "Hannah Till, a coloured woman, then aged over one hundred years . . . She had been cook to Washington and La Fayette for several years. The General learned that 'Aunt Hannah's' home was encumbered with a mortgage, and arranged before he left the city to have it paid off."

Friday, October 1st, there's an evening meeting of the Philosophical Society and a reception for the General at Nicholas Biddle's house.

Saturday, the 2nd, is another busy day—breakfast with John Quincy Adams, a visit to the Navy Yard, with much entertainment there and, in the evening, a dinner at the Masonic Lodge, with 400 guests present.

On his way to the Navy Yard, the Marquis passes under another of the triumphal arches, receives an address from the Corporation of Southwark and, as he passes the barracks, 800 school children— all uniformly arrayed in their "Sunday best"—from the Southwark Free School, ":chaunt suitable pieces of music in honour of the hero." To follow the review, inspection and reception, the Officers have got up a sumptuous collation in the mould loft, at which are about 700 guests.

The Marquis finds the festivities at the Navy Yard so engaging that he's over an hour late for the Masons' dinner. For this dinner, Robert Waln tells us,

> "the decorations and arrangements of the table were prepared by Mr. Haviland [one of Philadelphia's foremost architects]" and "that every thing was done in good taste. Before the General entered, the gas lamps were so arranged as to shed a pale and mild lustre, like that of soft moonlight. When he entered, the vessels being instantly filled, a splendid blaze of light burst forth over the room. . . ."

Before there's any municipal gas supply, the Masonic Lodge has its own individual gas plant, which it can manipulate as desired to regulate the lights.

On Sunday morning, the 3rd, the General goes to Christ Church, attends vespers at St. Augustine's and dines at Belmont with Judge Peters.

Notes on p. 363.

Monday, October 4—Another exacting day for the General. In the Yard this morning about 3000 school children, both boys and girls, are drawn up to receive him. They speak several speeches to him; then he addresses them. At this function,

> "one of the youthful orators was Henry Cadwalader, a son of General Cadwalader, a pupil of the academy of Tappan and Staples, and another was Malvina Kay, a pupil of T. T. Smiley's school, 29, Church Alley."

Butler says "the spectacle was beautiful and interesting."

Following this engagement, la Fayette dines with the surviving Revolutionary Officers at the Mansion House—a reunion greatly to his satisfaction.

To-night, to wind up the festive doings for the Marquis's Philadelphia visit, there's a grand State Ball at the New Theatre. For this they've been making elaborate preparations. Everybody says it will be a brilliant affair. Belike, they'll not be going home "till daylight doth appear."

The Marquis leaves to-morrow for the South.

The so-called "New Theatre," on the opposite side of Chestnut Street—just half a square away from the State House—is the second building to bear that name. The first "New Theatre," finished in 1794, and called "New" to distinguish it from the old Southwark Theatre, burnt down in 1820. William Strickland designed its successor, finished in 1822. In it the la Fayette Ball takes place.

Robert Waln, jr., an eye-witness says,

"the grand ball given at the new theatre, exceeded in all respects, any entertainment of the kind before known in Philadelphia . . . The lobby of the theatre was converted into a magnificent saloon, adorned with beautiful rose, orange, and lemon trees in full bearing, and a profusion of shrubbery, pictures, busts, banners, with classical inscriptions &c [the Federal Era was long on Classical inscriptions, as well as highfalutin language and plentiful superlatives] all illuminated with a multitude of lamps. For the dancers, there were two compartments, the house and the stage; the upper part of the former was hung with scarlet drapery, studded with golden stars, while the great chandelier, with two additional ones, and a row of wax tapers arranged over the canopy, shed over all a blaze of light.—The first and second tiers of boxes were crowded with ladies in the richest apparel, as spectators of the dazzling array on every side. Passing the proscenium, the other division wore the appearance of an eastern pavilion in a garden terminating with a view of an extended sea and landscape, irradiated by the setting sun, and meant to typify the western world. A great number of brilliant chandeliers rendered this scarcely less effulgent than the other part of the house. In front were three Latin inscriptions—*Advenit Heros—Olim meminisse juvabit—Hic domus; haec patria.*

The two retiring rooms connected with the pavilion, were fitted up with a degree of elegance and taste which drew expressions of admiration from every one that entered. Those who came to the house early were at once struck with the floor, which was brilliantly painted for the occasion, from designs furnished by Mr. Strickland.

The company consisted of two thousand or more persons, of whom six or seven hundred were invited strangers—Twenty-two hundred tickets had been issued. . . . General La Fayette appeared at nine o'clock.

He was conducted the whole length of the apartments, through an avenue formed by the ladies, to the bottom of the stage, where the governour of the state and the mayor of the city, waited to greet him in form; the full band playing an appropriate air during his progress. As soon as he was seated, the dancers were called, and at least four hundred were immediately on the floor. The dancing did not cease until near five o'clock, though the company began to retire about three."

A vivid description, this; likewise, a choice display of "language" —really an accomplished "derangement of epitaphs"—all in the manner of the day.

We're also told,

"the ladies were served with refreshments in the ball room, while the gentlemen feasted on the second floor. At twelve one of the managers from an upper box proclaimed a toast to the nation's guest."

Life of the Marquis de la Fayette, Robert Waln, Jr., 3rd ed. 372-383; *La Fayette in America*, Auguste Levasseur, 1829, *passim; U. S. Gazette, Poulson's American Daily, Democratic Press, Saturday Evening Post* and *Philadelphia Recorder* of September 28 to October 6, 1824.

INDEX